A naive young couple sets off across Asia and, somehow, against tall odds, ends up managing a publishing empire that straddles the globe. Therein lies a story. And the story is intermittently funny, full of false starts, frustrations, mistakes and numerous exotic locales. I think this book is ultimately more inspiring than a whole shelf full of self-help screeds. Go ahead, start on page one and follow your bliss.

—Tim Cahill

Now that we've all worked out how to get our bags off the airport carousels, it's time to find out how Lonely Planet really got started; Tony and Maureen Wheeler, to whom all world-wanderers now owe an eternal debt of gratitude, tell their unforgettable story with wit, wisdom and charm: their millions of admirers around what is now a distinctly un-lonely planet will love the tale they have decided to tell.

—Simon Winchester

As spirited and engagingly human as the books that have taught us how and why and where to travel, Tony and Maureen Wheeler's story describes a miracle (from 27 cents to a multi-million dollar empire) that is in its way as inspiring and wondrous as the temples of Pagan or Easter Island's statues. Whether penniless backpackers or heads of a global company, Tony and Maureen somehow always exemplify the very best kind of travelers' enthusiasm and curiosity.

—Pico Iyer

This is how it all happened, the adventures, the fun and the passion condensed into an enthralling read..."

—*Daily Telegraph*

UNLIKELY DESTINATIONS

In mid-1972, Tony and Maureen Wheeler set out on a year-long trip around the world, with the intention of getting the travel bug out of their systems. After following the 'hippie trail' from England across Asia to Australia, they recognized the need for a new sort of travel guide to suit the new breed of laid-back, independent travelers.

More than thirty years later, they are the owners of one of the world's largest, most successful and best-loved independent travel publishing companies. Lonely Planet Publications has offices on three continents, with 400 employees, 250 writers, more than 600 titles in print and annual sales of over six million books. Tony and Maureen Wheeler live in Melbourne, Australia.

UNLIKELY DESTINATIONS
the lonely planet story

Tony and Maureen Wheeler

PERIPLUS

Published by Periplus Editions (HK) Ltd, with editorial offices at 130 Joo Seng Road, #06-01, Singapore 368357.

First published by Penguin Group (Australia), 2005

Front cover photograph: Portrait of two young novice monks at monastery window
© Anthony Plummer, Lonely Planet Images
Maps by Malisa Plesa and Diana Duggan

ISBN-13: 978-0-7946-0523-0
ISBN-10: 0-7946-0523-0
Previously published as The Lonely Planet Story, ISBN 0-7946-0478-1

Distributed by

North America, Latin America & Europe
Tuttle Publishing
364 Innovation Drive
North Clarendon, VT 05759-9436, USA
Tel: 1 (802) 773 8930 Fax: 1 (802) 773 6993
info@tuttlepublishing.com
www.tuttlepublishing.com

Japan
Tuttle Publishing
Yaekari Building, 3rd Floor
5-4-12 Osaki, Shinagawa-ku
Tokyo 141-0032
Tel: (81) 03 5437 0171 Fax: (81) 03 5437 0755
tuttle-sales@gol.com

Asia Pacific
Berkeley Books Pte Ltd
130 Joo Seng Road #06-01
Singapore 368357
Tel: (65) 6280 1330 Fax: (65) 6280 6290
inquiries@periplus.com.sg
www.periplus.com

10 09 08 07   6 5 4 3 2

Printed in Canada

Contents

Introduction

Lonely Planet began because people kept asking us, 'How did you get from Afghanistan to India? Not get sick? Hitch a ride on a yacht? . . .' This book came into being for the same reason—people kept asking us, 'How did two backpackers with twenty-seven cents to their names end up running a multinational company?'

In much the same way as our initial journey sparked a great deal of interest in the minds of those people who dreamed of hitting the road, so the story of Lonely Planet seems to resonate with anyone who has ever dreamed of turning their passion into their work. Over the years we have given many interviews and public talks and we have often been asked the same questions: How much do we travel? How have we managed to remain business partners and married? How have we integrated our children into this lifestyle?

Lonely Planet has been on a journey for over thirty years and as it has evolved, so have we. We have grown from twenty-something backpackers with no money but a passion for travel to fifty-something owners of a multimillion-dollar company, still with the same passion.

Lonely Planet has been our life—we've lived it, breathed it and loved it—and while it hasn't always been easy or fun, it has never been boring. We've learned many lessons about business, about working and living together, about taking risks, working hard and what can happen if you throw yourself at the world with open arms and a lot of curiosity, so our story encompasses all of that: travel, work and relationships.

Tony was responsible for getting this book down, but the period of writing it was one of intense discussion and debate between us. We decided it made sense for the book to have one main voice (Tony's), except where the incidents being described were about me or had been observed by me.

Tony and I continue to travel. We still believe it is important to encourage others to go and see the world and we continue to love what we do. Of course, we could not have done it without all those travelers who've put their trust in all of us at Lonely Planet. For every person who has used and abused our books, sent us letters from the road and thrown one of our guides into their bag as they set out on an adventure, thank you.

Maureen Wheeler
Melbourne, May 2006

1

Asia Overland

'Twenty-seven cents,' I said, surveying the pathetic collection of coins in the palm of my hand.

A few minutes earlier, the last car we'd hitched had cruised into Sydney across the Harbour Bridge. The unfinished Opera House rose up beside the harbor to our left. As we rolled across the bridge, Maureen had leaned towards me in the back of the car and whispered: 'How much money do we have left?'

It was the day after Christmas, 1972. Maureen was twenty-two; I was twenty-six.

We stared at our small collection of coins. We were half the world away from home, friendless and jobless. How had we got ourselves into this fix?

I can pinpoint the place where our problem started. It was a park bench in Regent's Park in central London on the afternoon of Wednesday, October 7 1970. There are pivotal moments in many people's lives and this was one of ours. I was twenty-three and had just begun a postgraduate degree course at the London Business School. The school itself, now one of the best-known MBA factories in Europe, was only five years old, located in fancy new quarters in a restored Nash Terrace on the edge of Regent's Park.

I'd started the year working as a development engineer with the British division of Chrysler Cars, unaware that the company's American parent was about to commence a downhill plunge. We'd recently launched the Hillman Avenger; twenty years later, in a diatribe about the inspired awfulness of British cars of the early 1970s, British auto journalist Jeremy Clarkson would describe it as 'Britain's darkest hour'. I'd moved on from the Avenger, known within the company as 'B-car', to a larger version, code-named 'C-car'. A few months into 1970, the Chrysler high-ups decided that C-car was a dud and dropped it—along with all the engineers working on it.

'We'll pay you to quit,' my boss announced, explaining that it was cheaper for the company if we jumped, rather than waited to be pushed. So on a Friday in late May, I walked out of the Chrysler office and into unemployment. The year and a half I'd spent there would be the longest time I'd ever spend in a regular job.

I wasn't worried about losing my job. I had a redundancy check, a neat little fiberglass sports car known as a Marcos (a sort of two-seater Mini Cooper S), which I'd built myself, and, to hell with Chrysler, I was about to quit anyway.

A year and a half out of university I knew I wasn't cut out to be an engineer. Even while I was studying at Warwick University, I'd been distracted by other interests. The English faculty had a young Australian lecturer named Germaine Greer, whose course was such hot stuff that even engineers used to sneak into her classes. I'd taken up writing for the new university's fledgling newspaper *Giblet* and, as a result, neglected my studies, failed my end-of-year exams and had to resit them, only narrowly scraping back into the course. I passed respectably, although far from brilliantly, but my favorite part of the course had not been engineering, but a business elective in my final year.

So when Chrysler and engineering began to pall, I decided to go back to university and study business. I'd fired off applications to schools in Europe and the United States and, bolstered by a bizarrely high score in the entrance exam used by MBA courses, I'd been offered a couple of places, despite my relatively young age and lack of business experience. Sensing that Chrysler was about to perform its own crash test, I'd begun looking for a job to tide me over until I started at university in autumn. When the corporate axe fell, I took a summer job helping to run a go-kart track in the English south-coast seaside town of Worthing.

Two weeks before the go-kart season commenced, and the day after losing my job at Chrysler, I stowed my tent and sleeping bag in the Marcos and drove south through France to the Monaco Grand Prix. My engineering background has left me with gear-head enthusiasms which I've never quite shaken off and at this point in my life I was a regular at auto-racing tracks all over Britain, helping friends with their racing cars and motorcycles, and across Europe, where I spectated at grands prix from Monza in Italy to the Nurburgring in Germany. I spent the whole Grand Prix week in Monte Carlo, camping just outside the principality and driving into the city each morning to watch the practice sessions.

A week later, I took a ferry back to Dover, drove along the coast to Worthing and spent the rest of the summer collecting money from local leadfoots and repairing the go-karts after they'd bent them.

At the beginning of October, I headed north to London and back to university. A week into the course, on that fated autumn day, I was shopping for a new coat. It was unusually warm for October, so shortcutting through Regent's Park on my way back to the campus I paused on a park bench to look at a car magazine I'd bought. A young woman—of course she was beautiful!—noticed the same sun-lit park bench, sat down on the other end and took a Tolstoy novel out of her bag.

M: I'd arrived in London on the previous Saturday afternoon. My mother had come to the airport in Belfast to say goodbye. My plan was to go to London, find a job, stay for a year or so, then return home as thousands of Irish girls before me had done. London was the big city, full of excitement and possibility, but it was time out, not real life.

As I turned to say goodbye, my mother gave me a searching

look, then a hard hug, and said: 'You'll not come back.'

Secretly, I hoped she was right; I wanted to be one of those who got away.

I stayed at a women's hostel off Tottenham Court Road, an enormous place with a million rules. There were two to a room and communal bathrooms and kitchens. My mother was relieved that I had a curfew; I was just glad to have an address. I dumped my bag, then set out to look around. I wandered for hours, taking in the sights and sounds, trying to get my bearings, thrilled to the core at the thought that no one knew me here. In a small town like Belfast you couldn't go far without meeting someone you knew.

I had worked as a secretary at home so with my shorthand and typing qualifications, two weeks' rent paid in advance and about twelve pounds in my pocket, my priority was to find a job. I spent Sunday soaking up London, still buoyed by my freedom. On Monday, I hit the employment agencies. By the end of Tuesday I had accepted a job as assistant to the marketing manager of Peter Dominics, the wine merchants. I liked my boss, the office was a beautiful terrace at York Gate, Regent's Park, and the salary was twice what I would have earned in Belfast. I wandered home in a daze—it had almost been too easy.

I was to start work on the following Monday, so that left the rest of the week free. Since theater was one of my passions, I went to Drury Lane where *The Great Waltz* was playing, and I tried to buy a ticket. Although it was a Wednesday afternoon, there was not one seat left. My other passions were music and reading, so passing a bookstore I bought a copy of Tolstoy's *Boyhood, Childhood and Youth*. Then, since it was a beautiful day, I went to the park to read my book.

I found a bench that was in full sun. There was someone sitting there already, but I couldn't see until I was quite close that it was a young man. In the short time that I had been in London several young men had approached me, so I was a bit wary. However, I was committed, and it was the only bench in the sun. So I sat down on the extreme edge and purposefully opened my book.

Within a few minutes there was shuffling and sighing from the other end of the bench. 'Uh oh,' I thought, 'here we go.'

'So, is this the in place to read on a Wednesday afternoon?' he said.

I looked up slowly and deliberately, determined to freeze him off the bench with an icy response, and looked into the most beautiful green eyes I had ever seen. I quickly rearranged my expression, smiled and said, 'I don't know, I've only been in London since Saturday.'

That night, our first date was to see the movie *Mash*. It was the start of a magic year, although the evening concluded with what would become a familiar story in our relationship. Walking back from Leicester Square to Maureen's hostel, I decided to take a different route and got lost. I still do this on a regular basis.

The business school had rooms for students at one end of the building and during my first year this was where I lived. Maureen's office was literally a stone's throw from the school and soon we were meeting not only in the evening, but also for lunch. We spent much of our non-working time in bed, only emerging to buy the Sunday newspapers, newly heavy with special sections and magazines, which we would drag back to my room.

In the summer of 1971, between the first and second year of my course, Maureen and I took our first big trip together. We'd made a number of long weekend trips around Britain, but this time we packed camping gear into the back of the Marcos and set off across Europe. We went first to Czechoslovakia, a sad and sorry place after the fall of Alexandr Dubček, and then down through Austria to the rocky beaches and islands along the Croatian coast of what was then Yugoslavia. Then it was round to Venice and back up through Switzerland and France.

On our return, Maureen went back to work in central London

while I spent the rest of the summer doing a business study for a machine tool manufacturer at factories using their equipment in the Midlands and north of England. At the end of the summer we found an apartment in the suburb of Swiss Cottage, just north of Regent's Park, and moved in together. And on October 7 1971, a year to the day after we'd met, we got married.

My second year at the London Business School whizzed by as quickly and enjoyably as the first. In early 1972, the end of my second college phase was closing in.

I did the company rounds and was offered what seemed like the perfect job, product planning with the Ford Motor Company at their headquarters in Brentwood, Essex. In the European car market at that time, Ford was the market leader and far and away the most reputable of the British manufacturers. The job would allow me to use my engineering background and my new business qualifications.

But did I want a job at all, and did Maureen and I want to settle down to a nine-to-five existence? We'd loved living in London and the idea of moving out to the suburbs or commuting to work every day held no appeal. The more we talked about it, the less attractive it appeared. Eventually, we decided to put it off for a year. We'd go on a one-year trip around the world, and get travel out of our systems, then we'd settle down. I wrote to Ford and said I was thrilled by the job offer and would love to work for them, but could I wait a year before I started? They graciously offered to hold the job for me—I still have the letter.

So in late June, my second university career came to a close. A photograph of us taken in the early hours of the morning at the school's summer ball on the grassy college lawns shows a remarkably young-looking couple. Maureen looks more like sixteen than twenty-one and I don't look much older.

Asia had been on my mind in those last London months. My father had spent his whole working life in the airline business, so I'd had a peripatetic upbringing, rarely completing two years at the same school and spending most of my teenage years in the United States. Plus, I'd traveled every summer while I was at university and while I was at Chrysler. But those European trips had only whetted my appetite. Traveling across Asia would be the real thing. Three years earlier, shortly before I left Chrysler, I'd driven to Turkey, right to the edge of Europe, in a little proving run for my home-built sports car. We'd follow a similar route into Asia.

Chrysler had also provided some inspiration for the trip. In 1968, not long after I joined them, there had been a rally—really more of a race—from London across Asia to Sydney. The British division had entered a single car, a Hillman Hunter, and in a tortoise and hare rerun had managed to win the race. I'd pored over the maps which had been stacked in the car as it was being prepared in the experimental division's workshop, and mused about how much fun it would be to travel to India and beyond. I don't think we knew anyone who had been to Asia, although I recall a Chrysler engineer once telling us in a Coventry pub that he had driven clear to the other side of Turkey, not in some heavy-duty 4WD, but in his flimsy Triumph Spitfire sports car.

At the time, there wasn't much information available about making that long trek to the East. Bookshop shelves weren't groaning under the weight of carefully researched guidebooks to the Asia overland trip, but we eventually found a handy little book called *Overland to India*, written by a Canadian named Douglas Brown.

A much more useful information source, however, was the BIT guide. BIT (as in early computer speak for one bit of information) was a 1960s London institution, an underground center which could talk you down from a bad trip, book an abortion, find you a squat or get a lawyer to defend your drug bust. Finance for these public-spirited activities came from a variety of sources including the BIT guides, roneoed information sheets composed of 'letters from the road' sent back by travelers, a colorful farrago of truth and lies, advice and highs. I went round to the BIT office, paid my pound and came home to pore over the notes, names and addresses. (A few years later, Geoff Crowther, the bearded guru who presided over the BIT guides' production, would play a key part in Lonely Planet's growth.)

Gradually our plans came together. We would travel across Europe to Istanbul in Turkey, cross the Bosphorus from Europe to Asia, head east across Turkey into Iran. From Tehran, we'd head to Afghanistan, then to Pakistan and India, going through New Delhi and on up to Kathmandu in Nepal. We knew we would have to fly across Burma and then we would travel down through Southeast Asia to Australia.

We didn't have much money, but we hoped to stretch it out as far as Australia, where we would get jobs. At that time, British citizens didn't need a visa to enter Australia and could work there quite legally. We figured we'd soon save up enough money to get back to London. Perhaps we'd even have enough for a few stops in America on our way back. We'd travel around the world, taking about a year; it promised to be a lot of fun.

We immediately discounted the idea of joining one of the overland trips across Asia, although we probably couldn't have afforded to anyway. In the early 1970s overland companies were shuttling back and forth across Asia like city buses. There were small operators taking weird and wonderful routes with Land Rovers and big guys like Penn Overland, whose orange buses were at the luxury end of the spectrum. Then there were the crammed and renegade 'Magic Buses', privately owned and often operating out of Amsterdam. In between these extremes were companies like Encounter Overland, whose 4WD trucks are still a familiar sight on the subcontinent and in the backblocks of Africa.

On their Asia run, the assorted buses and trucks usually started in London and ended up in Kathmandu, where they picked up a new collection of passengers and retraced their tire tracks westbound. Overland companies were often operated by ex-British Army officers who ran them like military expeditions. They couldn't run the army the way they wanted to any more, but getting paying customers to behave like army recruits was no problem at all.

Having decided against an organized overland trip, public transport or our own wheels were the possible alternatives. Obviously we'd end up on public transport at some point along the way, but we decided we'd do the first stretch by car. We couldn't afford much of a car, so we decided to get something so cheap that we could leave it by the roadside and walk away from it if need be.

Having owned a couple of minivans and built my Mini-based sports car we decided to look for an old but solid Austin or Morris minivan. They were cheap to buy and run, reasonably reliable and surprisingly spacious. We bought a dark blue example, about ten years old, for sixty-five pounds. I collected some tools and spares and bought a second spare wheel and tire from a wrecker's yard.

There was a long weekend coming up and David Cooper, a college friend, invited us to his parents' beach house on the Atlantic coast of Cornwall. We set off after Maureen finished work on Friday evening and soon began to wonder if our bargain car was the ideal vehicle in which to travel all the way to India. There were typical English long-weekend traffic jams, then the fanbelt broke. Our box of spare parts included a fanbelt and in a short stop by the roadside I managed to change it by flashlight. About fifty miles later, the replacement fanbelt broke. Fortunately, I had a rather tatty second spare, but that was already on its last legs so having fitted it we stopped to buy yet another fanbelt. It wasn't long before I was fitting this fanbelt too. By this time the cause of our fanbelt consumption was making itself audible: a generator bearing was in the process of seizing up. We arrived at David's beach house well after midnight and next morning I fitted new bearings to the generator.

Our elderly vehicle consumed no more fanbelts for the rest of its life with us, but on the way back to London after the weekend there was another horrible noise. This time it was a rear-wheel bearing on its way to oblivion. With appalling screeching and squawking noises from the back we ground our way into London. If this little trip was a foretaste of potential mechanical problems, nursing our little car all the way to India was going to be no fun at all.

A few weeks later, term ended and we were ready to go. We had spare parts, the extra spare wheel, our two backpacks, an old tent, sleeping bags, cooking equipment and boxes of food. There were books and maps and about four hundred pounds in travelers' checks—not a lot of money even back in 1972. We spent our last night in England at my parents' place in Berkshire, to the west of London.

'We'll be back in a year,' we announced on the morning of July 4 as we backed out of their driveway. We wouldn't be. We turned the corner at the bottom of the road and set out to drive to India. Or somewhere.

'Europe,' I said, pointing in the ferry's wake. 'Asia,' I continued, indicating the direction we were going.

Crossing the Bosphorus from European Istanbul to the Asian side of that ancient city, sprawled across a continental divide, was the first great transition of the trip. Today there are two bridges linking European and Asian Istanbul, but in August 1972 the first Bosphorus bridge was still under construction. Driving our little van onto a ferry was the perfect way of making the jump to another continent, a major milestone on the road east.

We had driven into Istanbul a few days earlier and camped just outside the city walls where we spent long evenings talking with other travelers. They were British, Canadian, American and Australian travelers all heading east, many of them in VW Kombi vans. If we weren't already slightly nervous about what lay ahead, the Afghan horror stories we were fed certainly had us worried. Istanbul was our first taste of the exotic east and even though most of the city, and almost all of its historic parts, lies on the European side, there was a distinctly different flavor from the purely European cities we had passed through.

The Pudding Shop, a restaurant in the Sultanahmet area of Istanbul, was the first Asian 'bottleneck' we encountered, those places on the overland route where everybody and anybody was bound to pass through, if you waited long enough. It's still serving cheap meals and living on its footnote in the traveler's history book today.

Amsterdam's Dam Square had made a fine starting point for our journey, but we were soon watching every penny so tightly that we ran out of gas a few miles before the Swiss border. I hitched a ride into Switzerland, returning with a gallon of much cheaper Swiss fuel. Over the following months, my diary had many entries which read 'ran out of gas', as we tried to stretch every penny a little further than it could really go.

In Basle, a front-wheel bearing failed and the English amateur mechanic who helped me replace it solemnly informed me there were no roads where we were going. That was the last bearing failure for the trip, even though we drove over the Alps, through an unseasonal July snowstorm and down into Italy. In Italy, we were robbed, the only theft of the trip. Just like in the ads, American Express came to the rescue and, unfortunately, the thief was caught as well, delaying us for a day to appear in court. It wasn't until our second month in Sydney that we were robbed again.

A ferry took us across the Adriatic to Dubrovnik. Then we traveled to Athens, where we enjoyed a free shower from a laughing woman watering her garden as we descended, sweatily, from the Acropolis. We also drank far too much wine and dined on delicious leftovers at the city's annual wine festival. Wandering wine tasters would buy little cardboard trays of *loukoumades* (tasty little Greek donuts) and, economically, we filled up on the abandoned ones.

While the car took a break at our camping site in Athens, we made an Aegean detour to the island of Lesbos for a spell on the beach. On the ferry we made friends with Ivor Shaun, a lanky young South African, and we joined him on the bus to the ridiculously pretty village of Molyvos. Ivor was meeting some English and Australian friends who were renting a house there. One of his group was a young Australian woman named Barbara Aitken who, twenty-five years later, would be working for us in Melbourne.

We slept on the beach with a bunch of young travelers, including a pair of American hippies who'd adopted the names Sky and Blue for their trip to the east. We talked about the road ahead, skipped lunch every day to save money and spent the evenings drinking cheap retsina in Con's frenetically popular little café. In the early hours of each morning, we'd stumble home and later wake to see Sky and Blue going through their morning yoga routine on the beach, with Turkey looming up in the background across the straits.

Con was never in good enough shape at the end of the evening to tot up his customers' accounts so, after we'd crawled out of our sleeping bags and washed under a tap, we'd wander up to his café to pay the bill for the last night's excesses. We'd usually find him holding his head and swearing he'd never touch retsina again.

Back in Athens we retrieved the car and headed up the coast towards Thessaloniki. It's remarkable how travel leads to curious chance encounters which then lead to other meetings, sometimes years later. At a camp site just outside the small coastal town of Platamon we spent a pleasant evening with a young Australian, Simon Potter, who was doing his big tour of Europe. A few years later, the entire worldwide stock of Lonely Planet books would take up temporary residence under the sofa in his Melbourne apartment. Later still, I would be best man at his wedding.

We got our visas for Iran while we were in Istanbul, but we had to stop in Ankara to get visas for Afghanistan. From Ankara, we headed south to Göreme in the Cappadocia area with its strange rock formations hollowed out to form houses, churches and other buildings. Then it was north to the ancient Hittite cities of Bogazkale and Hattusa and on to the Black Sea ports of Samsun and Trabzon, south again to Erzurum, spending a freezing night in a camp site at Dogubayazit in the shadow of Mt Ararat and finally across the border into Iran.

M: I loved Turkey: it was my first experience of the 'East' and I found it completely enthralling. I was quite stunned the first time I saw camels grazing by the side of the road. We drove into villages which seemed to be sets for *The Greatest Story Ever Told*, places where donkeys walked round in endless circles hauling a huge stone wheel to grind the grain. The women covered their faces as we went by, their eyes wide in astonishment. I was too young and ignorant to understand how they saw me, but I was always touched by the instant friendliness and unforced generosity with which we were greeted.

When people ask us about that first trip, the most common question is: 'What was your worst moment?' It seems that people really want to hear about a dreadful attack or some similarly frightening incident. I don't have an answer. We have lost things, had things stolen, been scared on recklessly driven buses, and had unpleasant or unsavory characters annoy us briefly, but nothing really dramatic.

Except on the Black Sea coast. We had driven into a deserted park which had a camp site. There was no one there, it was quite remote and almost dusk, so we decided to quickly cook something then sleep in the van. As we were getting organized, two men appeared, both holding rifles. I was afraid they were soldiers or police and were going to tell us to move on, but they weren't wearing uniforms. They motioned us to go with them; we tried saying no thanks, but they were insistent. They led us along a wooded track and as we walked other men with guns appeared. They were talking to each other, but of course we didn't understand anything. Finally, we came to a clearing which seemed to be their camp: there was a hut and fire burning. Our escorts motioned for us to sit down. I was really scared. I didn't know where we were (nor did anyone else), all our worldly possessions were in the van and there were a lot of tough-looking men with guns all around us! One man went to the hut and summoned another man who came over, said something, then walked away, returning with tea and bread for us. That was all that happened, and eventually they led us back to our van, but I was really, really frightened—for a while.

We had other incidents in Turkey that began ambiguously and ended with gratuitous acts of kindness. Once we were camping by a lake, near a restaurant, when a tall youth appeared and stood by our tent, looking at us. We tried talking

to him, but he didn't understand. He seemed prepared to stand
there all night. We thought we might lose him if we walked up
to the restaurant. He quickly took the lead and ushered us into
the dining room where a man was waiting for us with a table
of food.

'What kept you so long? I sent Ahmed to get you a while
ago,' he said. We had a wonderful meal with the restaurant pro-
prietor, and he introduced us to a specialty—roasted sparrows.
I found it hard to choke these poor little creatures down, but
Tony has never had any trouble eating birds and was quite
intrigued. Sometimes I think that the 'bad' travel stories are
the result of miscommunication or misunderstanding but
maybe we have just been incredibly lucky.

In Tabriz, our first stop in Iran, we saw the Shah parading through
town in a motorcade before we continued south to Isfahan. Like so
many other visitors we were knocked out by the sheer beauty of
Isfahan; its immense square edged by brilliant blue-tiled buildings is
regularly cited as the most stunning in the Islamic world. There are
photographs of Maureen sitting on the river's edge beside one of
Isfahan's trademark bridges, looking very much the experienced
young Asian traveler, and of me at the camp site, sporting a beard
and laughing as I hold a wide oval of nan, the Persian bread which
was our usual breakfast.

Just before leaving Isfahan to go back north through Tehran, I ate
something which violently disagreed with me and for the next few
days I suffered from our first case of 'Delhi Belly'. I was lucky we
had our own wheels and I could avoid the familiar experience of racing down the aisle of a bus, clutching my stomach and waving a toilet roll in the air, much to the amusement of other passengers. From
the Caspian Sea we turned east and continued to Mashed with its
holy shrine and fiercely religious Muslims. The border with
Afghanistan was not far away, but what with customs officials,
health officials, immigration officials, police officials and insurance
officials (we had to buy car insurance, for a few dollars, at each bor-

der), simply crossing the border consumed three hours.

Herat was a delight with its beautiful Friday Mosque, brooding citadel and intriguing bazaars. This was a magical time to be traveling, and David Tomory's oral history of the trail, *A Season in Heaven*, which Lonely Planet would one day publish, captures the feel of Afghanistan in that era perfectly. Of course, the memories have faded (and if you can remember it clearly then you clearly weren't there), but Sigi's cafe in Kabul was undoubtedly the epicenter of the Afghan section of the trail. We sat on carpets, sipping mint tea, listening to music (the rumor was that if Pink Floyd released a record in London on Monday it was in Kabul by Friday), occasionally repairing to the courtyard to shift the giant chess pieces around the giant chessboard. Cool.

The Afghans were cool too. 'They were an example to us all, proving that you could be smart, tough, proud, broke, stoned and magnificently dressed, all at once,' according to *A Season in Heaven*. Our attempts to look magnificently dressed inevitably failed. I'd no sooner arrived in Herat than I wandered off to a tailor to be fitted out with a Europeanized version of an Afghan suit. A German traveler returning from the tailor at the same time donned his suit and reduced the Afghans hanging around the hotel to gibbering wrecks, laughing so hard they had to lie on the floor. 'No man would wear red,' one of them confided. It was the travelers' responsibility to entertain as well as be entertained and we certainly did our best.

We'd arrived in Afghanistan slightly spooked. We'd heard so many stories about wild men and craziness, there was no question that crossing borders in Asia seemed something to be measured on the Richter scale; the number goes up by one, but the earthquake jumps by a factor of ten. Leaving Europe for Turkey had been the first big culture shock, then it was shock times ten when we hit Iran and times one hundred when we crossed into Afghanistan. Well, that was the theory anyway. Once we spent some time in Afghanistan we relaxed, because it simply wasn't as scary as we'd convinced ourselves it would be.

Bruce Chatwin rejoiced that he visited Afghanistan 'before the

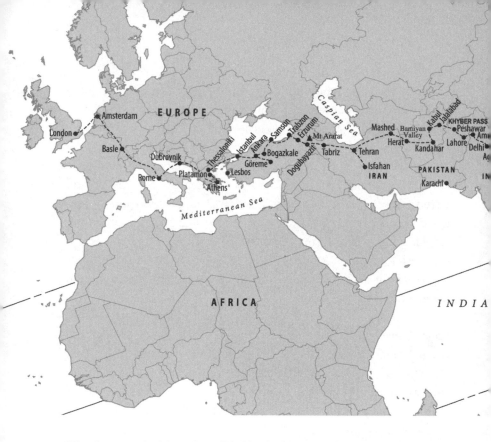

Hippies wrecked it'. They did this, he claimed, 'by driving educated Afghans into the arms of the Marxists', but Chatwin was a snob and never very happy about anybody who hadn't been to Oxford and didn't do their shopping at Sotheby's.

In fact, the Afghans look back to the hippy period as a golden age. Everything was peaceful and there was lots of money to be made: somebody was buying the carpets even if we weren't. One thing hasn't changed—our favorite hotel in 1972 Kabul was the Mustafa, the same one that everybody stays in today.

Like Istanbul, Kabul was another of the Asian 'bottlenecks', one of those places every traveler seemed to pass through. Kabul was the first of the three Ks (Kathmandu in Nepal and Kuta Beach in Bali were yet to come), places that serious Asian travelers felt compelled to visit.

Our minivan was going strong, but we were going to have to

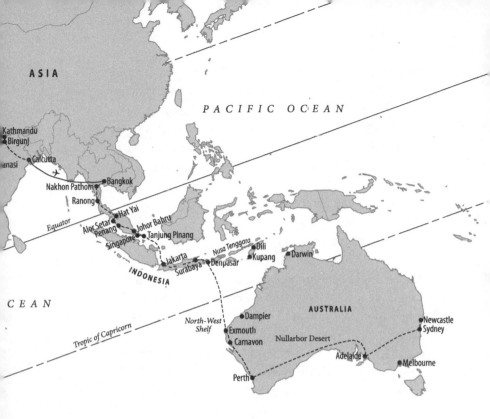

abandon it soon and when we were offered US$155 for it, a five dollar improvement on its purchase price, we took the money and pressed on east, regrettably foregoing the trip north to the great Buddhas of the Bamiyan Valley. In March 2001, the Taliban underlined their crazy brand of Islamic fundamentalism by destroying the age-old Buddhas. Now, I'll never be able to see them.

Our bus wound its way from Kabul through Jalalabad and up towards the Khyber Pass, but Maureen and I didn't spend much time enjoying the view. The meal our van purchaser had bought for us on our last evening in Kabul was doing terrible things to our stomachs.

In the middle of what became a nightmare trip, Maureen announced that she was either hallucinating or she could hear a Belfast accent wafting forward from a few rows back. It was indeed, although its purveyor, Carol Clewlow, was from Somerset in the south of England and had acquired her accent from a journalistic spell in the Northern Irish capital. An energetic slight blonde, Carol would later write one of our early guidebooks and then segue into fiction. Her companion, fellow journalist David Watson, was a real Belfast boy, but the third member of their small troupe, Joe Geddes, was a train driver and Vietnam vet from the town of Traralgon in the Australian state of Victoria. By the time we arrived in Peshawar in Pakistan we were a fivesome, and although David abandoned us a week later to head north to Kashmir the rest of us continued together to Kathmandu.

From Peshawar we traveled to Lahore, where each Wednesday night a traffic jam built up, jostling to cross the border into India the next morning. The war between Pakistan and India which had led to the creation of Bangladesh was only recently over. Relations between the two countries were at rock bottom and the sole land border crossing, between the Punjab cities of Lahore and Amritsar, was open once a week, for a few hours each Thursday morning.

We didn't hang around long in Amritsar, continuing to Delhi where Maureen and I enjoyed several days of real comfort—complete with hot showers—in the home of Ernie Carroll, a friend of my father's. We remember being incredibly intimidated by the platoon of servants—bearers, chowkidars, cooks, malis, sweepers and all those other reminders of the Raj. One night, Carol and Joe came round to dinner and we watched them equally flummoxed by this totally alien experience.

In Varanasi, the holy city of India, strategically situated on the holy Ganges River, we met up with Carol and Joe again to make the long overnight railway journey to Raxaul on the Nepalese border, with a change of train en route. Our first train arrived so late that we missed our connection and a large band of us camped out in the railway restaurant, calling for more and more rounds of toast, the only food they could provide that morning.

When the train pulled in, we piled on board and continued on towards Nepal. Until, that is, the ticket inspector gave us our first real experience of Indian bureaucracy. The missed connecting train was an 'express', but the train we now found ourselves on was a 'mail'. Neither of them moved very fast and, due to the missed connection, we would arrive at our final destination many hours behind schedule. Nevertheless, an express was an express and a mail was a mail, and half of our happy band had tickets which were good for an express but not good enough for a mail. None of us could work out why some tickets were acceptable, but others weren't, and when some of the guilty parties refused to pay the fines the train was halted while the ticket collector phoned (or more likely sent a telegram) for a ruling on this intractable problem. I can't remember if they all paid up, but eventually we continued on our way, arriving at Raxaul even more behind schedule. We then took a bicycle rickshaw to the border and another to Birgunj in Nepal.

It's hard to imagine a more miserable place than Birgunj. Even the name sounds, well, grungy. Worse still, there was no way of avoiding it. At that time, Birgunj was virtually the only entry point to Nepal and all the buses for Kathmandu left in a massed convoy around dawn each morning. Whatever time you arrived in Birgunj you were doomed to spend a night there before making an early escape the next day. Our group of four or five wandered around the small town until we found a hotel with only one room with one large double bed remaining. We took one look at the mattress and hauled it onto the floor before we all unrolled our sleeping bags crossways over the plank-like wooden bed base. We bought tickets for the next morning's bus and retired to our miserable hotel's miserable restaurant for a miserable meal. The menu was eggs, eggs or eggs, but the congealed mess, floating in grease, was more than I could face. I picked up the metal plate, walked into the kitchen and tossed it on the floor. Nobody looked up. Bad behavior from an exasperated traveler was presumably not unusual.

The next morning we headed north. The bus cruised across the Terai, the narrow strip of the great Indian plain along the southern edge of Nepal, then ground its way up the corkscrewing road into the foothills. The trip droned on all day with views getting steadily better as we climbed higher towards the Himalayan range, occasionally glimpsed in the distance. A couple of times we abandoned the crowded interior of the bus to join others, travelers and locals, for a ride on the roof. As evening drew in, the chill drove us back inside as we climbed the last rise towards the edge of the Kathmandu Valley.

Some places find their way into your heart instantly and Kathmandu was one of them. Perhaps the long ride up from the Indian plains helped, but as we topped the edge of the valley and dropped down towards Kathmandu it seemed like Shangri-La, with multi-tiered temple roofs punctuating the city skyline, oil lamps twinkling through latticed wooden windows and the setting sun warming the snow-capped Himalayan range as a backdrop.

We found a room at the Camp Hotel on a dirty little alley running from Durbar Square, the central 'Palace Square' of the town, to the Bagmati River. Officially, the street was known as Maru Tole, but to the travelers who congregated there it was either known as Pie Alley, from the string of pie shops, or Pig Alley, from the hordes of pigs. Even without the pigs it wouldn't have been very clean: Kathmandu wasn't noted for its hygiene. It was noted for its pie shops, selling apple pie, pumpkin pie, lemon meringue pie and many other creations which seemed out of place high in the Himalaya. It was said that a Nepalese cook set up the first pie shop in the Sixties, turning out the pies he'd learnt to cook for the local Peace Corps director. When his pies were an instant hit more pie shops quickly followed.

Kathmandu was also famous for its liberal attitude towards marijuana and hashish, freely available at outlets like the Eden Hash Shop which produced calendars and business cards proclaiming it was 'Your Favorite Joint'. On the pie shop menus there were 'special' cakes and cookies, special due to the liberal addition of dope. Lots of travelers in Kathmandu in 1972 were high in more places than the Himalaya.

We lounged around Kathmandu for a couple of weeks, switching hotels from Pie Alley to an even cheaper place on Freak Street, at that time the center for the town's ever-changing collection of hippies. We rented bicycles to ride out to the other towns around the valley and trekked up to Nagarkot on the rim of the valley, to catch sunrise over the Himalayan range. But all too soon we were packing up to continue our travels east. Carol and most of the other people we'd come up to Kathmandu with were flying out to Bangkok, but for us money was too tight for that extravagance, so we rode the bus back down to the plains.

Birgunj may have been a miserable dump, but the border town we stayed at on the Indian side was equally bad. That night, Maureen ate something which violently disagreed with her and she spent the long train trip to Calcutta feeling very ill. Calcutta was a shock to us. It was less than a year after the end of the violent and bitter struggle that split Bangladesh off from Pakistan and the streets of Calcutta were still packed with refugees. From Calcutta's chaotic Howrah railway station we eventually found our way across the densely packed Hooghly Bridge to the Salvation Army Hostel, still a backpacker's favorite on Sudder Street. I've since returned to Calcutta on numerous occasions and, like many other visitors, I've never developed a love affair with the city but I think I understand why Bengalis reckon this is the real heart and soul of India.

'What did he say?' we asked my father's friend.

The Indian butler had whispered something into our host's ear, something which was obviously very amusing. We were sitting on the veranda of his Calcutta apartment, having a pre-dinner drink, and Maureen had just asked for that perfect Raj-era tipple, a gin and tonic.

'He asked if memsahib was old enough to drink,' he explained with a broad grin.

That Indian interlude apart, the trip east had been distinctly alcohol-free. Since we'd left the pleasures of retsina in Greece, we'd only enjoyed the occasional bottle of beer in Turkey and, surprisingly, a shared bottle of Shiraz wine from the Iranian town which gave the grape variety its name, provided by some fellow campers in Isfahan. The Ayatollah, wherever he was at the time, probably felt a stabbing pain with each sip we took. At that time, buying a beer in Pakistan required a certificate indicating you were an alcoholic and had to have your fix, but in general our abstinence was the result of a far more fundamental difficulty—we simply couldn't afford such luxuries as alcohol.

There was no way of crossing Burma by land, so we bit the bullet and flew to Bangkok on Thai International, which was just developing a name as a sexy international airline and was the backpacker's carrier of choice. After those dry months on the road, a smiling Thai flight attendant coming down the aisle with a bottle of red wine in one hand and white in the other was like a glimpse of heaven. A very merry band of travelers was decanted onto the tarmac at Bangkok Airport to be met by three Thai shocks.

It was hot! Calcutta may have been hot, but this was an oven. It was cold! A blast of icy air hit us as we stepped into the terminal. The Thais like their air-conditioning set cold enough to keep ice-cream frozen. It was efficient! That was something we'd forgotten all about after a spell in India. The airport was brightly lit, there was a tourist desk and before we knew it we'd been told the perfect hotel was waiting for us and we were shoved into a bus and pointed towards Bangkok.

The Malaysia Hotel was, indeed, perfect. Compared to the ancient dumps we'd been staying in, the Malaysia was a dream: multi-storey, air-conditioned and with a swimming pool. Or at least that was our first impression; in fact, the Malaysia was a cheap box, quickly thrown up to cater to American soldiers on R&R from Vietnam. Now that Vietnam was winding down, the R&R business was disappearing and it was at this point that the Malaysia's owners had a brainwave. They'd cut costs to the bone and pitched their empty hotel at the nascent backpacker market. We'd arrived at introductory offer time: two dollars a night for a double room on your first night, three dollars thereafter. The sheer luxury—beds that didn't sag, no bed bugs or cockroaches, our own bathroom, air-conditioning, a swimming pool—was stunning, but three dollars was three dollars and after a couple of nights we shifted to a hotel that cost half the price.

It was November and our money was running low. If we were

going to get to Australia by Christmas and with any money left we had to accelerate. We decided to head quickly south through Thailand and Malaysia, perhaps coming back for a more leisurely visit after our working spell in Australia.

A few days later we took a bus to the outskirts of Bangkok, stuck out our thumbs and hitch-hiked south through Thailand to Malaysia and Singapore. Not far past Nakhon Pathom, and only about sixty miles from Bangkok, we spent several hours standing by the road watching the occasional truck rumble past and envying the Thais cruising by on their little Japanese motorcycles. It was early evening when a rowdy band of Thai students in two trucks picked us up. Hours south we stopped at a roadside restaurant and had our first introduction to the fiery heat of Thai food, crowded round a circular table and dipping into a communal bowl. Around midnight, they dropped us at a roadside hotel just outside Ranong on the west coast of the Thai peninsula. That night was not only our first introduction to real Thai food, but also to Thai friendliness—the students even negotiated our room rate before they went on their way.

Next day we thumbed our way further south to a small town beyond Phuket and the day after, giving up on free rides, we took a bus into Hat Yai, just north of the Malaysian border. AIDS has since taken the edge off the Thai sex business, but at that time Hat Yai's main purpose was peddling sex to visitors from strait-laced Malaysia. No doubt our cheap hotel moonlighted as a brothel.

In the morning, as a tropical downpour commenced, we crawled under a tarpaulin in the back of a truck for the ride to the border. At the Thai immigration control our passports were stamped, marking our exit from the kingdom, but then we made a horrible discovery: Malaysia was not just on the other side of the fence. A wide no-man's-land separated the two border controls. It was too far to walk, even if it was permitted, and there was no bus or taxi service to take us across the border.

Later we discovered that most travelers crossed in old Thai Chevy taxis which shuttled between Hat Yai and Georgetown on the island of Penang. A busload of Malaysian tourists leaned out the windows to photograph us: here were the long-haired backpacking hippies they'd read so much about. Eventually, a truck taking fish across the border took pity on us and we arrived in Malaysia smelling a bit fishy.

Maureen swears the Malaysian officials stamped 'SHIT' in our passports, for 'Suspected Hippies in Transit'. Well, we were in transit. After a night in the honky-tonk border town of Alor Setar we stood at the edge of town with our thumbs out once again. Our dwindling finances meant we had to get to Singapore as quickly as possible, as I'd asked my parents to send money to us there. An Indonesian mining engineer, with a colorful name which sounded like Golden Hoff, soon rumbled up in a Land Rover and told us he was heading south to Johor Bahru, just across the causeway from Singapore. He was the perfect introduction to Malaysia, explaining the food, introducing us to the amazing cold drink *es kacang* and refining our chopsticks technique. (*Kacang* means beans, *es* is ice, and this curious combination of red beans, shredded coconut, jelly and ice tastes far better than it sounds—or looks.) Late that night we arrived at his site camp in the jungle north of Johor Bahru and slept on the floor of his office. Next morning he dropped us at the bus station for the short trip to Singapore.

'How much money do you have?' was the first question we heard from the Singapore immigration official.

The city state's short-hair, buttoned-down, anti-hippy reputation was in full bloom and we did not get a friendly reception at the causeway border post.

'We have money waiting for us in Singapore,' we insisted.

'Well, phone the bank and prove it,' he responded.

Eventually we were allowed in, with a suggestion that I get my hair cut if we planned to stay more than twenty-four hours. At that time, post offices and other government buildings in Singapore sported signs announcing: 'Men with long hair will be served last.'

We found a room in a hotel we would get to know very well two years later, and next morning went in search of our money. I'd asked my parents to loan me fifty pounds and that was precisely how much they'd sent. Would it get us to Australia?

There was no direct shipping connection between Singapore and Jakarta, but there was a weekly service from the Indonesian island of Tanjung Pinang, just south of Singapore. This was the infamous *Tampomas*, operated by the Indonesian shipping company Pelni. In 1981, the *Tampomas* caught fire and sank. Today, Pelni's ships are rather classier affairs, but back then traveling deck class in Indonesia was the unhappy maritime equivalent of the discomforts of third-class train travel in India. We were relieved to see Jakarta, thirty-six hours later, but we knew nothing about Indonesia's capital city and spent most of the day trying to find somewhere to stay, never stumbling upon the street known as Jalan Jaksa, to this day the hub for backpackers in Jakarta.

Our task in Jakarta was to get tickets to Australia. We couldn't afford to fly there directly so we planned to make our way across Java to the island of Bali, then continue to Portuguese Timor. A couple of times a week the Australian airline TAA flew from Portuguese Timor to Darwin.

If you believed the worst of the wild and varied rumors, getting from Bali to Timor took a month of rough and ready travel. Four weeks of tough truck rides and bumpy sea crossings in leaky boats would only get us to the Indonesian half of the island. Travelers' stories kicked into overdrive when they described Timor itself: the roads were impassable, it was the wet season, there were unfordable rivers, the border was closed. Of course, they told us, you could fly Zamrud. This near-mythical airline had a weekly flight from Bali to Portuguese Timor—all we had to do was track it down and buy a ticket.

'Come back tomorrow,' we were told when we found Zamrud's Jakarta office, as if tickets could only be sold on certain days of the week.

'Why don't you fly to Kupang with Merpati?' we were told when we returned the next day.

This was clearly an airline which was not very keen on selling tickets. We did not want to fly to Kupang with Merpati. Kupang was at the other end of the Indonesian half of the island of Timor, and we wanted to get to the Portuguese half.

'Well in that case you're out of luck,' the agent said. Zamrud had gone bust.

Phoenix-like Zamrud rose from the ashes several times in the next few years, but regrettably we never set foot in a Zamrud aircraft. Their admirably battered old DC3s littered airstrips right down through Nusa Tenggara, the chain of islands sprinkled east of Bali, and for years a flock of partly assembled Zamrud planes were parked at the airport in Bali. It was said one of their pilots made his in-flight announcements by leaning round the open door to the flight deck and loudly enquiring if passengers would like to take the coastal route around an island or fly inland to check out the volcanoes.

We decided to worry about getting to Timor after we arrived in Bali, thinking that Zamrud may be back in action by then. We were still hurrying through, hoping to get to Australia before Christmas and, more importantly, before our money ran out. In Denpasar we found our way to Adi Yasa, a small hotel known as a budget traveler's favorite. It was the nicest place we'd encountered on the whole trip.

M: Bali was my perfect dream of a tropical island. We had driven all day from Surabaya to Denpasar and in the late afternoon we crossed by ferry from Java to Bali. I looked out the window and for a moment I imagined I'd stepped into the waterfall scene from *South Pacific*. By the side of the road, water was cascading down the hillside to where a beautiful Balinese girl was bathing, bare-breasted and surrounded by blossoming hibiscus and frangipani trees. Delicate, deer-like Balinese cows grazed by the road. It seemed almost too beautiful to be real.

Amongst the palm trees at Kuta Beach a half-dozen little *losmen*, small family-run Indonesian hotels, and a similar number of *warungs*, food-stall style restaurants, were reached by sandy roads running down to the sea. The beach was great and the food was wonderful, but we were troubled by how we would we get to Timor. If anything, the travel tales got worse the closer we got. It seemed the only way to do it was to island-hop south.

'I only need a couple more crew to sail south,' we heard a voice announce in a Kuta café the next morning. David was the skipper of a yacht out of Auckland, New Zealand, who wanted to head down to Australia to work while he waited out the cyclone season. He had us as crew within minutes.

We rented a motorcycle for an afternoon and rode round to Benoa to see the yacht, but didn't realize Benoa Village and Benoa Harbor were two entirely different places on opposite sides of the bay. Getting to Benoa Harbor, south of Denpasar and midway between the resort beaches of Kuta and Sanur, was no problem at all. Getting to Benoa Village was an entirely different situation and it was nearly dark by the time we reached the end of a long muddy trail and discovered Benoa Harbor was a couple of hundred yards away, across the narrow entrance to the bay. Today the village of Benoa is easily reached via the Nusa Dua resort, but in 1972 Nusa Dua was more commonly accessed by 4WDs than tourist buses.

A local boatman shuttled us across to the yachts anchored in Benoa Harbor and we had a look round the *Sun Peddler*, our transport to Australia. That confused bike trip should have been a warning, but a few days later we helped load supplies on board, sailed out through the constricted reef passage and turned south.

With the first slight swell Maureen turned an amazing shade of green and we discovered that anything slightly rougher than a ripple running across a bathtub had a severe effect on her stomach. We sailed south for a day or two, with no noticeable change in her coloring, and then we stopped. Dead. The water was flat and calm, but Maureen managed to remain horribly seasick. For several days there was barely a breath of wind and we drifted slowly in circles. Once we tossed a line out behind the boat and I have a photo of most of the crew swimming in the clear waters of the Indian Ocean, the rope as insurance in case a breeze should suddenly appear.

There were seven of us on board, and David, the skipper, was the sole Kiwi. There were two Americans, two Australians, and Maureen and I, two Poms (Australian slang for 'British').

By about day eight the wind began to pick up and Maureen felt a little better. This was terrible timing on her part because we'd estimated a six- to eight-day trip and had stocked the boat accordingly. As her appetite returned, the food ran out. By this time we were rationing water as well because one of our water tanks had developed a leak and a large proportion of our drinking water had disappeared. Then calm turned to gale until one night we were running through a real storm and our mainsail split. We limped on with a smaller storm sail, then hit another stretch of calm. When we tried to motor through it our engine wouldn't start, but eventually the wind picked up. This stretch of ocean was remarkably empty; we never saw another ship.

We dragged a fishing line behind us for almost the whole trip but the only catch was a flying fish which made a low altitude pass over the boat one night, crash landing through the hatch into the bunk Maureen and I shared. I woke to hear thrashing in our bed.

'We're sleeping with the fish,' I mumbled to Maureen.

'You're imagining things. Go back to sleep,' she wisely suggested.

I obeyed her, but we were indeed sleeping with a fish. In the morning we found a rather stiff finny friend wedged between us.

Our cash-enforced Christmas travel deadline was driving us towards Australia, but for Rob and Maggie, the Australian couple on board, there was a much more weighty reason for hurrying south. They wanted to vote. For nearly twenty-five years Australia had been run by the stiflingly conservative, and curiously named, Liberal Party. For most of that time, Robert Menzies had been the prime minister, a confirmed anglophile enamored of the days when Australia was a British colony. During the 1960s, the country had begun to loosen up, although the opposition Labor Party had narrowly failed to get across the line in the 1969 election. This time it looked like change was possible and indeed the party's slogan, regularly intoned by its charismatic leader Gough Whitlam, was: 'It's time.'

Unfortunately, we wouldn't dock in time for the Australian crew to vote. Gough Whitlam became Australia's new prime minister on December 5 when we were still several days' sailing to the north. Maureen and I were totally unfamiliar with Australian politics, coming from Britain where power had ricocheted between Labour's Harold Wilson and the Conservative Party's Edmund Heath with no discernible change, and we had no idea of the importance this election would hold.

Within days, Australia pulled its troops out of the Vietnam War. And quitting Vietnam was only the start. Whitlam's time in power was brief (his government collapsed in a morass of minor scandals and major money problems), but there's no question that he kick-started the new Australia which would emerge in the last quarter of the twentieth century. From being a quiet backwater which people wanted to escape, Australia became the place everyone wanted to visit.

We would arrive at an exciting time, but as the new government moved into office we were still trying to get into the country. The winds were finally blowing in the right direction, but the coast was still days away. The fresh supplies we'd bought in Bali were gone. The ice had long melted and there was no refrigeration. Even if there had been it wouldn't have been working since we couldn't get the engine started. We were reduced to eating the canned and dried supplies packed on board the yacht in New Zealand years previously. Dried meant powdered eggs, never a very satisfying dish, and canned seemed to mean one of three possibilities: asparagus spears, creamed sweet corn or Christmas pudding. It was no wonder we were keen to land.

That night a light appeared on the horizon, directly to the south. It was the first sign of life we'd seen since leaving Bali, now nearly two weeks past. All night we sailed towards it and as the sun started to rise we could make out, with binoculars, an oil rig and supply ship. Today the North-West Shelf fields pump huge quantities of natural gas ashore at Dampier, from where it's exported to Japan, but in

1972 the first experimental drilling was taking place and this was one of those rigs.

We made radio contact with the supply ship and, concerned that our water supplies were perilously low, asked if we could get water.

'No worries,' was the distinctively Australian response. 'Do you want some food as well?'

We certainly did and when we pulled up beside the ship a variety of supplies was tossed down to us. We clutched at these provisions with such wild-eyed exuberance that it was hardly surprising when someone made the next logical offer.

'Why don't you come on board for a meal?' asked a kind-hearted individual. We were up the ladders and on board in minutes. Food wasn't the only luxury on offer—there were also hot showers, something we didn't have on the yacht and for that matter hadn't seen too often for many months.

Next morning, after promising never to mention this highly unofficial visit to an offshore piece of Australia—technically we hadn't yet arrived in the country—we set sail again. We were heading for Exmouth, a remote town perched on Western Australia's North-West Cape. As well as being more or less directly south of Bali, the town had a US Navy communications base, used to keep in contact with American nuclear submarines, and for this reason had an immigration and customs post, so we could legally enter Australia.

Apart from being halfway around the world from our European starting point, Australia had a major attraction for us: we didn't need a visa to live or work there. British citizens could turn up uninvited, move in and find jobs, as if they were Australians. Back then, Australia even offered subsidized passages from England for suitable immigrants and for the next year we were regularly asked if we were 'ten-pound Poms', Brits who had paid that amount for their airfare down under.

From our boat anchored off Exmouth beach, David rowed ashore, tracked down Exmouth's immigration official and brought him back to the yacht. We were ferried ashore in an outboard-powered dinghy and Maureen and I got our photograph taken standing barefoot in the sand at the water's edge.

'So, are you visitors or immigrants?' the official asked.

'Is there a choice? What's the difference?' Maureen queried.

'Well, nothing really,' he replied, 'except if you're an immigrant you get three months' free medical insurance.'

'I guess we'd better be immigrants,' we chimed, spotting a bargain too good to miss. It was a wise decision, since only a year later the visa regulations were comprehensively changed.

Once our passports were stamped, we discovered how fastidious Aussie customs officials could be. Our toothpaste tube was unrolled and the plugs on our backpack frames were removed and the tubes inspected. We put it down to the fact that yachts arriving from Indonesia were not an everyday occurrence. Unfortunately, the customs guy found something interesting belonging to Rob.

A few nights earlier, Rob had decided to work off the last of his small collection of pre-rolled joints. It was passed around, its distinct lack of potency commented upon and then it was forgotten. The reason for its failure as a joint was fairly straightforward: it wasn't one. We'd smoked one of his roll-your-owns. The last joint was still in the cigarette pack where it was discovered by Exmouth's enthusiastic customs official. Rob was arrested and charged with possession of a few grams of marijuana.

Later on, the rest of us repaired to a pub for our first Australian beer. Maureen commented to Maggie that her boyfriend's chosen place of concealment was pretty dumb and our voyage together finished with a small but noisy argument. It shouldn't have ended like this because they had been remarkably helpful to us from the moment we first met, but it was not surprising. We'd been together long enough that at least one good yelling match was well overdue and it was certainly time for Maureen and me to hit the road. We were uncomfortably close to penniless by this time so employment was in order.

'How far to the main road to Perth?' we asked the barman.

'One hundred and thirty-five miles to the bitumen,' was the reply.

So, late in the afternoon, we walked to the edge of town and stuck out our thumbs.

Later we were to discover that Australians complain about visitors who expect the place to be like a *Crocodile Dundee* movie, with kangaroos bounding off in every direction. Paul Hogan was still more than ten years away from killing a croc at this time, but those myths were alive and kicking on the edge of Exmouth. We saw our first roo lolloping away before we'd even thumbed a ride.

And what rides we thumbed. We soon found ourselves bouncing along the road with a friendly Yugoslav truckie (truck driver) who periodically hauled a cold stubby (small bottle of beer) from his esky (ice cooler) and removed the top with his teeth. Some time later we turned off the road to stop at a beachside pub which I remember being full of Aborigines and road workers. Later still, we once more found ourselves with the Yugoslav truckie, heading back towards Exmouth. By this time it was getting very late and we had no idea what we were doing, or even where we were going. Our truckie friend flashed his lights for an oncoming car to stop, then he got out and talked to the driver. Returning to the truck, he told us the driver was the local Beaurepaire tire company rep, heading home to Carnarvon, and he'd be happy to give us a ride. So we climbed into his ute (another new word for us) and headed south.

'I was planning to pull over and sleep by the roadside,' he explained, 'but if you can keep me awake I'll drive home. My wife's pregnant so she'll be glad to see me. It's about 230 miles.'

We rolled into Carnarvon after midnight. We slept on a mattress in the back of a station wagon in their garage, lulled to sleep by the gentle noises of a joey (baby kangaroo) sleeping in a canvas bag hanging on the garage wall. The young kangaroo's mother had died after being hit by a car and our tire rep had rescued it and brought it home. Next morning, we were given breakfast and dropped at a truckstop on the edge of town where we soon convinced a truckie to give us a ride to Perth, another 600 miles south.

A day and a half later we arrived in Perth. The drive had been furiously hot and we'd spent one night sleeping beside the truck just off the road. We rode a train into the town center and as we came out of the station a passing driver saw our backpacks and offered us a ride, further confirmation of that legendary Australian friendliness.

Later, we bought a newspaper, found a boarding house up the hill from the city center towards King's Park and rented a cheap room. Sometime in that week, I entered our weights in my diary. Between England and Australia I'd lost more than fifteen pounds, falling from 123 pounds in my birthday suit to 108 pounds with clothes on. Maureen was equally skinny: in July, she'd weighed 117 pounds (naked) but now she was down to 106 pounds (clothed).

We should have phoned home. We'd sent a postcard from Bali, nonchalantly telling my parents we'd scored a ride on a yacht and would be in Australia in a week. A week later, when the card landed on their doormat in England, we were sailing round in circles and nowhere near Australia. Another week later, when they were beginning to wonder why they hadn't heard from us, we were still sailing south. Another week passed before we arrived in Australia and made our way to Perth. And now another week would pass before we got to the east coast and, finally, made that overdue call to my frantic parents.

After the sheer emptiness of the highway south from our landing point, Perth seemed bright, modern and, after Asia, tidy and quiet. Maureen quickly got a job as a 'flying domestic', rushing round Perth on a pre-Christmas house spring-cleaning mission, while I devoted myself to getting a refund on our unused Timor–Darwin airline ticket. We were down to our last few dollars, but the eighty-dollar ticket refund, minus a cancellation charge, plus the money from Maureen's cleaning job, was enough to point us towards Sydney.

A find-a-ride service put us in touch with Brian, a young guy in the Royal Australian Air Force planning to drive home to Sydney for Christmas, and with Rod, another young English traveler. We agreed to split the fuel costs for a quick trip across the Nullarbor Desert to the east coast. Brian and I would share the driving as neither Maureen nor Rod could drive. The long east–west track across Australia was unsurfaced back then; it wasn't until 1976 that it became a smooth bitumen road. Three days of more or less nonstop driving, with a short pause in Adelaide, saw us at Brian's parents' place on the north side of Sydney. It was the day before my twenty-sixth birthday.

In the morning we went to have our first look at Sydney and in the afternoon set out to hitch-hike north to Newcastle, where we were going to spend Christmas with Paul Myall. A neighbor and good friend from my last few years at school, Paul had been a keen motorcycle racer and I'd gone along with him to help out at tracks all around England when he was racing an old AJS 7R. Paul's racing career had ended after we'd parted ways when I'd gone to university. He'd won a race which gave him free entry to the Manx Grand Prix, the junior racing week at motorcycle racing's Mecca, the Isle of Man, but in a practice ride on that notoriously dangerous course he'd crashed badly, spent days in a coma and never raced again.

I'd sporadically kept in touch with Paul while we were both in college and then heard from him again shortly before we set out on our big trip when we were invited to a post-wedding party at his parents' place to the north of London. That crowded occasion was the only time we'd met Paul's new wife and this next meeting was not a happy one. We felt that we were looked upon as unwanted guests, come to sponge off an old friend, or perhaps we just brought some unwanted competition to the scene. I guess we were not the only ones she didn't like because eventually she and Paul were divorced.

Christmas Day was a rather icy occasion, despite the summer heat, so we announced that even though Boxing Day (the day after Christmas) was a public holiday we had a pressing engagement in Sydney. The next morning once again found us by the roadside with our thumbs out. A few hours later we crossed the Sydney Harbour Bridge into the city which would be our home for the next year.

Our ride into Sydney had a curious influence on our yet-to-be-created business. The friendly young couple who drove us into the city said that if we had trouble finding a place to stay we were welcome to sleep on their apartment floor. They dropped us off in the center of Sydney, outside the place where they both worked, the head office of the Bank of New South Wales.

'What nice people,' we thought. 'When we open a bank account we'll use that bank.'

For twenty-five years, Lonely Planet banked with Westpac, the Bank of New South Wales one name change later, and our line of credit grew to ten million dollars before we switched banks.

This was the finishing line for the first part of the trip we'd begun back in July. We'd set out with the simple aim of traveling overland from London to Sydney, stretching our money as far as it would go and arriving pretty well broke.

'How much money do we have left?' Maureen asked.

I fished in my pockets and brought out a handful of small change.

'Twenty-seven cents,' I said.

2
Southeast Asia

Even in 1972 twenty-seven cents didn't go very far, but it did buy us a copy of the *Sydney Morning Herald* newspaper and pay for a five-cent phone call. We found an ad for a single furnished room for sixteen dollars a week, phoned to check it was available, then walked from the center of Sydney up to Kings Cross, where we pawned my camera for twenty dollars. Past 'The Cross' on Darling Point we found the room, in a fine old house looking out over Sydney Harbour and across to the partially constructed Sydney Opera House. We paid the first week's rent and walked to a nearby supermarket where we invested some of our remaining four dollars in sausages and potatoes.

Within a few days both of us had signed up for temporary jobs with an office employment agency. Soon we were trekking back and forth to city offices delivering messages, typing invoices and digging ourselves out of our financial hole. Each evening we'd meet in Hyde Park in the center of Sydney and walk back through Woolloomooloo and Kings Cross to our tiny room. After dinner we'd wander back up to the Cross, Sydney's sex and sleaze center. One night, walking back through Darlinghurst with an armful of books from the Kings Cross library, we were accosted by one of the strip show touts who suggested we get rid of the books, come inside and get a real education!

By the end of January both of us had full-time jobs. Maureen was back in the wine business, working for a small company in the inner-

Sydney industrial suburb of Marrickville. Terry Donovan, the father of actor Jason Donovan, was friends with the general manager and did late-night television ads of the 'buy a case of wine *and* get a free barbecue *and* a set of steak knives *and* we'll even throw in the sun lounger' variety. During the year Maureen worked there, the company was taken over by Bernie Houghton, who, it was alleged by several people, worked for the CIA during the Vietnam War. He had come to Australia and set up several bars for GIs on R&R, including the iconic Bourbon & Beefsteak in Kings Cross. Years later, his name was connected with the Nugan Hand Bank scandal in Sydney, but in those days he was just the large American who arrived at Maureen's office a few days each week, often accompanied by young ex-soldiers from the Deep South who seemed to be his bodyguards.

Meanwhile, I had a job doing market research for Bayer Pharmaceuticals. We soon escaped from the Darling Point rooming house to a colorful basement apartment in nearby Paddington. We got around in an old Austin-Healey Sprite sports car which we'd picked up for only $350, mainly because it had no second gear. Over the next year I was called upon on many occasions to repair that less than reliable sports car, but we felt that if we were going to spend a year in Australia's sunny harbor city, having a convertible was the way to do it.

So far almost everything had gone to plan. We'd made it from London to Sydney, arriving as near to penniless as you could ask for, and now we had jobs so we could save up money to fly home. Except we had no intention of flying home.

Even now, more than thirty years later, I can almost recount day by day what we did during the last six months of 1972. How often in life is every day lit up so vividly? Most of the time we're lucky to be able to tell one year from another. We were having such an amazing time; there was no way we were going to rush back to Europe and into the nine-to-five routine. Even before we arrived in Sydney it was clear to us that this was no longer a one-year trip around the world. Three years seemed a much more sensible time span. Instead of working to save enough money for a few months' travel on our way back to Europe, we decided to spend a whole year in Australia and save enough for another year's travel. We'd explore some of those places in Southeast Asia which we'd scurried through in our rush to get to Australia before our last dollars disappeared. Then we'd go to Japan; maybe we'd buy a motorcycle there and take it to the United States, perhaps we'd even get down to South America.

We knuckled down to saving money, living on one salary and saving the other. Our bank balance put on weight even faster when we started working after hours on door-to-door market research projects for a North Sydney company. That still left us time to explore Sydney, nurse our ancient car down to Melbourne and back, and rack up many miles of bushwalking in the wonderful national parks which border Sydney to the north and south and in the Blue Mountains on the inland side. We even managed a skiing trip to Thredbo in the Snowy Mountains.

Soon after our arrival in Sydney we went to a slide show put on by a recent visitor to Iran and met two couples, Dave and Jane Shaw and Tony and Lena Cansdale, who have remained friends ever since. Casual meetings like this were to have a life-changing effect on us. Every time we went to a party or met people at a work function, questions would come up about our trip to Australia. How did we do it? How much did it cost? What's Bali like? Can you really hitch through Thailand? Are the trains in India as bad as they say? Is Afghanistan dangerous? Can you really get all the way to Europe by land? We found ourselves scribbling down notes so often that we began to draw up lists of the most frequently needed responses.

We began to think about selling this information instead of giving it away. Why didn't we produce a collection of mimeographed notes on the overland trip? Those notes soon grew to more than a handful of pages and we began to think bigger.

'Why don't we write a guidebook?' I suggested to Maureen one evening.

'But how would we find a publisher?' she asked, sensibly.

'We don't need a publisher,' I responded. 'We can publish it ourselves. I know how to put a book together.'

This was almost true; the unofficial newspaper publishing course I'd spent far too much time on during my first year at university was about to pay off as we put together our first primitive book. On weekday evenings we wrote by hand and each Friday Maureen would borrow her office typewriter so we could work on the book over the weekend.

At this time the battle to preserve Victoria Street in Sydney's Kings Cross was an ongoing drama. Today Victoria Street is the center for young international backpackers, a strip of small hotels and hostels, travel agents, restaurants and travelers' meeting places, populated by an ever-changing tribe of overseas visitors. Back then it was a street of decaying Victorian houses threatened by a city government redevelopment plan. Lots of Sydneysiders objected to a swath of the city's fine old Victorian houses falling to the wreckers. The adjoining suburb of Paddington, where we lived, was a shining example of how beautiful those old houses could be, given a little love, attention and money.

On weekends, Victoria Street was the setting for a street fair and protest meetings. One Sunday we took a break from working on our guide and strolled over to see what was happening. Sitting on the curbside we saw a young guy with a sign that read 'Traveler's Notes to Indonesia'. We asked him about them.

'I've traveled all over Indonesia,' he explained, 'and these are notes about how to do it. Where to go, where to stay, how to get around the islands and from one to another. It's an amazing place. I'm going to make my notes into a book.'

'That's a real coincidence,' I said. 'We're writing a book about our travels as well. We did the overland trip from London to Australia.'

The Indonesia information purveyor introduced himself as Bill Dalton and, of course, these notes were the forerunner to his famous *Indonesia Handbook*. Bill beat us to press with his first 32-page Moon Publications guidebook, typeset by Cathy Quinn at Tomato Press, a small counter-culture printing works on Glebe Point Road in the avant-garde suburb of Glebe. I can't remember if Bill introduced us to Tomato Press or if we found our own way there, but soon Cathy was typesetting our book as well.

Deciding to write a book and deciding to publish it ourselves were not totally one and the same decision. We did think about following the conventional route of taking our book to a publisher, but our initial enquiries didn't generate much interest and we had to get our book out fast. We'd set early January 1974 as the departure date for the next leg of our trip and it was already August. One other event inspired us to continue along the self-publishing route. I went in to Angus & Robertson on George Street, the biggest bookshop in Sydney at the time and still one of the largest. I spoke to John Merriman, the manager in charge of the small travel section, and told him about the book I was planning to publish. He promised to take fifty copies.

Our proposed book was too big for Tomato Press' small printing press, but they put us in touch with David Bisset who had a larger press in his basement and agreed to print 1500 copies. I drew maps of the countries we'd visited, crudely drew illustrations and we pasted up the typeset galleys to produce a book which came out to precisely ninety-six pages. We needed two more things—a title for the book and a name for our fledgling publishing house. The title was easy; the book was about traveling across Asia on a tight budget, so we called it *Across Asia on the Cheap*.

Finding a name for our publishing business was less straightforward. We ran through dozens of names over bowls of spaghetti and glasses of cheap red wine in a small Italian restaurant on Oxford Street in Paddington before inspiration hit. I'd been humming a line from the Matthew Moore song 'Space Captain', sung by Joe Cocker in the classic rock and roll tour film *Mad Dogs & Englishmen*.

'Once while traveling across the sky,' I sang, 'this lonely planet caught my eye.'

'No,' said Maureen, 'you've got the words wrong. As usual. It's *lovely* planet.'

She was right, I always got the words wrong, but lonely planet sounded much nicer. I sometimes wished we'd come up with a more business-like, more serious name, but it's certainly a name people don't forget.

Finally the sheets of our book were printed, but we'd only ordered the printing; turning the sheets into a finished book was our responsibility. We organized someone to fold the printed sheets into sixteen-page 'signatures' and these were delivered to our basement apartment. We borrowed a foot-operated stapling machine from Tomato Press—it rode home in our convertible, peering over the windscreen. A weekend's work collated the sections into books and Maureen and I stapled every copy. Then we ferried them round to Tomato Press's office where we used their guillotine to hand trim the finished books.

Finally we had 1500 copies of our little baby-blue book stacked on the floor. *Across Asia on the Cheap* was ready to hit the shelves. I'd even drawn a logo, the words 'lonely planet' written in lowercase with a circle behind them, which looks remarkably like it still does today.

I took a day off work and went to Angus & Robertson to fill that promised order for fifty copies. That may have been the biggest order, but by the end of the day I'd sold several hundred copies. Maureen followed up with the next bookshop circuit, including one very important sale to the New Edition bookshop in Paddington, a stone's throw from our Oatley Road apartment. The bookshop-owner's girlfriend, Nancy Berryman, was a journalist. She wrote the very first story about Lonely Planet for the Sydney *Sun-Herald*. A review of our book followed in another Sydney newspaper and then we were invited to appear on a breakfast-time television program. This was a useful first lesson for us about the power of publicity. Soon our book was not only on the shelves, but sitting by the cash register and in shop windows. Ten days after the review was printed we delivered the last of our 1500 copies and planned a reprint.

This time we printed 3500 copies and we left the collating, stapling and trimming to the professionals. We also changed the cover to a glossy white one, since we'd discovered the blue one quickly got dirty. We put quotes from our first reviews on the back cover. 'If you're thinking of going to Asia, do yourself a favor and buy this book. You'll be glad you did,' advised the *Nation Review*. 'The hardest thing about making a trip like this is reaching the decision to go. I think even people who never work up the courage will enjoy the book,' suggested the *Sydney Morning* Herald.

Most of the first batch had sold in Sydney; now we began to take our book further afield. I flew to Melbourne with two suitcases full of books, took the airport bus into the city, parked the suitcases in left luggage at the railway station, marched around the city bookshops in the morning taking orders and in the afternoon went back and forth to the railway station collecting books and delivering them. In the following weeks I used up more vacation days to repeat this technique in Adelaide and Brisbane, while Maureen made another trip to Melbourne to restock the shops there.

Soon we were planning another 3500-copy reprint and the thought occurred to us that we could make a living out of this. Perhaps it was presumptuous to imagine we could go from that first little book to making travel publishing our livelihood. It's more likely we simply thought that writing another book might help pay for more travel. In any case, *Across Asia* had been a totally unplanned success; we certainly hadn't set out from England thinking we were going to write a book about our adventures. But we did now wonder if we could repeat the act, this time with the intention of producing a book from the very start of a journey.

We looked north to Southeast Asia, at that time almost a terra incognita. It's hard to imagine how little known the region was less than thirty-five years ago. Today Thailand is one of the world's most popular tourist destinations, but in the early 1970s it was still stamping out a smoldering Communist insurgency and tourism meant R&R from the Vietnam War. Singapore was newly independent, still vaguely exotic and taking the first tentative steps towards becoming today's air-conditioned mega-city. Indonesia was emerging from the Soekarno years and was better known for burning down the British Embassy in Jakarta and threatening to invade

Malaysia than for welcoming with open arms the tourists who would soon be flocking to Bali.

Thailand, Singapore and Indonesia may have been relative unknowns, but to Americans at the time the words Southeast Asia conjured up none of those names. Southeast Asia was synonymous with Vietnam, the site of a long, divisive and still unresolved war.

Given this unhappy background it was scarcely surprising that guidebooks to the region were nonexistent, but we sensed the situation might soon be changing. In the final month of our Asia trek we'd hurried through the region, our anorexic moneybelts dictating the rapid pace, but we'd witnessed Bangkok starting to substitute international backpackers for vacationing American soldiers. We'd enjoyed the food and flavors of Singapore. We'd seen Bali when Kuta Beach was just the odd *losmen* (local hotel) dotted amongst the palm trees and rice paddies and visitors were mainly adventurous surfers. It was virgin territory and time somebody did a guidebook.

'Let's not just travel back to London,' I ventured. 'We could spend a year traveling around Southeast Asia and write a really good guidebook.'

'OK,' agreed Maureen, ever ready to join my mad plans, 'but what do we do at the end of the year?'

'I guess we'll go back to London,' I mused. 'We don't really need to make our minds up until the end of the year.'

So our plan was simple: we'd spend a year exploring the region and at the end we'd write the definitive guide. In December, we bought a used 250cc Yamaha DT2 trail bike, big enough to haul both of us around Southeast Asia, but small enough to load on and off boats and even airfreight if necessary. TAA (Trans-Australian Airlines), now the domestic wing of Qantas, operated flights between Darwin and Baucau in Portuguese Timor. I contacted the editor of their inflight magazine and he arranged to fly our motorcycle from Darwin to Timor in exchange for an article about traveling around the island.

In early January 1974, we packed our publishing business into a couple of boxes and dropped them off with friends who'd agreed to fill any orders and bank any checks that came in. Everything else filled up a suitcase and was sent to my parents in England. Before heading back towards Asia, however, we made a diversion east to New Zealand. We shipped the motorcycle to Auckland and followed it a few days later by air. From Auckland we rode south to Wellington, took the ferry across to the South Island and did a circuit of the island, ending up back in Wellington from where we shipped the motorcycle back to Melbourne. Our month in New Zealand included a number of press, radio and TV interviews and *Across Asia on the Cheap* was soon on sale in bookshops all around New Zealand as well.

Our New Zealand distributor was one Alistair Taylor, a name which would come back to haunt us a year later, although we've long forgiven the unreliable Mr Taylor for the problems he caused us. We stayed a couple of nights at his house at Martinborough, in the country-side outside Wellington, where another guest was a poet named Sam Hunt, already on his way to becoming a flamboyant national character in the land of the long white cloud. Years later Alistair took up wine-making from the house, an enterprise which evolved into the popular Te Kairanga winery.

Back in Melbourne, we slept on the floor at a friend's house for a few nights while we waited for the ship carrying our bike to arrive, then we loaded up and headed north. Our whole world was strapped on to that small motorcycle. There was a container bolted on the side, another box on the rear carrier, a bag and two sleeping bags went on top of that, another small bag sat on top of the fuel tank and our tent was strapped across the handlebars. We rode north through Canberra to Sydney and then along the New South Wales coast to the Hunter Valley, Port Macquarie, Byron Bay and across the border to Surfers Paradise in Queensland.

From Brisbane we continued north through Rockhampton, Mackay and Townsville, making excursions to a couple of Barrier Reef islands along the way. North Queensland was still many years away from its present role as a swish international playground for scuba divers and sunseekers. In Ingham, we had a first-hand brush with Queensland's redneck reputation, discovering why it rejoiced in the sobriquet 'the Deep North'. A few days earlier we'd met a young French couple at a Townsville camp site who'd bought an old car and were traveling round Australia. They were definitely pioneering visitors: meeting foreign tourists was unusual in Australia in those days, and meeting them in north Queensland was even more unusual, so a French couple at a north Queensland camp site was well nigh unbelievable.

We'd befriended them because the woman running the campsite shop had complained to us that their English wasn't good enough for her! In fact their English was absolutely fine and when we bumped into them again in Ingham we suggested we have dinner together. I went with the French couple to the small town's supermarket to buy food while Maureen dropped in to the pub to get a bottle of wine. Fifteen minutes later I found her by our motorcycle, in tears.

M: I'd gone into the pub, walked up to the bar and been met with silence. Nobody in the pub said a word and the staff behind the bar simply bypassed me. I was absolutely ignored. I couldn't understand what was going on, so for several minutes I stood there, puzzled.

Eventually a woman leaned in from a small hatch and said, 'You're never going to get served in there love. You have to come round here to the women's side.'

So I walked out of the bar, found my rightful place in Ingham's male universe, peered in through the hatch and the barman came over to me and asked what I wanted as cheerful as can be. The conversation resumed, I paid for the bottle of wine, life went on as usual. Except that I was shaking—I had never been so completely dismissed before, not just as a woman, but as a human being.

Fortunately most of Queensland was nothing like Ingham, although a telephone engineer we met at another camp site, further north, had his own tale of far-north pub sophistication. He'd been installing a phone system in a small town and was staying in a housetrailer at the local camp site. One night he'd gone to the town's only pub and ordered a meal and a bottle of wine, a nice change from the usual beers. A dusty bottle was found under the counter, uncorked and slid across the bar to him.

He waited a moment for a glass to be offered, then asked, 'Could I have something to drink this with?'

'Oh, yeah, sure,' replied the barman, and handed him a straw.

An overnight stop in the delightfully laid-back little settlement of Port Douglas stretched into several days. One day, in the small shop at the corner of the main street, we were invited to join an outing to Low Isles, a sandy little islet topped by a pristine lighthouse kept fastidiously neat by the house-proud lighthouse keeper. Only a few years later Port Douglas would metamorphose into a popular resort and today high-speed catamarans whisk boatloads of tourists out to Low Isles and the Barrier Reef every day.

Our route up the coast ended at Cooktown, where, two centuries earlier, Captain Cook made an enforced stopover to repair the badly damaged *Endeavour*, after colliding with the reef. We bumped into our French friends once again in Cooktown before we left the coast and turned inland to Charters Hill and Mt Isa. In Mt Isa, our camp site was raided by the police, hoping to find drugs in the beaten-up old Holden car of the 'hippies' camped next to us.

Leaving Queensland, we crossed into the Northern Territory and from Three Ways headed south to Alice Springs. By this time, we'd had to work out a solution to our fuel problem. The motorcycle tank held about two gallons, good for not much more than 100 miles from full to empty and it was frequently much further than that between fuel stops, so we added two containers of fuel to the top of our jumble of bags.

Alice Springs was a delightfully sophisticated oasis in the desert and, although it's become far more touristy over the passing years, we still enjoy going there. Desert or not, our arrival heralded a couple of days of solid rain. We were fortunate that the camp-site owners took

pity on us hunched in our tent and let us use one of the housetrailers parked at the site. We whiled away a day watching a mouse complain about our invasion of its home, then headed south again towards Ayers Rock. The road south was still dirt back in 1974 and the rain had turned long stretches into muddy quagmires. On our final run to the Rock we passed numerous cars bogged by the roadside.

Ayers Rock was far more interesting than the big red rock in the middle of a red desert we'd expected. We walked around it, climbed up it (still politically correct in those days), ventured out to the Olgas with an American couple who had also arrived by motorcycle, and the day or two we had planned could easily have stretched to a week. The long period of remarkably wet weather in the central desert that year had turned the landscape a lush green with beautiful pools dotted around the rock.

Eventually we headed north again, stopping once by the roadside to replace a worn-out rear chain, and once to kneel down and kiss

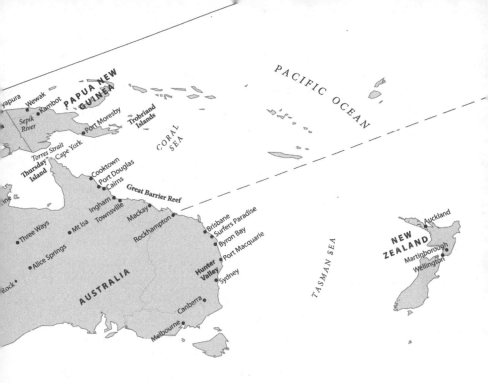

the tarmac surface when we finally left the dirt road behind. This time, we only paused overnight in Alice Springs before continuing north to the Katherine Gorge and finally to Darwin, still nine months away from its almost total destruction on Christmas Day 1974 by Cyclone Tracy.

The camp site near Darwin airport was home to an ever-changing collection of vagabonds, swapping travel tales and selling cars and camping equipment before heading up to Indonesia or arriving from Asia to set off around Australia. We didn't plan to camp after we left Australia, since we knew camp sites would be almost nonexistent but cheap hotels plentiful, so we sold our camping and cooking equipment. Some travelers weren't so lucky in finding buyers. One fellow camper still hadn't disposed of his dodgy old Holden car on his last day, so he announced he was going to drive south and give it to the first hitch-hikers he picked up. The Holden's new owners dropped him back at the camp site an hour later and headed off to Sydney.

Our motorcycle was stuffed into the little Fokker F27's front luggage compartment for the hour-long flight to Baucau. From there we headed west along the coast to Dili, the capital of Portuguese Timor. Dili was Timor's big city; it even had the country's only gas station. There, like most backpackers making the trek from Darwin to Bali, we unrolled our sleeping bags on the concrete floor of a metal-roofed shed on the beach, graced with a small painted sign announcing that it was the 'Hippie Hilton'. Somebody came round once a day to collect a dollar or so from all the happy campers. At night, we frequented Dili's small selection of Chinese restaurants where we washed meals down with cheap beer from the Portuguese colony of Mozambique or Mateus Rosé wine from the mother country. One night I ordered a chicken fried rice and was a little surprised to find it had prawns, but no chicken. Undeterred, I tucked in, but only a couple of forkfuls later the waiter scurried back, announced he'd brought me the wrong plate, glanced over at the adjacent table occupied by Portuguese soldiers and, confident they weren't looking our way, tidied my plate up and reassigned it to its original destination.

We rode south almost to the other coast, stopping en route at the mountain settlement of Maubisse where we stayed in an airy Portuguese *pousada* (hotel) before we continued west towards the Indonesian side of the island. The road got progressively worse as we bounced along rocky stretches more like dried-up riverbeds than any highway. It was no wonder buses were so few and far between. At each river we waded across first to check the depth and search for surprise drops before we rode the bike across. There were no bridges.

Our last night in Portuguese Timor was spent in the remote village of Balibo. There was a small Portuguese army contingent here and they fed us and let us sleep in the officers' mess, which was nothing more than a small wooden shed. In the middle of the night, plagued by rats stampeding over our sleeping bags, we beat a retreat to the veranda.

This little village took on a sinister importance for Australians a year later. When Portugal's long military dictatorship crumbled, the threads holding their ramshackle empire together quickly fell apart and Portuguese Timor, like Mozambique and Angola, was cast adrift. By 1975 Timor was in turmoil, with Fretilin trying to steer the ex-colony to independence while the threat of Indonesian intervention hovered in the wings. Five Australian-based journalists arrived in Balibo in October of that year, and during the invasion of the town by the Indonesians they were killed. Officially, they died in crossfire, but in fact they were summarily executed by the Indonesian troops, intent on keeping secret a takeover which was not yet formally under way.

We bumped on along the rocky road towards the Indonesian border and crossed to Atapupu. Our plan was to continue to Kupang, right at the western end of the island, but the Catholic mission cargo ship *Stella Maris* was due to depart westbound towards Java in a couple of days so we decided to wait. The veranda of the Atapupu police station was the only accommodation on offer and there were a couple of people there already. At dawn each day, a motley little band of backpackers crawled out of their sleeping bags to stand up while the Indonesian flag was hauled up the police station flagpole.

When the ship was finally ready to go, our small group, now reinforced by several more travelers, climbed on board and our motorcycle was lifted on by the ship's derrick. That night, we made the short crossing to Larantuka on the eastern end of the island of Flores. Unfortunately, when we arrived another ship was already tied up to the small dock and a second waited in line to unload and reload. We stayed in port for two nights, meeting travelers off the other boats, eating at a small Chinese-run *warung* (one step down from a *rumah makan* in the Indonesia language) and walking out to a nearby beach to swim.

This sudden influx of such a large band of *orang putih* (white folk) was obviously the most exciting thing to happen all year. The crowds jostling at the window of the *warung* were so large that the owners erected screens around our table to dissuade spectators. Our group included an opera singer from Sydney who one night put on an impromptu performance which left his Indonesian audience open-mouthed in amazement. We eventually became friendly enough with the owners to venture into the kitchen and introduce them to the wonders of French fries.

Crowds of children would follow us to the beach where one afternoon our opera singer, clearly an inveterate performer, went through a torturous routine removing his shorts from under a towel before discreetly putting his swimsuit on, only to drop the towel at the critical moment. His staring audience fell back in shocked horror, only to dissolve into laughter when it was revealed he already had another swimsuit on beneath the towel.

We sailed on to Maumere where there was no dock and our motorcycle had to be lifted off onto a small boat and shuttled ashore. We stayed overnight at a delightfully friendly small *losmen*; we have a photograph of Maureen with the whole family clustered around her. In 1992, Maumere was almost wiped off the map by a disastrous earthquake and tsunami which killed more than 2000 people.

As we traveled inland next morning it was clear the roads on Flores were nearly as rocky and rotten as those on Timor, but by midafternoon we were in the village of Moni, at the foot of Keli Mutu. Keli means mountain in the local dialect and Keli Mutu, one of the natural wonders of Indonesia, is an extinct volcano with not one, but three separate crater lakes. That would be wonder enough, but each lake is a different color due to some curious combination of chemicals in the ground. The small lake was a dark black while the two larger adjacent lakes, separated only by a narrow stretch of crater edge, were turquoise blue and a deep brownish-maroon. A few years later the brown-maroon lake changed color and today it's green-blue. My photographs from this visit in 1974 make a strange contrast with the ones I took on a return visit in 1991. In the 1960s, it is said, the lakes were blue, red-brown and café au lait.

We rode up to the craters that afternoon, but only caught glimpses of the lakes through occasional gaps in the cloud. The next morning at dawn it was crystal clear and after wandering around the craters we went back down to bask in a hot spring just outside the village with Rene and Ursula Kloeti from Switzerland, the only other visitors that day. In 1974, finding your way to Keli Mutu was still a reasonably rare feat, but today there's a host of small hotels and restaurants and a dawn bus service up to the crater rim.

Ende, on the north coast, was the main town on the island. Soekarno was exiled here by the Dutch for a spell in 1933, but I remember Ende on that occasion principally for its amazingly grubby beach. Houses along the waterfront backed on to the beach and used it as garbage dump and toilet, confident that tidal action would eventually wash it clean. More travelers turned up here including Mark and Debbie van Praagh from New Zealand and John and Jenny Templin from Australia. We had met them all in Portuguese Timor and would see a lot more of them in the next few months.

From Ende, we bumped westwards across the island through Ruteng to Reo, where the terrible road simply ended. We had intended to continue west all the way to the port town of Labuhanbajo, but after a long search for the road out of town we were told that no road existed. This was unbelievable: our map clearly showed a road along the coast and comparisons with other maps showed the same road. What had happened to it? The explanation was simple. In 1940, just before World War II spread to the Pacific, the Dutch had planned a road along the coast and showed the intended route on their survey maps. Then, after Pearl Harbor, the Japanese invaded and occupied Indonesia. After the war ended, the Indonesian independence struggle finally concluded with Dutch withdrawal. Thirty-five years after its original conception the road had still not been built, but every map of the island continued to show it. Later we discovered that we were far from the first to be stymied by this imaginary road. The August 1962 issue of *National Geographic* recounts a trip through the islands of Nusa Tenggara in an amphibious jeep which came up against exactly the same problem. Today a road has finally been built to Labuhanbajo, but it runs along an inland route from Ruteng, not along the coast as originally planned a half-century earlier. The 'Trans-Northern Highway' closer to the coast is still under piecemeal construction.

John, Jenny, Mark and Debbie turned up a day after us, having endured a rough trip from Ende perched on top of a variety of trucks. Our small party camped out on the veranda of the police station and a couple of days later we negotiated with the captain of a small boat to take us west along the coast to Labuhanbajo. The tidal flows around these islands are powerful and capricious and our trip entailed leaving late in the afternoon then stopping at an island en route for several hours in the middle of the night. We slept on the beach where crabs scuttled across us. Next day we arrived in the small fishing port and again camped out on the police station veranda.

From here we chartered another boat to take us via the island of Komodo to Sape at the eastern end of Sumbawa. This time we found a sailing *prahu*, and the next day, after endless delays and rescheduled departure times, set off with our motorcycle tied to the mast. The four-day charter would cost us forty dollars. We only sailed for a few hours before putting in to a small island to wait for the tide to change. Early the next day we were approaching Komodo, but again fierce currents stopped our progress. We spent an afternoon snorkeling in the crystal-clear water, then another night sleeping on a beach with brilliantly pink sand.

Komodo is famed for its 'dragons', huge lizards which can grow up to ten feet in length and weigh over 200 pounds. A guide led us several miles to a dried riverbed, tied some smelly fish that were past their use-by date to a tree and within ten minutes an ominous crashing in the undergrowth signaled the arrival of the first dragon. Soon more followed and over the next three hours from our hideaway on the riverbank we watched perhaps a dozen different *buaya* ('crocodile' in Indonesian; in the local dialect they were *ora*) arrive and depart. At times, there were as many as five gathered together and we encountered another one on the beach on our way back to the village.

That evening, after more tidal delays, we sailed away from Komodo. By early morning, we were in the strait where a stiff breeze pushed us towards Sape.

Indonesia, with 'unity in diversity' as its slogan, is home to an amazing blend of religions. From Christian Timor and Flores we would now cross Muslim Sumbawa and Lombok before arriving at Hindu Bali and continuing to Muslim Java.

The roads on Sumbawa were much better than those on Timor or Flores, and after two weeks of sleeping on boats, beaches and verandas, our dollar-a-night *losmen* felt like five-star luxury. And, while our boat charter had included food, we'd mostly lived on cold rice and dried fish, so the culinary delights of Sumbawa were also impressive. Good roads, beds and food were a welcome treat.

From the western end of Sumbawa a ferry whisked us across the narrow strait to Lombok and we crossed the island to the extended town of Ampenan-Mataram on the west coast. From there we could look across to towering Mt Agung on Bali, the obvious conclusion for the first leg of our foray through the region. Today, Lombok has become a popular alternative to Bali, a handy escape with its own selection of beaches and the engaging Gili Islands to draw visitors away, but in 1974 it was untouched by tourism and still recovering from a disastrous Soekarno-era famine, prompted by a horrifying plague of mice.

We set ourselves up in a small hotel and bumped into John and Jenny again. The first night a thief quietly made his way into their room and stole Jenny's birth control pills! They hadn't cost much, but they were hard to replace in the backblocks of Indonesia. They soon moved on to Bali, while we had an enforced pause when Maureen came down with food poisoning. She was stuck at our small *losmen* while I searched for the island's immigration officer to renew our visas, their one-month validity rapidly coming to an end. The officer was friendly and charming—clearly renewing tourist visas wasn't a regular activity in Lombok—but he wanted to know why Maureen hadn't turned up in person. I explained that she was incapacitated and, after informing me that women were simply unsuited for riding on motorcycles, something to do with the position of their wombs, he announced that he would come to our *losmen* to see if he could help.

He duly turned up, prescribed *bubur*, a rice porridge concoction, as an appropriate dish for a fragile stomach, and then opined that perhaps what would really help was a visit from the local *dukan*.

'The *dukan*? What's a *dukan*?' we enquired.

'You might say witch doctor,' he replied, going on to describe the trouble he'd had from *dukans*, since he was a good catch and local women had employed *dukans* to make him fall in love with them. He promised to return the next day with a potion or charm.

Fleeing the Lombok *dukan's* attentions we rocked and rolled across the choppy straits to Bali, crossing the Wallace Line which divides Southeast Asia and its flora and fauna from Australasia. The straits to the east and west of Bali are equally narrow, but while the channel to the west, separating Bali from Java, is only 200 feet deep, to the east the waters between Bali and Lombok plunge to more than 3000 feet. The imaginary geographical line is named after Alfred Russel Wallace, an English naturalist who observed that the monkeys and other animals of Southeast Asia concluded with Bali, while the parrots and other birds of Australia commenced with Lombok.

The ferry docked in the small port of Padangbai and we were soon back in Denpasar, in a room in the Adi Yasa Hotel, the first familiar point from our previous trans-Asia trip. Denpasar has become such a congested, noisy hellhole it's hard to imagine anybody staying there of their own free will, but in 1974 it was a fine alternative to Kuta Beach. The Bali Hotel dated from the Dutch era and at one time was probably the only hotel on the island. It still retained some of its colonial charm, but for backpackers Adi Yasa was the number one attraction. We'd paused there on our way through Bali in 1972, now we settled down for a longer stay, foraying out for meals and dance performances and talking with the band of visitors who were studying batik painting, teaching English or practicing their Indonesian, learning Balinese dance or gamelan music, or, in our case, writing a guidebook. The delightful little Three Sisters Warung, right across the road, was a regular dinner destination.

Travelers often ponder the weird coincidences which prompt unlikely reunions in strange places and over the years we've had quite a few, but none to match our second morning at Adi Yasa when the door of the next room opened and Carol Clewlow stepped out. We'd met Carol on the bus over the Khyber Pass from Afghanistan two years before and had last seen her in Kathmandu. We hadn't kept in touch. We had continued south to Australia and she had made her way to Hong Kong, where she worked for a year as a journalist on a Hong Kong daily. Like us, she'd been furiously saving to continue her travels and had spent evenings and weekends dubbing English-language soundtracks onto Hong Kong kung fu movies.

During the next few months our paths would cross regularly, and a couple of years later Carol wrote a guidebook for us, book number nine on our list: our first Hong Kong guide. Today Carol lives in England and has become a successful novelist with books like *Keeping the Faith, One for the Money* and *A Woman's Guide to Adultery*.

We spent about a month in Bali, dividing our time between Denpasar, Kuta, Ubud and other places around the island, but for many reasons Denpasar sticks in my mind. We spent endless hours having endless conversations while joints circulated around the Adi Yasa's comfortable courtyard. Getting Maureen stoned proved a near impossibility until Carol rolled the largest spliff of all time. It worked, briefly. One of our stays at Adi Yasa coincided with Nixon's departure from the White House and the American residents put on a 'goodbye Nixon' party complete with a 'Farewell Tricky Dicky' birthday-style cake produced with true Balinese artistry by a local bakery.

Bali in 1974 provided many other fine memories. It seems unbelievable that electricity had not yet arrived in Ubud. Today it's still the 'cultural capital' in the hills, but at that time there were only a handful of places to stay and eat. Like so many things in Bali they were often run by women. Oka Wati's little *warung*, across from the entrance gate to Pura Merajan Agung (a private palace temple), was our favorite breakfast place. We often had dinner (tacos a specialty) at Canderi's popular *losmen* at the top of the Monkey Forest Road. Canderi's looks remarkably unchanged even today while Oka Wati now runs a fine little hotel, complete with swimming pool, just off the Monkey Forest Road. In 2003, our German travel publishing friends Stefan and Renate Loose took over the whole hotel and invited a roll call of friends to come to Bali to celebrate their twenty-fifth wedding anniversary.

We didn't neglect Kuta Beach, although it had already expanded dramatically since our first visit. The adjacent village of Legian was beginning to get into the same game but in 1974 the evening stroll from Kuta to Legian still involved a quiet walk through the country between the two villages, along sandy laneways lined with coconut palms.

Poppies was a popular little *warung* when we passed through in 1972; now it was a slick garden restaurant which, remarkably, is still going strong today. Later it spawned a beautifully designed boutique hotel across Poppies Gang (*gang* is Indonesian for a pedestrian laneway) from the restaurant. In years to come we often stayed at Poppies on our first or last night in Bali.

Nearby was Made's Warung on Kuta Beach Road, to this day the most popular place in Kuta to sit and people-watch. The Balinese have a delightfully straightforward process for dishing out names. The firstborn, male or female, is called Wayan. Number two is Made (so the café was run by a second-born child), number three is Nyoman and number four Ketut. If a fifth child comes along you simply add a second Wayan to the roster. Later we would befriend an Ubud family with a Ketut Besar and Ketut Kecil—Big Ketut (fourth born, a son) and Small Ketut (eighth born, a daughter).

Not all the Kuta places we became familiar with have survived. Mama's, an enormously popular restaurant, famous for its nightly buffet, disappeared within a couple of years. We were regulars at the Garden Restaurant, noted for its pizzas topped with mushrooms which, if eaten at the appropriate time, ensured Kuta sunsets had a special potency. We remember the owner's little daughter appearing periodically at the kitchen door holding a pizza and calling out, 'Hello vegetable pizza,' in the hope that whoever ordered it hours earlier had hung around and still wanted it. So much hard work went into those small establishments; to this day, when I see a fast-food counterhand casually stuff a handful of paper napkins into a bag, my mind flips back to Kuta in 1974 when napkins were always carefully torn in half to economize.

M: Walking back to our *losmen* in Ubud one night we were surprised to see what looked like the entire village sitting in a large dusty square. It was dusk and in the center of the unsealed road rows of young girls were moving slowly and hypnotically to music from a gamelan orchestra. An old man was walking amongst them, positioning a hand here, tilting a head there, rearranging a foot. He was the dance master for the village. Each village on the island had a dance group which performed at temple ceremonies. They also competed against each other every year and tonight they were practicing for the upcoming contest. They were dressed in everyday clothes and we sat by the side of the road totally entranced while they rehearsed.

We saw many other dancers after that evening. Once we were returning late at night on our motorcycle and almost ran into a group practicing by oil lamps right in the middle of the main road. At that time, many of the villages couldn't afford the elaborate costumes, and the orchestras were also expensive to maintain, but once they realized how fascinated tourists were by this art form, putting dances on for paying spectators made it possible for many villages to continue their traditions.

By the time we were ready to leave Bali, we'd accumulated quite a circle of friends. Many of them joined us for dinner on our final evening. Halfway through the meal, we were surprised by the arrival of Phil Milner, a classmate of mine from the London Business School, and his French wife Marie-Hélène. They'd made their way across Asia, following our route from two years before in the red ex-post office Morris Minor van which another classmate, American Peter Schulz, one of the witnesses for our wedding, had used as London transport!

We headed west, to climb Mt Bromo at dawn, pause in Surabaya, explore Solo and, in Yogyakarta, run into Carol Clewlow once again.

Yogyakarta was another long stop with forays to the nearby temple sites of Prambanan and Borobodur, and a longer trip to the Dieng Plateau.

We arrived at the temple-studded Dieng Plateau in the mid-afternoon, but as night fell we quickly realized this was a very different place from sweaty Yogyakarta. There was no electricity and once the sun set the temperature plummeted. Carol was supposed to be joining us, but when she had not arrived by nightfall we concluded that her bus connections had not worked out.

We went in search of a meal with other travelers who were staying at the hotel. One look at the three old crones hunched over a simmering cauldron in the hotel's kitchen (obviously rehearsing to play the witches in some local production of *Macbeth*) crossed the hotel off as a place to eat. One of our group had heard of a restaurant down the street and we set off to find it. Halfway there, stumbling through the moonless dark, we heard somebody swearing and stumbling in the opposite direction, vainly attempting to keep on the road. It was Carol.

She joined our group and a little further down the street we found the feeble light which identified the restaurant. We ordered food (there was no menu of course) and hungrily worked our way through a fine meal. At some point, we put two and two together: the lack of a sign or menu, uncertainty about what was available, surprise at our arrival—this was not a restaurant! We'd simply turned up at somebody's front door and said, 'Feed us.'

'What would my mother say if a bunch of Indonesians turned up at her front door and demanded to be fed?' asked a Canadian in our party.

We continued west to Bogor and Bandung for a longer pause at Jakarta. This time we did locate Jalan Jaksa, the backpackers' street in Jakarta, although at that time the name referred to just one popular hostel on the *jalan* (street). From Jakarta we continued to the western tip of Java and took the ferry across to Sumatra, passing close to Krakatoa, the volcanic island which exploded catastrophically in 1883.

Palembang was the first stop in Sumatra; after that, travel got very rough. The Trans-Sumatran highway was still under construction and long stretches of road through the jungle were bumpy, muddy and near impassable. We ran out of daylight between Palembang and Jambi and ended up sleeping on the floor of a villager's hut by the roadside. In Jambi my camera was stolen: we think somebody reached through the window with a pole and lifted it off the table.

The roads got worse. It took us three days between Jambi and Padang and the first night found our spirits at their lowest. The rocky roads had broken the frame supporting our motorcycle's side pannier and I'd had to jury-rig a repair with bits of bamboo and wire. Then the rain started, becoming a downpour until it felt like Niagara was cascading down upon us. The road turned into a muddy boghole and when we finally crawled into Muaratebo, well after dark, we were soaking wet, plastered with mud and completely exhausted.

Naturally there was no hotel, but as so often happens when things seem to be at their worst, the situation suddenly reversed. Our enquiries about somewhere—anywhere—to stay prompted nothing but head-scratching until a friendly local took us down the road to a darkened house and called out to somebody inside. Remarkably, a woman appeared at an upstairs window and before we knew it we were being welcomed inside, given buckets of hot water to wash in and shown to a room with an elegant bed with mosquito nets and real sheets. We couldn't believe it!

Next morning, this lifesaving woman marched off to the market with Maureen, to show her off, and after profuse thank-yous we gratefully paid for one of the best rooms we had all year and completed the trip to Padang. Then the rain really started.

For three days we hardly ventured outside and when we did we were usually soaked to the skin in seconds. With the small collection of backpackers stranded in Padang we whiled away the hours over long meals of fiery, chili-packed Padang food, reputed to be the hottest in Indonesia. When the rains eased, we continued up into the hills to colorful Bukittingi and finally beautiful Lake Toba and Samosir Island.

We'd no sooner come ashore on Samosir Island than we bumped into John and Jenny, whose first words were commiseration about the loss of our camera in Jambi. How on earth did they know that, we enquired? They said the news had simply made its way along the traveler's grapevine—a couple on a motorcycle lost their camera, who else could it be? Samosir was just starting to take off as a travelers' center and we settled in for a break in the most laid-back place we'd been in since Bali. Every night involved long meals and endless conversations with our fellow travelers and our cheerful Sumatran hosts.

One night another monsoonal storm washed through and we peered out through the deluge from our little guesthouse, wondering how we were going to get down the road to our regular dining spot, when we saw one of the restaurant owner's young daughters emerging through the downpour. 'Hello umbrella,' she announced as she appeared at our door, ready to escort us to dinner.

One of our group had some American magazines and later that night our hosts crowded around us to stare at an advertisement showing a well-muscled stud lounging in a plumped-up four-poster bed. We stared in equal amazement. It was a reality from another planet.

John and Jenny moved on and for a few days we took their room at Losmen Carolina, a miniature Batak house perched on a rise overlooking the lake. It was absolutely the best room on the island. Our final Sumatran stop was at Medan, a noisy, dirty town with a miserable choice of cheap hotels. The ferry service across the narrow Straits of Melaka from Medan to Penang in Malaysia was out of operation so the only alternative was to fly. We turned up at the Malaysian Airlines office to enquire about airfreighting our motorcycle and were so clearly delighted to discover that the freight charges for the short hop would come to only fourteen dollars that the office staff recalculated the cost at eighteen dollars.

We'd not even paused in Penang on our rushed trip through the region two years earlier, so this time we settled in for a longer stay in delightful Georgetown, the main urban center on the island and still one of our favorite towns in Southeast Asia. Today Penang is the Silicon Island of Malaysia, a major center for computer manufacture and assembly, but somehow Georgetown has managed to retain its laid-back Chinatown atmosphere. We found a room at the New China Hotel, went to the tourist office and found—Carol Clewlow!

From Penang we headed south and climbed up into the hills to stay at the Cameron Highlands. This Malaysian hill station will always be connected with the Jim Thompson story. During World War II, the American architect worked for the Office of Strategic Services (the OSS), which later metamorphosed into the CIA. After the war he moved to Thailand, where he is credited with launching Thai silk onto the world stage. The beautiful house he built on a Bangkok canal in 1959, stuffed with antiques and art and with its walls turned inside out, is a major tourist attraction. In 1967 he paid a visit to the Cameron Highlands, went out for an afternoon stroll and was never seen again. Kidnapped by a band of the Malaysian Chinese communists? Eaten by a tiger? We'll never know, but it's something to think about when you go out for a walk in the highlands.

We continued south to Kuala Lumpur then forayed up the east coast, meeting our Swiss friends Rene and Ursula for a spot of turtle-watching at Rantau Abang. After riding north to Kota Bahru we U-turned and rode back south to Singapore. With helmets firmly on head we didn't have any long-hair problems this time, but our motorcycle celebrated by jamming in top gear a couple of hundred yards before our intended destination, the Palace Hotel. Very conveniently, the Palace was situated above a Yamaha motorcycle workshop so we pushed the bike straight in to be fixed.

The Palace was a mile or two from central Singapore, and there's still a hotel there today, but it's an ordinary, low-priced, modern creation with tiny rooms, totally devoid of the old-fashioned character the Palace had in spades. It was painted a garish shade of green and cream. There must have been about ten rooms, but the ones at the front were very noisy from the traffic pouring into downtown Singapore along one-way Jalan Besar, Malay for 'main street'. The upstairs room at the back, however, was much quieter and with windows on two walls it was bright and spacious. Our room was simple in the extreme: a sink and mirror, a double bed, a cupboard to hang clothes and a small round table with two chairs. The floor was red tiled and the walls whitewashed with the green trim which ran right through the place. The showers and toilets, which were Asian squat style, were off the corridor.

The Palace was certainly no palace, but it was spotlessly clean. The gruff old man who ran the place, slouching around in the standard attire of elderly Singapore men at the time—rubber flip-flops, baggy shorts and a singlet—had an instantly winning practice of plonking down a cold bottle of Coke in front of each sweaty new arrival as they were filling in the registration form. That cold Coke probably won him the instant appreciation of thousands of backpackers. Cleanliness and a free Coke apart, the Palace's major attraction was that it was cheap.

A couple of nights after our arrival, we celebrated our third wedding anniversary by splashing out on a fancy meal at an Italian restaurant. That dinner was a memorable reminder of how tightly we hoarded our cash that year. Once or twice in Indonesia we had allowed ourselves a beer as a special treat and this night we even had a bottle of wine. Today, when I really can't imagine dinner without a bottle of wine, it seems unbelievable that it was probably the only wine we drank between Portuguese Timor in May and Laos in December.

Our next stop was Brunei, the oil-rich kingdom wedged between the Malaysian states of Sabah and Sarawak on the island of Borneo. For long spells in the 1980s and '90s, the Sultan of Brunei was a regular contender for the title of 'world's richest man', although more recently he's slipped well behind Bill Gates. In 1974 he was still in his twenties and his much less profligate father was on the throne, but the Sultan was already working on his collection of expensive sports cars. Our Brunei-bound ship's cargo included a shiny new Italian De Tomaso. Maureen and I were traveling deck class so we unrolled our sleeping bags right beside the Sultan's new toy.

Bandar Seri Begawan was a strange place, dominated by its huge and glossy new mosque, and totally unsuitable for shoestring travelers. The handful of hotels were squarely aimed at the oil merchants starting to follow a pipeline to the Sultan's bountiful reserves, so their prices were right out of our reach. BSB did, however, have a luxurious new youth hostel, built to show how the kingdom was plugged in to the needs of its young people and young visitors from around the world. Of course, hardly any young visitors ever found their way to Brunei so the hostel, with its huge male and female dormitories, remained completely empty. Which was exactly the way its staff liked it. We turned up at the hostel and after long and patient attempts at dissuasion (our hostel cards were out of date, our nationalities were wrong, we were too old, we hadn't prebooked), we were eventually ushered in to the deserted hostel. Maureen was the only resident in the female dormitory, and I was the only one on the male side.

Alcohol was, of course, discouraged in the staunchly Islamic kingdom, but a request for a pot of 'special tea' in the town's Chinese restaurants brought a teapot full of beer. Despite random delights such as this, we soon exhausted BSB's possibilities so we continued on from Brunei into the neighboring Malaysian state of Sabah, made a loop of the state then continued back through Brunei again and into Sarawak.

We journeyed up into the jungle where we stayed at longhouses and eventually ended up at Kuching ('cat' in English) in the northwest corner of Borneo. From there, another Straits Steamship took us back to Singapore. This time we forked out for a cabin and, since the ship only had three cabins and a grand total of six cabin-class passengers, we ate every meal at the Captain's table. It's a shame we all fly these days—only a couple of years later the ships to Sabah, Sarawak and Brunei all stopped taking passengers.

Back in Singapore we stashed another boxful of notes at the Palace Hotel. Even today, when guidebook writers are more familiar creatures, carefully copying menus, prices, timetables and descriptions into notebooks and painstakingly drawing little maps and charts rarely raises much interest (thankfully). My miserable skills as a linguist hadn't hampered us, although by the end of the year I could query room prices and ask about bus or train departure times in a useful variety of languages. On October 30 1974 on a television in the garage under the Palace Hotel, I watched Mohammed Ali beat George Foreman in the 'rumble in the jungle', with the mechanics who had just fixed our bike. It was time for us to head north.

Months earlier in Bali we'd met an Australian friend-of-a-friend who was staying at the guesthouse of the recently constructed Hyatt Hotel; he had some connection with the hotel's architect. Out surfing one day, he found himself waiting for a wave next to Charles Levine, at that time the editor for APA Insight Guides in Singapore. (People tried to make APA stand for something, usually starting with 'Asia Photo', but it was just the Indonesian word for 'what?'.) The friend suggested I contact Insight in Singapore, where I met Charles, showed him our first primitive guidebook and was asked to help out on the forthcoming *Insight Thailand* guide.

In late 1996 Hans Hoefer, creator of the APA guidebook series, sold out to the huge German publisher Langenscheidt for a rumored fifty (or was it eighty?) million dollars, but back in 1974 APA was a tiny company, working out of an apartment and with a list of only five books: Bali, Singapore, Hong Kong, Malaysia and Java. Book number six was to be Thailand, but the writer couldn't complete the job. I was handed a list of places which needed covering and offered the princely sum of US$160 to complete a fairly large chunk of the book! Still, we needed the money so I took the job.

We left Malaysia and returned to Thailand, stopping first at Hat Yai, the honky-tonk southern metropolis, before continuing to Phuket. Today, with its multitude of beach resorts catering for every category of visitor from penniless backpackers to the wealthy Aman-resort groupies, it's hard to believe there was nowhere to stay at the beaches back in 1974. Well, there was an open beach shack at Patong Beach where you could unroll a sleeping bag, but since it rained almost the whole time we were in Phuket, we opted to stay in a Chinese-style hotel in town.

En route to Phuket we'd had an island excursion to tick off our Insight Guides' wish list. Their Thailand editor had heard about an island with beautiful beaches and a huge cave from where birds' nests were collected for that Chinese delicacy bird's-nest soup. If bird's-nest soup doesn't feature in your regular recipe list let me warn you—the small swifts whose nests are such a taste delight construct them out of the usual material which they glue to the roof of caves using bird saliva. It's the adhesive, not the twigs, which is the magic ingredient, so bird's-nest soup is really bird-spit soup.

At the port of Krabi we negotiated with the owner of a fishing boat to take us to the mysterious hideaway. On the island we admired the beautiful beach, swam in the crystal-clear water and inspected the towering cavern with the nest collectors' rickety ladders reaching up into the shadowy heights. The villagers on the island crowded around us—clearly *farangs* (foreigners) were a most unusual sight—and they were amazed and delighted with their peculiar visitors. Little did we know that we had 'discovered' Ko Phi Phi, now one of the most popular tourist destinations in southern Thailand. If you've seen the movie of *The Beach* you've seen Ko Phi Phi, although sadly the island would hit the headlines again when it was devastated by the tsunami on December 26 2004.

There were more stops and more rain before we rolled into Bangkok. It was two years since we were decanted off a Thai International flight from Calcutta on our first visit to Bangkok and we headed straight back to the Malaysia Hotel. The management's plan to switch it from an army R&R hotel to a backpacker's center had worked perfectly. It was jam-packed. There were tour desks and airline ticket agencies in the lobby and near the elevators a notice-board had sprung up which would become known throughout the region. If you wanted to find out about anything, buy anything or simply track down some long-lost traveling companion, chances were there'd be a note about it on the Malaysia's famous board. Even the restaurant was doing great business, but one thing hadn't changed from the old days: the elevators were filled with gorgeous young prostitutes who seemed quite happy to have swapped American GIs for an inter-national band of backpackers.

We continued to return to the Malaysia for some years, but it gradually got more and more run-down, the prices kept low by the owners simply never doing any maintenance. Eventually the noticeboard disappeared, the crowds thinned out, the center of gravity shifted across town to Khao San Road and today, after some renovations and improvements, the Malaysia is another nondescript cheap hotel with no hint of its glory days.

For a week our trusty motorcycle sat in the Malaysia's car park while we made a seven-day circuit of Burma, falling instantly in love with that bizarrely disorganized country. Burma had recently begun granting seven-day visas; previously visitors could stay for only twenty-four hours. But we knew it was going to be a rush to cover the country in 168 hours. Perhaps it was fortunate that in those days there weren't many places you could explore.

The Strand Hotel, Rangoon's most famous hostelry, was way out of our range at ten dollars. (Today, in its new Aman-resorts guise, rooms start at the wrong side of US$300.) Like most of the backpackers, we headed straight for the trusty YMCA, where we were consumed by mosquitoes. Then it was the all-day train up to Mandalay and a dawn bus departure to Pagan. With only seven days and a constrained budget keeping our travel options firmly at ground level, we were pushed to pack Rangoon, Mandalay and Pagan into our itinerary, but the abandoned city of Pagan is one of those sights which sears itself into the memory.

The trip back to Rangoon from Pagan also stays with me. We ended up on a train which managed to take almost twice its already lengthy scheduled time to drag back into the capital. After sitting up uncomfortably all night and most of the next day we never wanted to see another Burmese train, but Burma would come back to haunt us in other fashions. Five years later we would publish the first guidebook on the reclusive country and twenty-five years later we would be pilloried for it, but more of that later.

Precisely seven days after our Bangkok departure we were back in Thailand's capital, back on our motorcycle and heading north again. This time we stopped at the ancient cities of Ayutthaya and Sukhothai, both featured in the interminable wars between Burma and Siam, and both were on my Insight Guides assignment list. In the mid-70s, Thailand and Malaysia still suffered from minor problems with anti-government rebels. In Malaysia they were the remnants of the old Malayan Communist Party, principally found in the jungles in the north of the country and apt to melt across the border into Thailand when pursued by the Malaysian authorities. In Thailand the insurrection was more like low-level banditry than anything political, but buses in the south were sometimes held up and the passengers robbed. At Sukhothai we were warned about visits to the more remote temples where there was the chance of getting robbed or kidnapped. It was much the same story in Cambodia when we finally visited Angkor Wat in 1992.

Chiang Mai was already a popular tourist town, but a long, long way from its current frenetic pace. After exploring the region we left the motorcycle locked up in a shed at our guesthouse while we made a loop out to Laos and back. It was great fun, but somewhat abortive since Laos, like the rest of Indochina, was about to slam the door shut and remain locked away from the outside world for the best part of twenty years. Laos would appear in the first edition of our Southeast Asia guide, but not reappear until eighteen years later in edition seven. We hung around in Vientiane for a few days, helping the local restaurants to get through as much of their French wine collection as possible. It was clear that wine cellars were not going to be in favor when the Pathet Lao took over, which they did only a year later. A small bakery down the road from our hotel turned out wonderful croissants and when the country reopened for business one of the first letters we received was from a traveler commenting on the superb croissants he found—they'd survived two decades of Communism.

The main topic of conversation amongst travelers in Vientiane at the time was safety. There was no question that some people did simply disappear, including, only a month or two before we arrived, a young American named Charles Dean and his Australian companion Neil Sharman who had been captured and killed by the Pathet Lao. In 2003, when their bodies were discovered, Charles' older brother Howard Dean had become governor of Vermont and at the time was the front runner to become the Democratic candidate for the next presidential election, only to be overtaken by John Kerry.

With travel by road so risky, we opted for the relative safety of an elderly four-engined DC4 run by Royal Air Lao, another airline now long faded from the departure boards. It whisked us north to Luang Prabang where we continued on an even more ancient DC3 to the border town of Huay Xai. At the Luang Prabang airport, the same busy staff member who checked our tickets also carried our bags out to the aircraft, checked our boarding passes as we climbed on board and, as a finale, jumped on a motorcycle and chased the water buffaloes off the runway.

Most of our fellow passengers were colorfully garbed Laotians who hunched down in their seats with their faces in sick bags even before we rolled down the runway. In the air, the flight-deck door opened and the captain, a balding Frenchman in jeans and T-shirt, looked down the aisle, spotted us as the only Western faces on board and beckoned us to come up to the flight deck. There, we were poured red wine from a Johnny Walker whisky bottle on ice and admired the view as the beautiful flight attendant wove the plane around the Laotian mountain peaks.

The next day we took a ferry across the river to Thailand. Our passports were stamped and we took a bus to Chiang Rai. After an overnight stop we headed back to Chiang Mai, where we encountered the biggest problem of our Southeast Asian year.

On our first morning back in Chiang Mai we wheeled our bike out of the shed and rode to Wat Suan Dok, a Buddhist temple just to the west of the old town moat. Fifteen minutes later, when we emerged from a quick look inside the temple, our bike was gone. Stolen.

Losing the motorcycle wasn't in itself a disaster. We'd bought it to explore the backblocks of Southeast Asia and we'd managed that to the tune of more than 20 000 miles. It had been hauled through rivers, pounded along rocky roads, been stuck in jungle mud and, hardly surprisingly, was no longer in pristine condition. Our circuit of the region was pretty well over, so losing our trusty transport was not too terrible, except for two words: customs duty.

We had imported one Yamaha motorcycle into Thailand, so when we left we had to export it again. If we wanted to leave it behind we had to pay customs duty, which was something like 150 per cent of the value—not of one beat-up, high-mileage old machine, but based on its *brand-new cost*. Instead of getting a few hundred dollars when we sold it, we were now facing a $1500 bill for losing it. The fact that it was stolen was no excuse: we'd imported it, and we were expected to export it.

A couple of days later, after filing long reports at the police station and asking the British consulate (there was indeed a consulate in Chiang Mai at that time) to cable us if anything turned up, we disconsolately boarded the train for Bangkok. On Christmas Eve 1974 we were at Penang airport to meet my parents who had decided to come to Malaysia to spend the holiday with us. The best Christmas present was our film. We'd been sending film back to Britain for developing and for the first time we were able to look through the slides from our travels around Borneo, Malaysia, Thailand and Burma. I wondered if some of my shots of Ko Phi Phi would find their way into the Insight Guide.

The day after Christmas brought one final end-of-year disaster, another theft that sent our spirits sinking even lower. My parents flew down to Kuala Lumpur while Maureen and I rode the ferry to the mainland to take a long-distance taxi south. We found a taxi needing a couple more passengers, slung our bags in the back, jumped on board and off we went. Mid-trip we stopped to drop a passenger off and when we looked in the luggage compartment later, one of our bags was gone. As we were getting in the taxi at our starting point, somebody had lifted our bag out. Inside the missing bag was my portable typewriter (not a major loss), the partially completed manuscript of our book (which could have been a major loss if I hadn't stashed a complete carbon copy in another bag) and all the film which we had seen for the first time the previous night.

Travel enough and you're bound to have things stolen from time to time. These days I'm warier and more cautious, but I have had other things stolen and, no doubt, there are losses yet to come, but never have I been so depressed by losing something as I was over that film. The shots of the bird's-nest gatherers in the caves at Ko Phi Phi faded from the pages in front of my eyes, the temple-studded plains of Pagan disappeared along with the longboats in Sarawak.

Maureen continued to Kuala Lumpur to meet my parents while I took a taxi back to Penang to enquire at the taxi station and report the loss at the police station. In Kuala Lumpur the paper did a 'writer loses typewriter, manuscript and film' story; it was useless, nothing was ever found. From Kuala Lumpur we made a beach stop at Port Dickson and spent New Year's Eve in Melaka before returning to Singapore and bidding my parents farewell.

After our Chiang Mai and Penang disasters we were somewhat subdued, but we soon settled down to a three-month working stay back at the Palace Hotel. Remarkably, its role as the birthplace of *South-East Asia on a Shoestring* is not the only claim for travel guide literary distinction for the back room we occupied at the Palace Hotel. A year later Bill Dalton wrote the second edition of his Indonesia guide in the same room.

We developed a routine during our time at the Palace: breakfast at one of the little cafés nearby, work all morning, noodles for lunch, work all afternoon, then dinner and a movie (or sometimes more work). We had two favorite places for our evening meal. Some nights we would have chicken rice at a small restaurant just down Jalan Besar. Chicken rice, a dish from Hainan in China, is a Singapore specialty and there are some restaurants in the city which turn out nothing else. It's a dish of classic simplicity: steamed chicken, boiled rice, sliced cucumbers, a bowl of clear chicken broth and chilies to give it some heat.

These older-style Singaporean restaurants were group affairs— the restaurant provided the table, chairs and drinks while the food came from a number of cooking stalls, each independently run and with their own speciality. We became such a fixture at our chicken rice place that as we came in sight, walking down the street towards the restaurant, we would simply hold up two fingers to order two meals and the food would be on the table by the time we arrived!

Our other favorite was Komala Vilas, still one of Singapore's best known (and cheapest) restaurants and a place we often return to on visits to Singapore. Serangoon Road is the Little India of Singapore, chiefly populated by Tamils from the southeast of India, and Komala Vilas is a fine example of a Tamil banana-leaf *thali* restaurant. A *thali* is a vegetarian meal and takes its name from the plate (in this case the banana-leaf substitute) on which a host of little pots and bowls known as *katoris* are arrayed. There's quite a ceremony to a good *thali* although there are neither plates nor eating utensils. We would sit down, a big banana leaf spread out in front of us, onto which rice was dolloped. Then, an array of dishes containing different vegetable curries, yoghurt, spices and other condiments would be lined up. With our right hand, we would tuck in. Eating with us at Komala Vilas one night Hans Hoefer, the towering founder of Insight Guides, commented that with some cuisines the smell of the food is an important introduction to the meal, while with others it's how the food looks on the plate.

'But with a *thali*,' he continued, 'it's how it feels.'

He was right, this is the original finger food. Apart from being delicious, *thalis* have another important attraction to hungry back-packers: when you've finished you haven't finished. Until you fold your banana leaf in half to indicate you can manage no more, circulating servers will continue to resupply the rice and refill the dishes.

Our daily excursions for food were not the only time we escaped from room five. Singapore's cinematic fare was pretty limited, but we watched what we could. One afternoon we heard on our radio that Professor J. K. Galbraith—author, pundit, economist, adviser to JFK and US ambassador to India—was delivering a public lecture at Singapore University in an hour or so. We rushed downstairs and caught a bus to the university to join a surprisingly small crowd of young students hear a witty speech which I chiefly remember for a bawdy tale from the professor about how Bangkok got its name. The succession to the throne of the Siamese kingdom, the professor declared with straight-faced seriousness, was decided by seating the pretenders to the throne on the floor in a circle around a pool of honey.

'Inevitably flies are attracted to the honey,' Galbraith explained, 'and at a signal, the princes try to kill as many flies as possible by banging on the floor with the first instrument that comes to hand. The prince who kills the most flies succeeds to the throne.'

Every two weeks we had to venture forth for a less pleasant reason: to renew our visas. I suspect that nowadays young travelers who want to spend several months in Singapore might be looked at with considerable suspicion, but in early 1975 I made sure my hair was short so that each brief visit to the immigration office (even then Singapore was efficient) was honored with another stamp in our passports.

Gradually *South-East Asia on a Shoestring* came together. Seated across from each other at our small round table, Maureen and I pounded out the text on our portable typewriter. I'd decided the *Reader's Digest* magazine was a handy size and its twin columns of text were easy to read and so had gone for a very similar design. Although we've continually refined the information organization, and in 2004 pushed through a complete reorganization and redesign, the pattern we established with that first serious book has remained remarkably consistent to the present day. Every day or two, the typesetter delivered another roll of galleys for us to paste up as completed pages and took away more typed pages to be set. I laboriously drew the maps and line by line we cut out the typeset street and place names and glued them down.

Our book was coming along fine, but one major problem hung over us—that missing motorcycle. If we had to pay $1500 customs duty it was going to make a major hole in our finances. Back in 1973 in Australia I'd been earning about $7000 a year, so this was the equivalent of a couple of month's work and, adding insult to injury, it was virtually a punishment for somebody else's wrongdoing. Even though we had left the country there was no escaping the tax; we'd had to arrange a bond through the Australian Automobile Association in order to secure the Thai customs clearance and if we didn't clear the paperwork we'd lose our bond. After a failed attempt to contact the Thai customs department in Bangkok, complete with a letter translated into Thai, we decided that a return trip to Bangkok was necessary.

We left Singapore and hitch-hiked north to Penang where Maureen would wait while I continued to Bangkok, saving the cost of one train fare and visa. In Bangkok, armed with paperwork and police reports, I spent a day in the customs office arguing my case. Eventually, we negotiated a much more reasonable import duty, about ten per cent of what I was initially looking at, and I could pay the duty via the Automobile Association back in Australia. I again took the overnight train back to Malaysia, met Maureen in Penang and we were soon back in Singapore putting the finishing touches on our book.

The money we had saved in Australia had paid for our year's travel, for our long stay in Singapore and for getting our book to the starting line, but now our reserves were running low. We knew we had to start selling this book as quickly as we could once it left the printer. Perhaps it would be possible to sell some copies in Singapore? There were certainly lots of young travelers here and Singapore was the place they bought airline tickets, stocked up with supplies and enjoyed some good meals before heading off to less-hospitable regions. Why shouldn't they buy a guidebook in Singapore as well?

Armed with page proofs and a mock-up of the book's cover I made an appointment to see the book buyer at MPH, at that time the only big bookshop in Singapore. I explained the book and how I thought it would appeal to the young visitors passing through. I was sure MPH would buy some copies, perhaps ten or twenty, maybe even fifty or a hundred if they really thought it would work. I made my pitch and the buyer listed intently. Eventually he pulled out an order form, filled it out and pushed it across the desk to me. I saw the title, *South-East Asia on a Shoestring*, with a number written in front of it. A one followed by a zero, and another zero, and another zero!

One thousand copies! ONE THOUSAND COPIES! I could have walked out of that office on air. Or perhaps it was simply proof of what astute businesspeople the Singaporeans already were?

We had one more decision to make. Once the book was finished, where were we going to go? Back to England or back to Australia? The airfares were much the same and wherever we went we would be pretty well penniless when we arrived. Australia had some distinct advantages: we still had some copies of our first book there which we could sell, there were bookshops which still owed us money, and we did at least have the flimsy foundations of a business. It wouldn't quite be starting from scratch. So the decision was made—we would return to Australia.

The last night in Singapore we were all set to go. Our book was at the printer, our bags were packed, the tickets were on the table by the bed, but Southeast Asia had one final surprise in store for us. Just after midnight there was a knock at the door and we were handed a telegram. Late-night messages like this are always received with trepidation, but I could never have guessed what this envelope would contain. The telegram came from Chiang Mai—our motorcycle had been recovered.

Next morning we delayed our flight departure and pondered what to do. Going to Chiang Mai and back would cost nearly as much as the bike was worth, but getting it out of Thailand would completely solve our import duty problems. I had been worried that even with the lower duty agreed to by the Thai customs department I still might find some surprise in store. By now it was late in the week, and to exit Thailand by land on my motorbike I would need a visa, which would take until after the weekend to be issued. To hell with it, I thought, I'll go without a visa. Visitors arriving by air with a return ticket didn't need a visa and by this time I'd gone back and forth across the border between Thailand and Malaysia enough times to bet nobody would notice my missing visa. So I bought a Singapore–Bangkok–Singapore ticket, intending to refund the return portion as soon as I got back to Singapore.

I flew up to Bangkok and took the overnight train to Chiang Mai.

At the police station I retrieved our bike, now repainted and bearing fake Thai license plates. An officer translated the police report for me, a dramatic tale of Thai derring-do involving encircling the culprit's village in the middle of the night and pouncing at dawn, grabbing the thief and the *farang's* missing motorcycle. They even offered to point out the young villain in their lockup.

I rode part-way towards Bangkok, locking the motorcycle up very securely at my hotel that night. The following afternoon I was back in Bangkok where I loaded the bike and myself on the overnight train to Hat Yai. The next morning I rode to the border and cleared the paperwork that proved the bike was being exported. Motorcycles and bicycles were cruising back and forth, heading towards farms and other businesses in the No-Man's Land between the two borders. I rode my bike slowly and steadily straight past the immigration building. Nobody looked up. I would worry about a missing Thai departure stamp on my passport another time.

Back in Malaysia, I rode to Butterworth and loaded the bike on a train for the overnight trip to Kuala Lumpur, then headed back into Singapore. We took the bike to a motorcycle dealer who bought it for a sum which almost matched my Singapore–Bangkok airfare plus the two train trips.

That night, we flew back to Australia.

3

Getting Going, Going Broke

We'd arranged a reprint of *Across Asia on the Cheap* before we'd left Sydney for Timor, leaving the books with friends to send out when orders came through. Now, we collected the remaining few hundred copies, chased up some overdue accounts from Sydney bookshops then flew down to Melbourne where we camped on the floor of our friend Simon Potter's apartment. (We'd met Simon in a camp site in Greece three years previously.) We soon found a nondescript modern apartment just off bustling Chapel Street in the trendy inner-city suburb of South Yarra. We'd decided to spend a year in Melbourne, little realizing that we'd still be there thirty years later.

Maureen found work with Trailfinders, in the Melbourne office of the London-based travel agent. Today Trailfinders is a much bigger adventure travel and airline ticketing specialist, but in the early 1970s they were concentrating on the booming overland business. Filling up the overland buses and trucks for the return trips from Kathmandu to London was the responsibility of their offices in Sydney and Melbourne.

Lonely Planet was consuming some of my time every day, but we desperately needed more money. I managed to obtain a taxi driving license, even though my experience of driving around Melbourne was almost nil. We also made contact with the local office of the market research company we'd worked with in Sydney, so soon we were involved in their door-to-door projects as well. We furnished the apartment at minimal cost and bought a weather-beaten old Ford Cortina.

After we'd paid for the typesetting and pre-production work in Singapore and our airfares back to Australia we still had a little money left, but not enough to pay for 5000 copies of our new book when it left the printer. We'd wanted to print 10 000 copies, but that was clearly going to be impossible. Raising the cash was our number one priority.

We soon sold off the remaining stock of our *Across Asia* book and chased overdue accounts from bookshops around Australia. My taxi driving, Maureen's full-time job and our part-time jobs also brought in cash, but our bank balance still wasn't big enough for the print bill. Sales projections and cash-flow figures failed to impress the bank, which refused our request for a loan. There was only one place to turn: New Zealand.

Our foray around New Zealand in early 1974 had sold lots of books, but Alistair Taylor, our distributor there, hadn't paid for them. Polite reminders had no effect and when we called in the lawyers they had no success either. Eventually, Alistair announced he simply had no money. Would we be interested, he asked, in some books he couldn't get rid of in New Zealand? Four hundred copies of a 'build yourself a geodesic dome' book titled *Great Circles* and three hundred copies of a book on Jimi Hendrix. I'm no salesman, but we needed the money and I soon sold the lot. Months later, Melbourne record shops were still asking if I had any more Hendrix books.

In May, our ship came in. I attached a rented trailer to the tatty old Ford and drove off to the docks to collect our books, straight into the arms of what would be one of my pet hates for the next few years—the Australian dock system. Australian dockers are still not the best in the world, but in the mid-70s they were among the worst. At that time, third-world workers equipped with nothing more than some tattered ropes and a wonky plank could unload a ship ten times faster than Australian dockers armed with everything from cranes to forklifts. For many years, the docks remained a last bastion of Stone-

Age unionism in Australia and their institutionalized inefficiency was a prime disincentive to doing more of our printing in Australia rather than in Asia. We airfreighted all our books from Australia to New Zealand, reckoning that the higher cost was more than balanced by the time and energy we saved in not having to deal with Australia's crummy dock system.

Long lines of trucks were always waiting at the docks with drivers, who did want to get on with the job, cursing the time they wasted waiting for the dockers to lift a finger. Fortunately, small operators like us could usually jump the queue of big trucks. Until we could afford to use a proper freight agent to clear our shipments, I made many pre-dawn trips out to the docks to be first in line when the gates opened. I got through a stack of novels while I waited for the dockers to hand over the goods.

It could have been worse: years later on the Pacific island of Tuvalu, a former seamen talked fondly of the good old days when a port stop in Australia could mean four or five days.

'And in New Zealand,' he went on, 'we were sometimes in port for three or four weeks.

'They didn't have enough stevedores, so when we were in port we used to unload the ship as well,' he continued. 'We would start work at eight in the morning and we were used to working hard, so by eleven the New Zealand foreman was complaining that we were getting too much done and we had to stop for the day. It was fine by us, we were being paid by the shipping company and by the docks. We'd sleep all afternoon, drink all night and next morning work another three hours.'

At that time, freight out of Asia was not completely containerized and the odd shipment still came through on more traditional ships. I recall on one occasion I picked up two cartons of books newly arrived from Singapore, and as I staggered towards the trailer I saw a large and hairy spider clambering across the cardboard and marching resolutely towards me at eye level. My initial instinct to drop the boxes was tempered by the cold reality that we couldn't afford to lose any books due to damage. I quietly, though not very calmly, put the cartons down and chased the hitch-hiker away.

With our books stacked in our apartment living room, I set off around the country to sell them. On the way north to Sydney, the Ford's windscreen broke. On the way down to Adelaide, the exhaust fell off. Next trip north, the clutch failed. On the way back from the next trip south to Adelaide, the battery failed. No wonder I never liked that car.

One book was never going to keep us afloat, so until more Lonely Planet titles came along we found other books and maps to sell as well. We didn't even have to look for the first title since Bill Dalton, founder of Moon Publications and author of *Indonesia Handbook*, turned up at our apartment before setting out to follow our footsteps towards Singapore. We gave him the name of our printer in Singapore and suggested room five at the Palace Hotel as a good writer's retreat. Bill asked us to take over the sales of his first book, all thirty-two pages of *Indonesia—a traveler's notes*.

We also had the *Asia Overland Map* and *The Traveller's Health Guide* from Roger Lascelles, our new distributor in Britain, plus a map of Kuta Beach which we'd seen in Bali, so almost immediately we had a small travel list to distribute.

In between selling books I rewrote *Across Asia on the Cheap* in the same format as *South-East Asia on a Shoestring*. The first half of our original Australia-to-Britain-by-land guide overlapped with our new South-East Asia guide so updating that was no problem, but we had been nowhere near the stretch westwards from India through to Europe. Fortunately, the first edition was very thin to start with, so using smoke and mirrors I managed to produce an updated edition.

In late 1975 we were ready to print 10 000 copies of the second edition of *Across Asia* and a 10 000-copy reprint of *South-East Asia* was also set to go. But how would we pay for it? We hadn't saved enough money to pay two printing bills and our bank was definitely not coming to the party. Fortunately, my parents in England agreed to guarantee a $10 000 loan and we eventually arranged a bank overdraft. For years this was the total extent of our bank borrowings.

Lonely Planet was not the only tiny publishing house struggling to keep its head above water. Australia became an independent nation in 1901, but as far as book publishing went it was still a British colony until the 1970s. Many of the grand old names of British publishing, along with a few recent American interlopers, dominated the Australian publishing scene, principally selling imported books and occasionally publishing a local title. It was strictly a one-way flow: the British publishers couldn't imagine anybody back home being interested in any Australian topic. Furthermore, the British domination of the market meant that many American titles, which would have been perfect for the similar Australian climate and culture, never found their way here. If it wasn't going to fly in Britain, the British publisher certainly wouldn't take it on purely for the Australian market.

This all changed with the election of Gough Whitlam's Labor government in 1973. A quarter century of conservative political control ground to an overdue end and a flood of new ideas swept the country. One of the new government's projects was funding for Australian publishing and a gaggle of energetic new publishers grabbed the government grants and headed for the nearest printer. Unhappily, none of those pioneering names would last the distance, but the writers and ideas that publishers like Outback Press, Wild & Woolley, Greenhouse and McPhee Gribble launched woke up the big boys from London and New York and helped establish Australia's active and healthy local publishing scene.

Lonely Planet wasn't in line to get government writing and publishing grants. Art and culture had to come into the equation before government checks were written and there wasn't much of that in our publishing lives. Nevertheless, those other struggling small publishers were all good friends and together we formed the short-lived Australian Independent Publishers Association or AIPA. McPhee Gribble, founded by Hilary McPhee and Diana Gribble, would have a curiously lingering effect on Lonely Planet. We had published a number of titles before we realized we really should have had a contract with our authors and we borrowed our first contract from Hilary and Di. McPhee Gribble was a feminist publisher before the word 'feminism' had come into everyday usage and as a result for many years Lonely Planet's contracts always specified she/he rather than vice versa.

With the new edition of *Across Asia on the Cheap* published, we had two up-to-date books, but if Lonely Planet was going to become a real publishing house we couldn't write all the books ourselves. In mid-1975 I heard of *Nepal on $2 a Day*, self-published in Kathmandu by the Nepalese writer Prakash A. Raj. It was already a second edition; the first had been *Nepal on $1 a Day*. I wrote to him to buy a copy, which, if nothing else, would be good research material for our *Across Asia* guide. It turned out Prakash was keen to have his book published in the West. The original book was a pretty rough and ready affair, but we figured if we made a trip to Nepal, added photographs and wrote some additional material, we could produce something interesting. Trailfinders booked treks in Nepal through Stan Armington, an American resident there, and Maureen's boss, Alan Collingwood, asked Stan to organize a short trek while we were there.

Lonely Planet was clearly going to have to lift itself into a higher orbit the next year because Maureen had decided to quit work and go to university. Her three-year course would commence in February 1976—from that date our fledgling business was going to have to support both of us.

M: At the end of our first year in Melbourne, Trailfinders was having financial problems and decided to close down the Melbourne office. I began looking for a new job, but found it difficult to get past a first interview. In 1975, a 25-year-old woman, married, and somewhat nomadic, was considered a little suspect. I didn't want to go back to secretarial work and I was concerned that Lonely Planet would never really support both of us. I had watched my mother struggle to support our family after my father had died far too young, and

I felt that I needed to finish my education and have some professional qualifications up my sleeve, just in case!

I applied to La Trobe University because it had a very good mature-age student program. I was one of the eight per cent of applicants to be accepted. I decided to study psychology, since psychology, politics and sociology seemed to offer insights into the experiences I'd had while traveling. I loved it all, even doing assignments. Having been in the workforce since I was seventeen, I reveled in the luxury of having time to read and think and discuss. I received a grant which just covered the rent, and for the first year I did some temp work with an agency during the holidays and, of course, I also continued to help out with Lonely Planet.

Lonely Planet was outgrowing the corner of our apartment so we decided that when we returned from Nepal we would look for a house big enough to include an office. We packed up our furniture and distributed it amongst friends. The business was still so small that we could load all the paperwork into the trunk of our humble Ford and hand over the keys to fellow small publisher Jim Hart. He'd fill orders and bank any money that came in while we were away.

We decided to visit Britain as part of the trip and set off just before Christmas, flying to Bangkok and buying an Aeroflot ticket from New Delhi via Moscow to London. We flew on to Kathmandu where we settled into the Kathmandu Guest House, in the Thamel area. Since our last visit, Thamel had taken over from Freak Street as the main travelers' center. On Christmas Day we had dinner in the Yak & Yeti Restaurant, the predecessor to today's luxurious Yak & Yeti Hotel.

Prior to World War II, Nepal was closed off from the outside world and the early expeditions to Mt Everest all approached from the Tibetan side. Then Tibet was shut down after the Chinese takeover and around the same time Nepal opened up and the first intrepid tourists made their way to Kathmandu and the mountain kingdom.

Back in the 1950s, the legendary Russian ex-pat Boris Lissanevitch ran the Royal, the only hotel in town. Later he founded

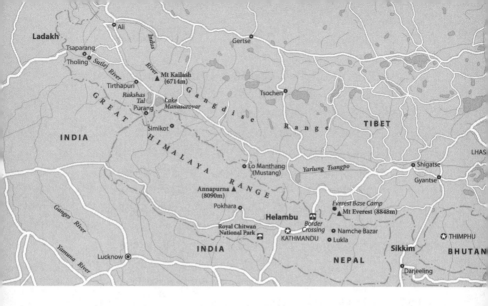

the Yak & Yeti Hotel and the Chimney restaurant. It's said Lissanevitch periodically fell out with the Nepalese bureaucrats and would end up in the local jail, where he happened to be when Queen Elizabeth visited Nepal in 1961. Prior to her visit, he was released to set up a jungle camp for the royal entourage, complete with toilets imported from Hong Kong. 'He was reminded of the visit of Queen Mary and King George to India where they installed toilets in a Maharaja's palace, but neglected the water,' according to Robert Peissel's book *Tigers for Breakfast*. On that occasion, so the story goes, the toilet with its elevated cistern was installed, but there was no way to get it to work. Eventually, a small boy was installed in the ceiling with a bucket of water and a spyhole. When the Queen or King completed what even royalty has to do from time to time and then pulled the chain, the boy would carefully hurl the bucket of water into the tank in a fine imitation of a flushing toilet. Or so the story goes.

Prakash was happy to work with us and for us to add material to his book, but Stan was initially very suspicious. I think he looked upon us as spokespeople for those unwashed hippies who wouldn't be booking on any of his treks. His initially prickly tone would soon soften and Stan became a firm friend who has visited us in Australia numerous times and walked many miles with us on treks in Nepal, Tibet and Australia.

We spent a month in Nepal, bicycling around the valley, going out to beautiful Dhulikhel, riding the bus to Pokhara and flying up to Namche Bazar. This turned out to be one of the highlights of all our trips to Nepal. We were planning to do the walk up from Lukla (a popular starting point for treks into the Himalayas) to the monastery at Tyangboche, but, as usual, Lukla was clouded in every morning and a backlog of unhappy trekkers was building up at Kathmandu's airport. It was here we met Michael Dillon, a young Australian free-lance film-maker also trying to get up to the Sherpa's Solukhumbu region, and we whiled away the hours at the airport together. Then somebody else's bad luck was our good: a Japanese trekker suffering altitude sickness had called for a helicopter rescue, and Stan used his contacts to get us on board. Michael, Maureen and I had a fantastic ringside view of the Himalayas as we flew up to the rarely used landing strip at Shyangboche, just above Namche Bazar.

Flying from the Kathmandu Valley at 4300 feet straight up to 12,400 feet is not a good idea and it took a day or two to get acclimatized, but we did some walking around Namche and further up the valley although we didn't go as far as the Everest Base Camp. It was 2003 before I finally trekked up to the base camp with Stan. Maureen and I appeared momentarily in the short film Michael made during that visit and from that low-key start he has become a well-known Himalayan documentary maker, working on several occasions with Sir Edmund Hillary.

Stan Armington had written a small general introduction to Himalayan trekking which had been published in the United States, but never sold elsewhere. We suggested that we should publish the book for the rest of the world. We would do so well with it that when Stan rewrote the book in a more comprehensive fashion he took it away from his original publisher and we sold it everywhere.

From New Delhi we joined the Aeroflot flight to Moscow. In 1976, Aeroflot was still solidly Soviet, with flight attendants who looked like they'd ship you off to a gulag as quickly as smile at you. Cheap tickets were the one and only reason people flew with the USSR's flag carrier. When I souvenired a teaspoon for a friend, I quickly discovered that an inventory was taken on each tray as it was collected after the meal.

'Vair ist your teaspoon,' the flight attendant hissed at me angrily.

'Where is it?' Maureen whispered as we trooped off the aircraft.

'In your bag,' was my traitorous reply.

In Moscow it was suggested by the Aeroflot staff that we might like to fly straight on to London, instead of taking our free 24-hour stopover, but we were keen to see Moscow, however briefly, and the way-below-freezing weather didn't deter us. The short stay consisted of nothing more than a bus to the hotel, lunch, an afternoon bus tour of Moscow and dinner. Next morning we were bussed to the airport, boarded the flight and then sat through an interminable passenger counting session before they decided somebody was missing and unloaded all of us onto the snow-covered tarmac where we had to identify our luggage piece by piece. The sari-clad Indian women coming straight through from New Delhi looked distinctly chilled. We never found out what happened to the missing passenger (the delay was put down to 'technical reasons'), but we were sure people wouldn't blithely 'no show' for flights from Moscow.

During our month in Britain we caught up with friends and Maureen flew back to Belfast to visit her mother. I hauled my little Marcos sports car out of its four-year hibernation, with the intention of shipping it to Australia. It was good to see family and friends and we were very busy chasing up contacts to sell our books and looking for other publications to import. The business was still so tiny it was hard for our friends to take it seriously and we were keen to get back to Australia, for Maureen to start at university and for me to get on with producing our new books.

Back in Australia, we moved in with Nigel Rockliffe, a friend from the London Business School, while we looked for a house. Soon after Maureen started at university, I found a crumbling little wooden Victorian-era house near the freeway in the suburb of Richmond.

The walls were grey, the floors were covered in grubby-looking vinyl, the backyard was entirely concrete with the toilet right down at the end of it, beside the back lane, but the rent was only twenty-eight dollars a week. Fearing it would be gone if I hesitated, I signed up and then took Maureen and our friend Simon to look at it that evening. There was no electricity and by matchlight it looked even more dismal than in daylight, but it was too late, we were committed.

Fortunately, seagrass matting and white paint can work wonders and within a couple of weeks 22 Durham Street was a very comfortable-looking place, with the small second bedroom functioning as Lonely Planet's fourth workplace (following on from our basement apartment in Sydney, the hotel room in Singapore and our modern apartment in South Yarra). The metal shed in the backyard became the warehouse and we had a phone installed, so it was no longer necessary to trek round to a nearby phone box when we wanted to summon a delivery truck.

Our third book, Stan Armington's *Trekking in the Himalayas*, was published in September and Prakash Raj's *Nepal—a Traveller's Guide* followed a few weeks later. More books would appear on our list as a result of our visit to Britain. While we were there, I'd contacted Geoff Crowther, the bushy-bearded Sixties character who was the driving force behind the BIT travel guides. The *BIT Guide to Asia* was their big seller, but there were similar productions for Africa and South America and Geoff was the person who ran the whole thing.

A university graduate with a degree in biochemistry, Geoff was a bit of a hippie, a person who would turn his hand to any good cause from fixing faulty plumbing in a squat to turning up at the registry office to marry someone desperate for a UK residence permit. He was also an inveterate traveler who had spent many months in India and traversed the Sahara. Now that the 1960s were over, BIT was fading away and I suggested that with his travel knowledge and our publishing house, Geoff could start making a living out of what he had been doing for free. Geoff set to work rewriting Africa as a guidebook, an activity which did not go down well with some of the remaining BIT stalwarts, but when we published the first 240-page edition of *Africa on the Cheap* it was the start of a long and mutually successful relationship. Remarkably, thirty years later, we still publish the only guidebook to cover all of Africa.

Our short visit to the UK had turned up several other useful publishing connections and our distribution list soon included books from small publishers like Vacation Work and Michael von Haag as well as a batch of back-to-the-land titles from Prism Press. We also picked up Nicholas Saunder's *Alternative England*, a less successful follow-up to his groundbreaking *Alternative London*. A 1960s visionary, Nicholas also created Neal's Yard, the wholefood zone of Covent Garden, and later became an enthusiastic evangelist for the drug ecstasy. He died in a car crash in South Africa in 1998.

Maureen was busy studying so she was only a part-time Lonely Planet worker, but in 1976 I was flat out working on our two new Himalayan titles and organizing distribution of our much longer list of imported titles, much of the work being done in co-operation with the Sydney-based small publisher Second Back Row Press.

The Australian tax year runs from the beginning of July to the end of June. Our Melbourne-based operation had got under way around July 1 1975, so mid-year 1976 saw the conclusion of Lonely Planet's first real year as a full-time business. Our sales—*sales* mind you, not profit—were $28 000. We could only go up. Of course, our two Lonely Planet titles retailed for only $1.95 so we had to sell a lot of books to make any sort of money.

In mid-1976 we made a very curious contact when a letter arrived from Andy Myer. He'd been a young high-flier at A&M records in Los Angeles, taken off on a year's sabbatical and ended up exploring the backroads of Southeast Asia with our book in hand. That first edition may have only sold 15 000 copies (later editions would churn through over 100 000), but it was already establishing itself as the guide to the region; when we discovered its users referred to it as 'the yellow bible' we were stuck with that color for the cover on every subsequent edition. Andy was an astute early observer of the book's influence and was convinced our books and his marketing expertise could go places. He was in Europe by the time this revelation hit him, but he suggested we get together and talk business. Andy, it turned out, was nearly as broke as we were, but he still managed to scrape together enough money to buy me an airline ticket so I could fly to Europe to meet with him.

The Frankfurt Bookfair in Germany is the annual get-together of the world's publishing business. I learned that by appearing at the bookfair I'd be eligible for a business grant from the Australian government, which I could then use to repay Andy for my airfare. So that trip to Europe in October neatly killed two birds with one stone: I could meet Andy to talk business and I could show off our books to the publishing and bookselling world.

Andy and I met in London and traveled to Frankfurt where we were so penniless the railway station booking service unhesitatingly directed us to a flea-bitten room in the city's red-light district. Our room for two was above a brothel and featured a single, fortunately rather wide, bed. It was years before I could afford to stay in good hotels at Frankfurt. A few times, I used the bookfair's accommodation bureau which arranges cheap B&B-style lodging in private homes around the city. One year, I found myself in the spare room of an apartment occupied by an attractive young woman and her son; she was recently divorced from an American GI. My second night there, I was astonished when my landlady hopped into bed beside me after a late-night toilet visit and immediately fell asleep! I surmised, correctly as it turned out, that I was sleeping in what was usually her room. No amount of nudging would wake her up so, eventually, I went back to sleep as well. In the morning, she leapt out of bed in shock and confusion.

Much later, swapping Frankfurt war stories, Bryn Thomas (an Englishman's Englishman who wrote for us and ran his own small travel publishing house, Trailblazer) confessed that for many years he could not afford a hotel at all. He'd camped outside of the city, putting on a coat and tie in his tent each morning and riding the train into the center. Staying in a hotel above a brothel in the red-light district was a big step forward for Bryn. The large New York and London publishing houses, comfortably encamped in the 44-storey Marriott across from the *Buchmesse* site, still have no idea what their smaller relations go through.

Nothing came of my meeting with Andy Myer in 1976, but I was encouraged by his vision that we were heading towards bigger things, grateful for his trust in advancing me the airfare and relieved when I could repay him, when the grant came through the following year.

A photograph I took of our small display at our first Frankfurt fair shows the whole Lonely Planet list on just a foot or two of shelf space. Going international with only four titles to our name was either foolhardy or careless bravado, but we knew people were going to want our books—we simply had to wait for the realization to sink in.

Guidebooks need to be updated. As our commentary on change goes: 'good places go bad, bad places go bankrupt, nothing stays the same'.

In late 1976 it was clear we had to do something about *South-East Asia on a Shoestring*. We'd researched the first edition in 1974, so it was overdue for an update. Writing the first edition had involved a year's travel, something we couldn't afford for an update. Updating our flagship book would have to be quick and dirty, not the comprehensive job we would have wished. In fact, that highly compromised first update trip would be typical of the way we were forced to do things for a number of years.

Just because we couldn't afford to do a perfect job of updating the material didn't stop us from expanding it by adding Papua New Guinea, Hong Kong, Macau and the Philippines. The update grew from 144 pages to 240, even though Portuguese Timor and Laos both disappeared from the new edition.

We flew to Papua New Guinea courtesy of Air Niugini. We'd contacted the airline, shown them our Southeast Asia guide, told them we'd do something similar for Papua New Guinea if we could only afford to get there and they'd offered to fly us to Port Moresby and through to Irian Jaya. It was a no-strings-attached offer which we greatly appreciated because PNG is an expensive, though fascinating, country. So in early 1977, Maureen and I flew into Port Moresby, then on to Lae, the port on the north coast.

We'd heard it was possible to get a free trip into the Highlands by contacting a truck importer and offering to deliver a recently unloaded vehicle. Sure enough, the local Toyota agent had a pickup truck waiting to be delivered, so we drove it up the Highlands Highway through Goroka to Mt Hagen. From there we flew down to beautiful Madang on the north coast and then on to Wewak, further west along the coast. We made a rather pointless and uncomfortable trip up to the Sepik River—pointless because we didn't have the time to explore further up the river and uncomfortable because we couldn't afford the high cost of accommodation and food in Papua New Guinea. In some towns there were mission hostels and other reasonably priced alternatives, but when we had to rely on motels and hotels catering to business visitors we were in big trouble. One night in Maprik we ate canned meat on crackers, sitting forlornly in our overpriced room.

A small plane carried us from Wewak to Jayapura in Irian Jaya, the Indonesian half of New Guinea, where costs immediately tumbled to more affordable levels, although they were still much higher than we had been accustomed to in other parts of Indonesia. Again, our tight schedule prevented us from exploring further afield, so we never got to the Baliem Valley. We flew to Biak and then took an ancient, four-engined turboprop Vickers Vanguard across to Makassar in Sulawesi. Indonesian visitors to Biak often bought parrots to sell in other parts of the archipelago and during our flight a passenger's recent purchase escaped and flew, squawking, up and down the cabin.

From the port of Makassar, we traveled by bus into the amazing Toraja land area to the north with its cliffside graves like theater boxes and its houses with their sweeping bowed roofs. Then it was back to Makassar and another flight to take us south to Bali. Kuta Beach had changed amazingly in the two-plus years since our last visit: tourism was clearly booming and ugly development was already beginning to sprawl out to Legian Beach and beyond. We rented a motorcycle, rode around the island, stayed in Ubud, still quiet and peaceful, and then took a bus to Surabaya where, for the first time, we witnessed the influence our little book could have. When the owner of the Bamboo Denn discovered we were staying at his lodge, he made an all-out effort to bribe us to ensure our recommendation stayed positive. We had to work hard to convince him that we didn't accept bribes. In any case, he had the only cheap place in town.

After Surabaya, we traveled by train and bus through Yogyakarta to Bogor and then Jakarta before another flight to Singapore. Our first trip through the region had been a laid-back cruise compared to this one—we hurtled through, grabbing information on the run. An early-morning train carried us from Singapore to Kuala Lumpur where we spent the day rushing around the hotels, restaurants and other places that needed rechecking and then took a late-night train to Penang. Around midnight, as we stood waiting for a ferry across the strait to Georgetown, I realized Maureen was all but asleep on her feet and quietly crying from pure exhaustion. I managed to almost carry her onto the ferry and install her in a bicycle rickshaw on the island side.

M: During this trip, I began to suspect that travel for us had changed forever. No longer were we simply following the road suggested by our curiosity and dictated by our financial state; we had a purpose, we were laying down the roadmap for like-minded travelers. We took this responsibility very seriously. We had to go further, higher, harder than anyone else, in order to document it all, but it was hard. By the time we arrived in Penang I was exhausted, but Tony wasn't very sympathetic. I remember getting off the ferry in Penang and walking to the waiting rickshaws. I think I was whimpering with sheer fatigue; I was also stumbling a little. Tony grabbed my arm and hissed in my ear, 'Walk straight, the customs guys are watching, they'll think you're on drugs!'

We had a short break in Georgetown, that fascinatingly old-fashioned city, then took a battered old Thai Chevy across the border to Hat Yai, where we caught an overnight train to Bangkok. The Malaysia Hotel's famous noticeboard provided lots of interesting update information before we flew to Hong Kong.

We'd been buying our various transport tickets as we went along, but Papua New Guinea's high costs had made an unexpectedly large dent in our reserves and by the time we hit Hong Kong we were near to penniless, an all-too-familiar condition for most of Lonely Planet's early years. We'd cabled our Australian bank from Singapore and requested money to be transferred to Hong Kong, but arriving on a weekend we had to survive until Monday without cash. This was before Visa and MasterCard had conquered the world and we certainly weren't eligible for an American Express or Diners Club card. Fortunately we had a Hong Kong distributor by this time, Geoffrey Bonsall, who worked as the director of Hong Kong University Press. Geoffrey invited us to lunch at the Hilton and was charm itself, refusing to let us pay for anything, establishing a tradition of looking after impoverished Lonely Planet authors who were passing through. In later years, Geoffrey's kindness was much appreciated by our writers who blazed new trails into mainland China as Mao's long-closed doors began to slowly creak open.

We explored Hong Kong and its islands, visited nearby Macau and got to know the intricacies of Chungking Mansions, the rabbit warren of cheap boarding houses which has been home to generations of budget travelers in Hong Kong. Cozying up against the Kowloon Holiday Inn and right across Nathan Road from the Hyatt, the Chungking Mansions guesthouses offer an entirely different Hong Kong accommodation experience. The shops, businesses and guesthouses in the seventeen-storey building attract an astoundingly international mix of occupants and visitors who throng the shopping arcade and spill out onto the street. We pushed through young backpackers from Australia, North America and almost every country in Europe, hearing snatches of Indonesian and breathing in the heady aroma of Kretek clove cigarettes. Africans in colorful but utterly incongruous tribal clothing towered over the Chinese, who almost seemed out of place in their own city. Curry smells wafting down the stairwells reminded us that upstairs there were countless little restaurants with origins from the Indian subcontinent. A bright flash of purple and orange would give us advance warning of a bevy of Tibetan monks pushing through the crowds.

A visit to Chungking Mansions is still a heady experience. The shops all seem to have a travel connection. There are numerous money changers, some of them giving the best exchange rates to be found in this city of money. Abundant luggage shops exist to help visitors who need extra capacity to lug all their purchases away. Virtually anything from a new battery for your camera to a cheap laundry service can be found here. Upstairs, interspersed between those aromatic Indian restaurants, are local gem-cutting businesses and airline ticket 'bucket shops' and travel agents. Today, Chungking Mansions is a center for agents specializing in Chinese travel (and experts at obtaining visas for China quickly and cheaply), but back in 1977, China travel had yet to begin. Also upstairs is accommodation ranging from backpacker dormitories offering the cheapest beds in Hong Kong to some quite respectable guesthouses. The only trouble is getting to them . . .

The upper floors of each of Chungking Mansions' five blocks are even today served by just two slow and undersized elevators. Inevitably there are long queues to board the elevators and regular stayers soon learn the Chungking trick to goad overloaded elevators into action. When the warning buzzer sounds and an elevator grinds to a halt, leaping in the air may momentarily reduce the weight and fool the elevator into continuing its journey. In one of the elevators a sign announces: 'The Irresponsible for Accident to Overloading'.

Impatient visitors sometimes decide to walk down (or even up) the stairways. Bad decision. In later years our Hong Kong guide succinctly described this Blade Runneresque vision:

> For a real-life vision of hell, take a look down the light wells of Chungking Mansions' D block. It's dark, dirty, festooned with pipes and wires covered in what looks like the debris of half a century. Why bother to put rubbish in the bin when it's so much easier to throw it out the window? Discarded plastic bags fall only halfway before lodging on a ledge or drainpipe. Soon they're joined by old newspapers, used toilet paper, underwear, half-eaten food and an expired rat (was it too dirty for him too?)

Any visitor to the Mansions soon recognizes that the building is a horrible fire risk, a disaster waiting to happen. A few years ago, a minor fire prompted some new rules and this travelers' talking point looks like soldiering on for years. We've visited Hong Kong many times since that first visit and I'm very glad to have outgrown the necessity of staying in Chungking Mansions. But every time I return to what is now, in Chinese official-speak, the SAR or 'Special Administrative Region', I always drop into Chungking Mansions to change money, get some laundry done or grab a quick Indian meal.

From Hong Kong, Maureen had to fly straight back to Australia, to restart university, but I carried on to Manila in the Philippines. In Singapore, I'd dropped into Insight Guides and was unexpectedly back on their payroll, tying up some loose ends in their forthcoming Philippines guide. On our shoestring budget, the extra few hundred dollars was invaluable.

I soon worked out the jeepney routes in Manila and found my way to Hobbit House, the folk music club entirely staffed (apart from the musicians) by dwarfs. Nearly thirty years later it's still there and as popular as ever, particularly with the little people, who reckon this is a place all their own.

From Manila I headed south to climb the Mayon Volcano on the main island of Luzon. Although I have a number of friends who are deadly serious about mountaineering, I've been happy to constrain my mountaineering interest to the armchair variety. I have climbed plenty of 'tourist mountains' over the years (Mt Fuji in Japan, Mt Bromo in Indonesia, Adam's Peak in Sri Lanka) but Mayon was a more serious tourist ascent. The 7900-foot climb starts right from sea level and getting to the top really requires an overnight halt on the way. The fact that the volcano is still regularly, and often dramatically, active adds spice to the ascent.

I met Ricardo Dey, a 'Mayoneering' guide who provided camping equipment and recruited a young Filipino to carry it. We chartered a jeepney to get to the starting point where we set up camp some distance below the summit. Before dawn, we started off to the top, only to be thwarted by heavy clouds draped over the volcano's shapely summit. Hunched down shivering behind huge boulders, we munched on the sandwiches we'd brought with us for lunch and Ricardo demonstrated his useful technique for warming his frozen hands by peeing on them. Shortly after we'd given in and started back down, the clouds whipped away and the summit of Mayon appeared above us, standing out against a clear blue sky.

We rushed to the summit, racing to get there before it clouded in again. It was freezing cold on the top and after looking down into the cone and marveling at the view down the volcano's flanks, sweeping straight down to the sea, we started back down to our base camp. By now, I was more than just tired; shattered would be a better word. The rest of the descent was a combination of walking a little bit, stumbling a little bit and sitting down to wait for my legs to stop feeling like jelly. We eventually got to the road and flagged a ride into Legaspi where even a cold beer didn't do much to revive me. Back at my hotel room, I flung my shoes into the bin and myself into bed, wondering why I was so completely beat. It was probably the result of two months of running too fast.

In March, 10 pounds lighter and more than slightly exhausted, I flew back to Australia to be greeted by what was to become a regular welcome home for the next couple of years—a strip search by customs officials convinced I was in Southeast Asia for some less-than-honest purpose.

It had been a tough trip and by the meticulous standards we would later establish it was horribly incomplete, but we had been back to most places and we'd been able to gather a great deal of additional information as we passed through. Noticeboards like the one in the Malaysia Hotel, guest books, letters and suggestions had all contributed to the update, and when it hit the bookshop shelves later in 1977 we weren't ashamed of the job we'd done. With its now familiar yellow cover the second edition of *South-East Asia on a Shoestring* went on to sell another 15 000 copies, like the first edition.

That flat-out trip around Southeast Asia was symptomatic of the whole year, a year which in retrospect was crucial for Lonely Planet. In 1975 we had two books, in 1976 we'd doubled that list to four and now, in 1977, we doubled the list again to eight books. It was a rate of production we simply could not sustain. Looking back at those books, they were often fairly shoddy productions, but simply getting them on the shelves helped make the business viable. Furthermore, they were often filling empty niches so even if they weren't very good, by our later standards, they were still better than anything else around.

Book number five was our first Australia guide and it was a seriously under-researched effort, most of it written from our back-room office in Richmond with little field research. International tourism to Australia at that time was very small and the backpacker boom was still years away, so it was scarcely surprising that sales of the first couple of editions of our Australia guide were pretty disappointing.

Mid-year I did another high-speed book, this time on New Zealand. The New Zealand Tourist Board supported this project, which basically meant organizing a free rent-a-car for me. Today we make a point of always paying our own way, but in these early days the little help we did get from airlines (like Air Niugini) and tourist boards (like New Zealand's) was absolutely vital. Lack of time and money again constrained how much effort I could put into the New Zealand guide, but although it was only 112 pages long, it was properly researched, unlike the Australia book.

When I came back from New Zealand I also had a slightly more reliable car than our dreadful Ford clunker. My little home-made Marcos sports car had finally been shipped out from England. It was now almost ten years since I'd built it myself, but I would end up driving it for nearly twenty-five years. The Ford now became Maureen's regular transport to university, although she took the Marcos from time to time.

Our sales had more than doubled to $60 000. Thirty years later, our retail prices are often ten times higher, so that would be more like half a million dollars today. Nevertheless, our cash flow was appalling and every morning I frantically opened envelopes, hoping one bookshop or another had paid their account. We chased bank loans, counted pennies and lost sleep.

The first local credit card system, Bankcard, was introduced in Australia in 1974 and Maureen and I were assiduous early users, although unfortunately it couldn't be used overseas. Every time we found ourselves at a restaurant with friends or Maureen's fellow university students, we would wait until everybody had put in their cash for the meal, grab the lot and pay with our credit card. For months this was the ready cash that kept us afloat from one week to the next. We never resorted to borrowing money on our credit card, being too frugal to face those high interest rates, but we regularly calculated how many weeks our card could keep us afloat if it came to grim necessity.

In September 1977, Lonely Planet made a major step forward when our first employee joined us. Although Maureen and I were still doing a large part of the writing and all the editing and book production, we certainly weren't doing absolutely everything any more. Tom and Wendy Whitton of Second Back Row Press were handling our book sales in Sydney and we were organizing representation in other states. Peter Campbell, a Melbourne art teacher whom we had met fleetingly in London years previously, was doing illustrations and some other work on the books. But we were still handling all the paperwork, the invoicing, parceling up and dispatch of orders, sending out monthly statements, banking, and all those other highly necessary, but time-consuming tasks. Keeping my head above the rolling seas of paper was becoming near impossible and Maureen couldn't provide as much support as she would have liked. At this point, Scottish-born and raised (and female!) Andy Neilson came into our lives.

M: We first met Andy at a party in her apartment in London. A mutual friend had a birthday and Andy had invited everyone and baked a cake. Had I realized at the time what a portent that was, I would have recorded what kind of cake it was. As our den mother for many years, Andy has baked thousands of cakes. Until there were so many Lonely Planet staff that birthdays occurred every day, every employee had a cake from Andy, and every special occasion, from sending a book to the printer to getting a good review, was celebrated with one of her cakes.

When we arrived in Melbourne, we met up with some of our Aussie friends who had returned home from London and we reconnected with Andy. She had come to live in Melbourne with her baby son, Torquil, the result of a relationship with one of those traveling Aussies in London. The relationship hadn't worked out, but Andy had decided to come to Australia anyway and was working as a nanny to support herself and her child.

On one occasion, we were in my kitchen having a coffee when Andy mentioned she needed to earn some more money. I was finding it difficult to juggle my Lonely Planet and uni work, especially when Tony was away traveling, so I asked her to come and help us out. I thought we could manage seven hours a week; she could choose her own times and bring Torquil with her. She jumped at it, but I was afraid Tony would

say we couldn't afford it. However, he was totally won over
when he found Andy carefully steaming unfranked stamps off
incoming mail and reusing envelopes—her Scottish frugality
completely matched his fiscal conservatism and they got along
just fine.

Thirty years later Andy is still working with us, still the Lonely
Planet den mother and still as frugal as ever. Occasionally we tell
new hands how, in the old days, all book orders were dispatched in
packages wrapped up in brown paper scavenged from Coles supermarket bags. Anytime we ran out of paper, we used to scoot round to
the Swan Street outlet, buy a carton of milk and bag it liberally.

In late 1977 we had to do something about updating *Across Asia
on the Cheap*. The 1975 update was based only on the work we'd
done for *South-East Asia on a Shoestring*; the other half of the book
from India westwards had been done purely from letters and desk
research. One of the major overland companies, operating trucks and
buses across Asia, was based in New Zealand and I'd met with them
while I was in New Zealand earlier in the year. They'd offered to let
me join one of their trips. Perhaps this could be a way of updating the
rest of the book.

We also continued to push our overseas sales, so I decided to go
to the Frankfurt Bookfair again in October 1977, then join up with
the overland trip in Istanbul and travel through Turkey, Iran,
Afghanistan, Pakistan and India, updating *Across Asia on the Cheap*
as I went. This neat plan came crashing to the ground just days before
my departure, when there were printing bills and other accounts to be
paid and we simply did not have the cash. For days we made phone
calls and chased up overdue accounts, but the money simply was not
there. Our sixth wedding anniversary was on October 7, the night
before my departure for Europe, and we decided to eat out anyway,
using that hard-worked Bankcard yet again, but the mood was definitely downbeat.

The next morning, I drove around Melbourne to the bookshops
who'd offered to pay me on the spot if I came to collect the checks!

I rushed to the airport and, for once, I was relieved to find the flight was going to depart five hours late, long enough to go back home and relax for a while. When we got back to the airport, the delay had been cut back to four hours and I got on board with minutes to spare. It was a gloomy flight. Was our baby business about to crash to the ground, before it even got airborne?

4

Near Disaster

Despite the pre-departure gloom, Frankfurt Bookfair 1977 was encouraging. In what was to be typical Lonely Planet fashion, we managed to give the appearance of being much bigger than we really were. A year earlier, we had a handful of books on the Australian government-funded stand. This year, when far bigger Australian publishers were still just getting their patch of shelf space on the government stand, we had our very own stand. Well, our very own shared with Michael von Haag's London-based Travelaid, whose books we distributed in Australia. More people were becoming aware, in a small way, of our books and we made lots of contacts and lined up more international distributors. We were pretty much on the rocks, but it certainly looked like we were going places.

I could not afford the time to take the planned overland trip back across Asia, but I did manage to stop in Istanbul, Tehran (in the dramatic last year of the Shah's rule) and Singapore, so there was at least some minimal updating for our neglected Across Asia title. It now only covered the western part of Asia, although in greater detail, since we'd chopped the Southeast Asian countries out. In early 1979 we reprinted it with a 'bad news supplement on Iran and Afghanistan'. The old Asian overland trip was about to implode as Afghanistan tumbled into twenty years of anarchy and Iran transmuted from the Shah's rule to the Ayatollah's.

Despite our straitened financial state, we also had a ninth book under way, to be written by our journalist friend Carol Clewlow. We'd written to Carol earlier in the year and suggested she write a Hong Kong and Macau guide for us. She'd agreed and was back from her research trip when I saw her in London, just prior to Frankfurt.

Arriving back in Australia, I was welcomed with another thorough search by airport heavies, still convinced that my comings and goings must have some ulterior motive. The illegal business the customs people imagined was nonexistent, but in our real business we knew we'd pushed things too far and decided to have a summer of consolidation. Maureen's second university year was finishing (she was switching from psychology to social work) and we decided to stay at home and concentrate on putting books out.

We met Don and Sheila Drummond, operators of a local publishing house specializing in primary school texts, as their business name Primary Education suggested. They had an IBM Composer, a glorified Selectric golfball typewriter with a very limited electronic memory, like an extremely primitive word processor. The 'golfball' was the round, metal type-element with all the characters on it. There wasn't a screen or anything high-tech, but you could type about a page of text, inserting signals when you wanted to change to bold or italic, then output the page as a typeset galley. In pre-desktop publishing days 'galleys' were long strips of text which you cut up and pasted down page by page.

Once you'd typed in a page of text, you could press a button and, like a player piano, the IBM Composer would type it out again, obediently stopping at the signals so you could change the golfball to produce the desired typeface. When you'd output the text, you cleared the memory and typed in another page. In 1977 this was the cutting edge of electronic technology and this primitive device cost around $7000! In 1977 dollars! We rented the Primary Education Composer by the hour, using it at night after they'd gone home. We typeset our sixth and seventh books ourselves and were soon doing all our own typesetting. By 1978 we were spending so many hours on the Primary Education IBM Composer we decided to buy our own.

This fancy typewriter was our first tentative step into computers. We installed it in the one-room office in our house and Maureen, Andy and I churned out galleys for our books. Despite its drawbacks, doing our own typesetting was economical, speedy and enabled us to make last-minute corrections with ease.

T: Producing text using an IBM Composer was a fraught affair. Since the memory was live only as long as the power was on, all it took was a power cut or somebody tripping over the cord to wipe it out. Once you'd output your page of text and started on a new page, the old page was gone. If, later on, you found a spelling mistake, the only way to fix it was to retype the line in question, cut it out and glue it over the old line. If the spelling correction required an extra character, it might make the line longer than before, so you would have to reset the next line as well. And the next line, and the next line, until eventually you ended up with something you could cut out and stick down.

A bigger problem, however, was those damned golfballs. We had a little plastic cabinet of alternative golfballs and for each point size and typeface you had to have three golfballs—one in *italic*, one in **bold** and one in the normal face. We used one face (Times Roman) in two point sizes (eight point and ten point) plus some Universe golfballs for headings. Since we put all hotel and restaurant names in italics (the *Grand Hotel* or the *Curry House Restaurant*), there was a lot of switching back and forth between golfballs. If we forgot to put the stop signal in after putting *Pizza Hut into italics, the Composer would merrily continue in italics until someone stopped the damn thing*.

That was annoying enough, but changing the golfballs required care and precision, rare in the early hours of the morning. If the golfball was not locked down properly, when you pressed the button to restart the Composer, the ball would go spinning into orbit like a frisbee, often breaking off a tooth as it went. Sometimes we had a spare golfball in the cabinet, sometimes the broken tooth could be fished out of the Composer's innards and reattached with superglue, but all too often we had to drive across town to the IBM office to fork out thirty-two dollars for a new golfball. Curiously, golfball emergencies seemed to happen most often around 4.30 pm on a Friday afternoon, allowing only half an hour to get there through rush-hour traffic before the parts department shut down for the weekend.

The Composer only handled text up to about twelve point. For bigger text for a chapter heading, map title or a book cover, we would have it photoset, usually at a friendly little place called Currency Productions run by Tess Baster, a friend to all the city's small publishers. We regularly rushed across town to collect galleys of typeset headings or 'bromides' of maps from Currency.

The summer of 1977–78 was somewhat like our time in Singapore in early 1975. We worked all day at our office and half the night round at Primary Education, breaking for souvlaki, salad and retsina at the Laikon, a popular local Greek restaurant conveniently midway between our house and Primary Education's office. It was a surprisingly enjoyable time of hard work and late-night walks from Primary Education to our house and office, not much more than a mile apart in the inner-city suburb of Richmond. At that time, Richmond had a large Greek population (today the Greek immigrants have given way to Vietnamese and yuppies), and as we strolled the back lanes there were night noises of Greek music and talk, the smell of flowers, lemons and barbecues.

Perhaps it was the frantic speed with which we pumped out titles during 1977, perhaps it was that summertime period of consolidation, but to our pleasant surprise we began to notice things getting easier in the early part of 1978. There was often a little money in our bank account and we rarely had to delay paying bills. It was a wonderful feeling because we had endured two years of serial financial crunches. Throughout 1976 and 1977 we never had enough money and constantly worried about every expenditure, and would often wake in a cold sweat.

We celebrated this liquidity by buying a near-new car. The horrible old Ford Cortina, easily the worst car I have ever owned, was sold for $530, a thirty-dollar improvement on what we paid for it, and I was delighted to see it driven away. In between times, we'd spent a small fortune keeping the wreck moving and we'd slept by the roadside many times after it had broken down on the way to or from Sydney or Adelaide. With a little help from the bank, we bought a thoroughly practical and utterly boring year-old Mazda 808 station wagon for $3850.

By now, much of our worldwide distribution had been sorted out, some of it for a long time to come. Peter Bleekrode, our man in the Netherlands, would still be running our biggest continental Europe market when the next century rolled in, although the original company, Meulenhoff-Bruna, had been subsumed into Nilsson & Lamm.

We produced two new books in 1978: Carol Clewlow's Hong Kong guide and a new guide to South America from Geoff Crowther. We'd suggested that Geoff follow his Africa book with a South American guide, but BIT's South American guide, which he would use as a basis, was a pale shadow of the other BIT guides. Geoff's own extensive travels had not extended to South America so the BIT guide was totally based on letters. Geoff went to South America to research his new book for us then came to Australia to write it, staying in a commune on an old banana plantation outside Burringbar in the north of New South Wales. He liked the lifestyle so much that he bought a share of the commune and established himself in Australia.

The one trip I made during 1978 was to Papua New Guinea to write a book on that country. Our trip through PNG in the previous year had been a less than comprehensive and rather rushed affair, but Air Niugini had been happy with the exposure it gave the country in our Southeast Asia guide and they agreed to fly me around again. My first two single-country books (we called them travel survival kits)—Australia and New Zealand—had been researched and written with too little money and even less time. I was determined to do PNG properly.

From Port Moresby I flew north to Lae, but before continuing up into the Highlands I took PMVs—public motor vehicles, the pickup trucks which functioned as a local bus service—to Wau and Bulolo, old gold-mining centers, then to Goroka and Mt Hagen. I then flew from Mt Hagen down to Madang on the coast and explored that area, some of it by bicycle.

From Madang I flew to Wewak and had a wonderful time on the Sepik River. With its crocodiles, cassowaries, pretty villages and towering *haus tambarans* (spirit houses), the Sepik was one of the highlights of the trip and is certainly the most interesting part of the country. Our riverboat guide was a retired crocodile hunter and one night he took us out to enjoy a little reptile hunting. His technique was very simple: he zoomed along the river in an outboard-powered dinghy, sweeping the riverbanks with a massive spotlight. The sly eyes of a basking crocodile appeared as two bright red dots in the dark. He would grab the croc and wrestle it on board the boat. Or at least that's what he did if it was small enough. He guesstimated how big it was by the distance between the two red dots. If the dots were too far apart it meant the crocodile had a very wide head, and presumably a body to match.

Once on board, we had to hold the crocodile firmly down to the bottom of the boat. Soon we had a half-dozen small crocs on board, at which point we got stuck on a mud bank. Two of us stayed on board, each holding down a crocodile with a hand and a foot, while the others pushed us off the bank. The crocs ended up, later that night, in a village crocodile farm where they would be fattened to handbag size.

PMVs carried me back to Wewak, then I flew via Manus to New Ireland where I hitch-hiked along the long narrow island, sleeping overnight at one point in a police station, then took a local flight from Namatanai across to Rabaul in New Britain. I had a thoroughly enjoyable time in that beautiful South Seas town, climbing up to the top of the volcano which devastated the town in 1994. I continued on to the island of Bougainville and visited the huge open-cut copper mine at Panguna. I was glad I had the chance to see it since for years after 1989, the whole island was off limits due to a smoldering local liberation movement.

From Bougainville I returned to Port Moresby and made a final trip out to the Trobriand Islands, another of Papua New Guinea's unusual attractions and a place subjected to intense scrutiny by anthropologists. Margaret Mead is perhaps the most famous of many who turned out PhDs from the Pacific, but it would be hard to find a more vivid character than Bronislaw Malinowski. Born in Krakow, Poland, Malinowski had the misfortune to be in the wrong place at the wrong time at the start of World War I. Or perhaps it was the good fortune? Whatever the case, he avoided internment in Australia as an enemy national in exchange for a spot of self-exile in the remote Trobriand Islands.

There, Malinowski studied the islanders, their intricate trading rituals, their yam cults and their sexual habits. His investigations led to a trio of classic studies. *Argonauts of the Western Pacific* and *Coral Gardens and their Magic* were certainly sturdy titles with a more magical touch than the average dry academic discourse, but it was Malinowski's third title which really hit paydirt. Who—anthropologist or not—could resist *The Sexual Life of Savages*?

Waitress seems the wrong term for a young woman wearing nothing but a short grass skirt and a flower in her hair, the same 'outfit' she wore when performing with the village dance troupe, but why did she always ask me if I'd like a beer with such a knowing leer? Reading through the hotel's copy of Malinowski's masterpiece one day I discovered the awful truth. Just as Eskimos have myriad terms for snow and Tibetans can roll out a dozen words for yak, the Trobriand islanders had a host of names for male and female genitalia. It's my *kwila*, your (singular) *kwiga* and your (that whole bunch of you) *kwim*. For women the equivalent was, of course, *wila, wiga* and *wim*. How any man could be so unfortunate as to be named '*wila*' was clearly beyond belief. Colloquially I was Tony Cunt.

Back in Melbourne we produced a very good book: there was a lot of research in it and it was well received. I particularly enjoyed that it was appreciated by the ex-pats who had been so suspicious at first.

M: While Tony was traveling, I looked after the increasingly time-consuming business end. I had decided that 'rats and stats' (Psychology) wasn't for me and applied to the new graduate social work course at La Trobe, headed up by Herb Bisno, a charismatic and dynamic American. Although I hadn't completed my bachelor's degree, he offered me a place in the course. This was much more interesting to me: we had placements in real organizations and worked with real people. Some of my placements were fascinating. I worked with Aboriginal Child Care in Fitzroy, my first real contact with Australia's indigenous people and an inspiring experience. I also worked with young unemployed people, drug addicts, kidney dialysis patients and even did a stint in Beechworth at the hospital for the mentally ill.

I enjoyed social work—I really felt that I could make a difference—but I remained committed to making Lonely Planet work. I believed that somehow Tony and I would be able to follow individual careers—Tony as travel writer, me as social worker—and come together as publishers. I hadn't really thought through how this would work, but I still didn't really trust that we could both be supported by Lonely Planet alone.

For seven years we had been together very intensively, traveling and working, and desperately trying to raise enough money to just keep moving. I think we both needed to step back a bit from our relationship. That didn't make it easier when Tony was away. Apart from missing him, I resented the fact that he was traveling and I was at home working, even though it had been my choice to go to university.

Having worked since leaving school at sixteen to help support my family after my father died when I was twelve, I had missed that irresponsible teenage phase and I was enjoying the whole university experience. I had many friends and although they were younger than me, I enjoyed their enthusiasm and freedom, and I envied their irresponsibility. I guess I tried to retrieve my lost youth. Tony didn't like this period at all, and found more and more reasons to travel. He wasn't really happy with my having another life and refused to be involved. When I came home at night after a particularly draining day working with an abused child or strung-out junkie, Tony didn't want to hear about it. He would retire to the office, while I worked in the kitchen. It wasn't easy, but we were both so committed to Lonely Planet that we got through it.

Andy would work two or three days a week and we would typeset, edit, proofread, send out invoices, sort out books, and pack up and mail orders. Torquil would sit on a beanbag and watch *Sesame Street* and Andy would stay until he got too bored or tired.

Back then, none of our overseas distributors seemed to understand that we were on a different time zone. I would often get calls at 1 or 2 a.m. asking for information. I tried to be polite since I didn't want people to dismiss us as difficult to deal with because we were in Australia, although I do remember becoming quite curt with Michael von Haag one night. Three nights in a row he rang at 2 a.m.; each time he called me Sheila (well, I was Australian and female) and then, to add insult to injury, he querulously complained that I had taken too long to answer the phone. On that third night I snapped at him: 'It's bloody two o'clock in the morning!'

We tried to deal with orders on the day we received them, partly to impress the booksellers with our efficiency, but also to avoid them backing up. I remember one Thursday afternoon I opened the mail and realized that I had to pick, pack and invoice a total of 800 books to a catalog of different book-shops before the post office closed for the weekend. I had just got home from university and it was late afternoon, so I rolled up my sleeves and got to it. Several hours later, I realized I couldn't manage it by myself. I hated disturbing Andy at home, but I rang her and explained the situation. She was there in thirty minutes with Torquil tucked up in a blanket. By 1.30 a.m. we had finished. When people wonder at the long association between Andy and us, I always relate an anecdote like that. She was always there for us.

Despite our more solid financial situation and growing sales, Lonely Planet was still a severely understaffed business demanding huge sacrifices and impossible workloads. We never seemed to have a moment free and every working day was conducted at a breakneck pace. I'd decided to learn some German, so the Frankfurt Bookfair conversations would not be strictly in English, but getting to my weekly class was always stressful. The drive there took twenty minutes if the traffic lights co-operated, so I would rush out of the office eighteen minutes before the class started and break speed limits all the way. At this time I was always in a hurry and, hardly surprisingly, accumulated a fine collection of speeding tickets. At one point I had been caught exceeding speed limits in almost every state in Australia and in New Zealand, but remarkably never in Victoria, the state where we lived.

At other times, life slowed from warp speed towards somnolence. Saturday mornings we used to meet friends in Jimmy Watson's, a wine bar near Melbourne University, where hours passed in a blur of newspapers and talk before we retired across the road to Café Paradiso for lunches that often lasted until evening. The sun always seemed to be shining in those lazy interludes.

Our relationship wasn't always smooth. Maureen's university course seemed to be driving us in opposite directions. I was no help: I didn't seem to get on with her uni friends, partly because I was working flat out most of the time, partly because I felt I was always outside the circle and partly because I didn't make enough effort. I remember listening to lots of late-night Leonard Cohen at that time, wondering when Maureen was going to get home from some university function. Ten years later, it would have been the Smiths or Nick Cave supplying the downer music; I read recently that Joanne Rowling, before she created Harry Potter and became seriously rich, used 'Everybody Hurts' by REM in the same way. By the end of 1978, we were back on a reasonably even keel and in an expansive mood.

M: Towards the end of 1978 I thought about what I'd do when I graduated. I wasn't sure we could make a go of Lonely Planet, but I did know that if I decided to make a career in social work, Tony and I would be living parallel lives and the relationship may not survive. I decided to spend the summer working with Tony on a trip to Asia and put the decision off until after we got back. It was the first long trip we had made together for a while and when we got back we seemed to be back on track. During my last year at university we realized that we both wanted to start a family—clearly a vote of confidence in our relationship.

That year brought a clear indicator of our level of financial maturity and stability: I got a credit card I could use overseas. Credit cards are such an everyday item these days it's easy to forget that just as there was a time before cell phones or laptop computers, there was a time before credit cards. Like 1978. Oh sure, Diners Club had been around since 1950, when it started with two hundred customers who could use their cardboard cards in twenty-seven New York City restaurants. American Express cards came along a bit later in the 1950s, the first plastic credit cards appeared in 1959 and the magnetic strips made their appearance in 1970. Visa and MasterCard only expanded onto the international stage from the mid-70s and neither appeared in Australia until 1984.

Our penniless arrival in Hong Kong in 1977, when we were working on the second edition of *South-East Asia on a Shoestring*, had been a wake-up call. We were perfect candidates for using a credit card overseas and would have found one really useful. So I applied for an American Express card on our return home, and our accountant sent in figures to show how well our business was doing and how financially sound we were. American Express rejected me. These days, when credit cards are dished out like McDonald's discount vouchers, it's easy to forget how fussy they were only twenty-odd years ago.

I forgot about it until 1978. When I was about to try again, Geoff Crowther casually announced that he had an American Express card. Years later, Geoff's royalties from the books he did for Lonely Planet paid for a stunning home inspired by the Minangkabau houses of Sumatra. This house featured in architectural magazines and was a beautiful example of hand-built craftsmanship, much of it courtesy of a young Japanese carpenter who had dropped out of the Nipponese rat-race to live in Geoff's idyllic corner of sub-tropical Australia. That, however, was years in the future. In 1978, Geoff was as penniless as we were and still bedding down in a disused banana shed! Why could he get a card when I couldn't?

I applied again, our accountant sent off all the facts and figures again, they rejected me again. A month later I got a Diners Club card and swore that I would never, ever, no matter what, have an American Express card. Over a quarter of a century later I still toss all those American Express 'you have been pre-approved for a gold/platinum/titanium/uranium card' letters straight in the bin.

The last week of 1978 and the first months of 1979 saw us researching two small but relatively important books which kicked our sales along and reinforced our image as a publisher on the cutting edge. They were small (Burma) and middling (Sri Lanka) sellers, but this trip laid the foundation stones for a much bigger project which we would throw ourselves into a year later.

We left Australia in mid-December, soon after Maureen had finished her third year at university. In Bangkok we checked the travel scene then took a bus down to Pattaya Beach, the resort to the south of the capital. De-jetlagged, we returned to Bangkok a couple of days later, only to discover that due to some conference there was not a hotel room to be found, certainly not in our price bracket. Fortunately, our charming, capable and mildly eccentric Thai distributor, the enigmatic Brigadier General Jumsai, came to our rescue and whisked us away to his family compound. There, his son, with an architecture degree from Imperial College of London, had designed and built a library to house Mr Jumsai's library of original editions. We had a comfortable bed in the library, but sleep was impossible with his amazing collection of rare titles on Southeast Asian history and exploration to dip into, not to mention the collection of large and colorful lizards which popped out from behind the books.

Our Burmese visas had come through while we were at Pattaya, so a week before Christmas we flew into Rangoon, our first visit since 1974. Visitors to Burma were still restricted to a seven-day visa, but we figured that two hard-working visits would be enough to put together the first modern guidebook to the country. After all, there weren't many places we could visit. After one night in the YMCA Hostel we left Rangoon and took the train up to Mandalay, then continued north by jeep to the colonial hill station of Maymyo. There we stayed in Candacraig, the 'chummery' or bachelor's quarters of the Bombay Burmah Trading Company, already immortalized by Paul Theroux in his *Great Railway Bazaar*. The utterly surreal nature of this place, where roast beef, roast potatoes and Yorkshire pudding were still on the menu thirty years after the British had left, was reinforced when we were summoned to the front veranda to hear a passing chorus of carol singers serenading the guests. We stood outside in the chill air, and for a moment it felt as if World War II, the Japanese invasion and the subsequent departure of the British had never taken place.

Next morning, in the pre-dawn gloom, our jeep started off down the hill towards Mandalay, but the glow-worm intensity of our headlights soon faded to black when the electrics failed. It was a relief to break down safely by the roadside rather than plunging down the steep and winding track in near total darkness. By the time the driver had sorted out the shoddy wiring, dawn was coming up like thunder and we made our way to the plains quite safely and flew down to Pagan. We had no time to waste now if we were going to cover Burma's short list of attractions in our allotted days.

Pagan was as exciting on our second visit as on our first, although the disastrous earthquake of 1975 had rolled by in the interim. On our first day in Pagan we teamed up with David Bennet, an impossibly English-looking gentleman wandering the ruined temples immaculately clad in a linen suit and clutching a briefcase. On rented bikes and horse carriages we covered all the main sites, even making an excursion north to the holy peak of Mt Popa. We flew back to Rangoon on Christmas Eve where we decided to make two nights at the Strand Hotel our Christmas present to ourselves. In those days, a double at the Strand was less than US$20, so we were clearly still very budget-minded.

With David, we rented an elderly Chevrolet taxi (payment in dollars, but quietly please) to make a Christmas Day excursion to Pegu, returning to a dinner of lobsters at the Strand. Lobsters seemed to be the best possible substitute for a conventional Christmas dinner and afterwards we retired to the Strand's musty lobby with a handful of other travelers to drink bottles of the People's Brewery's Mandalay beer, cached in a semi-secret locker behind the reception desk for guests' consumption after the bar closed.

We inspected, once again, the Strand's lost-and-found showcase in the lobby. Like Cinderella fleeing the ball at midnight, colonial ladies seemed to have been in the habit of losing dainty evening slippers during the course of regimental balls. Late in the evening, as we tottered off to our decrepit rooms, the hotel's stable of muscular rats came out to play, speeding from one side of the lounge to the other, sometimes stopping to play leapfrog on the way. One of our party, not used to hotel rats of such magnificent proportions (Rangoon rats are like American toothpaste, they come only in L, XL and XXL), took to standing on his chair every time a particularly hefty specimen hurtled by.

When I stopped by in 1997, the hotel had been taken over by Adrian Zecha, guiding light of the luxurious Aman Resort group and a worthy successor to the Strand's founding Sarkie brothers. He had restored the hotel to its original glory, and then some, and rooms now started at US$425. There was no hope of a rat showing its face in the

7 October 1971—Maureen and I had known each other for precisely one year so we celebrated by getting married at Hampstead registry office in London. *(Photo: Peter Schulz)*

At the London Business School's end-of-year ball in 1972. Maureen looks more like sixteen than twenty-one, and I certainly don't look much older. A few days later we set off to drive to Asia.

Maureen on the riverbank in Isfahan in Iran with the Khaju Bridge behind her. Today she would have to be wearing a headscarf and something all-enveloping. I returned to Isfahan in 2004 and the city is as beautiful as ever. *(Photo: Tony Wheeler)*

7 October 1972—We managed to arrive at the Taj Mahal (that symbol of enduring love) on our first wedding anniversary and began a tradition of having our photograph taken on every anniversary, hopefully in some interesting new location.

Moored at Benoa Harbour in Bali, the yacht *Sun Peddler* out of Auckland, New Zealand, was our transport to Australia. Maureen is perched on the rail talking to another of the volunteer crew members. *(Photo: Tony Wheeler)*

Our arrival in Australia on the beach at Exmouth, Western Australia, in early December 1972. When this photograph was taken we had been in Australia for 30 seconds and Gough Whitlam had been Prime Minister for about one week.

7 October 1973—Another anniversary shot, this time with the nearly completed Sydney Opera House as the backdrop. We were just about to publish the first Lonely Planet guidebook when this photo was taken.

Across Asia on the Cheap, the very first Lonely Planet guidebook, was published in October 1973 and this was the photo that accompanied a story in the Sydney *Sun-Herald* about how we came to write it. *(Photo: Fairfaxphotos)*

Our home in Sydney and the first Lonely Planet 'office' was the basement of 19 Oatley Road in Paddington, just off busy Oxford Street. We paid $350 for the red Austin-Healey Sprite parked in front of it. *(Photo: Tony Wheeler)*

In early 1974 we rode our Yamaha motorcycle up to Darwin and airfreighted it across to Portuguese Timor, today East Timor. Maureen is sitting in front of the 'Hippy Hilton', on the beach at Dili where all the passing backpackers stayed. *(Photo: Tony Wheeler)*

As we traveled through Southeast Asia we met all sorts of interesting people. On a back road in Java, Indonesia, we stopped to talk to this Belgian cyclist who had pedaled all the way from Europe.
(Photo: Maureen Wheeler)

We spent the first few months of 1975 in the Palace Hotel on Jalan Besar in Singapore, putting together our second book, *South-East Asia on a Shoestring.* Maureen is working on the maps for this book on the small table where the whole book was produced.
(Photo: Tony Wheeler)

In early 1976 we were back in Nepal working on the next two Lonely Planet guidebooks. We're on the trail from Namche Bazar to the Buddhist monastery at Tyangboche and the summit of Mt Everest is peeking over the ridge directly above Maureen's head. *(Photo: Michael Dhillon)*

Ladakh, the region of India to the north of the Himalayas where the people are Tibetan, was the final stop while we were researching the first edition of our India guidebook in 1980. *(Photo: Tony Wheeler)*

In 1978 Lonely Planet was still a very small business and we were doing a large part of the work on the books ourselves. Maureen's stroll down the beach in Tangalla became the cover photograph for our first Sri Lanka guidebook.

Sri Lanka book cover.

The whole Lonely Planet team in early 1981 outside our office in the Melbourne inner-city suburb of Richmond. From left to right there's Peter Campbell with his son Reuben on his knee, our business partner Jim Hart, Maureen with Tashi, Andy Nielson (who is still with us today), author Geoff Crowther, our typesetter Isabel Afcouliotis, and me in front.

Our India guide was a popular and critical success and was a real turning point for Lonely Planet. It won the 1981 Thomas Cook Guidebook of the Year award, which was presented by Lord Hunt, leader of the 1953 expedition which put Tensing Norgay and Edmund Hillary on the summit of Everest.

We were fairly pioneering in our adoption of computer technology in the early 1980s, although our first Century T10 computer looks pretty Stone Age today.

Checking the mail with Andy in our Rowena Parade office in the early 1980s. Andy was the very first Lonely Planet employee and since she's still with us today that makes her the longest survivor.

In late 1983 we made another trip to Nepal, the country we have probably returned to more times than any other. Maureen and I were walking in the hills outside the Kathmandu Valley with Tashi (a few days before her third birthday) and Kieran (about 8 months old). *(Photo: Tony Wheeler)*

7 October 1984—This time it's our thirteenth wedding anniversary and we're living in Berkeley, across the bay from San Francisco, while we set up Lonely Planet's first overseas office. The whole Wheeler family is backdropped by the San Francisco Bay, Alcatraz and San Francisco itself.

In early 1985 we had to make a hurried exit from the United States because our visas were expiring, so we traveled around South America with our two young children. Here, Tashi and Kieran are being transported from the railway station to our hotel in Puno (on Lake Titicaca in Peru) on a delivery bicycle. Puno is at 12600 feet altitude and when we got off the train from Cuzco the air was so thin we simply didn't have the energy to carry the kids and our bags.

(Photo: Tony Wheeler)

A rainy day at the great Buddhist temple at Borobodur in Java, Indonesia, in 1988. We were on another updating trip for *South-East Asia on a Shoestring*.

Outside the Hindu temple at Pashupatinath in the Kathmandu Valley in 1989, Kieran gets some lessons on yoga from an Indian sadhu. *(Photo: Tony Wheeler)*

A little fishing expedition off the island of Lamu in Kenya caught plenty of fish to grill on the beach. This photo ended up as the cover shot for the second edition of Maureen's book *Travel with Children*. *(Photo: Tony Wheeler)*

In 1995 Kieran and I walked the circuit of Mt Blanc, the highest mountain in continental Europe. The week-long walk took us through Switzerland, France, Italy and then back into Switzerland.

(Photo: Elizabeth Honey)

comfortable new bar where the products of the People's Brewery had been joined by a host of international beers. Curiously, Mandalay beer was now a dollar more expensive than Foster's, Tiger, Budweiser, Labatt's, Asahi, and others. The only catch was the hotel was all but deserted. The musical trio in the bar had nobody to entertain and photographer Richard I'Anson and I dined alone.

Back in 1978, after our Strand stay, we flew to Kathmandu for a brief visit between Christmas and New Year. The morning after our arrival provided one of those classic traveler's chance encounters which happen only a handful of times each lifetime. We left our Thamel hotel and walked across to KC's for breakfast. As usual, this popular Kathmandu restaurant was packed out and we had to share a table with a visitor who was already tucking into his meal. He looked up and enquired, 'Tony, Maureen?'

It was Harvey, the Bleecker Street anthropologist with whom we had shared a KC's table three years ago! It was as if time had been frozen since our last visit, but this was also Harvey's first KC's breakfast for several years. In the interim, he'd finished his investigations in a remote Nepalese hill village, returned to the United States and completed his PhD thesis. An academic convention in India had brought him back to the subcontinent and while there he'd decided to return to Kathmandu to revisit old haunts.

New Year's Eve we were back down on the plains, pausing briefly in Delhi and meeting up with Ashok Khanna, a friend from the London Business School who we had visited in India on our first overland trip. In London, Maureen and I had often borrowed Ashok's Volkswagen Beetle when we needed more seats than our little sports car could provide. Ashok had brought it back to India and it felt strange riding around Delhi in that familiar vehicle.

Our trip to India was not to work on a guidebook, but to think about one. It was to be some of the most important preliminary research we had ever done. When our India guide emerged two and a half years later, it immediately kicked Lonely Planet into a higher and more stable orbit. India's future importance to us wasn't really on our mind as we lazed on the beach for a few days in Goa, still essentially a hippy hang-out and years away from blasting into orbit as a major international tourist destination.

Madras was the start of a temple-hopping trip through the Dravidian temple towns of Tamil Nadu. We stopped at places with delightfully multi-syllabic names like Mahabalipuram, Kanchipuram and Tiruchirapalli. Eventually we ended up at Madurai, from where we would head south to Sri Lanka, our other guidebook destination on this trip.

The mere fact that getting down to Sri Lanka proved to be so difficult was an indicator that this was the perfect time to do a guidebook. The flights from Madras and Madurai directly to Colombo, the capital of Sri Lanka, were booked out weeks ahead. Even the train to Rameswaram, from where a daily ferry crossed the narrow straits to Sri Lanka, was hopelessly crowded. Not only was it impossible to get a sleeper, even reserved seats were out of the question. In true Indian fashion, we engaged one of the station porters to sneak on to the train before it was brought up to the platform. After the mad scramble to get aboard had subsided, we strolled through the train until we came to our porter, sprawled resolutely across a couple of spaces, tipped him handsomely and settled in for the night. It was a hard-slog trip, one of those nightmare journeys which seem endemic to lower-class travel in India.

Things didn't improve when we arrived in Rameswaram, soon after dawn. We walked to the port and queued for tickets and to get through the bureaucratic Indian departure formalities. The *Ramunajam*, a surprisingly well-kept ship even though it was nearly fifty years old, sailed in the late afternoon and we settled down for the crossing of the strait. A few years later, when the north of Sri Lanka tumbled into violent turmoil, this popular ferry service was suspended and hasn't operated since.

We docked at Talaimannar in Sri Lanka soon after dark and a mad rush started from the ship to the dockside railway station platform. We weren't looking forward to another long overnight grind by train—we were still exhausted from the previous night. This train was clearly going to be crowded and we'd been forewarned about theft. We, however, were in luck. On the ferry we'd had a long conversation with a friendly Sinhalese Tamil, on his way home to Jaffna, the Tamil capital in the north of the island.

'Don't join the rush to change money and buy tickets,' he'd advised. 'There are only a few sleeper compartments and everybody wants one. You can book a sleeper before you get your ticket, so go directly to the station master's office and grab one of those compartments.'

It was great advice. While most people were changing money and clamoring for tickets we had our reservations in hand and could buy tickets at our leisure.

That night we locked the door of our compartment and fell blissfully asleep. Next morning we slid the window shutters up and gazed across a pristine scene of green rice paddies backed by waving palm trees. We fell instantly in love with Sri Lanka and that initial high persisted for the next month.

Only one thing would spoil that pleasantly exotic glow—the buses. Almost every bus trip in Sri Lanka was horrific. At that time there were no private buses in the country. Every bus service, from a short village hop to a traipse from one end of the island to the other, was operated by the one monolithic state-owned bus company, the Ceylon Transport Board (CTB). The CTB was a nightmare: their bus depots housed rows of broken-down vehicles waiting for repair while those on the road were few and far between. Waiting was frustrating and the travel was often even worse so my initial bad mood regularly escalated until we finally arrived at our destination.

Asian bus trips almost always feature somebody whose stomach cannot handle the conditions, and who spends much of the trip leaning out the window to throw up. But in Sri Lanka, merely getting to the window of a CTB bus was often a near impossibility. On more than one occasion, wedged tightly in the crowd, we'd watch with horror as somebody tried desperately not to throw up, while everybody around them tried equally desperately, but with equally little success, to edge away.

On our second return to the capital, Colombo, we rented a car for our third and final island circuit. Lonely Planet was still such a penny-pinching operation that this was the first time we'd contemplated such an extravagance. Nowadays we (and most of our writers) rent cars without a moment's hesitation and, to save time or get otherwise unobtainable views, I've even chartered aircraft and helicopters. But in 1979 I'd never rented a car in Asia, not that there were many places you could rent one. Sri Lanka did have cars to rent, but only with drivers attached, so we set off from Colombo comfortably ensconced in a Peugeot 404 complete with chauffeur at the wheel. He soon caught on that this was not the normal tourist trip and even got quite good at dropping us at one end of a small town and picking us up at the other, after we'd worked our way from hotel to restaurant to hotel along the length of the settlement.

On this final loop we hit the beautiful beaches of the south coast. I took a photograph of Maureen strolling topless along the beach at Tangalla, which eventually became the cover shot of our first Sri Lanka guide and, for a while at least, resulted in the sandy strip being renamed Bikini Beach. Today a zealous editor would undoubtedly be quizzing a cartographer if that should be 'Half a Bikini Beach'. Our Sinhalese idyll ended with a few lazy days at Hikkaduwa, at that time the perfect traveler's beach, developed enough to make choosing a restaurant a tantalizing problem, but still sufficiently undeveloped and remote to make staying there a real pleasure. Hikkaduwa also seemed to have attracted a quite unfairly high percentage of the most beautiful women on the road in Asia, all of them wearing very little at all. Trying to write up my notes as I lazed on the beach was not easy.

Weighed down with countless files of notes, collections of maps and a small library of books on Sri Lanka and Burma, Maureen flew back to Australia for the start of term. I spent a few more days finishing our Sri Lankan research then returned to Madras and Calcutta to think about India some more and to continue updating our West Asia guide. From Calcutta, I flew back to Burma for another seven-day circuit. This time I covered Rangoon, Inle Lake and the scattering of temple towns around Mandalay.

Burma's dreadful state-owned airline had an appalling reputation, one that has scarcely improved since. Sure they didn't have as many disastrous crashes as Aeroflot or Indian Airlines during that same period, but they had far fewer aircraft to start with. Touch retrospective wood, we never had any Burma Airways disasters, although sudden jolts or unexpected turbulence while flying with them always left me clutching my seat more tightly than on any other airline. My best Burma Airways experience, however, was a much more serendipitous one. Their flight schedules were known to be unreliable, so a group of us turned up at Heho airport, near Inle Lake, in the hope there might be a flight to Mandalay that day even though there wasn't one scheduled. The staff at the airport confirmed there wasn't a flight, but said that in about an hour's time there would be a plane passing overhead en route to Mandalay. When it came within radio range, they volunteered to tell the pilot there were half-a-dozen potential passengers clutching cash to see if he'd drop down and pick us up! He did.

In Mandalay I teamed up with two couples. Judith and Richard Herzig were from America, no real surprise there, but the other couple was from Mexico. Burma was an unlikely place to meet Mexicans and until 2001, when I bumped into a Mexican couple in Fiji, they remained the only travelers I'd ever met from that country outside of North America. Meeting unusual travelers in unusual places is always a pleasure and a few days after my Burma encounter I was in a Bangkok backpackers' hang-out where I met a young guy from an even more unlikely country: Libya. He'd been in Australia studying dry-climate agriculture and was taking the opportunity to explore Southeast Asia on his way home.

This long Asian loop wasn't yet over. I then city-hopped my way down through Thailand and Malaysia to Singapore and across Java to Bali, completing an update of that part of our Southeast Asia guide. While I was away, Papua New Guinea had been printed and Andy met me at Melbourne airport waving the first copies.

When I finally arrived home we had done the research for two new guidebooks and also much of the update research for our West Asia and Southeast Asia guides. It's another indicator of how far we've come that I could even contemplate taking on so much research on one trip. Today we insist that our writers get back from every trip as promptly as possible and get their research recorded with equal speed, aware that information can date by the day.

In 1979, however, we were pretty certain that nobody else was likely to come up with a guide to Burma or Sri Lanka, so even if the research was a little older than we would have wished, it was still going to be the best available. Our new-found financial stability meant bills and rent were paid on time, but producing the books still came down to the two of us. Peter Campbell lent a hand illustrating both these new books, producing an evocative series of thumbnail identification pictures of the great Burmese temples of Pagan, and he also provided some of the Burma photographs. Linda Fairbairn drew three quirky illustrated-style maps of Rangoon, Pagan and Mandalay, and Andrena Millen did the design and paste-up. Anything else was our responsibility. We wrote and edited the books, I drew most of the maps, I'd taken most of the photographs and we even did the typesetting ourselves.

Doing what we wanted was still much more important than doing what made the most sense financially. Burma was published two months before Sri Lanka, even though we knew Sri Lanka, emerging as the traveler's flavor of the month, was clearly the more important book for our bottom line. Burma was more exotic, more exciting, more out on a limb. Burma sold adequately and reinforced our cutting-edge image, but Sri Lanka took off. Once again, and probably far more from good luck than good judgment, we'd done the right book at the right time, although Sri Lanka's popularity was short-lived. The second edition did even better than the first, but the increasing instability in the country led to the terrible massacres of 1983, when large swathes of the island became no-go areas and tourism nose-dived.

In mid-1979 we abandoned the back-room office at 22 Durham Street and took over the 41 Rowena Parade shopfront office from Primary Education. Lonely Planet finally had its own real home. It was still a miniature business: just Andy, Maureen and me. Andrena Millen, who had been designing our books for the past year or two, rented one of the rooms to use as her studio and worked for us on a freelance basis. By this time we were producing more typesetting than we could handle ourselves, so the next employee would be a typesetter.

Lonely Planet was a real business now. If I was traveling, Maureen and Andy made sure that orders were filled, statements were sent out and checks were banked. When we both traveled, during Maureen's university vacations, Andy kept the ship afloat by herself, but it was down to us to produce the books. When we were both away, no books got produced. If the business was going to grow further and faster we needed somebody to stay home and mind the shop, somebody who could push books through while we were away.

On trips down to Adelaide, selling books or visiting Maureen's cousin who had moved there from Ireland, we often met up with Jim and Alison Hart. In the heady days of the Australian Independent Publishers Association a few years earlier, Jim had been one of the small Melbourne publishers, packaging books for larger publishers and producing his own version of STA's *Student Guide to Asia* under his own imprint, Acme Books. When Maureen and I had gone to Nepal in early 1976 he'd looked after Lonely Planet, when the whole business had fitted into the trunk of that awful Ford Cortina. Jim had wound up his own publishing efforts and moved to Adelaide to take up a position as senior editor at Rigby Books, at that time the largest independent book publisher in Australia.

Corporate life didn't suit Jim and we suggested he move back to Melbourne and join us. Jim and Alison had two young children and we knew Alison was not at all keen about moving back for Jim to dive into our little start-up. What none of us realized was that Rigby's was about to implode and Jim would be the first of a number of their employees to leave the sinking ship and join us.

At some point in 1979 it was agreed that Jim would come back to Melbourne at the end of the year and would buy twenty-five per cent of Lonely Planet Publications, for a somewhat indeterminate figure to be paid at a somewhat indeterminate time in the future. The major problem was how Lonely Planet would pay for Jim. Our sales for the year before Jim joined us were just $120 000. That was paying our bills, meeting the royalty payments to authors, covering salaries and supporting us quite nicely, and in the second half of 1979 our sales were running a hundred per cent higher, but paying for Jim as well was not going to be easy. We were confident that with him aboard we would be able to take on more and larger projects and we'd soon 'grow' the company enough to pay all of us. We didn't realize that we were heading towards some very heavy weather.

Jim joined us around Christmas, but as a parting gift from Rigby's he'd brought with him one last project which he was going to finish for them on a freelance basis. This seemed like a perfect arrangement: he'd ease himself into working with us while Rigby helped to foot the bill. In fact, the project turned out to be much larger, more complex and more time-consuming than anticipated and for weeks Jim remained almost a full-time Rigby employee, even though he was now working from the Lonely Planet office in Richmond.

We had a variety of new books under way including guides to the Philippines, Israel, and Kashmir and Ladakh, all being translated from German guidebooks. Several of our books had been translated into German and we decided it was an experiment worth trying in the opposite direction. Plus, there were new books by our own writers on Japan and Pakistan. But the major project was India. After that last big trip to produce *South-East Asia on a Shoestring*, Maureen and I simply could not get away from the office for the long period of time which a major book like India would take. Nor could we afford the expenses which such a long period of travel would have required. As a result, we'd had to concentrate on books which could be knocked off with only a month or two of travel, although today, as the books have become more thorough and complex, even those small books take longer to research.

In 1979, we decided we could afford to tackle India by dividing the country between three writers. For a paltry thousand dollars of expense money each, Prakash Raj, our Kathmandu-based Nepal author, agreed to research north India while Geoff Crowther took on the south of the country plus Darjeeling and Sikkim in the extreme north-east. Maureen and I would cover the middle plus the extreme north-west regions of Himachal Pradesh, Kashmir and Ladakh. Geoff and Prakash started their travels in late 1979, but Maureen had to finish university before we could head off. We had also decided to start a family, and figured that if all went well, and Maureen had passed the first trimester before we arrived in India, we could handle the situation. Maureen became pregnant almost immediately, but our plans fell apart when she miscarried.

For several years we had dreamed about an India book. It was clearly our sort of destination and nobody had done a really good new guidebook to India for years. There was a Fodor's guide, but our sort of travelers, who were the people going to India, were not Fodor's readers. There was also a Frommer's India-on-some-number-of-dollars-a-day title, but once again this wasn't the sort of book to appeal to the travelers who were on the road in India.

That left the truly wonderful *Murray's Handbook for Travellers in India*. This magnificent tome was not exactly up to date since it was written in the mid-nineteenth century! *Murray's Handbook* was a true Raj-era creation; the first edition came out in three separate volumes, published between 1859 and 1882. A fourth volume was added in 1883, but in 1892, for the first time, the handbook was squeezed into one volume. By 1978 the handbook had progressed to its 22nd edition and although it had lost most of its wonderfully detailed and colorful fold-out maps it was still resolutely Victorian in its organization and material. The information was arranged in an often completely useless route system: take Route 29a Bangalore to Mysore City, the book advised, which was ideal if you were traveling between those two cities by the prescribed route, but utterly useless if you weren't. Furthermore, the information was often as engagingly out of date as the organization. According to Murray's, India's towns were dotted with stern statues of Queen Victoria, when most of them had, in fact, been replaced by sandal-shod Gandhi figures.

A couple of days before our intended departure another do-it-yourself test revealed that Maureen was pregnant again. Obviously fertility was not a problem for us, but was going to India when she was only a few weeks pregnant, and after one miscarriage, a good idea? We were committed to doing a book on India, and if Lonely Planet was going to grow—in fact, if Lonely Planet was going to survive—it was a book we vitally needed. Geoff and Prakash were already working on their sections of the book and it was too late to recruit a replacement writer, even if we could have afforded one. So, pregnant or not, hot season or not, we set out in early 1980.

We started in Bombay, then looped south to Pune, home of the colorful orange-clad devotees of Bhagwan Shree Rajneesh. His ashram was like a college campus and was Pune's major tourist attraction, although much of the appeal seemed to be for Indian tourists come to gawk at the Bhagwan's Western devotees. From Pune we zig-zagged north through the states of Maharashtra and Madhya Pradesh all the way to Delhi; we even stopped in Bhopal, four years before the town became famous as the site of the world's worst industrial accident when poisonous gas leaked from the Union Carbide chemical plant.

In Delhi we reversed direction and meandered back south to Bombay again, this time making our way through Rajasthan and Gujarat. The exotic state of Rajasthan quickly became one of our Indian favorites. Nowhere is India more romantic, more colorful, more dramatic. For us, one of the highlights was the desert city of Jaisalmer which, at that time, felt virtually untouched. Everybody made their way to Jaipur, most continued to Ajmer and Pushkar, some got as far as Jodhpur, but in 1980 few people made it as far as Jaisalmer.

From Bombay we flew across the country to Orissa to cover the coastal temple towns and then stopped in Khajuraho on our way back to Delhi again. This was really in Prakash's territory, we simply wanted to see it. By now it was uncomfortably, horribly hot and luxuries like air-con were still beyond Lonely Planet's means.

M: I had set off on this trip to India with trepidation; I was worried that I might miscarry again, but this time in some miserable Indian hotel in a town in the middle of nowhere. I did think of staying at home, but the idea of missing out on this adventure and spending five months alone did not appeal. So I read up on what I could expect, carried all the vitamins and iron pills I thought I might need, and set off. At first it was fine, but gradually I noticed that I was always hungry. We were eating local, mainly vegetarian food, which was quite healthy and sustaining, but over time becomes very boring. Although Indian food is associated with spices and chilies, we seemed to encounter bland rice and dhal with curried vegetables far too often. I enjoyed the delicious yoghurt and lassis, but I never seemed to get enough. After a few months of the same basic meals, Tony would push his plate away in disgust and I would descend on it and polish it off. I wasn't getting much bigger, but I was definitely eating for two.

Traveling in the hot season is difficult at the best of times, but I was finding the heat and the travel particularly tiring. All-night stints on trains were exhausting and after a while I realized I needed to rest every few days. Khajuraho was probably the hottest place we stayed. During the day the town baked in the heat and there was no relief at night—at midnight the temperature was still over 40°C. We had the ceiling fan going and the door open, but there was not a breeze. The only way we could get through the night was to jump up every half-hour or so and stand under the cold shower with our sheets wrapped around us. Within half an hour we were completely dry again, but during that time we could cool down.

Khajuraho was also the first time someone noticed I was pregnant. We were having dinner at an outside restaurant when

an Indian gentleman joined us. He told us he was a Brahmin and could only eat in restaurants where another Brahmin prepared the food.

During the conversation he turned to me and said: 'You are pregnant and it will be a girl.'

He was right on both counts.

Khajuraho may have been the hottest place we stayed, but it really wasn't cool anywhere. I used the 'soak your clothes' trick in Delhi. I washed my dress, put it on, walked outside into Connaught Place, dripping all the way, and ten minutes later the dress was totally dry and I felt just a little more comfortable, at least while it was drying.

In Delhi I decided I should have a pre-natal check up. I found a female doctor and made an appointment. When I arrived I was shown into a large room with three very pregnant women. The doctor told us all to get undressed, put on gowns and lie on the beds, then proceeded to examine us, one after the other, giving her comments. We got dressed and she gave us each a few minutes to ask questions, one at a time, then she gave us the bill and that was that.

It was reassuring to know that nothing seemed obviously wrong. Apart from constantly needing food, getting tired and needing to use toilets frequently (a bad thing to need in India), I was absolutely fine, and when the baby began to kick at the proper stage, very relieved.

Fortunately, our last spell was in the hill stations of the north-west, where the officials of the Raj used to retreat to escape the heat of the plains. Once again we headed out of Delhi by bus and train up to Chandigarh (where we were not impressed by Le Corbusier's architectural vision) and on to Kullu and Manali in the Kullu Valley, then on to Dalhousie and finally Dharamsala, home of the Tibetan government in exile. In McLeod Ganj we saw the Dalai Lama passing by in his elderly Mercedes.

From Jammu we bussed up to Srinagar where our Indian friend Ashok Khanna flew up to meet us. Unhappily, by the end of the decade Kashmir would be racked by violence, and tourism there would virtually grind to a halt, but in 1980 the houseboats were in full swing. Raj-era colonists making the hot season retreat to Kashmir had dreamed up houseboats as a way to circumvent restrictions on property ownership in the hill station. They were an exotic and surprisingly comfortable place to stay and a big part of the attraction of Kashmir. Staying outside Pahalgam, at that time a popular trekking base, we met trek leader Garry Weare who would later write *Trekking in the Indian Himalaya* for us.

There was one final piece in our Indian jigsaw puzzle: the legendary Tibetan region of Ladakh. Ladakh is across the Himalaya, on the Tibetan plateau. Culturally, religiously and linguistically the people of Ladakh are closer to the people of Tibet than to the Indian population of the plains. Today, with Chinese rule forcing so many changes upon the people of Tibet, the Ladakh region is probably more like traditional Tibet than Tibet itself. The only trouble for us was getting there.

From Srinagar it was a two-day bus trip up to Leh, the capital of Ladakh, with an overnight stop in Kargil. The buses climbed over the Zoji La Pass, but in late May the pass was still snowed in and it sometimes wasn't open until mid-June. The alternative was to fly, but at this time of year the flights were not only heavily booked but also notoriously unreliable, with frequent cancellations due to cloudy weather. We got used to traipsing out to the airport only for the flight to be cancelled.

Ashok decided enough was enough and flew back to Delhi. We had enough information to write something about 'little Tibet' for our book and decided we'd cover the place properly for the next edition. We were way down the wait list for flights anyway, taking our chances with all the other people desperate to get to Ladakh. Except it wasn't even called a 'wait list'; with Indian Airlines you joined a 'chance list'. Our chances were distinctly slim: we had numbers 282 and 283 for a Boeing 737 which probably wouldn't carry more than 100 people.

One day dawned crystal clear so the possibility of the flight getting through seemed good. Perhaps there would even be a big enough window of opportunity for two flights to cross the range to Leh? In the terminal there was chaos, with crowds milling around the check-in desk and rumors flying back and forth: the plane was going to go, no it wasn't, the weather was clear here, it wasn't in Leh, or perhaps it was, who knows? Finally the flight arrived from New Delhi and it was announced that it would continue to Leh today. They began to issue boarding passes to the confirmed passengers and the numbers began to thin. Finally all the confirmed passengers were checked in and they began to handle the chance list. What hope was there for us? A mob still swayed around the desk and, after all, we were 282 and

283. There didn't seem to be any pattern to the process and it was clear they were only going to take a handful more passengers. We all frantically waved our tickets above our heads. The guy behind the counter looked out over the mob and, like some school sports captain picking his team, decided he'd take that fellow over there, the woman in the sari to one side, and ourselves.

Maureen and I had no idea why we were the lucky ones, but slinging our bags onto the scales we didn't wait to find out. Half an hour later we were winging our way across a limitless expanse of mountains, then sailing down over the dry high-altitude desert of Ladakh and landing at Leh airport. A jeep took us into town and we quickly found a delightful little guesthouse with a green patch of garden outside.

The next day we bumped into the two Canadians we had talked to in the tourist office in Srinagar a few days earlier. They'd made it across the still-frozen Zoji La, but had spent most of the day floundering through the snow to get from the roadblock on one side to the buses waiting on the other. Both of them had been painfully burnt by the high-altitude sun and one, without proper eye protection, had been suffering from snow blindness. A few days later, however, the first buses started to come through and the summer season was clearly under way.

That visit to Leh gave our daughter her name. Although we had never been to Tibet we'd always enjoyed our contact with the Tibetan people; there are lots of them in Nepal. Many of the Ladakhis, both male and female, had that most Tibetan of names, Tashi. It translates roughly as 'a blessing'. One day, after talking with just about the one hundredth Ladakhi Tashi we'd met, Maureen suggested it might be a nice name for our daughter. Despite the Khajuraho Brahmin's prognostication I wasn't convinced we would have a daughter, but I did like the name.

We backtracked to Srinagar, took the bus to Jammu and the train to Delhi, met up with Ashok once more and then flew to Calcutta to end our India research. The monsoon arrived at the same time, but after weeks of heat and dust, torrential rain was a sheer pleasure. On earlier visits to Calcutta we'd stayed on Sudder Street, but never in the legendary Fairlawns, run by an English couple (well, Edmund Smith is English; his wife Violet is Armenian). At Fairlawns one felt the Raj had never ended, the Empire still stretched from sunrise to sunset, and Victoria was still on the throne. Staying there is like playing a part in a theatrical performance and while standards, service and food can be decidedly eccentric it's a small price to pay for the opportunity to join the cast. (But how much longer can the run last?)

From Calcutta we flew to Bangkok then straight back to Australia into yet another full-on search from Australian customs. Maureen's bulging stomach was easy to prove to be real and our equally bulging bags were stuffed full of nothing more suspicious than mountains of files, notebooks, maps, brochures, timetables and business cards, but still they insisted on sifting through every last envelope and package. Midway through this farce, the exit doors from the customs hall slid open. I spotted Jim standing outside and mimicked a striptease act for him. It was another forty-five minutes before we had indeed concluded with a striptease and then shambled out of the airport, our bags spilling their contents onto the baggage trolleys and Maureen seething loudly.

M: By the time we got back to Melbourne I was obviously pregnant, although still not very large. I told my doctor I was five months pregnant. He didn't think I was that advanced until the next appointment, a month later. He was very alarmed at my weight gain. I had put on pounds, which didn't surprise me, or anyone else who knew me, since I hadn't stopped eating since I'd arrived home. I said I was simply catching up, but he insisted on seeing me weekly. He was very relieved when successive months showed a more normal weight gain.

A couple of months after our return my parents arrived in Australia. We'd agreed to take a trip up to the Great Barrier Reef with them and along the way I'd do some updating for the long-delayed third edition of our Australia guide. Perhaps doing a new edition at this time wasn't a good idea. The Aussie tourist boom was still a few years away and putting our current weak production to one side and concentrating on getting the India book out may have been a more sensible idea. On top of the sheer volume of Lonely Planet work, we should have been concentrating on our forthcoming offspring's arrival. But we had another problem: Jim.

Jim had been with us for nearly a year and we had imagined that with him sharing the driving we'd be covering a lot more publishing miles. It hadn't worked out that way. There'd been that long hiatus after he'd joined us when he was finishing up the project from his former employer. And then there simply had not been the burst of activity we'd expected. It seemed to take a lot of thinking and deliberation before things happened with Jim, when what we wanted was action and lots of it.

While we'd been in India only one project had gone through and we were less than happy with how that looked. Joe Cummings, an American Peace Corps volunteer in Thailand, had approached us with the idea of a Thailand guide. That country's tourist boom was still a few years away, but Joe spoke Thai, he'd used our Southeast Asia guide and knew the region, so the idea seemed perfect. Unfortunately, it was Joe's first attempt at writing and in some places, it turned out, his experience was more limited than our own. That wouldn't have been a problem if I'd been there to supplement the material, but I was in India and Jim didn't know Thailand at all. As a result, readers were soon complaining. With future editions, Joe made dramatic improvements to the book which became an incredibly comprehensive publication, but the first edition was a sorry affair.

One rather thin and disappointing book seemed a poor return for the time we'd had a partner, but only days after we got back from our Australia trip a reason for his inactivity became clear. Jim came in to work one day complaining of double vision; he went to an optician, who sent him to a doctor, who sent him to a specialist. There were brain scans and then Jim was in hospital with a cerebral aneurysm, a swollen vein in the brain which could easily rupture and lead to a stroke or worse. Jim was wheeled in for major brain surgery as Maureen was about to give birth.

Maureen wanted to have the baby at home. I read the books, met other homebirth people and my initial suspicions were finally overcome. There were, however, only two doctors in Melbourne who were willing to do homebirths. We signed up with Dr John Stevenson, who turned out to be a perfect delight and a cool head when things went very wrong.

With Jim sidelined I found myself with a double workload just when I least needed it. We knew money and time were going to be tight for a time after Jim joined us. We took on lots of extra projects in order to expand the company to the stage where it could support more of us. Now we had the extra work, but not the extra hands to handle it. In the days leading up to our first child's birth I was working until all hours, writing the India guide, trying to push through the new Philippines and Israel translations, and doing a major rewrite on our Pakistan guide when I should have been spending more time with Maureen. Well, actually I *was* spending time with Maureen since she was roped in to proofread and fact-check when she should have been home taking it easy.

Like any first-time parents we were nervous as hell as the birth approached. Maureen's labor pains started soon after midnight on November 6, but at first they were a long way apart. They lasted all morning and into the afternoon, but by late afternoon it was clear our baby was on the way. Sally Keogh, Maureen's friend from her days at Trailfinders, and Bernadette Prunty, our midwife, turned up at nightfall and while Maureen had a bath I fixed spaghetti carbonara for all of us.

In the evening, Dr Stevenson turned up and, many hours later, all hell broke loose. Suddenly there was a baby—a girl as predicted— and Maureen started to hemorrhage. The doctor worked frantically, but Maureen was so weak she was barely conscious. Everybody looked worried and I was terrified. For what seemed like an eternity, I thought I might gain a daughter and lose a wife.

Eventually, in the early hours of the morning, I cut the cord and I held our baby daughter, who signaled her arrival by depositing a small shit on me. Eventually everybody left and we finally settled down—a very worn-out Maureen, a very relieved Tony, and a tiny Tashi with a very curious nose.

Like any expectant parents we'd mused on what we might produce. 'I don't care what she looks like,' Maureen had said on more than one occasion, 'as long as she doesn't have your nose.' It was a reasonable wish. Nobody's ever said I have a good-looking nose, but if there was one thing people would say about our new offspring it was that she looked like her father: she had my nose.

Welcome to parenthood. Maureen was as weak as a kitten, I was faced with so many bloody sheets to wash (that's real blood we're talking about) that on the morning of 7 November I bought a new washing machine, Tashi was already showing what a noisy and wakeful baby she would be, Jim was in hospital and once again Lonely Planet looked like it was going broke.

M: The morning after Tashi was born, I was very weak. Our recently purchased house (which we had been renting for several years) had an outside toilet, right at the bottom of the yard, and I wasn't supposed to stand up unassisted, nor move very far. I had a third-degree tear which required fifteen stitches, I'd lost a lot of blood and I didn't feel terrific. Tony had to get some supplies, so he asked Andy to sit with me while he was gone. Andy cuddled Tashi, made me tea and helped me to the toilet.

I remember our whole conversation was about Jim and how we were going to manage with only Tony and Andy. I was so worried that we were going to lose the little financial security we had just achieved. Andy put it into perspective: 'You're still here, and the baby is healthy and beautiful. Shouldn't you concentrate on that for now?'

5

More Headaches

In early 1981 Lonely Planet was still teetering on the brink of disaster, and our new daughter never slept. She was up all hours of the day and night and quickly developed an uncanny ability to know exactly when we needed a break, so she could interrupt it. We would spend hours getting her to sleep, creep quietly into the kitchen and then, the instant we put fork to food, she'd be awake again. Nor was Maureen in good shape after the difficult birth—she'd lost a lot of blood. We went out to lunch when Tashi was a week old, but before we crossed the road to the restaurant, I could see she was ready to drop.

I was trying to be everywhere at once and as a result running myself ragged. Early in the year my doctor announced I had developed high blood pressure, not the news I needed to hear at that moment and particularly with my family history (my father had a heart attack when he was only a few years older than I was then and subsequently had to retire early). On top of all this, we were worried about Jim. How could the company afford to pay him when he wasn't working? Only two years ago we finally felt the business was up and running, and now it was going straight down the drain.

We were temporarily bailed out by Jim's parents who advanced us $15 000 so that we could keep paying Jim until things could be sorted out. But would they sort out? I went to see Jim in hospital the night before his operation and he looked like death was staring him in the face. When I visited him immediately after his operation, his head had been shaved so they could cut his skull open and he really did look terrible. I visited him several times, bringing in new books as they emerged, but Jim was desperately weak and clearly had trouble concentrating or even understanding what was happening. He'd always been very thin, but a week after the operation he looked like a Holocaust victim and regularly reached for the oxygen mask beside the bed.

Soon after the operation he was moved to a rehabilitation hospital, but there was no indication when he would be fully recovered, if ever. Apart from India I was struggling with four other books. José Roleo Santiago, a Filipino citizen-of-the-world who had spent far too long in Pakistan, had written a book about the country for us. His English was less than perfect so I was rewriting his terrible prose. I was also adding material from our India trip to the translation of Kashmir, Ladakh and Zanskar and struggling with Israel and the Occupied Territories, an awful book which we had not realized was so bad until we were too far along in the translation to back out.

The hospital announced they were going to start sending Jim to daily classes, basket weaving or something to get him using his hands again, and take steps towards getting him back to work. Why not send him back to the office, his wife Alison suggested? He might as well mess around there for a few hours as mess around making baskets. So Alison started dropping him off at the office in the morning and he'd take the tram back home when he faded. Then the miracle took place; day to day we watched him getting better, getting back on top of things, cracking jokes, recovering.

Within a few months Jim was back at work full time, although he still looked desperately thin and worn and was clearly exhausted by the end of the day. The business also recovered, our financial fears started to melt away and within the year we had repaid his parents and were once again forging ahead. Although our sales stayed fairly static in 1981, after nearly doubling the previous year, publishing involves long lead times and the work we did that year would pay off the following year (1981–82), when our sales nearly doubled again.

Still, the last three months of 1980 had taken their toll, and it was a long slog getting India finished. Geoff came down from banana land, as we'd dubbed northern New South Wales, and moved in with us to work on drawing the maps. Many of our books had been 200 or 300 pages, but India was soon heading towards 700 pages, a monstrous tome at the time. We could see this was going to be something special, an extraordinary book which might just be a miracle as well. By mid-year, India was finally off to the printer and we sat back, very confident and very enthusiastic.

A photograph of the Lonely Planet team at that time shows a pretty small company. There was Peter Campbell (the artist friend who did a lot of illustrative work for us, including the cover of the first edition of India, and who sadly died of cancer in early 2003) with his son Reuben on his knee, Jim (still looking very washed out), Maureen with Tashi (Tashi trying to escape as usual), Andy, Geoff (on his map-drawing visit) and Isabel Afcouliotis (our typesetter). I'm kneeling down at the front. The shopfront window of the Lonely Planet office featured cut-outs designed by Peter Campbell, including a figure pointing in the (wrong) direction towards Kathmandu.

As soon as India was published, Geoff and I set off on further projects. We planned a Malaysia, Singapore and Brunei guide. I'd write up the Malay Peninsula and Singapore while Geoff would do Brunei, the Malaysian states of Sabah and Sarawak in North Borneo and then continue on to Taiwan and Korea. We weren't certain what we'd do with his research in those countries, and as it turned out we put those two very different countries together in one book.

Maureen, Tashi and I arrived in Singapore, collected a rent-a-car then drove all over the Malay Peninsula, proving to ourselves how difficult it could be to travel with an eight-month-old baby. After Malaysia we flew to London to show Tashi off to her grandparents in England and Ireland, then continued on to the east and west coasts of the United States to visit friends including Bill Dalton of Moon Publications in Chico, California. Bill and Mary Dalton also had a young daughter; Sri was only a few weeks older than Tashi and was also born at home. Tragically Maureen and I were with Bill in Bali twenty years later on the night Sri was killed by a hit-and-run driver in San Francisco.

It was late September when we got back to London where the first copies of India had arrived just in time for the Frankfurt Bookfair. The initial reaction in Frankfurt to our book was enthusiastic, but I remember being equally delighted when I arrived back in London—Maureen met me at the airport and Tashi teetered unsteadily over to me. Now that was a trick she hadn't performed a week earlier! Maureen and Tashi went back to Australia while I paused in Sri Lanka to update that book and multi-stopped through Southeast Asia to work on updating that as well.

The long-delayed Japan guidebook finally emerged in late 1981 as well, but it was India which lit up our sales charts. Within weeks we scheduled a reprint and India returned to the printer with encouraging frequency throughout the next year.

If 1980 was our year of disasters and 1981 our year of miracles then in 1982 and 1983 we sat back a little, dreamt up some big new projects which, post-India, felt within our capabilities, and engaged in what became jokingly known as 'consolidation'. We'd attempted it before, but 'consolidation' has never really been a long-term possibility at Lonely Planet so by the end of 1983 we were planning a major step forward and lining ourselves up for some major headaches.

After the previous year's surfeit of activity, Maureen and I didn't go anywhere very much in 1982 except for a week in Fiji, which was probably the closest thing to a holiday we'd had since the day Lonely Planet started. Tashi was up-and-at-them by this time, but Maureen was feeling a little odd when we got back to Melbourne, a slightly unwell in the morning feeling . . .

Top of our agenda for that year was to complete the long-overdue update of Australia. Our trip up the coast in 1980 with my parents was intended to be a step towards a major third edition rewrite, but Jim's illness and Tashi's birth had put the project on hold. Now I had the time to do a proper update and Lonely Planet had the money to let me do it in a proper fashion. We had also unwittingly picked the perfect moment to produce this expanded new edition. Paul Hogan was about to start tossing prawns on the barbie and Australia was revving up to take flight as a major international travel destination. Until the mid-1980s tourism in Australia meant Australians traveling around their own country, some New Zealanders and a handful of international visitors, generally very wealthy or very adventurous.

When I set out in late 1982, eastern Australia was in the grip of the deadly drought which would reach its disastrous conclusion in the Ash Wednesday bushfires on February 16 the following year. The morning before my departure, drought was not on our minds. I'd come back from the pharmacy with the results of a pregnancy test—positive results. We hadn't planned on a second child, but then we hadn't not planned on one either, so we couldn't claim to be surprised.

Leaving Tashi and her pregnant mother behind, I flew down to Adelaide and worked my way around that city before renting a car and heading north through the Barossa and Clare Valleys to remote Broken Hill. With perfect timing I pulled up outside the post office at the same moment as a Rolls-Royce bearing the license plate PH1. Pro Hart, the heavy-weight gentleman in stubbies, a T-shirt and flip-flops who climbed out of the Roller, may not have looked like an artist anywhere else in the world, but that was how a 'brushman of the bush' looked in Broken Hill.

The Road Warrior, the second of the three Mad Max movies that first made Mel Gibson's name, had been filmed the year before, just outside Broken Hill at the mining ghost town of Silverton. There was another film under way when I passed through, but soon I was heading south towards the Flinders Ranges. On the way north to Broken Hill I'd been astounded by the number of dead kangaroos along the roadside. When there's a drought, kangaroos cluster along roads because the run-off from any rain brings a faint fringe of vegetation, and then they get killed by passing vehicles. Driving south I counted 115 dead roos on one typical five-kilometer stretch. Only three years later, when that 1982–83 drought was a fading memory, I drove that stretch again and counted only one or two each five kilometers.

I covered the Flinders Ranges, dropped the rent-a-car back in Adelaide, flew west to Perth, took a train inland to Kalgoorlie and rented another car to explore the surrounding outback area. Back in Perth another flight took me north to Port Hedland and then to Broome and Derby. Only weeks before I arrived in Broome, the stretch of road up to the isolated ex-pearl-diving town had been sealed, the final missing link in a surfaced road right the way round the coast, and Broome had instantly become a tourist attraction. It was hardly surprising, as this raucous town has a long and colorful history.

From Western Australia another flight took me to Darwin, my first visit following the cyclone on Christmas Day 1974. We'd come through Darwin earlier in 1974 en route to Indonesia to research our first Southeast Asia guide. Eight years later Darwin was an even busier hub for travelers heading to or from Australia's nearest neighbor. That Friday night I joined the staff at the Book World bookshop for a beer in their storeroom. Their suggestion that we publish a phrasebook for the Indonesian language led, a year later, to the launch of the first phrasebook from Lonely Planet. Today, we like to say, we cover more languages than Berlitz.

After Alice Springs I quickly covered Mt Isa's fairly limited possibilities, only to find there were no flights to Cairns the following day. There was, the ticket agent volunteered, an Air Queensland DC3 flying Mt Isa–Cairns the next day, but they suggested I'd have to be desperate to take it because it flew via a host of Aboriginal outstations and Gulf of Carpentaria prawn-fishing ports and as a result the flight would take over six hours instead of one. That sounded absolutely perfect to me and I quickly got my ticket written over to Air Queensland. Next morning I undertook what is still one of the most interesting flights I've ever made. We landed at outstations where the whole settlement came to the airstrip to see the flight come through. I spent an hour sitting up on the flight deck while the captain pointed out the winding estuaries leading through eerily dry mud flats into the gulf and, at one point, the remains of a World War II B17 bomber. The flight attendant came round with cans of beer in styrofoam coolers and just before sunset we dropped down over the lush green hills of the Atherton Tableland into Cairns.

Port Douglas was busy (but still nothing like it is today), so I continued north up the muddy road to Cape Tribulation, trying to ignore the sign prominently posted on the rental-car's dashboard announcing 'This vehicle is not to be used on the Cape Tribulation road'. Then it was south to Townsville, Mackay and Rockhampton, with forays out to the Barrier Reef Island resorts, Brisbane, the Gold Coast, Sydney and Canberra and finally back to Melbourne.

With help from Simon Hayman and Alan Samagalski, this hasty but comprehensive circuit of Australia transformed the book. The sickly 192-page guidebook became a muscular 576 pages and once again we managed to perform the feat with perfect timing. Backpacker hostels were suddenly popping up all around the country, young travelers were beginning to discover the Barrier Reef and the outback, and the movie *Crocodile Dundee* would soon help turn Australia into one big tourist attraction. By that time our new Australia book was out and the statistics tell the story: the first edition sold 10 000 copies in two years from 1977; the second edition got through 15 000 copies in four years; the third edition was launched in mid-1983 and skyrocketed to 60 000 copies. Amazingly, that was only scratching the surface, since subsequent editions of the guide to our home country have all easily topped 100 000 copies and even a quarter of a million copies for the tenth (Olympic year) edition. Of course, these days it takes a team of ten writers to charge around the country for each updated edition.

Our son Kieran was born on February 23 1983, only a week after the terrible bushfires of Ash Wednesday. Kieran was also born at home, but thankfully his arrival didn't involve any of the hassles which had made Tashi's birth such a scary experience. Tashi was there to witness her brother's entry into the world, definitely a big surprise for a two-year-old.

A photo taken of the Lonely Planet team standing in front of the

41 Rowena Parade office soon after Kieran's birth shows a rather different company from two years earlier, although the background is unchanged. The photo shows Jim (looking much healthier), me with Tashi, Andy, Maureen holding a very tiny Kieran, Mary Covernton (our first full-time editor), our typesetter Isabel, Joy Weideman (our temporary although almost full-time art person), Evelyn Vyhnal (who also worked on art) and Alan Samagalski (our full-time researcher-writer). That's nine people in all.

Lonely Planet was certainly growing and our office, an old Victorian-era shop building with a veranda out the back looking onto an overgrown patch of weeds, started to grow with it. We walled in the veranda to create a storage room for our burgeoning stock of books, refurbished a back room to become a second office and knocked a hole through the wall to what would become a photographic darkroom.

Later in the year all our boats seemed to come in at once. We won a state small business award and a few weeks later I flew up to Canberra to shake hands with Andrew Peacock, the Deputy Prime Minister, and collect a national export award. A couple of weeks later we hit the guidebook jackpot when India picked up the Thomas Cook Guidebook of the Year award. In early December I made a flying visit to London where Lord Hunt, leader of the 1953 Everest expedition which put Edmund Hillary and Tensing Norgay on the summit, presented the awards at the Royal Geographical Society.

It was a thrill to receive an accolade at such a place—explorers such as David Livingstone, Ernest Shackleton and Sir Richard Burton (the source-of-the-Nile Burton, not the serial-husband-to-Elizabeth-Taylor Burton) all spoke about their adventures at the Royal Geographical Society. Years later, when I was invited to speak there, I sat at David Livingstone's table and afterwards I realized that my talk, in late 1999, was to be the last speech at the society for the century.

On the way back to Australia I paused for a day in Hong Kong to meet up with our charming distributor Geoffrey Bonsall and then, back at Melbourne airport, I was put firmly in my place. Once again the Australian customs officials showed in the clearest terms possible that my frequent arrivals and departures were a subject of deep suspicion. My bags were checked with the customs' department's proverbial comb and I was marched off to a private room to be subjected to the indignity of a body search. Drawing yet another blank must have finally convinced the department that we were legitimate because we've never been hassled again.

Later that day Maureen and I lazed by the banks of the Yarra, watching a group of elephants from a visiting circus standing on the opposite bank and drinking from the river. We pondered how even in your home town you can see amazing sights.

It was a good time for us. With our bank balance firmly in the black, books pouring out the door, government awards hanging on the wall and our India guide, already a terrific commercial success for us, getting critical acclaim as well, it was hard to believe that only two years before we were at our lowest ebb.

Two things happened in the early 1980s that would have a major effect on our future: competitors and computers. One of the runners-up in the Thomas Cook awards was *The Rough Guide to Greece*, the first title from the publisher which we would soon consider our number one competitor.

The other change had begun to occur early in 1981 when we'd decided to computerize our invoicing and sales accounts. It's worth remembering that microcomputers were still in a somewhat primitive stage of development back then. IBM and Bill Gates were yet to launch MS-DOS and the early Apple IIs weren't really very businesslike. At the other extreme there were 'real' IBM computers, but they were quite out of our price league. Our annual sales were only around $250 000 and 'real' computers started at around $25 000.

We'd eventually decided to buy a Century T10. This clunky device from the desktop Stone Age had a combined screen and keyboard and a huge metal box with twin floppy disk drives. Remember the 5¼-inch floppies that came before the smaller 3½-inch floppies? Well, this machine ran on ten-inch floppies, which were the computer equivalent of 78 rpm records. Our cutting-edge computer used the cutting-edge language of the day, CPM. Finding a suitable computer was pretty difficult, but finding accounting software was an even bigger problem. We contracted with a programmer to write our own accounting software for our new toy. We were poised to join the wired world.

Coming up with the accounting package we'd mapped out proved totally beyond the capabilities of our software expert and the technology of the time, but eventually we did get the whole box of tricks up and running quite satisfactorily, even if it never did everything we'd originally hoped for. With many rewrites, extensions and a wholesale changeover to MS-DOS we managed to live with that original sales and invoicing system for over ten years, by which time it handled all our Australian and international sales in a whole range of currencies, even plugging in the exchange rates every time we did a new invoice. It was a clever program for something we'd virtually had to create from scratch.

That clumsy old computer still sits, gathering dust, in a storeroom cupboard at Lonely Planet. We've slung in one example of each generation of computers, thinking that one day they might make an interesting little museum tracing our technological development. In 2003, over twenty years after we took that first tentative step into the computer world, I spoke to an audience of geeks at a conference, recounting our story, using as many pictures featuring computers as possible in my slide show.

'The programming for the early US nuclear aircraft carriers was written on the same sort of computers,' one of the attendees told me after my talk. 'Every now and then some programming problem pops up and they have to drag one of those relics out of a museum, dust off those big floppy disks, fire up the machine and get it working again. They've never bothered to transfer the code to new systems.'

In late 1982 I was hammering out the new Australia book on an electric typewriter when Jim suggested I have a go at using the computer instead. This seemed a rather novel concept, but it was a fantastic idea. Our big and bulky accounting computer could also be a glorified typewriter or, to use the new buzz word, 'word processor'. Within hours of first sitting down at the keyboard I was completely at home with WordStar and I wrote most of the new edition of Australia on the computer.

We didn't immediately realize that the value of writing with a computer was not simply the ease of getting the text down and correcting it, but the fact that the text was permanently recorded, ready for easy updating. However, word processing at that time did not offer choices of typefaces and type styles so once the material had been typed in it still had to be printed out and then typed in again on the IBM Composer.

It was time to dump the Composer and move on to more modern photo-typesetting. The inspiration we brought to this straightforward idea was to link up our word-processing computer with the photo-typesetting machine. No doubt other people were having the same brainwave at the same time, but what we were doing was pretty pioneering. In 1983 we spent $25 000 on an ITEC photosetter which we linked up to our computer so that word-processed text could be output as typeset galleys without having to be keyed in a second time. It was a primitive form of desktop publishing. Converting to modern photo-typesetting technology spelt the end of using golfball typing elements and meant we no longer had to have larger type set externally and pasted in, although the final text still came in long 'galleys'. These yard-long strips of text had to be cut to size and pasted down on the layout sheets which were eventually photographed to make the printing plates. At least we'd moved beyond pots of glue— the galleys were fed through waxing machines which coated the back surface with a thin film of hot wax.

We had to devise a detailed system of instructions for the computer to tell the photosetter when to switch typefaces or type styles, but we were very pleased with this great leap forward and soon all our books were produced this way. In fact, the problems of going from computer to typesetter had been so complex that even after we started to switch from CPM to MS-DOS computers we still made the computer-to-typesetter link with CPM and had to first convert all MS-

DOS text to CPM.

Our authors were still submitting their text on paper so we had to retype their manuscripts and very soon our single computer couldn't cope with sales information, my use of it as a word processor, and for inputting and editing writers' text.

One day Jim marched into the office and dumped an ugly grey metal box on my desk. 'Darth Vader's lunch box,' he announced. It was our first Kaypro computer: we eventually owned eighteen of them.

Before long our $25 000 photosetter was showing its technological age, so out the door it went, to be replaced by a $50 000 lasersetter. But something quicker and cheaper was already looming on the horizon—desktop publishing. Electronic typesetting was a long way from hot metal setting where type was produced from molten metal, but it was still a complex business requiring fairly extensive training. Desktop publishing would leapfrog beyond our computer-to-typesetter linkage, eliminate the messy business of cutting and pasting galleys, and let us produce finished pages straight from a computer, although for a while we were still pasting in illustrations and maps.

We bought our first Ventura Publisher desktop software package in 1988 and produced the second edition of our Tahiti guide with it. Once again we were pioneering and amongst the many problems we encountered was how to output the text. Our first computer printer was essentially a daisywheel typewriter, but we'd since moved on to dot matrix printers. These were fine for correspondence, invoices and the like, but they weren't good enough for a book. We could have sent the pages out to be typeset, but that would have been time-consuming and contrary to our policy of doing as much as we could ourselves. We could have used our laser-setter as a printer, but it seemed crazy to use a $50 000 machine this way. The first laser printers were, however, making their appearance at this time. They allowed us to produce books by outputting the pages fifty per cent oversize and then photographically reducing them.

That first desktop-published book ran into so many problems and took so much effort to produce that we questioned the advantages of the technology, but the next book was much easier and within a remarkably short period of time our laser-setter was standing idle. So were most of our layout sheets, scalpels, waxing machines and pots of glue. Ann Jeffree, our now redundant typesetter, was retrained as a cartographer-designer, but desktop publishing threw the whole editing and design side of the business into turmoil.

Previously there had been a neat division between editorial and design. The editors handled the words, the designers put them on the pages in the appropriate places. Of course the division wasn't really that simple: there were maps which designers drew, but which had words on them; there were illustrations and photographs which had to appear at appropriate places relative to the text; and so on. Suddenly the decisions on these questions were often being made by computers rather than people, and who oversaw the computers?

Around the same time, we began to draw our maps with computers using AutoCAD. Our Eastern Europe guide, published in 1989, embodied our tentative first steps into computerized mapping. Today, mapping is one of the prime uses for AutoCAD, but that application had not really occurred to AutoCAD's creators back then. Our software development was further complicated by having to create our own type fonts to cope with curious Eastern European characters and accents. Fortunately, Todd Pierce, eighteen years old at the time, who'd joined Lonely Planet a couple of years previously, was turning out to be a computer whiz and performed mapping miracles on the book. The arrival of AutoCAD signaled a switch in the company from employing designers who also drew maps to employing cartographers who also did some design.

We began to think about setting up an American operation. In May 1983 I went to Dallas for the American Booksellers Association's annual shindig. I stopped in San Francisco on the way back, with the thought of moving there in 1984. Looking back, the decision to expand overseas by opening a sales and distribution office in the

United States was either very brave or very foolhardy because at the time the Lonely Planet workforce was still less than a dozen people—not the sort of base from which to launch a multinational operation. By this time the United States had become our biggest single market, but it was only marginally larger than our Australian or British markets. When you considered that America had twenty times the population of Australia it seemed crazy that we couldn't sell at least two or three times as many books there.

We reasoned that we would never develop the market we deserved until we had a real presence in the United States. As long as we were just another overseas publisher we'd always be a marginal operator in a big game. Of course, having an American office would provide more advantages than simply a phone number for local bookshops. We'd be able to promote our books more effectively and store supplies of books there, avoiding shipping delays from Australia or Asia. Despite this logical reasoning, other publishers to whom we mentioned our plans would point at the disastrous experiences of overseas publishers who had tried to establish themselves in the States. Plenty of British publishers had burnt their figures with abortive American operations.

'You guys have been lucky so far, but you can't just set up in the US,' advised Bob Sessions, publisher at Penguin Books in Australia. 'It hasn't worked for anyone else, why should it for you?'

We had started selling books in the United States in 1975 with the first edition of *South-East Asia on a Shoestring* and the second edition of *Across Asia on the Cheap*. Our first foothold in the US market was with Bookpeople, a wonderful Berkeley, California-based operation and very definitely a creation of the 1960s. Bookpeople was an employee-owned wholesaler which specialized in small press books with many laudably high-minded principles such as equal salaries across the board and free lunches for everyone. This sort of flower-power business should have gone down in flames with the end of the 1960s, but although there had been some pragmatic compromises along the way, Bookpeople saw out the century before finally collapsing in 2004.

Bookpeople sold respectable quantities of our books, but nothing like what we were selling in Australia or Britain, since it was a wholesaler, not a distributor. In the book business, wholesalers and distributors both sell to bookshops, but a wholesaler is usually a passive operation, a distributor an active one. Bookpeople put out catalogs listing all the titles they carried and a monthly update listing new books. A bookshop could then use Bookpeople as one handy outlet for all their small press needs. But nobody was saying: 'This is new, this is good, buy it.' Distributors actually went to the bookshops and convinced them to buy.

We needed a book distributor (which handles lots of book publishers) or another publisher (which sometimes takes on a compatible book publisher's list). Finding that company wasn't easy—travel is too small, too risky, too specialist, we were told when we approached American distributors or publishers. Or we were too small. It simply wasn't worthwhile taking on a tiny publisher with less than twenty titles and located far away in Australia. Or our titles weren't commercial enough, nobody was going to those places we were doing books for, we'd never sell enough copies to make it worth doing.

A new company called Two Continents was interested in getting overseas books into the US market. They looked worth going with although the distribution deal was very one-sided. They wanted a big discount and they only paid us after they got paid themselves, so if a bookshop was slow in paying we had to wait and if the bookshop never paid, then we were the ones who suffered, not Two Continents. We couldn't be choosy so we threw our lot in with Two Continents.

For a short time all went well; our sales were climbing and although the money was slow in arriving we were prepared for that. Then they went bankrupt. How they could manage this feat when we were taking all the risk has always eluded me, but we found ourselves with no US distributor and a lot of books in warehouses which we had to fight to get back. When a company goes broke creditors, like vultures, try to pick over the remains. Of course Two Continents didn't own our books—they sat in their warehouse, but until they were sold they remained our property. Unfortunately, proving this could have been a time-consuming business and it would have been a fairly Pyrrhic victory to get our books back just as we were replacing them with a new edition. Fortunately, Two Continents had books in two warehouses and while the books in one warehouse were tied up with creditors' claims, the books in the other weren't. By a stroke of luck our books were in the second warehouse.

We soon tied up a new deal with Hippocrene, a small New York–based publisher with a compatible travel list. Hippocrene was run by George Blagowidow, who had escaped to the United States from Lithuania after World War II. George was an aristocratic gentleman and his books were very different from ours, but although his operation lacked the pizzazz which was really needed for selling our books he was solid, reliable and honest. Hippocrene became our distributor in 1980 and our American sales began to climb slowly but steadily.

Our US plan was simplicity itself: Maureen and I would go to San Francisco, open an office, find people to run it, return to Australia, and sell lots more books. How this would all take place was unclear, but we knew the first step was to get US visas and at this point we ran into a catch-22. If we already had a US operation then we could arrange visas to go and work with our US company. But since we didn't have a US company it was impossible! The fact that we wanted to go to the US to set up a US-based company made no difference. If we were a company the size of GM or IBM or even BHP this wouldn't be a problem, but little companies aren't supposed to go around setting up international subsidiaries.

Eventually an American embassy official told me, strictly off the record, to forget about doing it properly, legally and officially. 'Go over there on a tourist visa,' she said, 'and set up your operation. If it takes longer than six months you'll have no trouble extending your tourist visa to twelve months. Leave before the twelve months are up and everything will be fine. But forget about doing it legally. We'll tie you up in red tape and never issue the visas.'

And you wonder why America (or anywhere else for that matter) has immigration problems?

Meanwhile, in mid-1983 we went to Bali for a very pleasant month working on the first edition of a new guide to Bali and the neighboring island of Lombok. Kieran was four months old and Tashi was only two and a half so they weren't the ideal ages for rushing around researching a guidebook, but Bali proved the perfect place for working with the family.

Every locally run hotel on the island is just itching to adopt your kids, so there's always a babysitter on tap. Our small guesthouse was run by an enormously helpful young man named Ketut Suartana and his twelve-year-old sister (also named Ketut) attached herself to us, going everywhere with us. Every morning our daughter would be whisked off to the market for the morning shopping trip and we'd look out of our room to see her putting out the offerings for the spirits, an element of the Bali day which I've always loved. I did notice, however, that Tashi was never allowed to tend to the good spirits; it was generally offerings for demons and bad spirits, the little woven palm-leaf trays of flower petals and a few grains of food which are derisorily deposited at ground level (where demons hang out), which she was allowed to manage.

We spent weeks in Ubud, during which time I rode out to all the centers around southern Bali on a motorcycle.

We drove up through the mountains in a small Suzuki jeep and established ourselves at Lovina Beach on the north coast, from where I went out to cover the north side of the island. Meanwhile, Mary Covernton was working her way around Lombok.

Back at the office, Lonely Planet was continuing to grow. Graham Imeson had joined us as our first full-time designer and the Bali and Lombok guide, published in January 1984, was the first book he produced for us. Graham is still with us today as our production manager.

A few months later we traveled to Nepal, India and Sri Lanka. Tashi had her third birthday in Kathmandu. We spent several weeks driving around Sri Lanka, stopping in pleasant beachside hotels where Maureen would stay with the children while I explored the surrounding country. Sri Lanka is small enough that I could even drive up from the coast into the hill country for a day or two before returning to the seaside. One day I drove along the coast from our temporary headquarters in Unawatuna to visit the old fortified port town of Galle. On this occasion Tashi came along and demonstrated that she'd already learnt what guidebooks were all about.

Our final stop around the town was a visit to the charming old New Oriental Hotel, originally built in 1684 for the Dutch governor. I'd visited the hotel several times before so I only needed to see the new swimming pool and one or two other improvements since my last visit. We said our goodbyes, but as we walked out to the car a worried look crossed Tashi's face as she pulled at my hand. 'Daddy,' she whispered urgently, 'aren't we going to check the bathrooms?'

In February 1984 we were ready to shift to the United States. Kieran was coming up to his first birthday and Tashi was still only three (too young for a few weeks of roughing it while we found a place to live), so Maureen stayed in Australia while I went ahead to house hunt. Within a few weeks I'd found a house in Berkeley, bought a Honda Accord and the first of a new family of Kaypro computers. Soon after Maureen turned up with the kids and Frances Wombwell in tow.

M: Tony and I tended to make decisions quite spontaneously, and the one to go to America for a year was no exception. We needed to sort out distribution in the States; ergo, we go! However, with two small children in tow, I did need some sort of plan for who would care for them while I was working. I really didn't want to choose a career in a hurry, and I was nervous at the idea of leaving them with a stranger, no matter how well referenced she was.

I didn't have any family in Australia. Jim Hart's wife Alison had taken on the role of elder sister—she also had two children, one of whom was two years older than Tashi, and she'd really helped me find my feet as a new mother. Alison believed in routines for children and I learned a lot from her. She was very kind to me and would often look after Tashi, even keeping her overnight on occasion, which Tashi loved. I wasn't sure how I would manage in the States without her. Alison had employed a young woman from country Victoria for the past few years and had sung her praises so compellingly that all her girlfriends now had Frances working for them.

Frances was in her late teens and was cheerful, smart, totally reliable and trustworthy. She looked after Tashi one day a week and helped with housework, so I decided to ask her to come to the States with us for the first three months. None of my friends were happy with me for taking her away, but Frances was very excited—this was her first trip out of Australia, and her first time on a plane.

But then Frances began to get cold feet. She vacillated between yes and no. On the day we were due to fly out, I told her to come by Alison's, where the children and I were staying, and tell me she was on her way to the airport. On that day she jumped out of her friend's car and called out, 'I'm on my way.' I was very relieved.

It needed the two of us to manage the children on the plane. Tony met us at the airport with a big station wagon and took us to our new home. We settled in quickly; Tashi was a very social child and one day, as we were exploring our new neighborhood, we passed a small kindergarten where a group of children were playing in the garden. Tashi stopped to look and I asked her if she wanted to go in. We went in and met the director who showed us around.

I asked Tashi if she would like to come back and stay a while and her instant reply was, 'I want to stay now.' The director said that was OK and I should come back in an hour. On my return Tashi wasn't the least bit interested in leaving, so I signed her up and she attended three mornings a week, which quickly became five and gradually built up to full time.

Frances very quickly took to life in California. Within a few weeks she befriended a gang of au pairs from Scandinavia who used our house as headquarters before descending on the bars and clubs of San Francisco. Frances was loving it and didn't want to go home at the end of three months. I was loving it too, because the kids were well looked after, Frances took care of the house, and we got on really well. She ended up spending the year with us and left just before we departed for South America.

When we returned to Melbourne, Frances came back to work for me, which she still does to this day. She is 'family' and we have seen each other through every major event in each other's lives.

We found a small office-cum-warehouse in the industrial enclave of Emeryville, on Park Avenue, so at least the street address had a publishing feel to it. Cartons of books were soon stacked in the warehouse while our first two American employees, Elizabeth Kim and Camille Coyne, joined us in the office. The 1984 American Bookseller Association (ABA) bookfair in Washington DC was our first bookshow as a genuine American publisher, but although our sales began to inch up it soon became clear we needed a better distribution system.

Doing our own distribution in Australia had worked wonders, since we'd kept control and avoided the unreliable delivery that is so often the Achilles' heel of small publishers. Would the same technique work in the US? Before we could find out, Robert Sheldon marched into our lives and quickly mapped out our American future.

Robert was a character you don't easily forget. He had an imposing girth, but his nearly waist-length grey-white hair and impressively shaggy moustache were even more striking than his rotundity. Robert knew his way around the book business, but it was no secret that his career had been, shall we say, colorful. When we first met Robert he was about to leave Bookpeople, and from the firework-like eruptions taking place it was clearly not a happy departure, on either side. I'm not sure to this day quite how Robert marched out of

Bookpeople and into Lonely Planet, but he was soon on the payroll as a part-time consultant, counseling us to drop Hippocrene and taking over our distribution.

Breaking up with Hippocrene wasn't easy for us, but Robert soon recruited teams of sales reps and in December 1984 we were installed in the Algonquin Hotel in New York and holding our first sales conference. We could see some of the reps were far from convinced about a small company which was dedicated to publishing books about countries that nobody ever visited. Furthermore, the Berkeley address seemed to be a cover to disguise the fact we were from Australia, of all places.

Fortunately for us, Robert commanded a lot of respect from the reps, one of whom, Howard Karel from San Francisco, said he was convinced we knew what were doing (even if some of our books did look a little strange). A few years later one of those suspicious reps told me he'd come to realize that it didn't matter how curious and unlikely the destination sounded—if we were publishing it, people would want it.

We bought more computers and installed a rather rough-and-ready invoicing software package and in January we supplied our first orders. By February we were starting to learn the distribution ropes, but in early March I was going to be facing a real problem: my year in America would be up. Maureen's and the kids' visas would expire soon after. We devised a simple way around this one-year limit: we'd leave the country for a couple of months, then come back and start again with another six-month stamp in our passports.

Getting away from the US office was going to be a major relief. We'd worked ourselves to the point of exhaustion for month after month and money seemed to be hemorrhaging out of our US operation. We could see sales were building up, but not nearly fast enough, and for the first time in years I was back to waking up in the middle of the night and sweating over how we would pay the bills. Going away for a couple of months would also give the office a chance to experience life without us and February 22 1985 seemed like a good time to make our departure. Not only was it a week or two before my

one year was up, but it was also the day before Kieran's second birthday. He could still fly out on a ten per cent fare.

So Kieran turned two somewhere over Central America, on a
flight heading south to Lima, the capital of Peru. Two months on the
road with kids that age is not easy and ours showed it was going to
be tough right on day one. Sleeping off the jet lag in a hotel in Lima,
Maureen and I woke to discover the children had been using the bed
sheets as an art gallery with the colored pens they'd been given on
the plane.

From Lima we flew up to Ayacucho and then to Cuzco, from
where we took a train to Machu Picchu. The kids loved Casco, the
'Kathmandu of South America', and we traveled out to other towns
and villages in the area. Our photo album is full of pictures of the
children with llamas, the children riding in the back of pickup trucks,
the children in the Inca ruins. Another train transported us to Puno
on Lake Titicaca at 12 600 feet altitude. Casco was only 1500 feet
lower, but we arrived in Puno exhausted and quite incapable of coping with the altitude and our children. At the train station we found a
young Peruvian with a delivery bike, dumped our kids in the carrier
on the front and asked him to cycle them round to the hotel. Another
photograph shows our children sitting in this pedal-powered taxi
clearly thinking it's the greatest joke on earth.

A bus took us around Lake Titicaca and into Bolivia, but that
notoriously unstable country seemed to be on the brink of yet another change of government and its currency was declining at warp
speed. In fact the Bolivian monetary authorities were reprinting the
currency with an extra zero added with such frequency that they'd
given up printing notes on both sides. One side was completely
blank. At the border I changed US$20 into Bolivian currency and I
have a photo of Tashi, clearly perplexed, holding as big a stack of
Bolivian banknotes as a four-year-old could reasonably lift.

From La Paz we flew back through Lima and straight on to Quito
in Ecuador. We continued up into the Andes and then descended to
Guayaquil on the coast and flew out to the Galapagos, where we
cruised around enjoying the wildlife attractions which have made the

equatorial islands so incredibly interesting. Then it was back to the mainland and down the coast to conclude our South American escape where it had started in Lima.

If you're going to get pickpocketed, robbed or mugged then South America has always been the place it's likely to happen, so it was entirely appropriate that our visit should end with a rip-off. By the time we'd returned to Lima we'd heard plenty of stories and, in fact, I'd had two close encounters early in the trip.

Walking down a street in Ayacucho, just days after we'd arrived in Peru, a well-dressed gentleman had come up to me and pointed out with great concern that a passing bird had deposited something on my shoulder. This is such a standard procedure—while you're looking at the birdshit on your left shoulder your right pocket is being picked—that I immediately edged away and nothing was lost.

The next morning there had been a more decisive attempt, but again it was a familiar approach. As I was leaving the market, a solid Indian woman had barged into me from one side with such force that I'd immediately turned the other way to find out what was about to happen. There had been a sharp ripping noise as my daypack was razored, but I'd grabbed the bag before anything fell out of the gaping hole and later that day a local tailor sewed it up for me. Stupidly I was not wearing my moneybelt—it was in my daypack, and the razor artist's cut had slashed that as well. For the next year or two I was able to top any theft story by showing how I'd not only been robbed, but got a free vasectomy at the same time.

In Lima we really did get robbed, and again it was a classic set-up. We'd rented a VW Beetle with the intention of driving south to see the Nazca Lines. Our small children were both sleepy so Maureen and I were carrying one each as well as our bags. As we collected the car from the hotel car park, two young men approached us and asked the time. Glancing at a watch was all the distraction it took for one of our identical daypacks to disappear. Fortunately it wasn't the daypack with passports, airline tickets and other vital necessities. For their troubles the two thieves got a bagful of diapers and other baby paraphernalia, all of which proved difficult to replace in Lima. As a result we never got to the Nazca Lines.

In mid-April we boarded the flight back to San Francisco, via Vancouver, and flew straight into big problems. Our plan to extend our stay in the US by another six months came crashing to the ground at Vancouver Airport. We'd taken this rather roundabout route because the cheapest flight to South America had been with a Canadian airline. If you enter the US from Canada, immigration formalities are handled in Canada; it's no problem to the American officials if they reject you, since you are not even in America yet. At Vancouver airport we ran into the immigration officer from hell. In retrospect, we should have been less honest. We should have had tickets to Australia for later in the year, and wallets stuffed with travelers' checks. We shouldn't have had a business card with an American address on it (even though the Australian Lonely Planet address was more prominent). We should have looked like innocent tourists passing through from South America on our way back to OZ.

We had a rented house in Berkeley, furniture, two cars and a US bank account. The fact that we also had a business in the Bay Area with an all-American roster of employees made no difference—we were up against an immigration officer who clearly enjoyed keeping people out of the US. As we argued that we had a house back in Australia and were intending to return there as soon as possible, the minutes until our connecting flight to San Francisco was due to depart were ticking away. Our kids had been cooped up in a plane all night, and were getting more and more restless when this uniformed ogre announced it was our responsibility to keep them quiet while he harassed us.

Finally, he decided we could stay in the US for only another three months, stamped in our passports that our visas were not to be extended again and then announced sadistically that our flight left in fifteen minutes and we might still catch it if we ran. We picked the kids up and ran, swearing under our breath. We were still fuming when Camille met us at San Francisco Airport. Sales were climbing, the computer system was not coping, but Lonely Planet USA was still afloat. To top it all, our Africa and South America expert Geoff

Crowther and his Korean wife Hyung Pun had turned up, en route to South America, and were living at our house.

In mid-May, a garage sale cleared nearly everything we weren't going to ship back, and a shipping agent picked up everything else. We flew out, heading home via Asia on a one-month jaunt designed to get us back to Australia at the same time as our clothes and household chattels arrived. It was a good plan, only slightly spoilt by the shipping company deciding to mail us the bill in Australia and then waiting for it to be paid before they dispatched the goods.

Unaware that we were going to get back to the southern winter with all our warm clothes still in San Francisco, we jetted off to Japan where we discovered yet again that kids have absolutely no conception of time zones and jet lag and simply carry on as if nothing has changed at all. In Tokyo I spent two rather dazed hours with Kieran between three and five in the morning wandering through the deserted shopping center beneath our hotel.

We looked around Tokyo, took an excursion to Nikko, bullet-trained to Kyoto, stayed in a *ryokan* (a traditional inn which had a Japanese communal bath the kids thought was definitely interesting) and flew business class to Hong Kong. It was the first time we'd experienced life at the sharp end of an aircraft and we were rather mystified as to how or why it had happened until we remembered we'd met up with my father's British Airways friend Jiro Yoshida in Kyoto.

In Hong Kong my aversion to making advance bookings for hotels paid off for once, when we asked at the airport hotel booking desk what late-night bargains they had on offer and a cut-price room in the ultra-ritzy Peninsula topped the list! We'd never asked for favors or special deals but that unrequested airline upgrade was a pleasant surprise and finding ourselves in the best hotel in Hong Kong, if only for a couple of nights, was a real treat.

From Hong Kong we took the jetfoil across to Macau for a short stay at the exotic old Bela Vista Hotel, still in its decaying pre-redevelopment condition. Our brief halt became an extended one when a typhoon blew by and all the shipping services were suspended. I had a meeting with Steve Fallon, editor of the Asian edition of *Business Traveller* magazine, back in Hong Kong and was worried about missing it until we discovered he was also stranded in the Bela Vista. Steve would later leave *Business Traveller* and set up Wanderlust, a wonderful, though short-lived, Hong Kong travel bookshop, before joining Lonely Planet as a writer; today numerous books (including London, Paris, Budapest, France, Hungary and Slovenia) carry Steve's name.

The final halt on our way home was in Bali where we lazed at Poppies on Kuta Beach and revisited our friends the two Ketuts at the Suci Guest House in Ubud. I rented a small motorcycle, and in true Asian fashion we'd zip down the road for lunch with the whole family on board, Tashi perched on the gas tank, Kieran slung on Maureen's hip.

In early July we arrived back in Australia. We'd been gone for over a year and Lonely Planet had done some growing up while we were away.

6

Quiet for a Spell

Back in Australia we reclaimed our house, which was not in the best condition since it had gone through a series of tenants in our absence. Despite Maureen's initial dismay, it was soon back to normal.

Of course, after a year's absence, slotting back into things was not completely straightforward. Jim Hart had done a fine job keeping things not only going, but actually growing. When I thoughtlessly acted as if we were back in the driving seat and everybody else could sit back and look at the scenery, it provoked the only really angry words from Jim in the first five years we worked together. Unhappily, there were to be more angry words ten years later.

The office was only a mile or so away from our home so I often went to work by bicycle. When Tashi started primary school I bolted a bicycle seat on the back and dropped her off at school each morning on my way to work. Things were not exactly going smoothly in the US without us, but sales were climbing steadily and our financial fears began to steadily recede. Even my blood pressure nose-dived back to where it should have been and where it has stayed ever since.

By the end of 1985, however, it was clear we had to do something about the US operation. Our precipitate departure had left many problems behind, computers being only one of them. I'd made a hurried switch to a more powerful Kaypro computer, but it was simply not powerful enough and our invoicing system was also inadequate for our needs. Robert moved us to a much more advanced system known as Deliverance which ran on an MS-DOS computer, but there was considerable data loss at the time of the changeover. Lots of loose ends had to be tied up.

Maureen and I went to America in early December to visit the office, do the New York sales conference and try to get the figures to add up. We were worried about how US immigration would greet us, but we had return tickets to Australia and not having the kids with us gave us extra brownie points. Our time at the office was an almost continuous number-crunching session and we took stacks of paperwork back to Robert's apartment (where we were staying) each night. Although we were not altogether successful in sorting out the confusion we didn't do too badly, and just before Christmas we flew home with the US operation in better shape, but still not completely stable.

We had problems in Australia too: we'd outgrown our building. When we moved into 41 Rowena Parade at the end of 1979 Lonely Planet essentially consisted of Andy, Maureen and me, a freelance designer and soon afterwards a typesetter and Jim Hart. By 1984 those, shall we say, five and a half people had expanded to ten. In the year and a bit we'd been away the numbers had grown into the teens, including a couple of full-time editors. We were bursting at the seams. We'd long ago run out of storage for the books and were renting space at a warehouse round the corner. The single unisex toilet didn't meet local office standard regulations, but our major problem was the building was falling apart.

The roof leaked. That in itself wouldn't have been a major problem. After all, we could put a bucket under wherever the rain came in, except we never knew where the rain would come in. The water would seep through the old slate roof tiles or back up under the roof edge, but then it would accumulate above the ceiling and slosh back and forth until it decided where to come gushing through. With uncanny precision it seemed to find exactly the worst place to pour out, on one occasion splashing onto some nearly completed artwork and another time ruining dozens of carefully hand-drawn maps for our China book. Jim and I would rush to the office in the middle of the night if rain threatened. It was clearly time to move.

Eventually a brand-new office-cum-warehouse was found only a mile or so away from Rowena Parade, still in Richmond and actually closer to our home. Inevitably there were building delays, but in 1986 we shifted into our new open-plan office, heated in winter, air-conditioned in summer and with a roof that did not leak. It was large enough that we figured we could easily double our headcount—this new space could handle twenty-five people and it would take many years, if ever, before we got that big. We were soon to discover that we were very bad at predicting staff growth.

In early 1986 I was in bad need of a travel fix. Apart from trips in Australia I hadn't traveled since the South America journey and the short Japan—Hong Kong—Bali interlude a year previously. I hadn't made a solo trip since Burma in 1983 so when India needed an update I was ready to go. When the second edition came around in 1983 I had been completely tied up with other projects (including fatherhood) and Geoff had volunteered to cover my region as well as his.

This time it was Geoff who was overloaded, so Prakash Raj and I would do the whole book. (Today, when we ask for much more careful and extensive fact checking from our writers, we'd consider this an impossible task for only two people, but things were still a bit rough and ready at Lonely Planet in the mid-1980s.) We decided to swap things around, so Prakash would cover the south of India, formerly Geoff's region, while I would cover the middle and the north. Increasingly our books were being put together by teams of writers. I was quite happy to see this change; although I'd launched many of our early titles by myself it didn't take long for books like Australia or New Zealand to become much too comprehensive for one person to handle.

I arrived in India, bought an Indrail train pass and zipped quickly through all of northern India from Delhi across to Calcutta and then up to Darjeeling. I'd often travel overnight by train then take a hotel room simply for somewhere to shower and park during the day. At night I'd take another train to my next stop.

During my stop in Varanasi I suffered a most inauspicious injury. In the most holy of Hindu cities, where cows are the most holy of creatures, I was attacked by one. In the late afternoon I was heading back to my hotel, bantering with a cycle rickshaw wallah who was peddling alongside me. We passed a cow standing by the roadside, a common occurrence in India, when suddenly it decided that in some previous incarnation it was a bull—a Spanish bull. A genuine Spanish fighting bull in fact. And I was (evidently) a vacationing Spanish bullfighter. The bull, er cow, unexpectedly stuck its horn in my side. There was nowhere to go, as I was pinned up against the cycle rickshaw, and I fractured two ribs. The rickshaw wallah leapt off his bicycle and gave the cow a most unholy kick and I limped back to my hotel, trying not to laugh because it hurt so much when I did.

In subsequent years I've fractured ribs while skiing and by falling off bicycles. There's nothing you can do about it; you just have to wait until it heals and try not to laugh or sneeze too often in the interim. On this occasion the main problem was I could only get out of bed by rolling onto the floor and standing up from a kneeling position.

The Indrail pass ran out when I got to Darjeeling so I carried on with Indian Airlines down to the Orissa temple cities, then on to Hyderabad and Madras, across to Bombay and up through Gujarat before reverting to land transport again through Rajasthan to end up back in Delhi.

The final week of this absurdly breakneck trip degenerated into a frustrating comedy around the mountainous northern state of Himachal Pradesh. In Shimla, the old British hill station where Raj-era civil servants went to escape the sweltering plains during the hot season, I rented a taxi for a rapid circuit up the Kullu Valley to Manali and across to Dharamsala before concluding at Chandigarh. The car was an ancient Hindustan Ambassador, the Indian version of a stout 1950s British Morris Oxford. We negotiated a fee for the three-day trip, agreed where we would go and then agreed that I would make a one-third deposit to pay for fuel and other expenses.

The other two-thirds would be paid at the successful conclusion of the trip. Naturally, next morning the driver and his offsider announced they'd spent all the money on vital repairs and needed more money for fuel. This was to be one of the recurring incidents of the trip.

The other recurring incident was punctures. Not far out of Shimla we had the first of many punctures and the rotten old spare was hauled out and put in place, where it promptly deflated. On-the-spot repairs were made to the original tire, which was pumped up so we could continue to a garage where the spare was also repaired. Looking at these tires I began to have severe misgivings. One glance at either tire in the West would have ruled this rickety old wagon off the road right away—they were so worn that the inner tube was showing through the canvas.

We spent the second night at Manali, right at the top of the Kullu Valley. I'd been in India for a couple of months by this time and, as usual, I was thoroughly fed up with the Indian predilection for triplicate form filling, boringly detailed documentation and silly questions. You don't simply fill in your name, address and credit card number on an Indian hotel registration form. They want your life story, including where your visa was issued, what date you arrived in India and lots of other pointless information. Pointless because you know that after a year or two of storage all these forms will be binned and end up as holy cow fodder. So, fed up as I was by the time I got to Manali, I wrote a work of fantasy on the form. I issued my visa in Rio de Janeiro, I chose a date of issue actually after my arrival date in India and I said my home address was Timbuktu.

Unfortunately, Manali was an important center for Indian marijuana production and very popular with visiting Western druggies, and the local authorities had recently staged a couple of spectacular drug busts on foreign visitors. My arrival, way out of season and with car and driver, had been noted. A day later, as I left town, we were stopped at a roadblock and pulled into an army checkpoint to be exhaustively examined. My bag was gone through item by item, which was of zero concern to me as I knew it didn't contain kilos of fine Kullu Valley hashish, only a few aspirin tablets. What did concern me was sitting on the table—in front of the officer in charge, and right next to my passport, was my totally fictitious hotel registration form with not a single detail coinciding with the reality in the passport. But naturally, India being India, nobody pondered that Rio de Janeiro might be a strange place for an Australian to apply for an Indian visa. Or that it was a little peculiar that I'd arrived in India several weeks before the date my visa was issued.

Eventually we were waved on our way to continue further episodes of the 'Hindustan Ambassador-en-route-to-oblivion' adventure. Down the valley in Kullu, I jumped out for twenty minutes more fact checking while my trusty crew went off for another session of tire repair. Two hours later, as I sat by the roadside chewing my nails, I questioned the wisdom of leaving my backpack and notes in the car with this pair of incompetents, but as usual they turned up and we carried on for another afternoon of harmless fun.

That night we arrived at Dharamsala, late on a Sunday evening. Could they have another cash advance, they asked, to add to the long list of cash advances for food, accommodation, fuel, tire repairs, cigarettes and general living expenses they'd already had?

'No,' I said. 'I've got barely enough to feed and shelter myself tonight, and there's no bank I can go to in Dharamsala on Sunday night, so forget it. I'll get cash tomorrow morning and give you more then.'

'But we'll starve, we'll have to sleep in the car,' they implored.

'Then starve and sleep in the car,' I heartlessly responded and left them to it.

Next morning they turned up on time, I handed more cash over, and we headed off for another round of punctures.

I think we were glad on both sides to part, when we finally arrived in Chandigarh. I'd completely lost interest in eating by this time, had shed pounds and was happy to board the plane home from New Delhi a few days later. Despite the hardships and hassles, I'd had a lot of fun and the new edition of India would be much improved and surprisingly comprehensive.

I didn't realize it at the time, but during this trip to India I had also done something which became a regular occurrence for several years. I died.

My first death, or at least the first place I heard about it, was in Puri, the seaside temple town in the state of Orissa. A group of us were sitting in our hotel's restaurant one evening when a couple said that a week earlier, in the south of India, they'd heard I'd been killed. I forget now how I met my end, I think it was in a train crash. We laughed it off, but a couple of weeks later, in a lakeside restaurant in Pushkar, another couple told me a similar story, except the nature of my death was completely different. Again I laughed it off, although hearing you've died once is odd and hearing about it twice is a truly remarkable coincidence.

I didn't die again during the rest of my stay in India, but when I got back to Australia letters started to arrive either asking if the rumor was true or recounting different versions of my death. Soon I was involved in buses hurtling into ravines in South America, ships going down off Indonesia, fatal motorcycle accidents in China, falling victim to deadly strains of malaria in Papua New Guinea and even losing in shootouts with the Mujaheddin in Afghanistan. The rumors became so widespread I eventually alerted my parents to ignore any tales of my death. One of our writers, working on the new edition of China, heard the tale with such certainty (the teller had met someone who had definitely read the account of my death in a newspaper) that he made a two-day trek back to Hong Kong to phone the office to check if the project would still continue without me around!

One day Maureen, talking to a friend on the phone about the latest version of the tale, was overheard by Tashi who asked, 'Mummy, has Daddy been in a car crash?'

'No, no,' joined in Kieran, 'he was in a cow crash, not a car crash.'

Mid-year, when I was in San Francisco, Roger Lascelles, our distributor in London, heard such a believable version of my death story that he phoned Maureen who, on this occasion, thought something might really have happened to me and called me in the middle of the night to check I really was alive.

Like Mark Twain, rumors of my death remained greatly exaggerated, but by far the funniest occurred in 1988 in a bookshop in Singapore. I'd wandered in to check our presence on the shelves and saw a woman holding a copy of *South-East Asia on a Shoestring*.

'I didn't buy it in Sweden because I was sure it would be cheaper when I got here,' she announced to her friend.

'Yes, it's a pity he's dead isn't it,' replied her Canadian companion.

Naturally I immediately scotched this rumor, but I thought afterwards they'd be able to go home and recount how they'd seen amazing temples in Burma, fantastic dances in Bali, beautiful beaches in Thailand . . . and a travel writer rise from the dead in a bookshop in Singapore.

I was still writing up my India research when we made a short family trip to the Cook Islands to fill in a gap on our Pacific map. Weird stories were appearing about a mishap in Chernobyl in the USSR on the morning we flew out of Melbourne. We all stayed on the main island of Rarotonga and made a trip north to the second island of Aitutaki. I also made short out-and-back trips from Rarotonga to other islands in the group. It was the perfect interlude to produce a pleasantly compact and practical little guidebook. The first laptop computers appeared around this time and I bought a brand-new Toshiba just before we went to the Cooks, making this the first time any of our writers had traveled with a computer.

We were only briefly back in Australia before I had to rush to the US on the fire-fighting trip which finally put our American operation on a long-term even keel. Our US sales were booming, the computer system was running smoothly and we had some good people working for us, but we had nobody to really run the show. Camille was great at managing the office, but asking her to manage Lonely Planet USA would have been far too much. Robert was great at setting things up and running special projects, but he wasn't the sort of person to manage things on a daily basis. Inevitably there had been clashes between Camille and Robert. Now Camille had quit and we needed a real manager.

Robert knew he wasn't cut out to manage the business; we'd taken him on as a consultant and that was where his expertise lay. Meanwhile he'd met Jim Hillis, an employee of Dalton's, the US bookshop chain, and thought he might be the right person for the job. I met with Jim and agreed, but first wanted to look further afield. We called in a corporate headhunter who lined up a number of potential candidates, none of whom clicked, so we appointed Jim as our new US manager.

During my month in the Bay Area I stayed near Berkeley university for part of the time (this was the summer vacation for the college) and out at Danville with our friends Sally and Boyd Roberts for the remainder. In between interviews and meetings I worked on the new edition of India and the new Cook Islands book.

The year 1986 was crunch time for post-war baby boomers, the year many of them, like me, turned forty. I'd scraped in to 1946 with eleven days to spare, so by the time mine rolled around at the end of 1986 I'd been to more fortieth birthdays than I cared to remember. Even surprise parties were becoming familiar events. I wasn't at all enthusiastic about joining the club, so when Maureen mentioned a celebration I poured cold water on the idea. Perhaps we'll have a nice meal out somewhere over the weekend, I suggested.

Nevertheless I was a little disappointed when Friday passed without any acknowledgment of the occasion. Lonely Planet was still small enough that we could make a fuss about every birthday and we joked that more artistic effort went into creating birthday cards than into our books. All through the day I half expected somebody to announce my birthday, with an interesting card or perhaps even a birthday cake. Nothing happened.

After work, as usual on a Friday night, a bunch of us retired to the nearby Cherry Tree pub for a few cold beers. The numbers dwindled and when we were down to the last half-dozen we all walked back to the office to lock up. I was entirely unprepared when I opened the door and stepped inside to see the room packed full of children, friends and workmates. I had been totally taken in and a photograph, taken the instant I stepped through the door, shows the shock on my face. Even more surprising was a diminutive birthday present peeking round the double doors from the office into the warehouse: a vintage Austin-Healey Sprite in shiny British Racing Green. Maureen had tracked down the classic little car, exactly like the one we'd owned in Sydney thirteen years earlier, and had taken it from place to place around Melbourne to have it overhauled, recarpeted, repainted and turned into a showpiece.

The mid- to late-1980s was also the culmination of Lonely Planet's era of colorful accountants. Very colorful accountants. In the early days when we'd needed an accountant we'd turned to other people in the same business for advice.

Outback Press lived above their accountant in the suburb of Collingwood. Ronald O'Riordan—let's call him that to protect the guilty—had a small practice, operating out of a Victorian-era building, and he rented the upstairs room to Morry Schwartz, Fred Milgrom, Colin Talbot and Mark Gillespie—the four young guys who had set up Outback Press.

I'd often drop round to Outback's office for publishing advice and when I needed an accountant Morry unhesitatingly suggested Ronald. He was the image of an accountant, with thick glasses, an intense stare, ink-stained fingers and a calculator on his desk; exactly what we needed. Indeed, for several years Ronald *was* exactly what we needed. He got the tax returns in on time, we never had any problems from the bank or the tax department, the bills were paid, our balance sheets and profit and loss looked fine. True, his sweet words and carefully tabulated figures may have failed to get me an American Express card, but overall we were happy with Ronald.

Jim joined us, Lonely Planet started to grow at a faster pace, the international side of our business became more and more important and we began to wonder if we had outgrown Ronald. Perhaps we needed something a little more muscular than a local small business accountant. The path to that decision was interrupted by a phone call one afternoon.

'Get a copy of the *Herald* and then find a new accountant,' said Morry.

'Surely this could not be our Ronald,' we thought as we read the newspaper story about jail breaks, helicopters, yachts to the Philippines and a small-time accountant. One of Ronald's clients, it seemed, had got himself involved in something highly illegal and ended up in Pent-ridge. Even heroin dealers need accountants I guess, so Ronald had been a regular visitor and, on his client's instructions, had chartered a helicopter and planned to get the villain out and to Sydney where a yacht was waiting to sail to the Philippines. Unfortunately, somebody had tipped the police off. The helicopter pilot's hotel room had been bugged and the incriminating conversation with Ronald was taped.

Ronald went to prison and we went in search of a new accountant. Let's call him Kevin Murphy to protect the guilty, guilty, guilty. Like Ronald, Kevin did a fine job for a spell, but when he went off the rails it was us, not him, who paid the penalty.

The first inkling that our second colorful accountant was about to drop us in the shit came with a dawn knock on the door and a notice being served on Maureen for not putting in a tax return. We were puzzled, but a phone call to Kevin cleared everything up.

'I was a little late getting the paperwork in,' he explained. 'You and Maureen were in the States and there were some details I had to check. Anyway, the tax department jumped the gun. Don't worry about it, everything's under control.'

Fine, we thought, until one month later there was another dawn knock on the door.

'This is a complete mystery,' Kevin responded. 'I simply cannot understand why it's happened again. I'll phone the tax department right away and straighten it all out.'

A month later there was another knock on the door, and this time I was also served with a notice to appear in court.

I phoned the tax department.

'I can't understand it,' I said. 'I'm told I have to appear in court for not putting in a tax return, but I've got the paperwork from the accountant in front of me. I've signed all the forms, I've paid him for putting the return in, there has to be some sort of mistake.'

'There's no mistake,' explained the voice from the tax department. 'You wouldn't believe how many people pay their accountants to do their tax returns and the accountant doesn't do it. You have not put in a tax return for the last two years.'

I made some enquiries and discovered that quiet little Kevin had got himself out on a financial limb. Unable to keep up with his expenditure he'd taken on too much work, billed customers for work he had not done and all in all caused a great deal of chaos. By this time he was not answering his phone and was not turning up at his office. One night I drove out to his home and parked by his driveway to wait for him. When he got out of his car I was standing on his doorstep, but despite his frightened promises that he definitely, absolutely, honestly, would sort it out that week, he didn't.

At this point I discovered that one of the clients consuming all Kevin's time and not leaving him with an opportunity to do the work he was billing people for was, believe it or not, the tax department. Yes, our weaselly little Kevin was appearing as an expert witness for the tax department.

We switched accountants to Coopers & Lybrand—big, safe, boring and the purveyors of various bits of not-always-ideal advice in the following years—and spent a great deal of money re-creating our last two years' financial records, doing our tax returns again, paying the fines for not putting them in and making no claim at all against the useless Kevin.

'It's not worth chasing him,' recommended Coopers & Lybrand. 'He could cause you more trouble and expense than you'll ever get back from him.'

Children certainly hadn't stopped us traveling. Tashi had her first trip around Southeast Asia when she was less than a year old and by her first birthday could claim she'd been to four continents—Australia, Asia, Europe and North America. Kieran did even better, since we took him to Bali when he was four months old and before his first birthday he'd also been to Nepal, India and Sri Lanka. Then we moved the whole family to the US, took them to South America and made several stops with them in Asia before arriving back in Australia. Travel with very young kids had been tough, but when we set off for Mexico between Christmas and New Year 1986 Tashi was six years old, Kieran was nearly four and things were much easier.

We'd had a Mexico guide since 1982, but it was a slim and rather idiosyncratic book, a reflection of its equally idiosyncratic author, Doug Richmond, a Californian who would have been a clear contender in any Ernest Hemingway look-alike contest. A falling out with Doug prompted the development of a major new Mexico guide, something more in line with the size and scope of the country. We lined up three experienced writers and Maureen and I decided to have a look around at the same time, and perhaps contribute some ideas and suggestions.

We spent New Year's Eve 1986 at a LAX airport hotel and on January 1 1987 we arrived in Cancún. We rented a car, a VW Beetle of course, at the airport and set off straight down the coast and straight into a big problem. Everything was full. I was still philosophically opposed to booking things, but those first couple of days in Mexico turned me around, especially because we were traveling with our kids. Maureen and I had done a tourist Spanish course before we left Australia, but by late that evening we were very familiar with the word *completo*, 'no rooms available'. Eventually we did find a room in a very pleasant beachside place, but for one night only.

The next morning we went straight back to Cancún and checked into a hotel where everybody else seemed to be on a Canadian package tour. By the time we set out again a few days later we had hotels pre-booked and the kids had become experts on the pleasures of swim-up bars. We arrived in the ancient Mayan city of Cobá to discover our reservations had not gone through and, surprise, surprise, the hotel was full. Eventually we found a room in a run-down fleapit, but that was the end of our Mexican problems. The rest of the trip was wonderful, and we stayed in everything from beautiful resorts to historic old hotels looking out over the town center *zocalos*.

Our month included a circuit of the main Mayan sites in the Yucatán along with visits to San Cristobal de las Casas, Oaxaca, Acapulco and finally Mexico City. Kieran had developed a consuming passion for the television cartoon series *Masters of the Universe*. To his delight he discovered that the toy figures from the series were made in Mexico and were on sale everywhere. To our delight they were much cheaper than back home. We bought him a few, but we left Mexico with a large collection hidden away in a ceramic pot, ready for his birthday when we got home. We weren't far behind him in the shopping stakes and when we arrived in San Francisco we had to move up to a bigger rent-a-car, the first car's trunk being too small to swallow all our purchases.

We'd met up with Dan Spitzer and John Noble, two of the three writers on the book, while we were in Mexico and of course I couldn't resist making some additions, but my contribution to this rewrite was minor. The end result was a huge improvement on the earlier editions: the second edition was only 256 pages long, the new edition was 944 pages and in subsequent years has become the most popular guidebook to the country and one of our best-selling titles in the American market.

I played a bigger part with the new edition of New Zealand later in the year. I'd written the first edition back in 1976, but had not been involved in editions two through four. New Zealander Simon Hayman had done a solid, workmanlike job on two and three and Mary Covernton, at that time a Lonely Planet editor, had handled edition four, but overall the book had not enjoyed the time and effort it deserved. In 1986 we had stopped for a few days in Auckland en route to the Cook Islands and I had been very disappointed with the book. It was time for a major rewrite and, as so often seems to happen, we made the decision just in time. Our New Zealand guide had been selling very comfortably, but the country was on the brink of a tourist boom (bungy jumping was about to become a worldwide craze) and we were about to face real competition from other guides.

I did a fast but thorough circuit of the North and South islands then flew back to Australia from Christchurch. We were still years away from flying anything other than economy, but the Qantas staff tagged my bag for priority handling and the flight crew moved me up to the sharp end of the plane because I had to get into Melbourne quickly that evening. Maureen and I were becoming Australian citizens.

There had been interruptions of over a year in Southeast Asia and in San Francisco, and regularly we were away for months on end, but there was no question that Australia was now home. We'd been in the country for nearly fifteen years, both our children had been born there and we'd lived in the same house in Richmond for over ten years. That alone was a serious commitment; until then, I'd never in my life lived in the same place for much over two years. Plus, Australia had been good to us. We never forgot that when we arrived in Sydney in late 1972 we had just twenty-seven cents between us. Now we had a business known all over the world, our books were on sale in almost every country we visited, and my informal aircraft surveys (walking down the aisle to see what people were reading) always turned up a few Lonely Planet guides. We may have been far smaller, but Qantas and Foster's were probably the only other Australian brand names which reached as many corners of the earth as we did.

It was an indication of how Australia was changing that Maureen and I were the only Anglo-Saxons stepping forward that night at the Richmond town hall. A few years earlier in Richmond, the most Greek suburb of the third largest Greek city on earth (only Athens and Thessaloniki have more Greeks than Melbourne), it would probably have been Greeks who predominated, but now they too were in the minority. Most of our fellow 'new Australians' were Vietnamese.

A few weeks later I was back in New Zealand, this time with Maureen and the kids, and we decided to travel by campervan (kiwi-speak for an RV). Lots of people get around New Zealand in this fashion so we thought it might be fun to try it, especially with the children. We picked up our campervan in Christchurch and set out on a circuit of the middle part of the South Island, including the west coast and its magnificent glaciers. The weather was not the best and I don't think Maureen would deny that she is not a fan of kiwiland, but we boated along the river in Christchurch, went walking at Mt Cook, had a great time at Queenstown, took a helicopter to the Fox Glacier and generally tried out everything going.

New Zealand was a place where I felt quite confident about picking up hitch-hikers and while working on the book I picked up dozens of them on both islands. They often realized who I was and filled me in on places they'd discovered. I even made a little statistical analysis of what nationalities I came across most often.

Having Maureen and the kids on board didn't shut out the hitch-hikers, since our campervan had plenty of room in the back and the kids were delighted to have a constantly changing circle of young travel companions. Driving out of Wanaka, a notorious dead end for hitch-hikers, we swept the road clean, picking up all the young people marooned on the edge of town. One young Englishman we picked up day after day, moving him by stages up the west coast.

Once again, it was a case of doing the right thing at the right time. My minimalist first New Zealand guide had just 112 pages and sold 10 000 copies, but the new (fifth) edition grew to 352 pages and sold 70 000 copies. Since then, tourism in New Zealand has boomed and so has our book. We struggle to keep it at 700 pages (I joked at one stage that for a country of only four million people our New Zealand guide had enough pages to list every person who lived there by name) and the sales now top 100 000 each edition. In 2003 and 2004, with *Lord of the Rings* mania sweeping the world, our New Zealand guide was often our top-selling title.

There were many trips in 1987. I'd always been a keen snorkeler, but had never learned to scuba dive, so I took a course in Melbourne that May, just as Australia moved into winter. It had taken me so long to acquire this useful skill that doing it in winter hardly seemed to matter. Having collected my scuba-diving ticket, writing a guide to Australia's Great Barrier Reef seemed an obvious move. We started visiting the Reef islands and resorts that year but it turned out to be an incredibly long-winded project. It took me two years to visit them all.

We also managed an outback trip, driving up to Ayers Rock and Alice Springs during the August school vacation, enjoying the newly sealed road. Leaving the Red Centre we put the car on the Ghan, the train named after the Afghans who used to run camels through the Australian outback before roads and railways arrived, and arrived back in Adelaide next morning. That night we drove to Melbourne, the kids asleep in the back seat and the Australian election results coming in on the radio. Bob Hawke was re-elected as prime minister.

I traveled to Frankfurt for the bookfair and to Hong Kong, Macau and the Philippines, working on the next edition of Southeast Asia. In January the whole family went to Bali and then Java for more work on that long-running guidebook. At the end of the month Maureen, Tashi and Kieran flew back to Australia for the start of the school year, while I carried on to Lombok and then north to Sumatra. Today, with phone offices everywhere, Internet cafés in every resort and cell phones in most daypacks, it's easy to forget how far international communications have come in the past twenty years. Of course they'd already come a long way by 1988—only ten years earlier making a phone call from many centers in Asia could involve all-night waits in phone offices and impossible reception when (and if) you did get through.

I'd phoned Maureen from Bali the morning she'd arrived back in Australia, to check they'd all got back ok. Then I was out of touch for ten days until I managed to get through from a phone box in the Sumatran port of Padang.

I sensed something was wrong almost as soon as Maureen answered.

'Tony,' she said, 'I've got bad news.'

Those seconds of horrified disbelief are still hardwired into my mind. Disbelief followed by relief (it wasn't the kids) and guilty shock (it was my brother). How could I feel both relief and such sadness at the same time? Patrick was only thirty-seven, four years younger than me, and he'd dropped dead from a heart attack, leaving his two sons, Gavin just six years old and Owen only four. My parents, vacationing in Australia at the time, had flown straight back to Britain and then spent a week trying to get in touch with me, hoping that I could make it to the funeral. But now it was too late, it was all over. I probably should have flown straight home, but there was nothing I could do so I carried on in a daze.

A month later, back in Australia, the phone rang again, and this time the tragedy was for Maureen. Her sister Lynne, three years younger than her, had died in a senseless, pointless accident. In many ways 1988 had not been a good year.

The next year started with our first African trip and led to another new title. We flew to Perth and stayed for a few days with our friends Mike and Burkie Eustace and then continued to Harare in Zimbabwe and on to Nairobi in Kenya. In Nairobi we stayed at the New Stanley Hotel, famed for its Thorn Tree Café and noticeboard. Ten years later, the Thorn Tree travel forum would become the most popular area of the Lonely Planet website.

From Nairobi we made a series of safari trips to see the wildlife, experimenting, in typical Lonely Planet fashion, with every type of safari possible. We started with a low-budget camping trip. As we were setting up camp in the Masai Mara Park we noticed our crew didn't seem to be in any hurry to get their own tents up.

'We're going to sleep in the van tonight,' they explained nonchalantly.

'But it'll be hot and uncomfortable and you've not slept in it before,' we said. 'What's different about this camp site?'

Eventually we squeezed an explanation out of them.

'There's a rogue elephant which hangs around here,' they confessed. 'Sometimes it comes into the camp looking for food. One time the cook had some pineapples in his tent, and the elephant picked up the whole tent, with the cook in it, and shook it to get the pineapples to fall out. When they didn't fall out, the elephant put the tent, cook and pineapples into a tree. Since then, the cook won't stay in a tent at this site.'

'It even broke in the back window of the van to get at food inside,' continued the driver.

'It's a really big elephant too,' said the guide.

'Like that one?' asked Maureen as a large elephant loomed out of the darkness around our campfire.

'Run,' yelled the guide, quite unnecessarily, as we scattered in all directions.

The driver chased the troublesome intruder off with the van and eventually the camp settled down.

African nights are always noisy with grunts, yowls and howls coming from all directions, but that night brought some quite unexpected sounds. First there was the noise of grass being pulled up and consumed, so close that it almost felt like it was being ripped out from underneath us. Then there was a loud and prolonged slurping noise from near the campfire.

'What on earth is that?' whispered Maureen.

I puzzled over the strange noise for a few moments. 'It's the dishwashing water,' I said. 'They must have left the used water in that big metal bowl and the elephant's drinking it.'

The pans and cooking utensils, cutlery and metal cups and dishes were all stored in a tin trunk and with a jangling crash we heard the elephant pick up the container and shake it vigorously. Finally, disappointed in its search for food, we heard it moving off into the night.

We followed the camping trip with a stay in a luxurious game lodge overlooking a waterhole and tried a more up-market safari staying at a 'fixed camp'. Finally we rented a car and put together our own safari trip, including the flamingos on Lake Nakuru (remember the opening scene in *Out of Africa*? That was where it was filmed) and on to Lake Baringo with its lakeside game lodge, resident hippos and rich birdlife. We visited Mombasa, traveled across the country by train and rented a house for a few days in the exotic old island-city of Lamu. Even Kieran, our less than enthusiastic six-year-old son, began to realize that travel could have its compensations. Finally it was back to Zimbabwe and quick trips to Victoria Falls and the amazing ancient city of Great Zimbabwe, the most impressive site in sub-Saharan Africa.

Our East Africa book was fine, but lots of visitors spent their whole time in Kenya so for them the Tanzania and Uganda sections were redundant. We decided to do a separate Kenya guide.

Driving through Zimbabwe and Botswana a few years later we became adept at reading the footprint and tire-track stories on the dirt roads. One time, another Land Rover left the camp ten minutes before us, and following its path we saw elephant tracks trampling across the tire tracks. An elephant must have crossed the road in the last few minutes. Sure enough, round the next corner we were confronted by an angry elephant, ears flaring out and trunk raised, its offspring tromping quickly away into the undergrowth. We waited until the watchful guardian had cleared off, but when I looked back in my door mirror there it was, like in the scene from *Jurassic Park*, materializing under the words 'objects in mirror are closer than they appear'.

Baby elephants are always great to see, whether it's at an orphanage or in the wild. At the Pinnewala Elephant Orphanage in Sri Lanka some of the orphaned animals were no taller than our three-year-old daughter when we visited in the early 1980s. Years later, from a hilltop lookout in Zimbabwe, we watched a herd moving down to the lakeside for a drink. One particularly energetic baby elephant was clearly excited by everything it saw, running ahead to get down to the water only to be brought back to the circle by its mother. Only minutes later it would spot a waterbird stalking along the bank of the lake and rush over to have a look; this time an elephant 'aunt' steered the runaway back to the herd, a protective trunk draped over the little elephant's back.

I've become used to seeing elephants in unusual places. I once saw one marching through the vegetable market in Kathmandu, casually scoffing up a cabbage from one side of the road and a basket of lettuces from the other while irate stallholders complained bitterly.

Of course, some of the most annoying wildlife is on the small size, particularly what we call 'hotel wildlife'. When we published the first edition of *South-East Asia on a Shoestring* there were still many small old-style Chinese hotels in Singapore. They were often quite charming places with big, spacious, sparsely furnished rooms, ceiling fans whisking smoothly round and verandas hanging over the street. The bathrooms were generally shared and the toilets were often Asian squat-style, but the better examples of these old hotels were spotlessly clean and surprisingly stylish. Today they've almost all fallen to the wrecker's ball as Singapore's relentless redevelopment mows down all the old buildings. New hotels in the city are multi-storey, air-conditioned and as modern as tomorrow. For penniless backpackers, like we were on that first visit, the choice is usually a characterless hostel made from a converted apartment with rows of bunk beds stuffed into each room.

Not all the old Chinese hotels were as well kept as they should have been, however, and soon after that first Southeast Asia guide appeared we got letters complaining that one establishment on Bencoolen Street, in subsequent years the center for backpacker hostels, was plagued by mice. We duly reported this small problem in the next edition and instantly letters arrived disputing my account.

'No, no,' wrote one disgruntled Singapore visitor, 'it's not the Hotel Tai Chi which suffers from the mice problem, it's the Hotel Chow Mein next door.'

No sooner had we identified the Chow Mein as mice central, however, than the problem seemed to move to the Hotel Gin Sling.

On my next visit to Singapore I made a concerted effort to assess the situation, staying in each hotel and sitting up in bed until late at night waiting for the mice to come streaming across the floor. They didn't. On my final night a single mouse made a timid appearance, but as for plagues of rodents-of-unusual-size, forget it.

Nevertheless the letters complaining about rodent infestations continued to arrive, topped by one from an intrepid woman who reported that her hotel was positively teeming with overly energetic mice.

'They played hopscotch across my bed,' she wrote. 'They used my pillow as a trampoline! But the worst thing was that the hotel completely denied their existence.'

Quite why she didn't shift to another hotel was unclear, but this was obviously not the sort of traveler who let acrobatic rodents scare her. Or perhaps she simply wanted to make the hotel manager eat his words.

'One night I managed to trap one,' she went on. 'I caught it in a box and next morning I marched up to the reception desk and whipped the lid off.'

'The manager looked at the mouse disdainfully,' she said, 'and announced, "well it is a mouse, but it isn't one of ours".'

A Kathmandu restaurant waiter was rather more honest when a visiting rodent was pointed out to him by a customer.

'That's not a mouse,' he explained, 'that's a rat.'

Cockroaches are, of course, the other renowned hotel wildlife. New York hotels of a certain style always have them, but Big Apple cockroaches are miserable specimens, flyweights compared to the Asian heavyweight contenders. There's a simple test to determine if a cockroach is the real thing: jump on it. If, after you've applied your full weight, concentrated on one foot and from at least a foot above floor level, the cockroach reels back slightly stunned, shakes three legs on one side and then three legs on the other, before continuing about its business, you know you've met a real cockroach. A messy brown carcass lying dead and squashed on the floor is just a bug.

We've seen our share of these ugly critters over the years, including one in the infamous Rex and Stiffles Hotels in Bombay (the two hotels shared the same building). A scream from the bathroom announced that Maureen had picked up the toilet roll and a cockroach lurking in the center tube had sprinted out, run across her hand, up her arm and down her back.

My most memorable cockroach encounter took place in Shanghai, at an airport restaurant. While we waited for our flight to Guilin we grabbed a meal. Three of us ordered noodles while Kieran, ever the optimist, decided to see what they could do with the concept of a hamburger. About halfway down my bowl I fished in with my chopsticks and brought out something large, brown, dead and six-legged.

I can remember quite clearly what I said about this unwanted ingredient in my dish: 'Urgh.' Quite loudly. Loudly enough to bring several of the restaurant staff running over to our table.

The cockroach was inspected, my bowl was removed and a long huddled discussion took place. More restaurant staff came and joined in what was clearly turning into a heated argument.

'I know what they're discussing,' I said to Maureen.

By this time we had been in China long enough to become uncomfortably familiar with the local propensity for overcharging foreigners at every opportunity.

'They're trying to decide if they can charge us extra for the cockroach,' I surmised.

Slapping on a supplement for extra 'protein' turned out to be even beyond the usually highly flexible rules for 'cutting the fat off foreigners', as the overpricing practice was known in China. We got a refund for my bowl of noodles and Maureen and Tashi lost all interest in continuing with their possibly cockroach-free meals. Kieran's hamburger had turned out to be the wise choice.

We finished the Great Barrier Reef book in 1989. Research for this guide had involved a combination of trips by myself (including a very interesting boat trip to Australia's remote northern tip at Cape York and to Thursday Island in the Torres Strait between Australia and Papua New Guinea), trips with the whole family and trips for just Maureen and me, including one to the very romantic Orpheus and Bedarra islands. In a small 'tinny', an aluminum dinghy with a small outboard motor, Maureen and I were motoring back to the Orpheus Island resort one afternoon when two dolphins, a mother and a young one, popped up beside us. We stopped, they stopped. We started again, so did they. We went round in a circle, they circled around us. For half an hour we played games, before they cruised off and we hurried back for dinner.

There are so many opportunities for dolphin encounters. I've often been on boats where they've joined in that favorite dolphin game of ride-the-bow-wave. At Rangiroa, the shark-diving capital of French Polynesia, a small group of us went out to follow the dolphins as they surfed the incoming tide racing through the Tiputa Pass, one of the narrow channels leading into the atoll's vast lagoon. As we powered in from the ocean side through the pass to the calm lagoon a half-dozen dolphins leapt and swirled in our bow wave as we excitedly leant over the bow, almost touching the dolphins' dorsal fins.

'That was fun,' we cheered as we slowed in the lagoon. 'Let's see if they want to do it again.'

We motored back out to the ocean side, turned round and headed in to the lagoon. Instantly the dolphins appeared at the bow, leaping and jumping like big show-offs. 'Again,' we demanded, so out we rushed again, and once more the dolphins were there, ready to repeat the game.

In October 1989 we took the kids on their first trek in Nepal, a short three-night walk out of Pokhara. Kieran was still only six years old, but any time he showed signs of flagging one of the young Sherpas, instantly dubbed 'big friend', took his hand and off they'd march. On occasion he'd be lifted onto the Sherpa's shoulders, but most of the time the children arrived in camp with more energy than us. One afternoon they also arrived with a pet chicken, but didn't seem particularly surprised or upset when it turned up fried with rice later that evening. The trip was to be the inspiration for a much longer walk with a much larger cast of characters a few years later.

Unhappily just as 1988 had started with family tragedies so did

1989 end with one. This time when the phone rang it was Maureen's brother in Ireland, to say their mother had died.

Apart from family heartbreaks the second half of the 1980s had been, for us, a comparatively quiet time. The business had achieved some sort of stability and we were feeling quite comfortable as well. In 1984–85, the year Maureen and I spent in America, sales were just short of A$1 million and our list of titles had grown to thirty-three. The following year all that hard work breaking into the American market really paid off. The list had grown by a third, but our sales grew a hundred per cent and for the first time we made a real, write-home-about-it profit. From $40 000 in 1984–85 our profits zoomed to more than half a million the following year. Sales continued to climb steeply to nearly $7 million in 1989–90 by which time we had more than eighty titles in print. Five years later our sales would be heading towards $20 million.

Our new office had felt wonderfully spacious in 1986, but within a remarkably short period of time it was even more crowded than its predecessor. It had taken us five years to go from five people to fifteen, but suddenly we had twenty-five, then thirty-five and then forty-five staff. We rented a house round the corner from our office and moved a half-dozen people in there while we frantically hunted for a new place. Melbourne was going through one of its periodic real-estate booms and 1988 turned out to be a terrible time to move. Eventually we bought into a new purpose-built office and warehouse complex in nearby Hawthorn. Over the next ten years we steadily expanded until we owned or rented almost the whole complex. By the time we made our next office move our Australian numbers had expanded to 300 and there were another 200 Lonely Planeteers in our overseas offices.

As our numbers grew we inevitably lost some enjoyable 'small company' activities. Once upon a time we could shut the whole office down at lunchtime and get everybody around a table at the local pub. Once upon a time every birthday was celebrated with a cake and card. Once upon a time we had regular formal presentations of the 'moving your car' teapot. Let me explain that last one.

'I'm going to move my car,' a new bookkeeper once announced. She had been our first step towards having a real accountant on staff, and on the Friday morning of her inaugural week with us she had to shift her car, which was parked in a two-hour zone outside our office. She never came back.

She wrote and explained that our bookkeeping was a mess and she would never have accepted the job if she'd realized how bad it was. Somehow this dramatic departure was commemorated with a teapot which, for a couple of years, was ceremonially presented to every new employee after they'd survived one week without 'moving their car'.

In early 1990, just twelve months before the Kuwait version of the Gulf War, we made our first trip to the Middle East. It was a trip where preconceptions were knocked over even before we arrived at our destination. We flew from Singapore to Amman in Jordan with Royal Jordanian Airlines and as the DC10 leveled out over Malaysia the captain came on the intercom to brief us on the flight ahead. It was a woman.

'So this is how it's going to be,' I thought. 'In the Arab world women can't drive cars, but they can fly wide-bodied jets.'

There were more wake-up calls as the trip went along. The Arabs were calm, polite, well mannered and honest; the Israelis were pushy and aggressive, and the taxi drivers had to be watched carefully. The trip started with a circuit of Jordan and continued across the Allenby Bridge to the West Bank and Jerusalem, where the first intifada was still under way. From Tel Aviv we drove along the Dead Sea to Eilat, then crossed into the Sinai and Egypt.

We visited St Catherine's Monastery, climbed Mt Sinai (no sign of any commandments) and paused at Dahab (still developing as the major Sinai backpacker center). I did some Red Sea scuba diving from the southern Sinai town of Sharm el-Sheikh and we continued to Cairo, up the Nile to Luxor and Aswan before returning to Cairo and making a final side trip to Alexandria.

Although Lonely Planet had many regular writers by this stage I still enjoyed working on guidebooks myself, and my big project in 1990 remains one of my favorites. We decided to rewrite our Japan book and I joined two talented linguists, both much better qualified to write about the country.

Robert Strauss, who had worked on our China and Tibet guides and seemed to pick up languages effortlessly, would cover Hokkaido and the north-east of the main island, Honshu. Chris Taylor, who had originally joined us as an editor and had lived in Japan and spoke Japanese and Chinese, would write most of the rest of Honshu. Despite my near total failure as a linguist, I held up my hand to be the third writer and ended up covering the western end of Honshu, the two smaller western islands Shikkoku and Kyushu, and the dribble of tiny islands that spill down to Okinawa and on towards Taiwan. My presence on the team wasn't a totally thoughtless decision. After all, few visitors to Japan are conversant with the language, so sending someone who was flummoxed by Japanese was probably a good idea.

Maureen and the children came along on the first leg where we rented a car out of Kyoto and drove west along the north coast of Honshu. We stayed in traditional *ryokans* (fancy Japanese-style bed and breakfast places) and *minshuku* (less fancy versions) where Tashi and Kieran soon got used to sleeping on the floor and hopping into the bath with the whole family. 'Ryokan dogs', well-behaved, compact creatures whose always-clean little paws had never ventured beyond tatami mats, were a firm favorite with our children.

When Maureen and the kids flew home from Fukuoka I carried on alone. I visited Nagasaki and Hiroshima, walked mountain trails, climbed volcanoes, soaked in traditional baths, was buried up to my neck in a thermal sand bath, sat through interminable traffic jams and sped along deserted mountain roads. I stayed in everything from business hotels to capsule hotels and a night (solo, I hasten to add) in a love hotel. I had a great time.

In August I was back for my second circuit. We'd just completed our end-of-year financial figures and for the first time our profit had topped one million dollars. In the days before my departure the papers had been full of stories about Japanese breweries investing in Carlton & United Breweries (CUB). When my flight landed in Tokyo I edged forward from economy in time to see John Elliott, head of Elders IXL which owned CUB, emerging from first class, followed by a posse of executives.

'So, I've made a million and fly economy and they're looking for a multi-million bailout from Asahi and fly first class,' I thought.

This time I started my travels by scaling Mt Fuji, along with thousands of predominantly Japanese climbers. August is the peak of the Fuji season and it's traditional to start the ascent late at night and climb through the night to arrive at the summit for an icy sunrise.

There were more towns to visit in Honshu before I explored the islands of the Inland Sea by ferry, made a circuit of Shikkoku by bus and train and finally flew down to Okinawa. From Okinawa I island-hopped to the southern end of this almost tropical chain of islands, then flew to Hong Kong and back home.

The new edition of Japan was a big and complex book, completely rewritten and with a huge number of extremely detailed maps. I was very pleased with it.

The following year I made a trip which convinced me that my relationship with *South-East Asia on a Shoestring* had to change. I had felt so inextricably tied to the book that even when it became so big that a whole team of writers was needed, I still wanted to be involved. Other writers did the real country-by-country work, but with each edition I made a trip right through the region: I was the unifying voice that pulled the whole book together. I'd planned to persevere through to edition ten, until a trip to Timor convinced me otherwise.

Earlier in the year the whole family had been in Bali, but it was not one of our favorite visits. The weather was consistently wet and miserable and for once the island seemed to be overwhelmed by the number of tourists. In March I returned to Asia to work on the seventh consecutive edition of 'the yellow bible' and I realized I was in serious danger of burning out.

Flying from Bali to Timor I took the wrong flight (nobody checked my boarding pass) and ended up in Kupang (West Timor) rather than Dili (East Timor). That night in Kupang I decided I'd had enough of Southeast Asia. The next morning, waiting for the damned Merpati flight to Dili, I knew it was time to make some changes. This would be my last complete circuit of Southeast Asia and 'furthermore', I jotted in my notebook, 'I'm too old. I don't want to stay in the really cheap places—I'll stay in cheapies with character, but otherwise I've had it with the rock-bottom places. I'm too old for the travelers there, too.'

That spell in Bali and Indonesia was overlaid by a greater unease. In mid-January 1991, on a Kuta Beach bar television, I watched the first air strikes on Iraq—the Gulf War kick-off. I remember being profoundly depressed by the whole miserable affair and in the following weeks I scribbled notes about how I hated 'the gung-ho jingoism, the endless hype about cruise missiles flying straight through windows'. Sure Saddam was a lousy, cruel, greedy, mindless dictator, but we were defending Kuwait, a slack, fat, lazy, corrupt, boys' club where, after it was all over, the slug-like Emir wouldn't even come back to his palace until the air-conditioning had been reconnected and the water was flowing properly. Even British Prime Minister John Major had dropped in to see his troops before the Emir deigned to return. We were also defending Saudi Arabia, a place where they're so ashamed of the nepotistic little Islamic paradise they've created that they keep the doors firmly shut to ensure nobody gets in to see what they've done.

Our own greed came into it as well. Would we have been rushing to defend everything that was right if right didn't hold the keys to the oil wells? I doubted it in 1991 and in 2003 I was even more doubtful.

In February, I walked the Overland Track from Cradle Mountain to Lake St Clair in Tasmania with four friends. It's a beautiful, wild and rugged walk, made even finer on that occasion by a week of flawlessly benign weather in a region famous for weather as ruggedly uncomfortable as the terrain. It was wonderful, but all the time the Gulf War hovered in the background, creating a feeling of unease that would persist until the one-sided farce ground to a halt. It would be ten years later, when two aircraft slammed into the World Trade Center in New York, before I would feel so utterly disheartened again.

7

First Europe, then America

Lonely Planet started in Australia in 1973, if you date it from our first book, or in 1975, if you date it from when it became a full-time occupation. In 1984 we opened our office in the San Francisco Bay Area. In the 1990s we moved into Europe.

By 1990 we'd been selling books in Britain for fifteen years. Our British distributor, Roger Lascelles, was an Englishman's Englishman (except he was a New Zealander). Roger had a decidedly militaristic bent—selling books was always a case of 'getting his men out in the field', although that tended to shift from the army to the navy once you were on the road. After driving from London to Frankfurt with Roger one year Jim commented how, 'once we were on the autobahn it was "both engines, full speed ahead".'

Roger also published books and maps, distributed for a small list of travel publishers, had a few useful import lines and was adept at picking up travel remainders. When the *Daily Telegraph* decided to drop their range of maps, for example, Roger bought up the lot. He had an affinity with 'Arfur Daley' from the British television series *Minder*.

We began to worry that we would soon outgrow Roger. We did a circuit of other publishers and distributors, but at the time decided to stick with Roger. 'His men' carried on their front-line duties, but the writing was on the wall and the person putting it there was Charlotte

Hindle.

Charlotte was English, and after finishing university had traveled across Asia, pretty much like Maureen and I had fifteen years earlier. She'd turned up in Australia, talked herself into a job at Lonely Planet and then, a few years later, convinced us we should open an office in London and let her run it. In 1991 Charlotte started Lonely Planet UK in an empty room above the Brentford warehouse where Roger was also located. That was a temporary home until we shifted to a slightly larger upstairs room in Chiswick, conveniently situated between Heathrow Airport and the center of London.

We shifted our distribution to the very efficient and enthusiastic (although appallingly named) World Leisure Marketing. Our UK office handled not only British, but also European, African and Middle East sales and soon our already healthy regional sales were growing faster and faster. Jim was heavily involved in setting up the UK operation, even migrating our home-grown accounting software package to the London office. We were in Europe, with an office, before we really got into Europe with our books.

We'd covered much of Asia, Australia and the Pacific, Africa and South America. We'd even done the odd book on North America, but Europe remained untouched. Should we start, we wondered, as we had in Asia, Africa and South America, with a continent-wide guide and then break it down into individual country books later on? Or should we start with the country guides and put them together as a whole continent guide?

By this time, our wider and narrower guides, in a geographical sense, were very much interrelated. We often researched both simultaneously, condensing the country guides to produce the continental guides. So we might do a 240-page Sydney guide, for example, while the city got ninety pages in our New South Wales guide, sixty pages in our Australia guide and would be squeezed further for our combined Australia and New Zealand shoestring guide. Of course, we wouldn't simply write up Sydney and then do repeat *Reader's Digest* efforts on the original. City guides are approached in a quite different fashion from country guides, with more emphasis on things like nightlife and shopping. Sometimes the same place in one book might be updated on even years, another on odd, but there are still savings to be made.

We started to think seriously about European titles in 1987, but it was 1993 before we launched our Europe series. By then we had a Europe book on the shelves and, with typically lucky timing, it was the right title at the right time, although it was also instantly out of date. Our author, David Stanley, was best known for his classic *South Pacific Handbook*, by Moon Publications. He was an experienced travel writer and a long-time friend, although he had never written for Lonely Planet. In 1987, David said he would like to write an Eastern Europe guide. We were more than happy to work with him and keen to dabble a toe in European waters, no matter at which end of the pool, but we had no idea the end product would emerge at such a historically critical time.

We were so interested in the project that Maureen and I edited the book ourselves. *Eastern Europe on a Shoestring* hit the shelves in April 1989 and almost immediately began to exceed our sales expectations because the whole world's attention was focused on the turmoil developing in the region and, true to form, we had the most up-to-date guidebook on the market.

In May 1989, the Iron Curtain started to rust away in Hungary and in November 1989 the Berlin Wall fell over and Eastern Europe was a whole new ball game. Sales of our book went through the roof, but it was also embarrassingly, well, wrong. David had bent over backwards to be understanding, even apologetic, for the Communist regimes and now that was all ancient history. The next edition of *Eastern Europe on a Shoestring* had to go through some major historical revisionism, quite apart from all the street names which had to be changed on the maps. We would hit even worse problems two years later when our USSR guide was published just as the very name of the country ceased to exist.

Finally, in May 1990, we made the critical decision to charge full speed into Europe, working to a plan devised by Richard Everist, who had joined the company as an editor and also looked after publicity, and was beginning to take over my publishing role. We would produce a series of regional Europe guides, dividing Europe into Eastern, Western, Mediterranean and Scandinavian regions, some of them overlapping.

There were two major factors in this decision: our customers and our competition. We felt that few people were going to combine Turkey (Med Europe) and Britain (Western Europe) in the same trip. Or Norway (Scandinavian Europe) with Morocco (Med Europe). On the other hand, Spain and Morocco did go together (so we put both in Med Europe), but so did Spain and Britain (so both were in Western Europe). The competitive reason was that we simply did not believe we could cram as many countries into the same space as *Let's Go Europe*, the market leader at the time. We'd made our name on the number of maps our books featured so, for that reason alone, we needed more space to cover a given country. Furthermore, our books weren't exclusively aimed at student travelers—we catered for a wider range of budgets in our hotel and restaurant listings.

Producing subsequent editions of a book is faster than a first edition; you don't have to rewrite the history from the birth of man, and you don't have to redraw every map from scratch. We would be competing with guidebooks that were well established and often came out in new editions every year, so it was imperative that we produce books which were absolutely up to date. The only solution, we concluded, was to do them twice. We would go to Europe in 1991 and research the new books, write and edit them, draw the maps, get them almost ready to go to the printer, but not actually print them. In 1992 our writers would return to Europe, each with a prototype guide in hand, and update that guide for production later in the year and publication at the beginning of 1993. The first editions which emerged would in reality be second editions with, hopefully, all the first edition problems ironed out.

During 1990 we worked out how much space we would allocate to each country and what maps we would need to draw. Then we lined up the writers, a blend of proven and experienced Lonely Planet authors and fresh new faces. Europe is a very seasonal destination. In some places in the world it doesn't matter what time of year you go. It's often said that Thailand has two seasons, the wet season and the wetter season; in Australia, summer is too hot in the north and just right in the south, while winter is too cold in the south but just right in the north. Apart from skiing and other winter sports, Europe, however, is essentially a northern summer destination. This complicates researching guidebooks to the region because it's no good arriving in Ireland in March, for example, since many places close for the winter. Don't even think of researching northern Scandinavia at that time of year either—the roads will still be snowed in. Fortunately, for our first round of research, we didn't have to actually print the books, giving us a little extra time. Longer term, however, we knew these seasonal constraints would cause problems. If we started research too early in the season many summertime activities would not be open, but if it was left too late we wouldn't have books to sell at the beginning of the next year.

I wanted to lend a hand since this was such an important new project so I took on writing the Ireland chapter for *Western Europe on a Shoestring*. In July 1991, with Maureen and the children, I flew into Dublin, picked up a rent-a-car and set out on two circuits of the island. The first half of the trip it rained almost continuously, confirming the Northern Irish weather test that if you can't see Cave Hill from Belfast it's because it's raining, and if you can see it then it's about to rain. Actually the rain did pause briefly, while we were staying with Maureen's brother in Belfast, but apart from that it kept up the downpour pretty much continuously. After I'd put Maureen and the kids on the plane back to Australia it only rained half the time as I completed the solo second half of the trip.

A month later, in mid-September, we were all back in Europe for a France–Italy–Switzerland circuit. By this time we had some preliminary material in from a number of writers and this was an opportunity to road-test parts of the book.

We drove our rented Citröen from Paris south to Lyon, ambled around Provence for a week, continued south to St Tropez, Cannes and Nice, spent a few days at an out-of-season Cote d'Azur resort, continued into Italy and headed down to Pisa before turning inland to Perugia where we met Helen Gillman, the author of the Italy chapter. Then we drove south to Rome and down to Naples and the Amalfi Coast before a long drive north to Venice, up through Switzerland and back to Paris. It was a lengthy and rushed trip, recalling our first explorations of Europe many years before, but that was part of the aim of our new series so this trial run was certainly authentic.

We celebrated our twentieth wedding anniversary in Paris before the kids flew to London to stay with my parents while Maureen and I went to the Frankfurt Bookfair. Maureen went straight back to Australia with the children after Frankfurt. I had planned to stop in Karachi on my way home, but I also had another unplanned stopover to my itinerary.

As usual, the Bookfair had been punctuated by long beer-drinking sessions in Frankfurt bars with our German travel publishing friends. One night a group of Berliners, including Stefan and Renate Loose, who produced German-language editions of several of our books, and Jens Peters, who wrote our Philippines guide at the time, were describing being in Berlin when the wall came down. Their tales of disbelief on watching the first television reports and then spending the night by one of the breaches in the wall and greeting arriving *Ossis* (East Germans) were enticing.

'For weeks after the wall fell you could not buy a hammer or chisel anywhere in Berlin,' recalled Stefan. 'Everyone simply wanted to make it disappear.'

'No matter where you were in the city you always knew which way it was to the wall,' went on Renate, 'because you could hear it being chipped away.'

'I want to see Berlin one day,' I enthused.

'Not one day, right now,' they insisted, explaining that less than two years after the *wende* (the 'change,' as the Germans call the wall's fall), Berlin still felt like two cities, but the east–west divide was rapidly fading. From a historical perspective, right now was the time to visit.

So I did. As soon as the bookfair ended I flew to Berlin and stayed with the Looses in their Kreuzberg apartment, close to where the wall had once stood. One day, Renate and I rode bicycles along the old route of the wall. In many places the wall had been built right down the middle of roads and nearly everywhere it was built straight onto the ground, without benefit of any excavations or foundations. Only two years after the wall's collapse it was already becoming difficult to trace.

Near the Brandenburg Gate the wall had cut through the area of central Berlin most badly damaged during the final assault on the city. Hitler's bunker had been somewhere in this area of utter destruction, and since the east–west boundary cut straight through it there had been no building or reconstruction since the war. With the wall gone, this empty wasteland was some of the most valuable real estate in Europe. Soon after I visited, the construction crews would begin creating a new commercial center on this former no-man's-land.

On the way home I stopped in Karachi, the city where I'd spent four of the first five years of my life. My father had been an RAF pilot instructor during World War II and then joined British Airways after the war, as ground staff rather than as a pilot. His first overseas posting was to Karachi and since he kept meticulous logs of every flight he ever took I can list all the details of my first time in the air: the aircraft, the registration number and even the pilot's name. I was eighteen months old when I departed England, not from Heathrow, but from Southampton, because Captain Allen was at the controls of a Sandringham flying boat. We flew first to Marignane, landing on a lake near Marseille in France. Then to Augusta in Sicily, Cairo in Egypt (where we must have landed on the Nile), Bahrain on the Gulf and finally to Karachi in Pakistan. There would have been a couple of overnight stops on the way because one didn't fly at night in those days.

When I returned to England in 1952 it was on a Comet jet. Unfortunately, I don't remember much about that pioneering flight either. I spent a year living with my grandparents while I started primary school in England, but then my father was transferred from Karachi to Nassau in the Bahamas and my next couple of years were spent there.

My family moved around so much that I never did more than two years in the same school. Of course at the time you always think your childhood is quite normal, but I hated leaving friends when I'd just made them and having to start all over again as 'the new kid'. I think it made me very cautious and uncertain when it came to meeting people; I've never been good at fitting in to new groups.

After that Caribbean period there was another brief interlude in England before my father was sent to Detroit and then Baltimore in the United States. As a result, almost all my high-school years were spent in the US, which I thoroughly enjoyed. Returning to school in England when I was sixteen, just as the Beatles appeared on the scene, was seriously dispiriting. In America you had elections for class president; in England the teachers appointed prefects. In America you chose your clothes; in England there were school uniforms. As for educational standards, schools in both countries have changed dramatically over the years but in the early Sixties I thought they were remarkably similar.

In Berlin I learned that I needed a visa to visit Karachi. Fortunately, the Pakistan embassy to the old East Germany was still operating so I turned up to apply for a visa. It seemed there had not been a big demand for them from the East Germans.

'How much does a visa cost?' I asked, after a yellowing application form had finally been located.

'That depends on your nationality,' said the visa clerk, flourishing a list of countries with their corresponding prices. A visa in my British passport would cost a pricey US$55, but nowhere on the list could I see a price for my alternative Australian nationality.

'How much for Australians?' I asked. 'I can't see it on the list.'

'You're right,' agreed the official, after studying the price list.

'Australians are not to be found. I suppose we will have to charge Australians the minimum price,' he decided, and I left the embassy with a bargain US$13 visa in my passport.

In 1947, when India was partitioned, Karachi was a sleepy seaport with a population of less than half a million. As Hindus flooded into India from Pakistan and Muslims trekked in the other direction to their new homeland, Karachi exploded in size. I had arrived in Karachi before my second birthday, just a year after the creation of Pakistan, and some of my earliest memories are of the tent city refugee camps which ringed the old town. Today the city has a population of over ten million and is often a seething hotbed of political violence, corruption and crime with the unrest regularly erupting into pitched street battles.

My younger brother Patrick and sister Coleen were both born in Karachi, but it had been forty years since I left, and none of us had ever returned. Fortunately I'd chosen a lull in the violence and with some photographs from the family album I easily tracked down our old house on Bath Island Road. It looked remarkably unchanged, even down to the flagpole from the top of which a large vulture-like buzzard used to peer myopically down at me each time I appeared at the front door. I remembered my mother driving home one day in our little Morris Minor and decisively squeezing the car between a little girl (a daughter of one of the cooks) and the rabid dog chasing her across the driveway. The servants had beaten the dog into one of the sheds which still stood behind the house and the police had been summoned to shoot the animal.

Each morning I used to go by bus to a pre-school by Clifton Beach, crossing what seemed like miles of empty flatland on the way. Now it was totally covered in sprawling urban development. Out on the harbor, however, things had not changed at all. I could still charter a little fishing boat for the afternoon, dangle a piece of string over the side and pull in sand crabs, which clutched fatally to the bait. The crew boiled them for immediate consumption.

The new year started in a more relaxed fashion—we'd really burnt out in 1991. With three trips to Southeast Asia, two to Europe and a final-round-the-world excursion in December, I'd spent more than half the year on the road. We spent a week on the beach at Noosa, the beachside gourmet ghetto and surf center north of Brisbane.

'Is this what people call a holiday?' our kids asked.

Although we went somewhere every school vacation, and usually somewhere further afield than up the east coast of Australia from Melbourne, our offspring had very normal school lives. There were one or two occasions when we were a few days or even a week late back, but until the mid-1990s, when we moved overseas for a year and put them in an international school, they had no interruptions or strange changes to their education.

In April I was back in Ireland, solo, working on the second round of research for *Western Europe*. I also gathered material for an Ireland country guide and wrote a Dublin city guide, so it was a very productive trip.

The Temple Bar area was turning into Dublin's party district and the city was becoming very trendy and European. I rented a bicycle and pedaled all over town, and stayed in backpacker hostels, traditional B&Bs and the five-star Shelbourne Hotel. I even spent one night at Dun Laoghaire, the Dublin port, and the next morning at dawn, like 'stately, plump Buck Mulligan' in Joyce's *Ulysses*, swam a lap of the Forty Foot Pool. Nude of course—the 'togs must be worn' sign only kicks in at 9 a.m.

For *Mediterranean Europe on a Shoestring* we had pulled the Morocco chapter from our Africa guide without putting it through the first cycle research in 1991. It needed work so in July 1992 I returned to Europe. Many budget travelers heading to Morocco from Britain buy last-minute charter tickets and I thought this would be an interesting way to get to North Africa. The London office bought me a £40 ticket to Málaga on the Costa del Sol departing from Gatwick. To comply with the rules, my ticket was round trip and included accommodation, although the return flight left half an hour after I was due to arrive in Spain and the hotel probably didn't exist. From

Málaga, I caught a bus for Algeciras, just beyond Gibraltar, where the ferries cross the straits to Tangiers.

All went well until the bus pulled to a halt in a small resort town and the driver announced he wasn't going any further due to a massive traffic jam blocking the coast road. I retired to a nearby English bar (not for nothing is the Costa del Sol also known as the Costa Fish and Chips), where I discovered this was not unusual—heavy tourist traffic combined with Moroccan workers returning home from France often brought the coast road to a standstill. At the time there was no alternative inland route although today a modern toll road parallels the coast route.

I was on a horribly tight schedule. Traffic seemed to be flowing smoothly through the town and Gibraltar was only twenty or twenty five miles south, so I decided to hitch. Shouldering my bag I set out, and just out of town reached the tail end of the traffic jam. In the summer coastal heat I walked on. And on. And on. Families were picnicking by the roadside. Some had abandoned their cars and headed down to the beach. Eventually, after five miles of nose-to-tail cars, I reached the police roadblock and found a taxi to take me to Gibraltar. I was weary, sweaty and still rather jet-lagged from the flight from Australia so it took a number of beers to restore my normally cheerful outlook. The next morning I continued by bus to the port, very early before any traffic jams appeared.

It takes only two and a half hours to cross the narrow straits from Spain to Morocco, Europe to Africa, one world to another, where I soon had my first encounter with Morocco's famous touts. I found my way to the Hotel el-Muniria and, to my delight, I managed to get room nine where William Boroughs had written *The Naked Lunch*. Jack Kerouac and Alan Ginsberg had also stayed here.

After drifting east along the coast towards Algeria and then south to Rabat I eventually flew to Marrakesh and took the train back to Casablanca on the coast. There I had a weird coincidental meeting when Michael Sklovsky, an Australian who owns Ishka, a string of Third World arts and craft shops, walked into my restaurant one night. He was on a shopping trip around Morocco (this guy shopped by the container load) and our chance meeting prompted the idea of arts and crafts sections in our guidebooks. Michael subsequently wrote these for several of our books, including Morocco.

I flew to Paris in late July to find the town strangely quiet—anyone not on holiday was indoors watching the Barcelona Olympics. Another week in Ireland, finishing up the Dublin city guide, followed before I flew home via San Francisco.

To ensure I didn't miss out on 'quality children time', Maureen left me to hold the fort on a number of occasions while she went to Europe, the USA and Asia on business trips. Despite Maureen's firmly held belief that my cooking abilities are nothing to write home about, the kids didn't eat badly when I was the resident cook. Comments about being forced to survive on 'Dad's dinner shakes', a reference to my enthusiasm for taking disparate leftovers from the fridge and blending them into entirely new combinations (Thai food with mashed potato, a sort of Siamese shepherd's pie, for example), are absolutely not to be taken seriously.

In October, with some friends and their children, we walked the eight-day Helambu circuit in the mountains of Nepal. We had Sherpas and porters and tents and a kitchen crew, but we also took along something quite unusual: a bunch of Nepalese kids. Stan Armington, our American trekking author and owner of Malla Treks in Kathmandu, suggested to the cook that he bring along his two sons, aged eight and nine, and a Nepalese trek operator sent along his twelve-year-old daughter, so in total we had thirteen kids, including two six-year-olds.

Halfway through the trek, we had one of those Himalayan down-down-down mornings followed by an up-up-up afternoon, only to discover the porters had unilaterally decided to keep going up-up-up for another couple of hours beyond our intended camp site. As the sun was about to disappear, Rosie, one of the six-year-olds, told me, with the seriousness that only a six-year-old can carry off, 'I think this is the worst day of my life.'

The view the next morning was stupendous, perhaps even more amazing because of the effort spent getting there, and at the end of day eight even the two youngest kids announced they'd like to do the whole thing again. They'd seen plenty of things not many Western kids get to experience these days. Nepalese trekking cooks turn out a special meal for the last camp dinner so we knew what was going to happen when we left a village on our penultimate day and glanced back to see some of the children leading a goat on a piece of rope.

'Goat curry for dinner,' I thought.

That afternoon, after we'd set up camp, the cook came over to the children who were playing with their pet, his freshly sharpened *khukri* (a large Nepalese knife) in his hand.

'Want to watch me get dinner ready?' he asked.

'Yes!' they all chorused.

The kids came back and said it was amazing how quickly the skin came off. And complained it was tough when dinner arrived. I wrote a piece for a British newspaper a couple of years ago about seeing a friend's car in Kathmandu getting a 10 000 mile sacrifice. Once a year a goat has its head chopped off and the blood is sprayed on the wheels (so they don't fall off) and the engine (so it keeps running).

T: I don't know how you say to an elephant, 'Look for a Nikon lens, 50 mm,' but our *pahit* (the elephant's rider and master, known as a *mahout* in Hindi) had clearly whispered some instruction into our elephant's ear because the ponderous beast swung around and began to walk back along the jungle path, swinging its trunk through the vegetation on each side.

Our children's trek also included a stay in the Chitwan, the jungle park in the lowlands of Nepal, along the Indian border to the south of the foothills which eventually climb north into the mighty Himalayas. At dawn and dusk each day we'd climbed on board our elephants—the camp had built high wooden platforms, rather like an airport boarding gate, to make getting on and off easy. Then we'd stomped (but quietly, very quietly) into the undergrowth to look for rhinos (quite easy to find), deer and, if we were very lucky, tigers. In between those cool-of-the-day forays we'd lazed around, read books, learned about elephants and even joined in elephant bath time in the river. Clambering over a lazily recumbent elephant, scrubbing its back with a large stone and getting a free shower from the trunk when the *pahit* said '*chhop*' was our children's idea of fun with a capital F.

When it was time to leave, we rode the elephants to the river which marked the park boundary. Once across the river, we would reluctantly return to more mundane motorized transport. Tashi, Kieran and two other children were on one elephant while Maureen and I joined a fellow park visitor on another. He was a European airline pilot and throughout our stay he'd been worryingly clumsy, forgetful and generally less 'handy' than you'd expect from someone in his profession. Now, true to form, he'd dropped his camera lens.

'I changed it about five minutes ago,' he announced. 'It must have rolled off my lap.'

'Well, I guess it's gone,' he lamented as we looked back at the dense undergrowth. 'There's not a hope of finding it in that.'

'No,' said Maureen, 'tell the *pahit*. We may be able to find it.'

We'd been repeatedly impressed by elephants' abilities to find and pick things up. One of the elephants had even shown us how it could pick up a ballpoint pen with its trunk. Another afternoon, as we'd forged through the jungle, an overhanging branch had swiped Maureen's cap off her head. The following elephant had nonchalantly reached down, picked it up and politely handed (well, 'trunked') it back to her.

Sure enough, a couple of hundred yards back, the elephant stopped, reached into the tall grass and triumphantly handed up a camera lens—Nikon, 50 mm. The *pahit* took the lens, wiped it on his sarong and handed it back to the astonished pilot.

Our first batch of Europe guides hit the shelves in January 1993. We didn't expect our entry into Europe to set the travel publishing world alight. We had studiously avoided the region for years because there were already so many books out there. Plus, we didn't feel that

European guidebooks would have that 'can't live without one' quality. (India and China are quite mysterious, while France or Italy seem fairly familiar.) So we didn't see our new European titles shouldering our Asian blockbusters aside to fight their way to the top of our sales charts.

Four years down the road, when the first Europe titles were coming up for their third editions, I noted that our Europe launch had gone very much according to plan and there had been no major hiccups or surprises. On the other hand, Europe books were expensive to produce, particularly when it came to research. A few months of trekking around Italy or France costs a lot, no matter how cautious your writer. And while the sales had not been disappointing, they hadn't been knockout either. A few years later that would change.

The reputation we'd won in Asia and other regions did carry us a long way in Europe, but there was no denying we were the new kids on the block and had to establish that we could perform as well in the old world as we had done in the various new ones. People were using our books, however. Kicking around the Greek islands in the summer of 1996 I saw lots of people poring over our Greece book. By 2001 there was no question that we'd carved out our place in the market. Four of our top ten titles were on Europe (the other six were Australia, New Zealand, three Asian titles and Mexico), and in Britain we were the number one publisher of titles on Europe.

That summer Maureen and I spent three weeks driving around Spain. In Córdoba I went for a late-afternoon wander while Maureen retired to the hotel room for a siesta. Sitting at a bar I pulled out the Spain guide to see where we might go for dinner. The couples sitting to my left and right both told me they had copies of the book. And Portugal and two other Lonely Planet guides between them, it turned out. All four lived in Canada, although one of them was English and one French. As I left I mentioned that I worked for Lonely Planet, which prompted one of them to suggest improvements to the maps.

'Don't hassle him,' said one of the group. 'It's not as if he owns the company.'

The best publicity wagon we ever managed to hitch a ride on was for the first edition of our guide to Britain, which we published in early 1995. The *Sunday Times* ran an article highlighting anything critical we'd said about Britain, from the Queen's bad taste in interior decoration to the shonky development of Land's End in Cornwall. The article was a beat-up—sure, we were critical of a few things in Britain, but overall we were amazingly enthusiastic. The *Sunday Times* story was only the start, however. Soon, local papers all over the country were running stories about how their town had fared in the 'horror guide'.

Our favorite reaction was from the 'beach resort' of Margate which Richard Everist panned, writing, 'Looking at Margate, God got so depressed she created Torremolinos.' (Torremolinos is a Spanish town on the Costa del Sol which is particularly popular with British holidaymakers.) Photographs of the mayor of Margate appeared in the press, wearing a World War II vintage tin helmet and clutching an old rifle, standing on the beach ready to repel incoming travel writers. His subsequent media appearances probably increased his re-election prospects a hundredfold. He sent us an autographed copy of his appearance on the beach. We sent an autographed copy of the book in return.

It was Sunday evening in Australia when the first *Sunday Times* article appeared, but demand for Monday-morning radio interviews from Britain was so great that Richard and I camped out at our office and spent most of the night on the phone. Eventually we had to airfreight more copies to Britain to meet demand and Jennifer Cox, our hard-working and imaginative British publicist, who had stirred up the controversy in the first place, persuaded me to fly to Britain to meet our critics. The *Daily Mirror* asked me to come to Blackpool to be confronted by seaside landladies, try Blackpool rock (hard sticks of candy for which the area is famous) and comment on the dismal state of Blackpool's beach.

I spent the best part of a week on the firing line, and enjoyed every minute of it, but the publicity wave spread far beyond Britain's shores. Perhaps the whole controversy only took place because of

British colonial attitudes, suggested an Australian newspaper, speculating that the British were touchy about any criticism from Australia. This launched another round of articles about 'Pom bashing' and once the Australian and British press had finished sniping at each other the Canadians took it up, intrigued by the stand-off between the two countries. Visiting our American office I suggested that when we got around to doing American guides we should get Californians to write about New York and New Yorkers to write about California, in the hopes of sparking a similar slanging match.

We basked in the success of our Britain launch for two years until the second edition rolled around. Once again the British press was full of stories about Australians complaining about British food, British tea, British bathing habits. We even scored three minutes on the top-rating television show *News at Ten* and had the pleasure of watching Germaine Greer, on another television program, postulating that perhaps the author of the Cardiff section (Bryn Thomas) had been laudatory about the city 'because he'd got laid there', but the author of the Coventry section (me) 'certainly hadn't been successful'. Well, it's an achievement to have Germaine Greer commenting on your sex life, or lack of it. And this time we made sure we had plenty of books on the shelves when we let the press pack loose.

By the late 1990s we had most countries in Europe covered, and had published guides to many of the most important cities. We were even starting to break up some countries into smaller regions. Scotland had followed Britain, for example, while France had spawned Provence and Corsica. We'd also expanded our London office from a purely sales and marketing operation to a fully fledged publishing house, specializing in these European regional titles.

Our push into Europe had been spurred by some unwanted competition. Penguin Books had bought a controlling stake in Rough Guides, so our main competitors in the British market now had a parent with very deep pockets. Each summer their books would be on sale with free offers of a Penguin novel to read while you were on your travels. Furthermore, Penguin seemed to be targeting some of our most popular titles for aggressive price competition. Where our title might once have been a pound more expensive than a competing Rough Guide, suddenly we were being undercut by three pounds. (Rupert Murdoch was engaged in the same activity in the daily newspaper field in Britain at the time, selling the *Times* at a knockdown price with the intention of grabbing market share, irrespective of what it might cost him.)

We couldn't compete with the new Penguin-owned Rough Guides when it came to price cutting, so we decided to do something cleverer. While we had started publishing with Asian titles and then moved through Africa and South America before tackling Europe, Rough Guides had gone in the opposite direction and their greatest strength was still with their European titles. We decided to hit Rough Guides head on. We ranked all their European books by sales and set out to produce a competing title for every one, starting at the top and working down. By the year 2000 we could claim that for all its European expertise we had more titles on Europe than Rough Guides.

M: By 1993, Lonely Planet had reached the stage in a company's life where business school students do a case study analyzing your success. One group from Melbourne Business School asked to see 'flow charts' and 'hierarchical structures', requests which Tony, Jim and I found quite entertaining since we didn't have any. We went to the group's presentation and listened while they explained what had made us successful and described the challenges we would face in the future.

Not long afterwards Steve Hibbard, one of the students, proposed he work for us for six months to identify areas that required our attention in order to take the company forward. I was concerned that we were not paying enough heed to the 'business' side. The lack of analysis and monitoring of expenditure made me uneasy—our decisions were made on a day-to-day basis with little overall planning.

So Steve joined us, although instead of staying for six months he was with us for the next ten years. At first as general manager and then later as our CEO he tried to instill some discipline in our business planning. I began to dislike the phrase 'the Lonely Planet way', which generally seemed to mean things couldn't be changed. If Steve had a problem at Lonely Planet it was that he was too much in thrall to the company's uniqueness to make the necessary hard decisions.

Around this time we were entering the 'tech boom'. The 'information superhighway' was the phrase of the moment and Steve was one of many people who believed that with Lonely Planet's information and the new technology we would become the travel 'content provider' for every type of media. I remember being told that in five years there would be no more books, that people would get their travel information from other sources, and paper would be obsolete. I didn't believe it, but I did believe that we should be exploring how this new media would affect travel.

We were regularly asked why we were headquartered in Australia. And with the whole world to choose from, why had Maureen and I made Melbourne our home? Pure accident on both counts. It was almost a toss of the coin which brought us back to Australia rather than the UK after we'd finished putting *South-East Asia on a Shoestring* together in Singapore. In Australia we'd tried Sydney first, then tried Melbourne and stayed there, but it could easily have been the other way around.

I wrote an article for Salon.com about 'terminal wanderlust', a term coined by Douglas Coupland, the guy who also came up with 'Generation X'. It was defined as a state of being so disconnected to anywhere that everywhere is home, or might as well be. That's me I thought. I've never found a city I didn't like or didn't think I could call home. I'm quite happy in Melbourne, but I was equally happy in San Francisco in 1985 and Paris when I lived there in 1996.

Lonely Planet could be anywhere too. We take a writer from X, send him to Y, he returns to Z to write it up, then we manage the publication from our London office, edit and design it in Australia, print it in Singapore and finally our US office sells it in Canada. Emails travel from one side of the world to the other as fast as they travel across the office.

Of course, Australia is a very nice place to be. The weather is generally pretty good, the country from beach to desert to mountains to islands is superb, the food is great, the wine is terrific, the prices are competitive and the people are friendly and hard-working. What's not to like? Plus we arrived in Australia at a particularly interesting time, when Gough Whitlam, for all his management faults, was about to wake the place up and kick off a boom which lasted for the rest of the century.

Meanwhile Britain was about to swing into a revolving door of political inertia and chaos, backed up by labor unrest, endless strikes and industrial collapse, and topped off by the Thatcher years. It's no wonder Germaine Greer whinges endlessly about how she can never come back to Australia—she can't admit she left at the wrong time. Watching the Thatcher years from far away had a macabre fascination, like watching a horrible car smash, but you certainly wouldn't have wanted to be in the car when it stalled at the railway crossing as the express came by. Poor Germaine, sitting in the front seat.

Concentrating on Europe in the first half of the 1990s didn't mean we neglected Asia or Australia, and our travels sometimes led directly to new books. In 1992 Cambodia was just reopening to tourism; very little of the country was accessible and even the limited areas that were open were not exactly safe. We contemplated visiting Angkor Wat back in 1974, but at that time the country was on a downhill slide into chaos and this huge and justly famous Buddhist temple city sat on the impossible list for nearly twenty years. Our 1991 Vietnam, Laos and Cambodia guide did a pretty good job of covering Cambodia, but within a couple of days of arriving in the country I began to muse about a separate guide. Many of the people we bumped into were only visiting Cambodia; it wasn't part of some larger Indochinese circuit.

The idea was reinforced at Siem Reap, the small town near Angkor Wat where the old Grand Hotel d'Angkor had just been reopened—the Swiss hotel manager was very enthusiastic about the idea of a small Cambodia guide. Flying back through Bangkok we dropped into the excellent little bookshop in the Airport Hotel, right across from the airport terminal, where the manager added further weight to the idea and suggested we should produce it in French as well. By the time we got back to Australia I was sold on the idea. We quickly pulled the Cambodia section out of the larger book, added material on the Angkor temples and other newly accessible areas and published a Cambodia guide which later became our first French-language guidebook.

In 1991 we set out to travel the Birdsville Track in Central Australia, but we didn't get very far because it was underwater. It happens every now and then. Instead, we followed the unhappy route of the pioneering explorers Burke and Wills up to Cooper's Creek where they died. It's one of the great tragedies of the heroic era of Australian exploration. In the nineteenth century it was believed that there must be a great inland sea in the center of the continent, waiting for some hardy explorer to penetrate the impassable desert that blocked it off from the coast. Funded by the Victorian colonial government, flush with funds from the region's gold rush, the two explorers set off from Melbourne in 1860 with the biggest and most lavishly equipped party ever assembled. They would try and solve the mystery of Australia's interior and make a pioneering south-to-north crossing of the continent. Burke and Wills established a base camp beside Cooper's Creek, near the present-day outback settlement of Innamincka in Queensland.

From Cooper's Creek, Robert O'Hara Burke, William John Wills, their young assistant John King and Charles Gray set off with camels to make a rush to the north coast and return to their base camp. The crossing took far longer than planned and the impenetrable mangrove swamps that fringe the Gulf of Carpentaria prevented them setting sight on the sea, although tidal movements in the river proved they were at the coast. As they straggled back south their supplies dwindled, their animals died off and eventually Gray also died. Burke had instructed their base-camp personnel to wait for them for three months, after which time they could presume they were either dead or had left the north coast by ship. The base camp hung on for more than a month beyond the deadline, but eventually gave up hope and on the morning of 21 April 1861 headed back to Melbourne. On the evening of the same day Burke, Wills and King crawled into the camp, starving and exhausted.

The departing group had buried a cache of supplies under a coolabah tree at their camp site and carved into the tree 'Dig 3ft NW'. Burke, Wills and King were too weak to pursue the base group, but fortified by the supplies they decided to head south towards Adelaide. This attempt proved futile and they returned to Cooper's Creek in worse condition than ever. It was symptomatic of the whole badly planned and tragic expedition that while they were away a rescue party arrived from Melbourne and then returned south without ever realizing that Burke's party had returned in the interim. Burke and company had not thought to leave any message themselves at the camp!

Burke and Wills eventually died of starvation and exhaustion at Cooper's Creek even though groups of Aborigines were surviving quite comfortably on the creek's fish and birds and native vegetation. The Aborigines managed to nurse the 22-year-old King until another search party rescued the group's sole survivor.

Australian author Alan Moorehead's *Cooper's Creek* is the classic history of the fatal expedition and I read passages from this book to Tashi and Kieran as we headed north. We followed the trail of the disastrous trip from the statue of Burke and Wills, looking suitably heroic, in the center of Melbourne all the way to the famous 'Dig Tree' beside Cooper's Creek.

The rains that prevented us from reaching Birdsville had also flooded the normally shallow Cooper's Creek until it was hundreds of yards wide and impossible to cross without a boat. Fortunately, the gas station in Innamincka had a small fleet of canoes to rent out, so we crossed the last thirty miles of desert to the creek with a canoe strapped to our rooftop and then ran a ferry service across the creek for other stranded visitors.

In 1993 we did get to Birdsville, but there our expedition took a totally unexpected left turn. Birdsville, named after the birds that flock to the area when the normally dry creek is in flood, is famed for being Australia's most remote settlement and for its annual horse races. For much of the year Birdsville has a population of about a hundred, but for that one weekend in September the town's airstrip becomes the busiest airport in the country and the Birdsville Hotel gets through more beer than any other pub. Thirty ton of beer slides down thirsty race fans' throats during the course of the cup—that's about fifteen cans for every man, woman and child present. The town is traditionally reached by the Birdsville Track, a rough and ready outback trail running 300 miles north from Marree in South Australia. Today any sturdy car can make the trip as long as the driver is reasonably careful and cautious. Not so long ago, however, a breakdown on the track could be fatal. In 1963 a young family's car ground to a halt on the track and, in the midsummer heat, they ran out of water. The couple and their three children were dead before help arrived.

Our trip was quite uneventful and we arrived in Birdsville at dusk, intending to continue north to the Plenty Highway and follow that dirt trail west until we hit the all-mod-cons road between Alice Springs and Darwin, then drive south to Alice Springs. There is a route directly west from Birdsville to Dalhousie Springs and on to Alice Springs, but it crosses the remote Simpson Desert. Although our 4WD Land Cruiser was quite capable of making a desert crossing, we would need more equipment and such a crossing should only be attempted in a party of at least two vehicles.

In Birdsville we drove straight to the town's famed hotel, in search of cold beers and square meals. There was one other party in the dining room, including two boys who turned out to be classmates of our children. Their group was planning to set out across the

Simpson Desert the next day, and their Land Cruisers were exactly the same model as ours (so spare wheels and parts would fit either vehicle if necessary), so before we knew it we had joined their expedition. Next morning we stocked up on extra jerry cans for fuel and water and in a few hours we were taking the first of several runs at Big Red, the huge sand dune which marks the start of the desert crossing.

Over the next four days, we had the time of our lives. Once again I mused on what wonderful adventure opportunities the Australian outback offered and back in Melbourne I sat down with publisher Rob van Driesum and we dreamed up *Outback Australia*. The book, one of my favorite Lonely Planet guides, came out in 1994 and subsequently won a Pacific Asia Travel Association Gold Award.

The launch of our European guides had been planned with almost military precision (well, military precision compared with our usual give-it-a-go process), but the familiar old USA didn't require such careful planning, or so we thought. After all, everyone spoke English, information was straightforward and easy to obtain, and we had already done Alaska and Hawaii as well as an abortive USA West guide. We'd complicated matters a little by setting up a US publishing unit as well, but that shouldn't be a big problem. Bad decision.

We chopped the US into a series of regional (rather than state) guides and looked for writers to tackle the first few titles. A guide to the whole country would come later. Our first failing was to underestimate how big these books would be. Usually you can get an impression of how much work is involved by the size of the population or by how much physical territory has to be covered. For some reason, neat equations don't work when it comes to the US.

We got four books under way in 1994. Rob Rachowiecki, resident in Tucson and author of guides to Peru, Ecuador and Costa Rica, was an obvious writer for the Southwest (Arizona, New Mexico and Utah) and that book came through quite smoothly, although many months late. The Pacific Northwest (Washington, Oregon and Idaho) also came through without too many headaches.

The Rocky Mountain States and Mid-Atlantic States guides, on the other hand, were complete disasters. The authors had worked for us before, but we've probably never paid out so much and got so little back as with the Rocky Mountains book. Although Montana, Wyoming and Colorado are three relatively lightly populated states progress was very slow. We like to see sample material as the project develops, but everything we were shown was sketchy and disturbingly badly written. Nevertheless, we were dealing with an experienced author and we were confident he would come through eventually. The alarm bells didn't ring loudly enough, even when he argued that the project was bigger and more complex than originally planned and wanted further advances and to renegotiate a higher fee for the completed book.

I met the author at our Oakland office to thrash out how much remained to be done. What about the mapping, I asked. I always organize the maps first, and the text builds up around them. He didn't have any maps, our worrisome author reported; he was going to put them together after he'd finished writing. I was shocked; there was no way he could produce accurate and comprehensive maps if they weren't done when he was actually there. As I pushed further, it quickly became clear that virtually nothing was completed. Our 'experienced' writer had been farming work out to an inexperienced second writer, without our knowledge. We had been taken for a long and expensive ride by a writer who had been overwhelmed by both the project and personal problems. If he'd asked for our help we could have supported him, but as it was we wrote off everything. We didn't get one line of text or one map.

The Mid-Atlantic situation was almost identical, although we should have realized right from the start that this bigger project was too much for one person. The book covered the densely populated corridor from Washington DC to New York, including Baltimore and Philadelphia. The author completed some text and mapping before giving up mid-project, leaving us to pick up the pieces. However, he also called in a backup researcher without our agreement and we got stuck with making further payments to his second writer even after the project had ground to a halt.

We wrote off ridiculous amounts of money on these books before we put a new team into the Rockies. They pushed it through in record time, but the Mid-Atlantic project never came out in its original form. It was eventually divided into two separate books.

Author disasters were only part of the US problem. We also managed to get things wrong in-house. Ten years earlier, Maureen and I had moved to San Francisco to set up our US operation on visitor visas because we'd been told it would be impossible to do it legally, but we were now an established and much larger firm with a US operation and American staff. Furthermore, new immigration regulations promised to make obtaining visas for inter-office transfers much simpler.

We decided to send Sue Mitra, an experienced editor, to recruit and train staff and establish the US publishing operation. We soon had our first American editor and cartographer at our Oakland office, but Sue, who should have been telling them what to do and how to do it, was still waiting for a visa. Faxes were flying around, but nothing came back from the US immigration authorities—it was strictly one-way traffic.

We gave up on the benefits of the new 'straightforward, simple, routine' process and called in an American immigration lawyer. And what advice did we get? To forget about doing it legally, to go on a visitor visa and get out within twelve months! Ah, *déjà vu*.

Years later, we discovered that the US immigration authorities are often weeks and months behind in their processing. Since they don't like to confess that they are backlogged, they ask for more information. They don't really need it and asking for it delays things even further, but it gives people the impression that things are happening. And you wonder why Mexicans sneak across the border?

Why can't countries make the whole process simpler, particularly for companies operating internationally who have a real need to shuffle people back and forth? When we set up our American, British and French publishing operations we sent in staff from Australia to install the computers, get the software up and running, recruit and train the local staff and generally get things running smoothly before handing over the keys. Why should we have to spend countless hours and large sums of money to prove we're not going to deprive an American of a job when what we are doing is going to create more employment in America?

These days millions of frequent flyer points are accumulated by people traveling between our offices. For a while we even encouraged staff to organize their own transfers if they had similar jobs. It was up to them to get there and if they wanted to swap apartments or houses that was a good idea, but we'd support the switch in any way we could. Surprisingly, one of the first swaps was organized by Dave Skibinski from the Oakland warehouse, who spent a spell packing books in the Melbourne stockroom. We reckoned this was a win-win policy: our staff got to live and work in a different country and we got the benefits of them exchanging local expertise and gaining a feeling for operations. Now why won't immigration authorities co-operate?

One of the benefits we foresaw from our US operation was a little competition, a little cross-fertilization, some exciting new ideas, particularly in computer technology. We'd follow the management buzz phrase of the time and 'think globally, act locally'. A few years later we would painfully discover that efficiencies aren't so easily found.

8
All About Guidebooks

Travel guidebooks are almost as old as travel. Pausanias wrote his *Description of Greece* back in the second century AD. If it isn't the world's oldest guidebook it's certainly the oldest guidebook still in print—you can get the English-language edition through Amazon, although some of the bars he recommended have been closed for a millennium or two.

The famous German Baedeker guides made their first appearance in 1829 and after Karl Baedeker's death in 1859 his sons expanded the business, publishing the first English-language edition of a Baedeker guide in 1861. The name 'Baedeker' would become synonymous with 'guidebook' and today old copies of the books are popular with collectors. During World War II there was even the 'Baedeker Blitz' between April and June 1942. In reprisal for allied raids on the Hanseatic League city of Lübeck, the Luftwaffe launched a series of attacks on English cities thought to be of more importance to tourists than to the military. It's said they were chosen from the Baedeker guide to Britain. Over a half-century later, when a 1999 American NATO raid on Belgrade accidentally targeted the Chinese Embassy, it was suggested the mistake might have been avoided if the mission had been planned with a good guidebook to hand.

Murray's Handbooks were an English competitor to Baedeker.

John Murray published their first guidebook in 1836 and eventually developed a list of 400 titles. They were 'less visually appealing' than Baedeker's guides, but superior in other areas. *Murray's Handbook to India* outlasted all the other books in the series. It was still in print, although often wildly out of date, in the late-1970s when we researched our first India guide.

The Victorian era may have been a high point in the history of guidebooks, but when it comes to travel literature, it's often said that the 1930s were the golden days. Travel guides at that time were not very exciting affairs. Baedeker's had been joined by the Blue Guides, books that told you in exacting detail about the history of a castle or the architecture of a church, but the 'how to' of travel rarely crept into these guides. If you were sufficiently well off to travel then you would have somebody to advise you on where to stay and where to eat. If you were going somewhere really outrageous, where there might not be anywhere 'suitable', you'd probably turn to your consulate or embassy. Accounts of travel in that era seemed to take it for granted that the ambassador would be only too pleased to see one of his countrymen passing through and the guest suite was always ready for their use.

Arthur Frommer's first *Europe on $5 a Day* in 1957 was a clear indicator of the change after World War II. Frommer started by compiling travel notes for his fellow soldiers and putting that advice on civvy street was a huge leap forward. Travel snobs may have looked down their noses at his guides, but suddenly how to get there, where to stay and where to eat was as important as the difference between a Baroque church and a Gothic one. At a time when you could get a room in Paris for two dollars a night and a three-course meal for not much more than a dollar, this was a major revolution in guidebook publishing.

Another travel landmark, also from America, was the first Let's Go guide which appeared as mimeographed notes in 1960 and metamorphosed into *Let's Go Europe* a year later. The first guidebook I ever traveled with was a copy of *Let's Go Europe* in the mid-1960s. Let's Go guides are researched and written by students at Harvard University in Boston, Massachusetts, and published by St Martin's

Press in New York. That single guide to Europe spawned numerous offshoots including individual guides to many countries and cities in Europe, guides to the United States and Mexico and to 'our' regions, Southeast Asia, India and Australia.

Let's Go has one major advantage over us: cheap labor. All the Let's Go writers are students, researching and writing the guides during their summer vacation as a labor of love rather than a real occupation. When you leave Harvard your days as a Let's Go writer also come to an end. Using students has some major advantages and some equally big drawbacks. There's a very disciplined approach to the production of Let's Go guides: the students travel during the summer, they have neatly segmented regions to cover and tightly defined schedules for delivering their material. At the end of the summer the Let's Go editors take over, feeding the numerous contributions into the tightly defined template for books which will be on sale before Christmas. Let's Go claim they completely update their books each year and they pack in a remarkable amount of information and get it out remarkably quickly.

The drawbacks are that the books are often produced from one perspective, during one season and for one market. If you too are a Harvard University student and traveling during the American summer vacation then a Let's Go guide may be precisely what you want. If you aren't an East Coast college student, or even an American, and don't happen to be traveling during the American summer, the story may be a little different. An amusing *Rolling Stone* story in 1995 followed a floundering Let's Go writer around Istanbul. An inexperienced, first-time visitor to Turkey, he was desperately trying to cover large areas of a totally unknown city. 'Let's Go, or Let's Not and Say We Did' was not a reassuring picture.

Given that Let's Go was aimed at such a rigidly defined market segment, it was interesting, and a slightly sad reflection of what a me-too business publishing can be, that somebody should try and grab a slice out of what was already only a slice. In the early 1990s Fodor's, part of the huge American publishing group Random House, announced the development of a new student-oriented series to be called Berkeley Guides. It was obvious that this was a copy of the Let's Go concept, substituting West Coast Berkeley for East Coast Harvard.

As with Let's Go, students researched the guides. When the material came back to the Berkeley campus, teams of student editors, guided by some experienced ex-Let's Go hands, whipped the books into shape and the Berkeley series was launched with four books in the fall of 1992. But in 1997 Berkeley Guides announced there would be no more West Coast student guides.

What went wrong? The guides were efficiently produced, and they were good books, worthy competitors to Let's Go. I suspect the American student market, even with some demand from young travelers in other countries, simply wasn't big enough and strong enough to sustain two such similar series. Modern guidebooks are expensive and complex products, and enjoying the benefits of cheap labor isn't always enough. The creation of the Berkeley Guides did have one useful benefit—we subsequently took on a number of ex-Berkeley students who'd taken their first steps into travel publishing courtesy of the series.

The French Michelin guides are certainly idiosyncratic. Produced almost as a sideline by the French tire manufacturer, the guides are available in several series including the old-fashioned 'green guides', which come in a variety of languages and cover the regions and countries in A-to-Z style. The connoisseur's Michelin guides, however, are the 'red guides' which come out annually and simply list hotels and restaurants with symbols detailing facilities and standards which are so complex it almost takes a CIA codebreaker to decipher them. The really important question in the red guide is which restaurants rate a Michelin star, an *etoile* in French.

Getting even one star is no mean feat. The whole Michelin rating process is shrouded in almost Masonic mystery. The Michelin restaurant critics are faceless people, eating their meals anonymously and returning to try a restaurant again if there are any questions about the absolute reliability of the cuisine. The red guide to France is said to sell over half a million copies and to make a loss on every copy sold. Dinner for two at a Michelin three-starred restaurant in France can easily top US$500 so with all those meals to pay for it's scarcely surprising that it's hard to make a profit. Other French travel publishers sniff that Michelin simply writes the whole guidebook business off as publicity for their core business, tire manufacturing.

Each year gastronomes queue up at midnight to get the first copies of the new red guide for France—it's only the French edition of the red guide which gets this obsessive attention—and next day there will be articles in the paper detailing whose star is on the rise, and which famous restaurant has been stripped of one. In 1996, the year we were living in Paris, there was national horror when the three-starred Tour d'Argent dropped down to two-star status and articles in the press discussed the strategies to be put in place to regain the missing star.

The 1970s saw a flood of new travel publishers, a number of which are now at the forefront of modern travel publishing. What prompted this explosion? Clearly it was more than a bunch of people simultaneously having the same good idea. A whole bundle of changes had prepared a fertile field for our ideas to take root. The coming of age of the post-war baby boomers was part of the package—suddenly there were all these young people looking for new horizons. Then there was sex and drugs and rock and roll and the feeling that perhaps all of those things were more interesting in India or Morocco or almost anywhere away from home. At the same time a travel boom was about to take off. In the 1960s, jets had made air travel more reliable; now the Boeing 747s, which first went into service in 1970, along with other wide-bodied aircraft, were about to make travel cheaper and more accessible.

We were certainly not the only new kids on the block. Moon Publications started the same year as us, APA Insight a couple of years earlier and Bradt Publications a few years later. Rough Guides, the publisher we look upon as our most direct competitor, came along in 1982. Mark Ellingham's travels in Greece inspired their first book which was, indeed, fairly rough looking.

'There were plenty of guidebooks to Greece which covered the history, the ruins, the art and the architecture,' Mark would later tell me. 'But they all managed to cover Greece from one end of the country to the other without ever mentioning the word "beach".'

Surprisingly, none of the new developments in travel publishing came from established companies. The changes in the air seemed to completely bypass them and when they did wake up to the upsurge in growth it was too late—they'd been overtaken. Much the same happened a decade later with computer books. Just as the travel book explosion was led by travelers who got into publishing rather than publishers getting into travel, so the computer book explosion was led by computer geeks getting into publishing. The regular publishers never saw it coming.

The boom in new travel publishers wasn't limited to the English language. All over France there are little stickers in restaurant windows or small plaques beside hotel doors proclaiming that the establishment is recommended by the Guide du Routard. If there's a French-language equivalent of Lonely Planet (apart from Lonely Planet France, of course!) then it's Guide du Routard. Philippe Gloaguen, who started and still runs the company, was another early 1970s startup. The first Guide du Routard was a guide to the Asia overland trip, just like our first book, and it also appeared in 1973.

When Lonely Planet started up in France, Philippe reacted with Gallic outrage to another example of the Anglo-Saxons trying to crush French culture. How could tiny Guide du Routard compete with this English-language juggernaut, he complained, conveniently forgetting that Guide du Routard was part of the gigantic Hachette organization. In fact, I think the competition in France has probably been good for Guide du Routard and Philippe himself confessed to me that soon after our French office opened he used this new threat as a convenient lever to get the Hachette management to install the expensive new computer system he had been unsuccessfully demanding.

You're likely to bump into Australian travelers almost anywhere on earth, in numbers completely disproportionate to the country's population, and the British have long had a reputation for exploring the furthest corners of their empire—and then the rest of the world when there wasn't an empire to explore any more—but when it comes to spending lots of money on travel the Germans are in the lead. Long vacations and, until recently, a very strong economy combined to make Germans the world's biggest travelers. So it's hardly surprising that Germany has lots of guidebook publishers, both old school (Dumont and Polyglott, for example) and new era. The German market was notable for the sheer proliferation of small publishing houses, like Stefan Loose in Berlin, Verlag Gisela E. Walther in Bremen (both of which also translated a number of Lonely Planet, Rough Guide and Moon titles) or Peter Rump's energetic Reise Know How operation, but none of them grew big enough to dominate.

The mountains of bad press Nike managed to create for themselves by their mishandling of the 'how are our shoes manufactured?' issue was certainly a wake-up call for anybody making something in the Third World. We do most of our manufacturing in the developing world, so how do we stand up?

Purely on image, we have a huge advantage over a company like Nike. We're not selling a product with a retail price which is a huge multiple of its manufacturing cost and we don't spend a fortune on advertising, promoting and pushing the brand in order to make people feel like they're complete losers if they're not wearing it or using it. We don't have any Michael Jordans promoting our books, so nobody is paid a thousand times as much per hour as the person who actually makes the damn things is paid per week or month.

We don't really advertise at all—the Lonely Planet 'brand' has got where it is totally by word of mouth. Those Nike ads proclaiming that winning was everything, only losers came second, were such a turn-off I swore I would (wherever possible) never buy Nike shoes again, although I've got no idea if the brands I've been buying instead are any more socially responsible.

We have worried about whether we are exploiting people for quite a while. Initially it wasn't a problem. Our first book was printed in Australia, our second in Singapore and our third in Australia again, but by the time we'd done half a dozen books we were pushing everything towards Singapore and Hong Kong. At that time printing in those countries was no problem—they were both Asian 'tigers' on the prowl and they were affluent; their employees may have been working hard, but they were generally competitively paid and their working conditions were equally competitive.

How do I know that? Well, when we started out Maureen and I were not only the authors and publishers, we were also the production staff, the accounts staff and anything else you care to mention. At the same time as we were researching our books we were also visiting the factories where they would be printed. We were very aware of what working conditions were like.

But then things began to change. The production began to move out of Singapore and Hong Kong. The Singaporeans started to treat Indonesia as their backyard and shifted production there. At the same time, 'printed in Hong Kong' began to mean 'printed somewhere near Hong Kong, most likely in China'. So factory visits became less easy to slot in. Plus Maureen and I weren't doing absolutely everything any more, and we were certainly no longer the production managers.

Why were we doing most of our printing in Asia anyway? Hardly surprisingly, price topped that list. We got much more competitive printing quotes from Asia. We still do. In any straight price battle we can count on Singapore or Hong Kong winning, even though they are emphatically not Third World countries. They also do it better. We quickly discovered our Singapore-printed books stayed in one piece when our Australian-printed ones were falling apart. This wasn't a simple question of high quality in Asia versus low quality in the West. The first books we printed in Asia were 'section sewn' while we were printing 'perfect-bound' books in the West.

A little technical explanation: 'perfect bound' is one of those great oxymorons, like 'management efficiency' or 'military intelligence'. A perfect-bound book is printed like a stapled magazine in separate sections, typically of sixteen, thirty-two or sixty-four pages.

7 October 1992—Anniversary time again. This time it's our twenty-first and we're high in the Himalayas above the village of Tarke Gyang on the Helambu Circuit in Nepal.

In 1994 we drove west-east and then east-west across the United States in a venerable old Cadillac. The car had no brakes to speak of but it did have a cigarette lighter for every seat and the biggest tail fins ever seen. *(Photo: Tony Wheeler)*

In 1997 photographer Richard I'Anson and I made a circuit of a dozen cities in Asia to produce our coffee-table book *Chasing Rickshaws* about those man- (and occasionally woman-) powered bicycle taxis. *(Photo: Richard I'Anson)*

The rickshaw project also took us to Yogyakarta, the cultural capital of Java. Here I'm trying out a *becak*, the Indonesian version of a cycle rickshaw. *(Photo: Richard I'Anson)*

I did a lot of walking while we were researching the first edition of our Britain guide. Here I'm crossing a field along the Cotswold Way, a delightful week-long walk from near Stratford-upon-Avon to Bath. *(Photo: Simon Smallwood)*

WESTEN EUROPE

In Lonely Planet's warehouse one sunny afternoon . . .

1st Warehouse Guy (stacking copies of new book on shelf): How do you spell Western?
2nd Warehouse Guy: W-E-S-T-E-R-N.
1st Warehouse Guy: There's an 'R' in it?
2nd Warehouse Guy: Sure.
1st Warehouse Guy: Well, looks like somebody ****ed up.

Later, in a publishing meeting . . .

Steve: How did this happen, surely somebody should have checked the covers?
Richard: Everybody checked the cover – designers, senior designers, editors, senior editors, Rob (publisher), damn it, I even saw it!
John: So what are we going to do? We look pretty dumb if we can't even spell Western.
Anna: Well we could pulp them, but I don't think we should sacrifice all those trees just for one 'R'.
Richard: We could sticker them, but unless you get the stickers on really straight it just attracts attention.
Maureen: And people peel off the stickers to see what you're trying to hide.
Steve: We could just confess, put an errata slip in the book, make a bit of a joke about it.
Tony: Make it a bookmark, then at least it's something useful.

looney planet

If you do want to bugfix your Westen Europe, the patch is available for download from
www.lonelyplanet.com/upgrades/oops.htm

The 'Westen Europe' Bookmark.

During 1998 I managed to get on a ship going to Pitcairn Island in the Pacific Ocean, one of the most remote and diffi-cult-to-reach outposts in the world.

'My other business partners take me out for beer or for lunch, not on a bloody three-week walk.' In 2001 we took our new partner, the colorful Sydney businessman John Singleton, on the Annapurna Circuit walk in Nepal. *(Photo: Richard I'Anson)*

Our London office had a taxi painted as a rolling Lonely Planet billboard to promote our new London guidebook in 1998.
(Photo: Tony Wheeler)

7 October 2001—Yes, another wedding anniversary, our thirtieth, popped up while we were on the Annapurna Circuit and our Sherpa crew baked a cake for the occasion. *(Photo: Richard I'Anson)*

Maureen and I have just reached the highest point on the Annapurna Circuit, the 17769 feet summit of the Thorung-La Pass, a smidge higher than the Everest Base Camp. *(Photo:Richard I'Anson)*

In early 2001 photographer Peter Bennetts and I were working on *Time and Tide*, a photographic book about the effects of global warming and changing sea levels on the low-lying Pacific nation of Tuvalu. We were marooned on the island of Nukufetau for a week when the boat which was supposed to collect us broke down. I'm giving thanks as our boat finally turns up. *(Photo: Peter Bennetts)*

Richard I'Anson and I worked on another photographic book together, *Rice Trails*, which told the story of the world's most important (and beautiful) food staple. I'm in Bali having rice for lunch in a roadside food stall with my Balinese friend Ketut Suartana. *(Photo: Richard I'Anson)*

Rice Trails also took us to Cambodia and Vietnam. Here I've just jumped on a motorcyle taxi near the market in Phnom Penh. *(Photo: Richard I'Anson)*

I had a go at doing some rice farming myself while I was in Bali, and I can confirm that transplanting the seedlings is backbreaking work. *(Photo: Richard I'Anson)*

We returned to Burma with our daughter Tashi, and villagers at Maing Thauk on Inle Lake showed us this bridge which Lonely Planet had paid for. *(Photo: Stan Armington)*

Lonely Planet moved to a new office in 2001, a renovated Victorian-era warehouse beside the Maribyrnong River in the Melbourne suburb of Footscray.

In 2002 I went back to East Timor to research the first guidebook to the newly independent nation. My travels took me all around the country, including to the top of Mt Ramelau, the island's highest point. *(Photo: Galen Yeo)*

In 2003 our German publishing friends from Berlin, Stefan and
Renate Loose, decided to celebrate their twenty-fifth wedding
anniversary by getting married again in Bali. Along with their other
guests, we dressed up in traditional Balinese style for the ceremony.
(Photo: Renate Loose)

Researching *Rice Trails* also took Richard I'Anson and me to Japan—the bowl of food I'm pointing at is a tasty dish of fried grasshoppers. *(Photo: Mitsuku Hibino)*

On a visit to Bali in 2003 we discovered our name had been appropriated for a billboard advertising Bintang Beer. *(Photo: Stefan Loose)*

Checking a map en route
to the Everest Base
Camp in 2003.

If we look slightly depressed it's because this was our last lunch
after a month of traveling around Spain and France in 2004. We're
at a café perched high above the Mediterranean coast on the Côte
d'Azur.

The Coliseum Bar in Kuala Lumpur has hardly changed from the days when colonial rubber planters used to gather here for a beer. In 2005 I had one too.

When I was traveling through Southeast Asia in 2005 I visited the monastery at Wat Kdol, just outside Battambang in Cambodia, and this elderly monk wanted to be photographed with me.

In 2005 I traveled from Singapore to Shanghai, sticking to surface-level transport the whole way. En route I stopped in Macau to talk about sustainable tourism at the PATA (Pacific Asia Travel Association) annual conference and took time out for a high-altitude stroll around the Macau Tower.

Traveling by train from Hanoi in Vietnam up to the border with China in 2005.

Not a lot of tourists get to Bangladesh so you certainly get plenty of attention. *(Photo: Richard I'Anson)*

7 October 2003—We celebrated Lonely Planet's thirtieth birthday by doing a reprint of our very first book, and when the Melbourne *Age* came round to photograph us at our new office it just happened to be our wedding anniversary! *(Photo:Fairfaxphotos)*

Each of those sections is known as a 'signature'. The book load of signatures is then clamped together, the folded edge is sliced off and the whole collection of now individual pages is glued into the cover. It's far from perfect because if you bend it back and forth enough times eventually those individual pages will start to fall out, one by one. Generally that's not a problem. You read a novel, you hand it on to your girlfriend or your mother and they read it too. Everybody flicks back and forth a few times, but this doesn't come close to testing it to failure. Unless the glue is really weak, or the book gets seriously misused, perfect binding is perfect for most books.

Guidebooks get opened and closed countless times. When you're in town you open it up a half-dozen times to the same place to look for that particular restaurant. On the bus you open it up over and over again to check how much longer this interminable trip is going to take. You drop it on the floor, you spill coffee on it, you throw it against the wall in exasperation when you cannot find the great hotel five minutes from the railway station. You use it outside in the rain, it sits and bakes in the sun and then freezes in the snow. Eventually, a perfect-bound guidebook falls apart.

Enter section sewing. Each of those 'signatures' is individually sewn down the fold, just like a magazine would be stapled. Then the signatures are glued into the cover. There's no way a single page can fall out. If a section-sewn book is going to suffer terminal collapse at least it's going to be in big chunks. We think our books should be section sewn; in fact we make a bit of a song and dance about it. Of course, lots of other books are section sewn as well; books that are going to get heavy use, like school textbooks or Bibles, for example. How can you tell if a book is section sewn? Just look at the spine— if you can see the individual, magazine-like sections then it's section sewn. It doesn't matter where it's produced: a section-sewn book is going to be more expensive than a perfect-bound one, but the difference is much less with our Asian printers.

Our Asian printers also win on shipping and that relates to Lonely Planet's international needs. If we were a purely American publisher it would make sense to print in the US. Sure it might be a bit more expensive, but we'd recoup that cost and could live with any quality difference because we'd have those books on sale while the Hong Kong–printed books were still crossing the Pacific. But we aren't a one-country publisher, so the time we'd gain in one country we'd lose in another and when it comes to shipping things the Asians are the champs. They pack the books better, they get them on the ships faster, the ships leave more frequently and they do the paperwork with more efficiency.

So there were very good reasons why we should be printing in Asia, but what began as 'Asia' started to expand beyond Singapore and Hong Kong and, at the same time, we were no longer regularly visiting the printing factories. We asked Graham to have a look. Graham Imeson had joined us as our sole book designer in 1983, but over the years his role shifted from design to production. At around the same time it became more and more necessary to visit the printers, whether it was to keep an eye on quality or to discuss paper purchases, print speed, packaging strength, shipping times or paperwork simplification. So we added 'check the working conditions' to Graham's list of responsibilities. We expected Graham to check what the print-workers' lives were like, just as he was checking the nature of the printing presses. So far it seems to be working—we can put our hands on our hearts and say that as far as we know we aren't exploiting people in order to get our books on the shelves.

That's the 'people exploitation' issue, but do we look after the 'environment' as well? With printing and books that usually comes down to their vital constituent: paper. That is to say, trees. It's a fairly simple equation. Pick up a copy of a 1000-page book like our India, Australia or Britain guide. It weighs a couple of pounds. Take a thousand copies of our India book and you've got almost a ton of paper or wood. Take 100 000 copies and you've got almost 100 tons. It's easy to see why forests fall to create books.

It's not all gloom. Books, unlike oil, are a renewable resource. You can plant more trees and grow more books. You can't create more oil. We use as much recycled paper in our books as we can, but recycled paper doesn't work well for guidebooks. It's heavier. We're always fighting weight problems with our books, trying to keep the weight down so they'll travel easier. We can do that by cutting the book size and that's something with which we wage a never-ending struggle. If we used more recycled paper they'd get bigger again. Then they'd cost more to ship from place to place—and more fuel would get burnt getting them shipped. Plus people would complain about having to carry those bulkier books about.

How about printing the books in sections so travelers only need to tote around the area they're actually visiting? That's one of the standard suggestions we field from our readers. Cost again makes it impossible, so if you really want to carry less book around you'll have to slice it up.

Our paper comes from all over the place and Graham also makes sure the paper we use has a history we can be confident about. The last thing we want to find out is that a Brazilian rainforest fell to provide the paper to print our Brazil book. Book paper comes from timber plantations and we use so much of it that we often buy it in bulk. Buying our own paper means we can be sure of where it comes from and we get a better price, but just as importantly it ensures we don't run out.

We do much of our business with only a couple of printers. Partly it's because we know and trust each other, but it's also very difficult for a new printer to get a foot in the door. Of course you don't want to jump into bed with a new printer and straight off ask them to do ten or twenty new books for you, but if you ask for a quote on only one job they're unlikely to be able to match the prices of a printer that's lined up for a hundred such projects in the coming months.

Guidebook writer. Sounds like a romantic occupation doesn't it? You fly here and there, explore unusual attractions, look for the perfect hotel, search for the most wonderful meal and write about it. It's like being on holiday all the time and getting paid for it. Think again.

For a start, you're constantly in a frantic rush. When the people who use our guidebooks are on vacation they may go to some of the places we cover and explore some of the sights. The writer who researched that guidebook had to go to every place and visit every sightseeing attraction. Writing a guidebook is rather like preparing a terrific meal. First you decide what you're going to cook and study your recipe book; that's the equivalent of the pre-trip research the writer has to do. Then you buy the ingredients, which for a writer means doing the in-the-field research. Finally, you bring the ingredients home and cook the meal, which is when the writer returns to base with notes, brochures, maps and memories and blends them into a book.

You don't buy the fish one day and a couple of days later shop for the salad ingredients. Nor do you leave the lettuce sitting around for a few days, watching the leaves turn brown, before you put the meal together. It's the same with guidebooks—all that freshly gathered information will start to go stale and curl up at the edges if you leave it for too long. Guidebooks are perishable commodities; the information quickly dates, so once you start work you must push through to the end as rapidly as you can.

As a result, guidebooks are researched at a breakneck pace. There's no time to sit around and soak up the atmosphere, no time for leisurely coffees, no relaxed romantic meals. Writing that a beach has sand like talcum powder lapped by warm, translucent water probably means the writer sprinted down to the beach and jumped in the water for just long enough to test the temperature before rushing off to the next beach.

Guidebook writers don't work from nine to five. At the start of the day they may find themselves checking if the sunrise over the temple really is spectacularly beautiful or if dawn is the best time to visit the fruit and vegetable market. At the other end of the day they may be exploring which are the hot nightclubs and discos. That's before they return to their hotel to write up their notes and to read up on tomorrow's program. To cover the places that their schedule requires may mean researching all day then traveling by night to the next destination. It's no wonder 'author burnout' is something we worry about.

Furthermore, guidebook research is generally a solitary pursuit; it's not good for relationships. We've got a few couples who work as a team and some writers have established a family base from where they fan out to cover the surrounding region, returning to base when they can. Generally, however, it's faster, more efficient and, of course, cheaper to work alone. Since a typical project may mean three months or more field research this can entail a large part of the year on your own.

The story doesn't get any easier when you finish the research and start writing. The information you gathered in the first town you visited is already three months old so it's imperative to write as fast as possible. (We sometimes suspect that airlines deliberately put up their fares, telephone companies change all the phone numbers and governments change the visa regulations as soon as we've got the current information into the system.) So, after months of solitary travel, the poor guidebook writer is now locked away with a word processor, tapping furiously to meet a deadline.

We're regularly asked how we find our writers (usually followed by a request to be one). Well, first of all, you've got to be madly keen on travel and have done lots of it. Don't plan on becoming a guidebook writer if you're not already an experienced traveler, and don't believe Anne Tyler's novel *Accidental Tourist* about a guidebook writer who doesn't like to travel. It's a nice book and some of her observations about guidebook writing (stealing the menu, for example) are spot on, but I can't imagine a guidebook writer who didn't like to travel. Give me a ticket, point me towards the airport and I'm gone.

The skills required for a guidebook writer are amazingly varied and our writers come from all sorts of different backgrounds. Writing is a basic skill and hopefully our writers can do it well. Sometimes we put up with a weak writer, but essentially we want someone who can do the job without lots of outside help. Having some unique skill or experience is a bonus. Writers who speak weird and wonderful languages are always interesting. Writers who have lived or worked in offbeat places are also looked upon with favor. Relevant experience helps—if you've been writing for one of our competitors we may be very happy to hear from you, although, in general, we prefer that our writers don't swap their allegiances back and forth between publishers. Being a computer whiz can be helpful and taking great photographs can make you popular, particularly if you're working on one of those really off-the-beaten-track destinations for which lots of images are not readily available.

A Lonely Planet guidebook writer must also be good with maps. We're very proud of our maps; there are lots of them and they often cover places for which no other alternative mapping is available. They're difficult, time-consuming and expensive to produce and, unfortunately, some people can be good at everything else, but mapping is simply not their forte. We spend an enormous amount of time cross-checking between the text and the maps. If the text says the hotel is two blocks to the west of the railway station, does the map tell you the same thing?

At the end of the day, however, being a good guidebook writer requires some really mundane skills. You'd be disappointed if a football player couldn't kick a ball straight, if a singer couldn't hit the high notes or if a model didn't look stunning, right? So a travel writer damn well better be able to instantly spot the best restaurant in town, zero in without fail on the hottest nightspots and at the very least go round the block without getting lost. Sorry, it doesn't always work that way.

I hate to think how many times I've been hopelessly lost with fellow travel writers. In fact, I don't know any group of people more apt to get lost than travel writers. It isn't that we're stuck with some genetic impairment to our sense of direction. It probably is a hard-wired problem, but it's not got a lot to do with knowing which way is north. No, the real problem is curiosity and the constant need to find something new or different. As a result, travel writers simply cannot bear to go from A to B by the same route twice. We're constantly turning off into previously untried back alleys and, sure enough, at least half the time they turn out to be dead ends.

And as for our unmatched ability to find the hottest nightspot, the coolest hotel swimming pool, the highest lookout point or the best shopping bargain? The truth is you cannot be an interested expert on absolutely everything. I know travel writers who are absolute philistines when it comes to art and culture, so how are they going to advice on the latest art-gallery trends? Others wouldn't know their Guccis from their Levis, so how can they spot whether this is the place for the latest fashions?

Some travel writers are night owls, keen to check out every night-club in town and always the last one to get kicked out of bars in the early hours. Others couldn't care less about late nights, but they've caught the sun rising over every mountain and temple in Asia and been there for a thousand pre-dawn market openings. A few years ago, two travel-writing friends ended up in Pyongyang, the hard-to-get-to capital of reclusive North Korea. One night writer A, the night owl, came rushing back to the hotel room of writer B, the early-to-bedder, to excitedly announce he'd discovered the location of North Korea's only disco and they should go there immediately. I'm not a real late nighter, but I would have been instantly on my way. Not writer B; he opted to stay home and catch up with his notes.

So how do we get away with being experts on everything? Surprisingly, you do get enthusiastic about the most unexpected topics. Put me with birdwatchers and I suddenly develop an interest in birdwatching. Working on a guidebook to Britain I developed a totally uncharacteristic enthusiasm for medieval church architecture. Kicking around Irish pubs for an Ireland guide I even discovered I liked Guinness. I've written about everything from unexpected encounters with sharks (Tahiti) to red-light district strip clubs (San Francisco) and what to do when your dinner tries to escape from your plate (Japan). Even the stay-at-homes write imaginatively about the glitzy night life. The atheists glory in the temple architecture. The late risers pretend they were there to see the market opening and the teetotallers wax lyrical about fine wines.

Which brings me to food. If you're writing guidebooks it does help if you like to eat out. Fortunately, I could happily eat out in restaurants every night of the year. Ask me about what I like to make, when it comes to food, and the answer is reservations, but of course there's no way we can eat out in all the restaurants we write about. A guidebook writer, spending a day or two in each place, cannot possibly eat out in a dozen restaurants in each town. Nor do we need to. I have a simple and generally infallible restaurant test. I look in the front window, and if it's crowded, noisy and people are smiling, laughing and enjoying themselves, then the food is good. If I look in another restaurant and it's almost empty, and at the few occupied tables there's not a smile to be seen, well, what do you think the food is like?

Once upon a time we did all our books on a royalty basis with the author holding the copyright. That's the conventional way novels and other 'author-created' books are handled. The book retails for $30 and the author gets a ten per cent royalty, so for each copy sold he or she picks up $3. The reasoning behind this is that the author and the publisher share in the success of the book. If it does well, the author does well. If it falls on its face then so does the author. When we were a penniless new publisher royalty contracts had a big advantage: we didn't have to pay until the book sold. Sure there's that magic word 'advance', money you hand over to the author as an advance against royalties, something to keep them going until the book hits the shelves, but in the early days we had no money to hand out and our authors, keen to travel and be published, were happy to go along with that.

This was fine in our early days and in some cases it worked out very well for both sides. On the first India book we gave Geoff Crowther and Prakash Raj US$1000 each as an advance for their expenses and agreed that they would each get a 2.5 per cent royalty from the sales of the book. It was a risk from both sides, but when the book started to sell in big quantities we all did very well.

As we grew and our books became more complex, there were all sorts of reasons why we could no longer live with royalties and therefore began to pay fees. Today all our guidebooks are prepared on a fee basis and Lonely Planet, rather than the author, holds the copyright.

In many ways a travel book is more akin to a magazine than a conventional book because it doesn't stay the same for ever and the writers on one edition of the book may be completely changed for the next edition. Even if the writers stayed the same from one edition to the next, those conventional contracts were impossible to administer when there was a big cast of writers on a book. Paying a royalty was also recognition of the author's creative role in the book and it soon became evident that we, the publishers, were the creators, not the authors. We thought the book up, we decided what it was going to be like, and then we recruited the writers to put our plans into action. The travelers who bought our books bought them because the Lonely Planet name was on the book, not the author's.

The issue of increasing complexity doesn't only apply to the number of writers involved with a specific book. Photographic quality, for example, became more important and we recognized that it wasn't right to pay two authors the same amount if one brought us back superb photographs while we had to pay photo libraries to bring the other author's book up to scratch. The books also spawned increasing numbers of spin-offs. If we were using material from the country guide to form the basis of a more detailed city guide, for example, or if it was distilled down to appear in a less detailed regional guide, there were problems with compensating the original creator. Once again, it was much easier if we owned the original material outright.

We do try to reward hard work even if it isn't with royalties. We don't want writers burning out and it's to neither side's advantage if our writers aren't making a reasonable return for their efforts. We're especially concerned about our dependable full-time writers, the ones who go straight from one project to the next and on whom we can absolutely rely. We're flexible when they insist they really need to be paid more for their project, and if we feel they've been having a tough time—because a project has taken longer than expected, because travel costs have escalated in their country, or for any of a host of reasons—then we may well decide to be unexpectedly generous with their next project.

We can be flexible, but we're not going to make a writer rich simply because they've landed the country that has become the flavor of the month. The big money that book pulls in is going to shore up the balance sheet for the book about the country which has suddenly fallen right off our sales charts, for reasons which might vary from political instability to an unexpected outbreak of disease or some natural disaster. We're going to keep that book going, on the expectation that things will turn round and the visitors return, and meanwhile it will be supported by the strong titles in our list.

Copyright was another issue we began to face at about the same time as the royalty question. We didn't want the author holding the copyright, as therefore they'd be able to take the book somewhere else if they fell out with us. If we decided they weren't doing a good enough job we wanted to be able to get somebody else to write the next edition.

The fee allocated for researching and writing a book is based on the amount of work involved (how long it will take) and the expense involved (clearly we have to allow more for three months in Italy than three months in India). Plus, of course, how much we love and respect the author. Experienced old hands (whom we trust and want to keep happy) get paid more than new writers on their first outing. The potential sales of the book may have some bearing on what we pay—the bigger and more successful the title, the more we can afford to pay for the project—but it isn't the total story. Sometimes we pay our authors more than the book is worth because it's a project we really want to do; perhaps it completes coverage of a region or perhaps it's a country which has temporarily fallen on hard times (political unrest may have scared visitors away, for example).

Some of our books have enjoyed a steady, long-term relationship with their authors and some have had a changing cast with each edition. There's a lot to be said for each approach. When an author (or authors) writes several editions of a book they really get to know their country or region and can do each subsequent edition more efficiently and quickly. On the other hand, they can go stale and fail to see when changes and improvements are needed. The best solution is a mix of stability and fresh faces. Properly managed, either pattern can work.

One of the writers in the team will always be the 'lead author'. He or she will be in charge of bringing the whole project together, making sure there's no overlap between writers or (much worse) something missed out in between. It's also their responsibility to ensure consistency—we don't want city A to be spelt differently in one half of the book from the other, or the bus fare from A to B being different from the fare from B to A (unless it really is).

We value long-term relationships with our writers, but sometimes books do go bad and sometimes the author simply has to leave. Sometimes it's the author's decision and we come to a quite amicable agreement over the split. Other times it may be because we no longer get on with the author, their approach is wrong or the country has changed but they haven't.

These days, with authors coming and going more frequently, egos don't come into it so much, but at one time they certainly did. We all like to see our names in print, but some authors seemed to have egos which got totally out of control once their name was on a book. They'd decide they were infallible, that we could not live without them and that their contribution to the book far outweighed anybody else's. This could lead to petty sniping over whose name was higher up on the title page. These days we simply list the lead writer first and then everybody else alphabetically. In one case an author complained that in the photos of the authors his head looked smaller than the other authors and he wanted his picture enlarged and recropped so his head was as big as anybody else's. We bit our publishing tongues and didn't comment that his head was already much bigger than anyone else's.

T: We had concerns about our Tahiti book, one of our most popular Pacific guides, so in 1994 Maureen and I gave it a thorough test. Well, somebody had to do it! We stayed in places from a Club Med to the luxurious Bora Bora Hotel, biked and drove around islands and sailed catamarans on lagoons. I did some scuba diving, flying with manta rays or quaking as the sharks streamed by in the Rangiroa Lagoon pass. We tried out plenty of restaurants and visited lots of *maraes* (pre-Christian Polynesian temples), and at the end of the day we decided to rewrite the book from scratch.

Working with Jean-Bernard Carillet, who worked at our Paris office, had lived in French Polynesia for a spell and was an even keener scuba diver than me, we wrote the book in English and French. I had a surprisingly good time. Far from the sybaritic South Seas vision of reclining on golden sands watching the waves lap at your toes, I found it exhaustingly energetic—from having to make a half-day 40-mile circuit of Tahaa by beat-up bicycle (the island's two rent-a-cars were both taken) to a series of sweaty climbs to the top of the picturesque mountain tops which tower over island lagoons.

Book covers often cause us angst. They inspire lots of arguments, and work well when we don't expect it or fall flat when we have high hopes for them. Finding the perfect cover is virtually impossible; you want something that is a cliché (one glance tells you where it is) and yet somehow isn't one. The last thing you want is yet another shot of the Eiffel Tower for a Paris guide, the Golden Gate Bridge for San Francisco or a Beefeater for Britain. We've done all three although one edition of Paris was the perfect 'cliché, but not a cliché'. The Eiffel Tower was certainly there, in the background, but what caught your attention was a guy in baggy pants doing a somersault in the foreground.

We have done some great covers over the years. On the very first edition of our Bali guidebook we used a bright orange naïve art painting in the style known as 'young artist'. The painting, from a little local gallery in Ubud, cost me only $20 back in 1983 and the artist I Nyoman Dana was delighted that his picture ended up on the cover of a book. It still hangs on my office wall.

One edition of our Africa shoestring guide had a lovely cover showing a robed North African about to ski down a Saharan sand dune. A German friend who runs an expedition equipment business in Germany (if you need a kayak outfitted for the Arctic or long-range fuel tanks for your Land Rover, he's your man) told me of leaving a worn-out pair of skis planted in the sand atop a remote Saharan dune. Years later, a customer turned up to say, 'you would not believe what I saw, miles from anywhere in the middle of the Sahara . . .'

We featured a whitewater rafting shot on our New Zealand guide once. A couple of editions later I was speaking at an adventure travel function in New Zealand and the oarsman Damien O'Connor who appeared in the shot introduced himself. He was now a politician and a member of the New Zealand parliament, 'I regularly used that cover in my election campaign,' he said. 'Tourism is really important for us and I was able to say, "I've played my part in encouraging visitors"!'

It's remarkable how often people who appear on the covers or in the photographs inside do see them. A photo I took of a young man and his fruit stall in the market in Kandy in Sri Lanka was proudly displayed in his stall for years afterwards. Unhappily, these days we have to be much more cautious about getting model releases signed before we can use photographs of people. It's one of the sad developments that go with getting bigger.

If there's a word any self-respecting publisher should dislike it's plagiarism. The creator of an original intellectual work has copyright in it and owns it. When somebody else copies (or plagiarizes) that work it's theft and the copyright owner can take action against the thief. First, however, copyright has to exist and second, the theft has to take place. The magic words in this game are 'intellectual' and 'creation'. Is putting together a phone directory an 'intellectual' and 'creative' act?

Essentially, the copyright lawyers have decided, you cannot copyright facts, but you can copyright the presentation of them. So, you can spend great effort to go to the back of beyond and find the only three hotels in existence there, but you can't copyright their details. All you can copyright is the matchless prose with which you described those three hotels. The names of the hotels, their addresses and phone numbers (if they have them) are simple facts. For the person who has gone to considerable effort to be the first person to track down those three remote hotels, this is very galling. Of course, if the clever author only found two hotels, and made up the third one, then creativity has come into it and the copycat who lists all three is guilty of plagiarism. Or if the hotel doesn't really have a name (there's no sign, no local phone directory, no advertisement), and the name is just what people call it, then finding that information is a creative act.

Any decent travel writer soon learns who has been there and who hasn't. Talking in a bookshop in Vienna one day, our Austrian distributor told me there were two types of guidebooks: the first-level guidebooks and the second-level ones. For the first-level books, like ours, somebody really goes there and researches it. They've seen it with their own eyes. For the second-level books, somebody sits down in an office with a bunch of other books around them and writes the text. Sling in some off-the-shelf maps and some pretty photos and bingo, you have a guidebook. A second-level book can even be quite legitimate—perhaps it's an author who has already written a more comprehensive first-level book and now turns to producing a condensed and simplified version—but it's not the product of that original research. Essentially, the second-level books ride on the first-level's hard work.

Writing about somewhere without going there is no problem when it comes to the Taj Mahals, Empire State Buildings or Eiffel Towers of this world. They've been described a million times, seen in movies and there are plenty of non-copyrighted materials (tourist office brochures, for example) which cover them very adequately. Writing about somewhere remote, when alternative descriptions are few and far between, is a whole different kettle of fish. This came home to me very clearly in 1983 in Burma. I was working on the third edition of our Burma guide and for the first time I went to the town of Prome (now known as Pyay). In the earlier editions I'd described Prome in very general terms, but I had never been there. The town was one of those curious places in Burma which wasn't really 'off limits', but certainly was not on the list of approved places for tourists to visit. I'd hired a pickup truck, driver and guide, in itself a rather borderline thing to do, and my companions were very cautious whenever we entered a town or passed by a checkpost. I was hiding under the tarpaulin in the back of the truck as we came into Prome.

We spent several hours in the town, visiting the Shwesandaw Pagoda in the center and the ruins of ancient Thayekhittaya (or Sri Ksetra) outside the town. I had several sources of information about Burma with me and I soon discovered that nobody had been to Prome! Clearly, everybody had rehashed some old and badly worded description which turned out to be misleadingly incorrect.

As we know to our cost, if you are charged with plagiarism sorting it out can be very time-consuming and expensive. We published our first China guide in 1984 and although it was not the first China guidebook on the shelves after the doors to Mao's reclusive hideaway first began to creak open, it was certainly a pioneering effort. Early visitors to China were strictly escorted and tightly controlled; our book was written for independent travelers at a time when independent travel in China was far from straightforward. The first edition went well, and three years later the second edition was at the printer when, with malevolent timing, a lawyer's letter arrived accusing us of a long litany of copyright infringements. We laboriously tracked down the relevant pieces and, of course, many of them turned out to be quite harmless. There are only so many ways you can say 'the Great Wall of China is very long' and it's hardly plagiarism if two books use that exact same wording. In other places, however, we were much less certain of our position and our book did sometimes look suspiciously like our accuser's publication.

Furthermore, all the tricky pieces emanated from the same writer whom we dragged into the office and questioned about his writing practices. Sure enough, he'd sat down with an armful of books on China and researched places which he had not visited himself (and in China in the early 1980s there were bound to be some of those), so it seemed conceivable he might have copied something. Lawyer's letters were flying back and forth and at the printers we'd stopped the presses and were busy not only rewriting questionable sections, but also scouring the rest of the book in case any other time bombs were quietly ticking away.

A couple of years had passed since that first edition was written and our possibly guilty writer was not at all certain what information sources he'd used and where, but after what seemed like endless hours of reading one description then carefully comparing it with the similar descriptions in half a dozen other books, we stumbled upon an ancient and long out-of-print pre-Communist guide to China which was clearly not only the inspiration for some of our writer's unoriginal prose, but also for our accusers. When faced with this new evidence the lawyer's letters quickly came to a halt, but we still put many more hours into ensuring the new book was squeaky clean. We didn't want our books copying anything—even antediluvian and long out-of-copyright material.

Our contracts stipulate that the work must be original, and our writing guide recommends that writers firmly shut all reference sources when they come to put their own words on paper, but still this case had crept through. We've also been pretty certain on occasion that something has been copied from one of our own books, although we've never let the lawyers loose. For one edition of our South Africa guide, our author had done a far less than careful job and the book was an embarrassment. We hauled our author over the coals and hired a new team of writers to make major improvements. Meanwhile, another publisher brought out a number of new titles with such speed that we had deep suspicions about how they had managed to research them. When we read their South Africa guide we could only laugh. All the worst mistakes, short cuts and abbreviated research in our own guide popped up precisely copied in the other publisher's book.

Plagiarism into another language is easier for the guilty party to do and harder for the innocent party to detect. Authors, well aware of their own style, quickly pick up when somebody else is copying their work. That's not so easy when the work is a translation, and we have on a number of occasions found whole books plagiarized in a different language.

Our Bolivia guide, for example, is a pretty marginal book. Bolivia doesn't attract huge numbers of visitors, ergo we don't sell as many copies as we'd like. That's in English, the biggest potential visitor pool, so what hope would there be for a Bolivia guide in another language? Well, perhaps it might get off the ground in German, always the travel leaders, but a guide to Bolivia in Dutch? It certainly cuts the cost if you simply translate our Bolivia guide into Dutch!

Most of these illegal translations come to our attention due to civic-minded readers. Without them we would never in a million years have found out about the Japanese publisher who turned our Moroccan Arabic/English phrasebook (price less than $10) into a Moroccan Arabic/Japanese phrasebook (price more than $50)! An outraged Japanese-language student wrote to us to reveal this very unprofitable crime—how many students of Moroccan Arabic can there be in Japan?

Plagiarized maps are often very easy to detect, particularly if our map is the product of original research and not available in any other form. The funniest case for me was while I was working on an update of our India guide in 1995. The map of the center of the city of Mysore was adequate, but not state of the art. The scale varied dramatically from one side of the map to the other and at one point a fictitious street popped into the grid. When I tried to buy a new map, however, nothing was available at a large enough scale to show the area I wanted. I was carrying some competitive guides with me so I looked to see what they made of the place. Only one other book had a map of the central area and to my considerable surprise it also had the same wild scale variations and the same fictitious street.

This curious map went right back to the first edition of our India guide and had been hand-drawn by Geoff Crowther. The competitive guide's map was clearly a straight copy of our map. I wasn't worried, since I'd put a lot of effort into correcting the old map, even going to the trouble of pacing out street distances and checking street alignments with a compass (today I'd do both with a GPS) and our new edition would have a much more accurate map. I also found an old pre-war British map which, remarkably, was better than anything produced in the subsequent sixty years although a number of new streets had been built during that time. I did, however, write to our competitor to tell them that they had a naughty author who had been copying our maps.

'But I won't tell you which one,' I added. 'Next edition we'll have it right, but you'll be stuck with the old one. And you owe me a beer.'

Next time I was in their city they bought me one.

Our longest-running plagiarism problem, however, was another case where we were the accused party. Nicholas Greenwood wrote a Burma (Myanmar) guide for Hilary Bradt's small publishing house. In 1996, when we published the sixth edition of our Burma book, he decided we had plagiarized his book. The first we knew about this was when a letter arrived from his lawyer. His claim seemed to boil down to his description of the toilet at a guesthouse in the remote village of Putao. Since, he claimed, he was the only person who had ever found their way to this isolated convenience, if anybody else mentioned its toilet they had to have copied it from him! Not surprisingly, this didn't get him very far and having refuted his claim we heard nothing more until one day in May 1996 I got a most curious fax.

I was living in Paris at the time and the fax was addressed to all four of our offices—Melbourne, London, Paris and Oakland—and appeared to have been written on official government letterhead by Lt Gen Thein Win, from the Ministry of Transport, Union of Myanmar. In what, at first glance, one would assume was curiously stilted Burmese English, the letter informed us that anybody found in Burma with a copy of our book was 'summoned to appear at a special tribune under Myanmar Penal Code Section 500' and would be punished with 'two years' imprisonment or with fine or with both'.

Furthermore, the letter continued, any Burmese citizen found with the book would be subjected to 'not less than five years' hard labour on Ye-Dawei rail line'. The letter then wandered off to make a few editorial corrections, complain about how we'd divided the country into chapters and, finally, get around to that tiny village of Putao (scrupulously avoiding any mention of the toilet facilities).

The letter was clearly a prank, but there was one final give-away—the fax answerback number indicated it had come not from Burma, but from London. I wrote a reply, dialed the number and discovered it was a dual phone and fax line, answered by someone with a very English accent.

'Nicholas?' I queried.

There was some noisy spluttering from the other end of the line before the phone was hung up!

For a time that ended our communications with Mr Greenwood, but before long he had found another way to exact his revenge upon us. He began to plague our website. One of the most popular parts of our website is the Thorn Tree, a travel forum where visitors can post questions and comments and get replies or, in some cases, abuse. Internet chat rooms are frequently plagued by 'trolls', computer nerds who spend endless hours being abusive or even pornographically rude to other visitors. Our Burma complainer became a grade A troll, usually operating under the 'handle' Kyaw.

Simply blocking any message from 'Kyaw' was, of course, hopeless. He would just send in messages from K*aw or Ky*w and he clearly had plenty of time to indulge his hobby. A lot of his abuse was directed at Lonely Planet and at poor Joe Cummings, who had been responsible for recent updates of our Burma guide, but anybody who took offence to something posted by Kyaw in his many impersonations was also fair game. We spent ridiculous amounts of time clearing off page after page of the same four-letter word, posted by the idiotic Kyaw. Then, for a time, he would calm down, and would even respond helpfully to queries about Burma.

At times we could imagine him bent over his computer keyboard, virtually frothing at the mouth. We had to clear out his garbage around the clock, with people in every office assigned to delete his postings in each time zone. Nor were we the only party to suffer the wrath of Kyaw. Anything connected with Burma, on either side of the political fence, appeared to be fair game.

By mid-2000 cleaning up after the foul-mouthed Kyaw was becoming a serious waste of time and energy, but legal advice counselled that taking action against him could be equally time-consuming and expensive. Setting legal precedents never comes cheap and this would be a case of an Australian company taking action against a UK resident who was a nuisance to a website hosted in the USA. Maureen and I were spending twenty-four hours in London in early August en route to Italy for the Verona opera festival, so at breakfast time on August 2 2000 I visited Nicholas' apartment.

Standing there barefoot on his doorstep, in shorts and T-shirt, looking rather flabby and pale, Mr Greenwood seemed more computer nerd than terror of the Internet. There was no question he was very surprised to see me, but he didn't slam the door in my face, although I could see the thought momentarily appealed to him. We talked, probably for over an hour, and I began to believe he could be persuaded to be more reasonable. We talked about the 'alleged' plagiarizing of his book and about his 'alleged' posting of garbage on our website, and we talked about the situation in Burma. Eventually we shook hands and said we'd meet again sometime, when he'd show me his extensive library of books on Burma.

I would like to say that doorstopping Nicholas had an amazing effect, and for a few months it did. He still spent a lot of time on our website, but generally his postings were reasonable, even helpful. Then suddenly, like flicking a switch, Dr Jekyll turned back into Mr Hyde (or good Nicholas turned back into bad Kyaw) and away we went again. In June 2001 we appointed UK lawyers to take the case to the London Metropolitan Police's Computer Crimes Unit, but that got nowhere. Years later, there are Internet tools which have made keeping the nuisance makers out or cleaning up after them much easier, but periodically people like Kyaw can still be a painful waste of time.

Lonely Planet books provide independent advice. Lonely Planet does not accept advertising in guidebooks, nor do we accept payment in exchange for listing or endorsing any place or business. Lonely Planet writers do not accept discounts or payments in exchange for positive coverage of any sort.

Until recently that warning appeared in every Lonely Planet guidebook, often accompanied by the same statement in the local language. We've always insisted that our writers pay their own way and we regularly underline how important it is that their reports are completely unbiased. Despite this, we have regularly received reports that Hotel A only got its rave review because they'd bribed our researcher. We usually put these complaints down to sour grapes on the part of Hotel B, which had not got a rave review, until we had a deluge of complaints from operators in Vietnam, building up to one angry restaurateur who raged that he'd got a good write up in the previous edition, but this time his business had not even been mentioned, 'despite paying the fee'.

We couldn't believe that Robert Storey, our straight-arrow Vietnam researcher, would have charged hotels, restaurants and tour operators for their write ups. The truth turned out to be much more straightforward and the sort of scam which, unfortunately, has become a byword for Vietnamese operations. Robert had engaged a driver-cum-guide and translator to speed his work, but as Robert was writing up his notes after each inspection his friendly assistant was handing out his own business card and invoice!

Touch wood, but until 1996 we never had a really serious accident, illness or other problem with one of our writers. There had been thefts from time to time, and Jon Murray got mugged more than once in Johannesburg. But fortunately, no author has ever lost all their notes (some of them, but never all of them).

At an authors' idea-swapping session one year Bryn Thomas mused about how he became increasingly paranoid about his notes as he got close to the end of a project. In India, he recounted, he took to hiding his notebooks in the wastepaper bin every evening before he went out, on the basis that the bin was the one place no thief would think of looking. In a similar fashion David Else, Lonely Planet's 'author liaison manager' and Africa expert, wrote of spreading them all over the room, not leaving them in a handy stack that somebody could quickly pick up. These days, many authors regularly email their notes back to head office or to some other safe 'data vault'.

Nor has any author ever got seriously ill, and although we've all had our share of Delhi bellies and Montezuma's revenges even that seems to become less frequent as writers gain experience and perhaps develop a little natural immunity. Geoff Crowther probably went through every disease on offer in his tough traveling early days on the road, including a spell of malaria in southern Sudan. When James Lyon rented a beach house in Mexico for his family to stay in while he worked on the guidebook, the whole lot of them came down with hepatitis. Steve Fallon developed malaria in Budapest, which was misdiagnosed until he realized it was a delayed reminder of a trip he'd made to Irian Jaya many months earlier. And more than one author has found the sheer long-term stress of producing a guidebook can threaten their mental stability, but life-threatening diseases? No, we all seem to have escaped those.

And then, in 1996, one of our writers had a real accident. I was in the London office when a message came through from Australia about Christine Niven. A New Zealander, she was working on her second Lonely Planet project. She'd updated Sri Lanka, had gone on to work on India and was returning from Ladakh to New Delhi. There was a lull in the ongoing unrest in Kashmir and Christine had decided it was worth stopping in Srinagar, even though tourism on beautiful Dal Lake had been virtually shut down for over ten years.

She'd rented a jeep and driver and had set out to drive back to Delhi, but soon after leaving Srinagar her driver pulled out to overtake a bus and collided head-on with an approaching truck. The driver was killed instantly and Christine was seriously injured. At first, she was dumped in a corridor at the local police station while enquiries were made, then she was transported to the sort of Third World hospital we all hope we never have to experience. Fortunately, the owner of the houseboat where she had stayed the previous night heard that there had been an accident and a foreigner was in hospital.

Since foreign visitors were few and far between, he surmised it might have been Christine. When he discovered that it was, he phoned her embassy in New Delhi. He probably saved Christine's life.

As well as two badly broken legs, poor Christine had also contracted malaria in the Kashmir hospital and was in such bad shape that she was put into hospital in Hong Kong between flights on her way home. She spent many months recovering in Australia, but remarkably she had kept hold of her notebooks throughout her ordeal and when I went to visit her one day her main concern was getting her updated text in on time.

Luck certainly came into Christine's escape—what if the houseboat owner hadn't heard about the accident?—but there was also one very important piece of planning on her part which had nothing to do with luck. She had good travel insurance. We repeatedly warn people that you buy travel insurance for one reason: catastrophic disasters. The stolen camera can be replaced. The cancellation penalty for a missed flight can be paid out. When you really want insurance is when something awful happens and you need to be flown home, stretched out over several seats and with a doctor at your side. That doesn't come cheap.

Christine's accident was a wake-up call. She had good insurance, but what if she hadn't been so careful? We would have been morally obliged to get her out of there, but we decided there and then not to leave ourselves so exposed. All Lonely Planet authors, as well as staff traveling on company business, are now covered wherever they are in the world.

Curiously, we'd no sooner put the policy in place than we had a minor spate of travel incidents. Peter Turner arrived in Jakarta in 1998 to update our Indonesia guide just as the riots broke out with the fall of Soeharto. Most of the Indonesian capital's Western residents were evacuated and Peter along with them. Your government may fly you out in that situation, but they're still likely to present you with a bill afterwards. Krzysztof Dydynski was checking a hotel in Venezuela when the floor of a partly constructed new wing collapsed, pitching him onto the floor below and leaving him with a broken arm. Even we had to make a claim on the policy when our son Kieran was bitten by a dog when he was trekking with Maureen to Lo Manthang in the remote north of Nepal in 1999. It was a very nice dog and he was only giving it a pat, but he needed an expensive series of anti-rabies injections when he got back to Kathmandu.

I often say a guidebook has to do three things.

First, it has to save your life. Perhaps not literally, but on those occasions when you emerge from the railway station in an unknown town at midnight the guidebook should say, 'turn left, walk two blocks and you'll find a good, reasonably priced place to stay. Turn right and you'll get mugged within a block.' That sort of advice may not exactly save your life, but it can certainly save you a lot of hassles.

Second, it should educate you. A little education not only helps you enjoy your travels more, it makes you a better traveler. A simple example is handicrafts: know a little more about them and you're more likely to buy something good rather than something trashy. Not only will you enjoy the transaction more, you'll also encourage the people who make those crafts to turn out good work, not junk for tourists. Maureen and I have a house full of what we call 'high-quality tourist art'. There's nothing especially valuable, nothing that would find a place in a museum—well, one or two pieces look like they might deserve a place with spotlights—but it's all been selected with care.

It's remarkable how a little knowledge can make simple sightseeing much more interesting. When our children were still pre-school age we'd make a game of identifying Hindu temples in Kathmandu.

'See that trident in front of the temple, that's the symbol of Shiva, the god of destruction,' we'd point out. 'So there should be a figure of a bull, his "vehicle", the animal he rides on, look, there it is . . .'

Before you knew it our kids could tell a Ganesh temple from a Vishnu temple and those strange-looking buildings became a game, something they were beginning to understand, appreciate and enjoy.

Third, a guidebook should be fun. We travel for all sorts of reasons, but most often it's for enjoyment and guidebooks should help your enjoyment. Even if you're not having fun they should lighten your load.

Guidebooks have all sorts of responsibilities to the people who use them. We're there to make life easier and more interesting as well as offer more serious advice about treading gently in new environments and strange cultures. A good guidebook should help you avoid hotels with bedbugs and restaurants with lousy food. It should tell you which museum is worth a visit and which tourist trap to walk straight by. It should also help you to avoid getting ripped off.

There have been travelers' rip-offs as long as there have been travelers to rip off and as soon as people get wise to one scam, another immediately pops up. The amazing thing is how long it takes some people to get wise to them.

The longest-running scam has to be the Thai gems one. The routine is simple: Thailand is a world center for semi-precious stones, so if you buy them at local prices, you can sell them at home for a healthy profit. Nobody jumps out of a gemshop and says, 'Buy these gems, you'll make a fortune.' Usually the unwary traveler is led into the trap so gently they never see it coming.

Travelers in Bangkok might find themselves sharing a table in a coffee bar with a local and after a few chance meetings there might be an invitation to look around a temple. Only after the traveler is quite convinced that the contact is entirely genuine and non-commercial will it slip out that there is a brother in the gem business and lots of people are making big money taking the gems back to Sydney or London or New York.

Then there are visits to the brother's gem business; letters from happy customers are passed around, explanations are proffered about why this business doesn't work on a large scale (probably something about import regulations) and to clinch the deal there are the addresses and business cards of the gem buyers in Sydney or London or New York who are waiting for people to turn up with their valuable gems. With dollar signs dancing in front of their eyes, the visitor is soon cashing in every traveler's check they can find to buy buckets of gemstones.

The reality check comes in Sydney or London or New York. Perhaps the dealer doesn't exist at all, but if they do they're not very interested in buying the unwary traveler's gemstones for the sort of money the unwary traveler is expecting. It's not that the unscrupulous gem dealer has sold anything fake. There are $5 emeralds and $50 emeralds and $500 emeralds and it's certainly no crime to sell $5 emeralds for $500, it's just rather foolish to pay such a big mark-up.

In the late 1980s this scam grew to amazing heights and we put more and more detailed descriptions in our Thailand and Southeast Asia guides of how this scam worked and how it was going to cost big money if you fell for it. Often, however, it seemed like we were whistling in the wind. One foolish traveler wrote to us at great length explaining how he had been sucked in to parting with ridiculous amounts of hard-earned money. Had he missed our carefully worded warning of the dangers he faced as soon as he ventured in the door of a Thai gem dealer? Oh no, he'd read it, but this dealer was so utterly convincing (and the dollars signs were dancing so brightly in front of his eyes) that he chose to ignore it.

Always ask yourself this: if it's such easy money, why aren't people doing it professionally? If gems in Thailand are a tenth the price they'll fetch in the West, won't there be big companies importing them? Of course there will.

Perhaps it's something to do with magic carpets and Arabian nights, but carpet merchants are undoubtedly the used-car dealers of the developing world. They'd sell their mothers into slavery if it would turn a rupee. Maureen and I have bought a few carpets over the years and generally we've been very pleased with them. We bought a Kashmiri carpet in India and we've bought a number of Tibetan carpets in Kathmandu that still look great.

We never set out to make a fortune from carpets. In fact, we only ever bought carpets that we wanted ourselves because, quite frankly, carpets are one of the dumbest things you could imagine buying. For a start they're bulky and heavy, so bringing one home is either a pain in the neck or, if you have it sent separately, likely to be expensive. Even more importantly there are lots of professional carpet importers—there's probably one round the corner from where you live right now. They import carpets by the hundred, get huge discounts from buying in bulk and ship them home by the container load. Why go to all the hassle of buying a carpet and hauling it halfway round the world, only to find your friendly local Ali Baba has the same carpet at a lower price? What's more, he's there to complain to when the carpet fades or the edging comes unstitched.

We've heard lots of sorry carpet stories over the years. Turkey is thick with them, but for a spell it was Agra and Jaipur in India where unfortunate travelers really lost out. Our prized letter was from a visitor in Agra who needed to get to a doctor urgently. A cycle rickshaw was called and he set off in haste to the doctor, only to find himself at a carpet dealer.

'This is a carpet shop, not a doctor's office,' he complained.

'Well, yes,' was the reply, 'but he's a doctor on the side.'

Remarkably, given the pitfalls, lots of people do make interesting livings from buying here and selling there. Germans still buy small diesel-powered Mercedes buses, drive them across Asia and sell them in Nepal—it may not make a living but it can help pay for the vacation. The business of relocating Peugeots from Europe to the taxi fleets of West Africa was badly hit by the turmoil in Algeria (you crossed to North Africa and drove across the Sahara), but I recently met an Austrian who'd driven from Vienna across Asia in an elderly Renault R4, then shipped it to East Africa and finally sold it for a profit in Zimbabwe where the Harare taxi fleet was once largely composed of R4s.

Krzysztof Dydynski, the Polish author of our guides to Colombia, Venezuela and Poland, managed to escape from Poland and travel the world when the iron curtain was still a formidable barrier and the Polish zloty was virtually worthless. He started by making buying and selling circuits around Eastern Europe and the old USSR. Gradually, over repeated circuits, he managed to convert soft currencies into semi-soft ones and semi-soft ones into small quantities of hard ones. Then he took his buying and selling instincts further afield and bought carpets in India to sell in Singapore where he bought watches to take back to sell in India and buy more carpets. In this fashion he saw the world!

At the end of the day, buying something on the road has one often overwhelming plus point, an upside that may well make all the hassles worthwhile. Buying exactly the same thing at your friendly local jeweler, Third World crafts shop or local carpet emporium is never going to reward you with those matchless memories. We can look at a piece in our house and think, hey, that's the Tibetan carpet we brought back to Kathmandu from the Tibetan center in Patan. We brought it back to our hotel strapped across the back of a bicycle with Tashi sitting on top of it. Or, that's the storyboard from Kambot on the Sepik River in Papua New Guinea which I bought on the beach at Wewak from some guy who'd brought it down from the river. And that's the Mayan-style piece we found covered in dust in the shop at the museum in Mexico City. And there's the Burmese lacquerware table we bought in Pagan that sat in our hotel room for three months while we worked on the first edition of South-East Asia.

Unpopular travelers? Loud Americans? Drunk Australians? Snooty Frenchmen? The haughty English (and their 'lager lout' cousins) or the pushy Germans? Yes, there are lots of contenders for the travelers you'd rather not know about. Curiously, it's often the locals. Almost anywhere you care to name, the least welcome travelers are the ones closest to home. Sometimes they're even, unofficially, banned, so Australians (and New Zealanders) may find themselves unwelcome at Australian backpacker hostels—if you can't show your passport and prove you're actually traveling, rather than just looking for a place to stay, forget it. The same thing can happen to the Irish in Ireland, Americans in America and, remarkably, Indians in India.

There are some national 'characteristics' which make certain people unpopular. Germans and their penchant for grabbing sun loungers, for example. At any beach resort anywhere in the world you can count on Germans to relive World War II and make one more territorial claim. Before anybody else gets up, the Germans will be putting their towels, sunscreen and beach novel on the sun lounger in order to book it for the day, irrespective of the signs announcing that they cannot be 'booked'.

Italians will complain about everything and run off in every direction while their poor tour guide is trying to get them all back on the bus. 'The Brazilians are even worse,' observed the owner of a Pacific resort.

For a spell it was travelers from the old East Germany who really racked up points in the unpopularity stakes amongst operators. 'They're used to thinking that everything comes from the state and that they've got a right to grab it,' complained an Australian hostel operator. 'They steal the sheets off the beds, they'll even take the lightbulbs.'

If one nationality gets the almost universal thumbs down, however, it's Israelis. Young Israelis, fresh out of the army, are used to being pushy, demanding and aggressive. Perhaps there's a national tendency to argue about prices as well, but in the developing world to get aggressive about saving fifty cents is not going to make you flavor of the month. Israelis have made themselves unpopular almost everywhere. It's become such a problem that Israeli embassies, fed up with making excuses for their bad-mannered nationals, have begged their travelers to behave themselves.

There are situations when even ill-tempered young Israelis can redeem themselves. In 1990, the democracy movement in Nepal saw young Nepali protesters being tear gassed. There are always lots of Israelis in Nepal and many of them certainly had lots of experience at tossing tear gas at Palestinians. Furthermore, they were well aware of how the Palestinians counteracted the effects of tear gas by squeezing onion juice or vinegar on their face masks, for example. So it was young Israelis who played a part in the devolution of power in Nepal from the monarchy to an elected government by teaching them exactly the same techniques which the Palestinians used against the Israeli army. Not that it did the poor Nepalis much good—democracy simply substituted corrupt and inept politicians for royalty.

9

All the Trouble in the World

Author breakdowns, author battles, total rewrites, political upheavals— you name the problems a guidebook could face and our Tibet guidebook had them. Guidebooks go through a pattern: they're never quite right at the first edition, there's always something you would have done differently, and it's not until the second or even third edition that you think it's a good book. It wasn't until the fourth edition of our Tibet book that we really had a second edition.

In 1985, I was at work in Emeryville, our first US office, squeezed between Berkeley and Oakland on the east side of San Francisco Bay. One day our author Michael Buckley phoned from somewhere in China.

'I'm here with Robert Strauss,' he announced. 'We've found out that you can get permits to Tibet, so we're going to go.'

'Fantastic,' I replied, enviously. 'Send us a postcard.'

'We can do better than that,' suggested Michael. 'We could send you the first guidebook to Tibet.'

'Go for it,' I said, very sensibly.

Years later, it didn't seem quite so sensible.

Michael Buckley had co-written our first China guide, which had appeared in October 1984. That was not fast enough to be first out of the gate when it came to China guidebooks, but it was still pretty early on. The first Western visitors to China started to make their way into the big red realm in the mid to late 1970s, years after Richard Nixon's pioneering visit in 1972. They were on tightly controlled, fully escorted, stage-managed tours and the starry-eyed visitors came back with tales of smiling peasants, precision acrobatic shows and multi-course banquets in solidly old-fashioned hotels. Not the sort of thing we could write a book about. Then we started to get letters from wide-eyed intrepid travelers announcing that they'd entered on highly questionable visas and wandered off on their own. Or gone to China on a tour and then disappeared.

It gradually became clear that visas for independent travel in China could be found if you asked the right people in Hong Kong. These rogue visas could only be obtained from freelancers, usually working out of the traveler's labyrinth of Chungking Mansions in Kowloon. Of course, the visas only let you go to a highly restricted list of cities; wandering further afield required more permits from the usually less than helpful PSB (Public Security Bureau). To complicate matters, officials in a given district often refused to recognize permits issued elsewhere in China. In fact, they were often blissfully unaware that someone back at head office had decided big noses were allowed to wander into their remote corner of the People's Republic.

Stories trickled back of travelers being arrested for turning up in places where they shouldn't have been and being made to write 'self criticisms' before going on their way. A self criticism might include a confession that you'd been a silly person, you were very sorry to have inconvenienced everybody and you definitely wouldn't break the rules again. One traveler reported that while heading from town A to town C he was arrested en route in town B. He was told he shouldn't have been there and would immediately be sent back to where he'd come from.

'And where was that?' queried the official.

Thinking fast, the traveler shamefully confessed, 'Town C.'

He was promptly sent 'back' to where he was going.

Clearly it was time for a China guidebook, but before we could move, the first guides had already appeared. In Hong Kong, pioneering backpackers realized nothing was available in print and quickly put their own travels down on paper. It was remarkably similar to what Maureen and I had done with our Asia book ten years earlier, but time had moved on and we knew if we put our minds to it we could turn out something bigger and better.

Alan Samagalski, our in-house researcher, had been packed off to Hong Kong to update that book and make a preliminary foray into China to visit Guangzhou (Canton). Around the same time we heard from Michael Buckley, a Canadian who seemed to work as a teacher solely to make the money to finance his travels. He'd been wandering extensively in China and suggested he write a China guidebook for us.

'Meet Michael in Hong Kong, go wherever you need to go, come back with the book,' we told Alan and off he went. Thanks to the success of our India guide, we could afford that sort of thing.

Months passed, and only occasional postcards and even more occasional phone calls made their way back to us. Travel in China was tough.

One card from Alan said it all. 'You know you've been in China too long,' he reported, 'when you're so desperate to talk to a friendly face that you find yourself talking to a sack of cabbages in a train compartment.'

Already the two words '*mei you*' were establishing themselves at the top of the China traveler's vocabulary. It means 'don't have', but as often as it meant 'there are no rooms left', 'the train tickets are sold out' or 'the food is finished', it could also mean 'I don't think you're allowed to do that', 'I can't be bothered dealing with you', 'I don't know if this is allowed or not and I'm certainly not going to risk saying yes' or simply 'go away, can't you see I'm trying to sleep on the job'.

The bureaucracy was horrific, the accommodation was often appalling, the food was generally terrible and communication was, well, difficult is probably too gentle a word. Periodically Michael and Alan emerged from China for short breaks in Hong Kong where Geoffrey Bonsall, our gentlemanly agent and distributor, offered

them shelter, nourishment and a place to store their research material before pushing them back into the turmoil. Eventually they came
out, wrote the book, and in October 1984 the first edition of our
China guide hit the shelves. It immediately became *the* guidebook
for China for independent travelers.

Michael was staying with us in Berkeley in late 1984 when the
first copies arrived for the American market. I remember him helping me unload the cartons from the truck and almost being crushed
by an unsteady stack. We joked about verbose authors being flattened
by their overweight books. Now, in 1985, he was back in China with
a second book in the works.

Robert Strauss, the Tibet co-author, was English and a linguistics
whiz. He'd studied Chinese at a university in Germany so his expertise in that difficult language came via a second language. My head
ached just thinking about it. Robert had traveled with Michael during that first China research spell and together they put together a
very effective guide to Tibet, although at that time travel to Tibet was
extremely restricted so in some ways it was as much a guide to how
to get to Tibet as a guide to Tibet itself.

Then the problems started. Michael, it turned out, was carrying a
chip on his shoulder from the China guide. The book was selling
very well and he didn't think he'd been paid enough. We were paying
him royalties on Tibet so that wasn't a problem, but his discontent
with China festered. Then he and Robert started to squabble. Author
disputes are not unusual. Writing a guidebook can potentially break
up a strong partnership even more effectively than getting married.
This dispute got worse and worse until it became clear we couldn't
count on them to work together on the next edition. We had to choose
between Robert and Michael, and by this time we'd worked with
Robert to rewrite our Japan book with Chris Taylor and myself. We
chose Robert.

Unfortunately, Robert couldn't simply update Tibet when the
time for a new edition came around. At that time we let authors retain
copyright on many books, including this one, so half the book
belonged to Michael. Which meant the second edition was going to

involve not only a complete update, but also a complete rewrite of one half of the book. All Michael's photos would have to come out as well.

Worse still, Robert had no sooner set off to work on the new edition in 1991 than he was taken seriously ill and had to be evacuated from China. He'd completed some of his research and went on to write the complete book, but it was a decidedly sketchy affair.

In 1993 Robert, now fully recovered, was in Japan working on an update of that book when he suffered a relapse of his earlier illness and again had to abandon the project. We pulled the project together by sending in Chris Taylor, who had already completed his half of the update, to finish the rest of it. This was hardly an ideal situation, but it was an emergency. A year later, when it came time to update Tibet again, we told Robert we were not going to send him there. It wasn't fair to him to be thrown into a region where travel is decidedly hard work. And it wasn't fair to us to risk having a third project undermined if Robert's health should fail again. We would buy out his copyright for the Tibet book and send someone else in to do it.

'No,' said Robert.

We negotiated, we pleaded, we cajoled, but Robert was rock solid. It was his book, and nobody else was going to work on it.

So we parted company, sent in Chris Taylor and started all over again from scratch. Our new Tibet guide finally emerged in 1995; it was not a bad book, but it wasn't the carefully developed, step-by-step improved, exhaustively road-tested publication we should have had after ten years.

In 1998 we produced a real second edition of Tibet. This time we owned the copyright so there was no need to argue about who was going to update it or how. We sent in Bradley Mayhew, a recent graduate in Chinese from Oxford University who had already worked on our China book, and John Bellezza, a Tibetan-speaking self-made expert on the region who had spent years exploring some of the most remote corners of the country on foot.

I'd first met John in Kathmandu a few years previously.

'Look at this,' whispered Stan Armington, quietly opening a door to a back room in his office.

Poring over a table covered in large-scale maps of Tibet, a hulking figure was painstakingly tracing lines across the terrain.

'He's marking all the routes he's walked in Tibet,' said Stan. 'I found him out on the trail and brought him back here,' he went on, as if John was some exotic creature he'd picked up and brought home to feed and look after.

To complete an unlikely trio, I went to Tibet as well. I'd always wanted to walk the Kailash circuit, the three-day route around the holy mountain, the completion of which is said to clean away all your sins. All your sins of this lifetime that is; a thorough clean-up of all the sins of all your lifetimes requires much more dedication. It's 108 times round for the all-lifetimes cleaning job and, presumably, an instant ticket to Nirvana.

With Stan, Eric Kettunen who ran Lonely Planet USA and his soon-to-be-wife Ingrid, neighbor and friend Don Whitford and 74-year-old Bob Pierce, a friend of Stan's, we flew to Simikot in the far west of Nepal and started to walk. Five days' walking took us to Sher on the Tibetan border from where two Land Cruisers and a truck took us and our Sherpa trekking crew to Purang, the important western Tibet trading town for Indian and Nepalese traders. From there we drove on to Lake Manasarovar and then Mt Kailash itself. With yaks to carry our equipment we spent four days walking round the holy peak, crossing the Dölma-la Pass to the north of the mountain which, at 18,466 feet, is a titch higher than the Mt Everest base camp.

We continued west, over roads worse than anything I'd seen for a good few years, to Tirthapuri and then to Thöling and the abandoned hilltop citadel of Tsaparang—quite the most amazing abandoned city I'd been to in Asia after Pagan and Angkor Wat.

'Why do so few visitors come here?' I thought, marveling at this little-known outpost. And then I thought about the roads we'd traversed to get there, calculated that there was another week of driving on similar roads before we arrived at the big-city security of Lhasa and knew why there were so few visitors.

There were more amazing moments on the way to Lhasa, but the most surprising of all was when a shape beside the road materialized into our Tibetan expert John Bellezza!

'I knew you were going to Kailash around this time,' he explained. 'And if you were going to drive back to Lhasa from western Tibet you'd have to come along this road. So I sat down by the roadside to wait for you. I figured I'd wait a week to see if you turned up, but I've only been here three days.'

For the next few days John entertained us with his fluent Tibetan and expert storytelling. He'd come from Dharamsala, where the Dalai Lama had blessed a large handful of those colorful woven threads which Tibetans give you to wear on the wrist or around the neck. On more than one occasion after quizzing Tibetans on directions or asking them to explain the significance of a building or natural feature, John would produce these blessed threads, explain their provenance and then hand one to each Tibetan. The result was always astonishing. If he'd written each of them a check for a million dollars they could not have been more overjoyed. The awestruck recipients would often fall to their knees, take the thread in both hands, press it against their foreheads, clasp John's hands, thank him repeatedly and leave wreathed in smiles. There is nothing wider or more genuine than a Tibetan smile.

It was an amazing trip and at the end of it I was confident we had a terrific book. Working from Chris Taylor's excellent foundations we'd put together something exhaustively researched and right up to date. Which was just as well, because it had taken thirteen years to get there.

Our Russia book, on the other hand, has been plagued by straightforward politics. In the late 1980s Gorbachev and *perestroika* were in full swing and it seemed the perfect time for a USSR book. Surely Russia was going to open up just like Eastern Europe in 1989? As if.

Gorbachev may have been chattering about *glasnost*, but that certainly hadn't had any impact on Intourist, the all-encompassing Soviet tourism monolith. If you wanted to visit the USSR, your travels had to be arranged by Intourist, stop by stop, hotel by hotel, so there was none of our usual 'get in, get the job done, get out' behavior. To make matters worse, Intourist charged like the proverbial wounded bull. The facilities may have been lousy, but if you wanted to go you paid what they demanded, no choice.

John King and John Noble (great surnames for writers working on a book to a Communist people's state) were two of our most experienced writers, but they soon found there were no short cuts in the USSR and there was a lot more to see than they'd expected. The project dragged on, extra trips from London to Moscow were scheduled and the break-even point receded ever further into the distance. Finally the project came in-house and our editors, cartographers and designers began to grapple with the complexities of Cyrillic script and untrustworthy mapping. The Russians were famed for secrecy when it came to mapping. It was said the best map of Moscow was by the CIA since all the Soviet maps had added an imaginary bend in the Moscow River so that it appeared to flow right over the site of the KGB headquarters. In fact, we found almost all the mapping was flawed.

What was probably the most time-consuming and expensive project we'd ever tackled moved towards completion just as the USSR self-destructed. With the book about to hit the press we were stuck with a country in turmoil, a country which no longer even had a name. After much discussion, we bit the bullet and called it the USSR, even though the USSR no longer existed.

It was a great book, 840 pages long, admirably comprehensive and praised not only by travelers, but by Russians. Over and over again we heard that Russians were amazed at how outsiders—from Australia of all places—had got a handle on their town, even producing the best map they'd ever seen of their remote outpost. The problem was that praise, approval and sheer hard work didn't translate into sales. Tourism to Russia did not boom, in fact quite the reverse. To outsiders the country seemed not only dauntingly difficult to travel around, but with tales of corruption and the Russian mafia, disturbingly dangerous as well. Furthermore, the bureaucracy and red tape remained as complicated as ever.

With subsequent editions, our researchers reported that travel in Russia was pretty straightforward, the general population was happy to have foreign visitors and it certainly was a place worth visiting. The fracturing of the union did have one benefit for us: it created lots more countries to produce books about. First, the Baltic states split off and we published a guidebook to Estonia, Lithuania and Latvia in 1994. Then we did a guidebook to the Central Asian Republics—all those 'stan' countries—in 1996. We even added Afghanistan to the 2000 edition and greatly expanded the country's coverage in 2004. Guidebooks to Georgia, Armenia and Azerbaijan and to Ukraine followed.

As for Russia itself, we were stuck with USSR as the title for the first edition, but the next edition in 1996 became Russia, Ukraine and Belarus. It was John King, one of the original authors, who had the final word on the 'what to call it' imbroglio.

'I know now what we should have called it,' John wrote, a year or so after the book had been published. 'It should have been the UFFR—the Union of Fewer and Fewer Republics.'

It's bad enough when individuals dislike your book, or hotels and restaurants get upset because of what you've said about them, but when you're up against a government you've got real problems. First-World countries are generally able to take criticism; it's the little Third-World places that get upset and nobody has got more upset than the government of Malawi. Back in 1977, in the first edition of *Africa on the Cheap*, Geoff Crowther commented that 'President for Life' Dr Hastings Banda was perhaps not the nicest politician in the world. As a result, not only was Geoff banned from visiting Malawi, but our Africa book was also banned, along with *Lady Chatterley's Lover* and a select list of other highly subversive titles. We had to print a warning in our book that copies should be hidden or disguised before arriving at the border.

Maps are a regularly sensitive point and nobody gets more sensitive about them than the Indian government. Satellites or not, Indian officials get palpitations if they think anybody has detailed or accurate maps to 'difficult' areas, which seem to be the entire coast, anywhere near the borders and most of the Himalayas. In an Indian hill resort on one visit to India I was searching for a better base map than the regular tourist handouts and Survey of India maps. I asked a bookshop owner if he had anything more accurate, an old map produced during the British period perhaps? Nothing of that sort was available he replied, but, ten minutes later, when we were alone in the shop, he reached under the counter and pulled out a British map from the 1930s.

'This is much more accurate than anything produced today,' he whispered. 'But, of course, it's illegal to sell it.'

A great deal of cross-checking was required to ensure we included all the changes of the past seventy years, but that old British map was better than anything produced today.

The Indian government gets really touchy when it comes to their external borders, particularly if it's a border between India and Pakistan or India and China. What the Indian government would like to believe is that Pakistan never ended up with half of Kashmir after partition in 1947 and that China never grabbed a large chunk of Ladakh in 1962. In fact, that piece of Ladakh was so remote and inaccessible that the Indians never even noticed the Chinese had taken it over and constructed a highway through it, until it was too late.

Unfortunately, saying that the border we show on a map is current reality, where you find Indians on one side and Pakistanis or Chinese on the other side, won't do. Showing the borders where the Indian government wished they would be isn't good enough either because even the Indian government isn't really sure where they'd like the borders to be. For years, all the maps in our India guide included the catch-all wording that 'the external boundaries of India on this map have not been authenticated and may not be correct' and that this was a 'Government of India Statement'. That worked fine until we had our book banned because the government decided that the statement might be taken to imply that only the Government of India really believed the maps were possibly incorrect, and that perhaps the publisher thought they were quite OK.

The Indian government's paranoia about what people might think about their borders grew so severe that it became all but impossible to buy an atlas in India. An Indian bookseller showed me an Indian history book with a map of India as it was under the great Buddhist Emperor Ashoka, 2500 years ago, complete with the statement that the borders on the map were 'neither correct nor authenticated'. The real absurdity is that you can turn on a television in India and watch the world news beamed down from some satellite with a newsreader talking about the latest India–Pakistan border skirmish while the map behind him or her shows the Kashmir borders exactly as they are in reality, not as some government official wishes they would be.

Of course, fixing the borders to please one side of the line only upsets the other side. So if you have Kashmir OK by the Indians, you have it wrong for the Pakistanis. Ecuador and Peru can't agree about their boundaries either. Don't even whisper the words 'Western Sahara' around the Moroccans. And don't pretend Taiwan is an independent country if you're in China. You'd better remember that those inhospitable islands off to the east of Tierra del Fuego are the Islas Malvinas, not the Falkland Islands, if you want to sell your Argentina guide, or your South America guide, or your Antarctica guide in Argentina. And if you're in the Arab world, for goodness sake don't try and think of a name for that blank space on the map west of Jordan and Syria. You can also cause considerable heartburn in the Middle East if you take a stand on that stretch of water bordered by Saudi Arabia, Kuwait, Iraq, Iran and others. Generally we diplomatically refer to it as 'the Gulf', certainly not the 'Persian Gulf' when we're dealing with the Arab world or the 'Arabian Gulf' if it's the Iranians.

Even two First-World countries can get upset when talking about that stretch of water bordered by Korea on one side and Japan on the other. A little Japanese diplomatic delegation turned up at my office one day to complain that we were not always referring to it as the 'Sea of Japan'. I was presented with a color brochure explaining why no other name was correct and a batch of UN statements about the subject, backing up their demands that we should immediately cease and desist from ever referring to it as the 'East Sea'. The trouble is no Korean wants to go down to the beach for the day and paddle in the Sea of Japan. Using that name is as distasteful to the Koreans as not using it clearly is to the Japanese. Our policy of referring to it as East Sea (Sea of Japan) in our Korea book and Sea of Japan (East Sea) in our Japan book didn't keep either side happy.

The border, front line if you wish, between India and Pakistan in Kashmir may have been a problem, but we also managed to offend the Kashmiris in general. Perhaps not in Kashmir, after all it was a Kashmiri who gave me the line that, 'Kashmiris are so fond of the truth they'll rarely part with it'. No, it was Kashmiris in Bradford, England, who took offence at the comment and had the book banned from Bradford public libraries.

For a combination of authors getting in trouble, governments getting upset and piracy, it's hard to beat our experiences in Vietnam. In 1990, when we were researching our first Indochina guide, *Vietnam, Laos and Cambodia*, our author Daniel Robinson went somewhere north of Hanoi that he shouldn't have, was arrested, dropped in the tourist version of the wartime Hanoi Hilton for a short stay and then flown to Bangkok, where he immediately spilled his story to the *Bangkok Post*. It wasn't that Daniel had deliberately gone somewhere off limits, since at that time in Vietnam you could easily get permission from one government department to go somewhere, only to be promptly arrested by another department. Daniel had simply organized permits in Saigon which weren't recognized in Hanoi.

Fortunately, his arrest came right at the end of his research and his notes weren't confiscated, so the book still came out as planned and was an immediate success. If imitation is indeed the sincerest form of flattery, then the Vietnamese government certainly forgave us for our sins in finding out things we shouldn't have and putting them in a book, because they promptly pirated our guidebook. It's easy to undercut our prices if you don't have to pay for researching and producing the book, or for covering the costs of having your writer deported.

For a time the government even tried to improve the sales of their pirated version of our book by banning our legitimate copies, ostensibly because of a comment in our second edition that Vietnam had 'the best police money could buy'. The pirated copies that were sold on the street and, for a time, in government tourist offices also carried that comment. They've stopped confiscating copies from visitors on arrival, but subsequent editions of our Vietnam guide have been pirated, as have the French version of our guide and our Vietnamese phrasebook. Unhappily, the quality of the pirated copies has improved with time, as has the speed with which they get them out. It takes less than a week from the release of a new edition to the appearance of a pirated version on the streets of Saigon and Hanoi. Over the years we've bribed all the right people in Hanoi to try and solve this problem, without success.

Vietnam isn't the only place we've had books pirated, and we were never able to track down what may have been the cleverest piece of piracy. Fifteen years ago we were suspicious of how many copies of our China book were finding their way into Hong Kong outlets and eventually decided that one of the printers producing the book may have run on some extra books for their own use. Our print broker in Hong Kong farmed out work to printers, binders and shippers all over the colony and across the border into China and it was difficult to keep a close eye on every step of the process. It reminded me of a report, years ago in India, that Wilkinson's Sword were concerned about the exceptionally high quality of pirated versions of their razor blades, until they discovered the fake blades were coming from their own factory, working a highly unofficial extra shift after hours. French fashion designers have reported experiencing the same problem in Vietnam.

Authors may give you headaches, governments may give you grief, bookshop thieves (they particularly target guidebooks) may severely piss you off, but we also trip ourselves up. We did it most thoroughly in 1999 with the fourth edition of our Western Europe guide. We printed 40 000 copies of this best-selling 1376-page work and then discovered that the spine proudly proclaimed it was not a guide to Western Europe, but to Westen Europe. Screw-ups do happen, but what amazed me about this one was how much ass covering went on—from all sides people rushed out to proclaim that it hadn't happened on their shift. Of course it had happened on everybody's shift. The designer had failed to key in an 'r', but he was only one of a whole string of people who looked at the cover, approved the cover, signed off the cover. It was simply one of those things. Far more important was what we were going to do about it.

'Scrap it. It's too embarrassing to have that sort of mistake right on the cover of the book,' proclaimed some people. The editorial department, always sticklers for getting every comma in the right place, led the 'pulp and reprint' chorus.

'No,' I said. 'Quite apart from the sheer cost of reprinting 40 000 copies of a big, thick book, there's the small matter of how many trees would have to fall to put one little 'r' onto each copy.' We had two trees outside the entrance to our office that grew so well we had to periodically get them trimmed back so you could see the Lonely Planet sign. I calculated the thirty-eight tons of paper that went into 40 000 copies of Westen Europe equated to about 500 of those trees. So no way were we going to reprint it.

'Sticker it,' suggested somebody else.

Putting a Western Europe sticker over Westen Europe was possible, but incredibly time-consuming, and unless it's done with absolute precision it's easy to see the book has been stickered. And then what do people do? They peel the sticker off to see what's underneath. A few years previously, Random House had launched their short-lived series of student-oriented Berkeley Guides. The first Berkeley Europe guide in 1993 had scribbles of graffiti on the cover, including one extremely politically incorrect announcement that 'Belsen was a gas'. This oversight must have been missed until after the books were printed because the finished books all had neat little stickers obliterating the offending graffiti. Of course, if you knew about it and were in a bookshop with friends you couldn't resist showing them.

'Don't do anything at all about our Westen screw-up,' was probably the most sensible suggestion. If we had done nothing, and kept quiet about it, I'm sure we would have only heard from a half-dozen people. The trouble was we had to do something, just to stop all the crisis meetings and get everybody back to work.

We would come clean about it, admit to the world, if the world was interested, that we'd goofed. But what would we do to fix it?

Westen Europe was clearly getting into my dreams because one night I woke up with the answer. We'd insert a bookmark, admitting our mistake, explaining how it happened and how we'd come to the decision not to pulp and reprint or to sticker. My laptop was right under the bed so I designed the bookmark there and then, before it disappeared with my dreams. It went through some editorial and design department improving, but what you see here is pretty much what I came up with that night.

WESTEN EUROPE

In Lonely Planet's warehouse one sunny afternoon ...

1st Warehouse Guy (stacking copies of new book on shelf): How do you spell Western?
2nd Warehouse Guy: W-E-S-T-E-R-N.
1st Warehouse Guy: There's an 'r' in it?
2nd Warehouse Guy: Sure.
1st Warehouse Guy: Well, looks like somebody ****ed up.

Later, in a publishing meeting . . .

Steve: How did this happen? Surely somebody should have checked the cover?
Richard: Everybody checked the cover—designers, senior

designers, editors, senior editors, Rob (publisher)—damn it, I even saw it!

John: So what are we going to do? We look pretty dumb if we can't even spell Western.

Anna: Well, we could pulp them, but I don't think we should sacrifice all those trees just for one 'r'.

Richard: We could sticker them, but unless you get the stickers on really straight it just attracts attention.

Maureen: And people peel off the stickers to see what you're trying to hide.

Steve: We could just confess, put an errata slip in the book, make a bit of a joke about it.

Tony: Make it a bookmark, then at least it's something useful.

Having decided what to do about it, the next question was how to publicize it. We didn't want some newspaper announcing we'd produced a book on Western Europe and couldn't even spell the title. Hats off to our publicists. Soon there were stories all over the place about Westen Europe, and bookshops were reporting that customers were asking for the book with the misspelt spine title. The book got so much publicity there was even speculation that we'd done it deliberately, simply to score all those column inches. Some articles suggested that the book might even become a collector's item. Of course, there was the occasional article in the British press sniffing, 'what could one expect from a publisher in the colonies', and the British bookshop chain W. H. Smith decided they'd only buy copies once we'd sold the first 40 000 print run and reprinted with the spelling corrected. They didn't have to wait long: the first printing sold out much faster than expected and subsequent print runs did get things right.

Did we learn from that mistake? Apparently not, since a few months later we printed our Bangkok city guide with not just one letter missing from the spine title, but all seven of them. I still don't know how that happened and, once again, the mistake wasn't caught until the books had been printed and bound. Fortunately, they were yet to be packed, and the printer devised some neat way of printing the missing word onto the spine of the finished books. I don't imagine a single purchaser of those 'repaired' books ever noticed that the title felt, to a finger run down the spine, slightly different.

Many countries seem to treat visas as a means of discouraging visitors, a way of creatively increasing employment or a handy way of raising money. Countries like the United States may require visas because they're afraid people would flock to the Land of Plenty if they weren't carefully vetted, but why do crumbling Third-World horror spots, where nobody in their right mind would want to remain longer than necessary, impose such bureaucratic, time-consuming and expensive visa requirements? Sure, some countries slap on visa requirements on a tit-for-tat basis, but why do countries make a song and dance about encouraging tourism while at the same time doing their best to discourage it? It's not as if visa forms weed out the people they're supposed to. Even in the computer data-banked First World, governments keep discovering they've let in the wrong person.

Getting visas can take for ever and cost a small fortune although on one memorable occasion the US set an all-time speed record for visa issuing and it was free. I was flying to the US via Sydney where I arrived with plenty of time to record a radio interview at the airport. After the interview I breezed over from the domestic to the international terminal, checked in for my flight and then reeled back when the ticketing agent looked at my passport and announced I wouldn't be able to fly because my visa had expired. I'd got a new passport just over a year ago and had immediately applied for a new US visa. In my old passport my US visa was valid for unlimited visits for the life of the passport. I'd assumed the same rules applied to the new visa, but it was only valid for twelve months and had expired ten days earlier.

'The flight departs in an hour and half,' she continued. 'There's no way you can get a new visa in time.'

'We'll see,' I replied, sprinting for the door.

I leapt into a taxi and told the driver to get me to the US consulate in downtown Sydney as fast as he could. Fortunately, Sydney airport is only six miles from the city, but two blocks from the consulate we ran into a street demonstration and I had to abandon the taxi and run.

Emerging, panting, from the elevator I sprinted into the consulate and gasped, 'I need a visa. My flight leaves in an hour.'

Somebody rushed off with my passport to get the visa stamped while I was filling in the application form. Literally minutes later they returned with the passport, but the application required a photo. I scrabbled through my bag and came upon a Youth Hostel Association membership card from which I ripped the photo. Then it was back into the elevator, downstairs, out onto the street, grab a taxi, back to the airport, check in again and onto the flight. With time to spare.

American efficiency isn't so impressive when it comes to the immigration form which visitors have to fill in for their US arrival. For many years this has remained one of the world's dumbest forms. For at least twenty years it was cunningly designed so at least half the form fillers would put the answers on the wrong line. Then the US brought in a 'visa waiver program' so citizens from nice dependable countries no longer need visas. They simply have to fill in an I-94W form with a list of questions of quite breathtaking stupidity. Are you coming to the US to deal in drugs? Or to engage in prostitution? Or to foment revolution? My favorite query asks if you were involved in Nazi persecution between 1935 and 1945? Presumably, if you made an early start or late entry, then Nazi activity was fine. I've always wondered if Holocaust victims would have to admit that they were involved in Nazi persecution, even if it was on the persecuted side of the equation.

T: I can count on the thumbs of one hand how many airlines have flown me places for free—Air Niugini, the airline of Papua New Guinea. Nor do the airlines see me coming and immediately usher me up front. Every time I've been upgraded it's been because of my healthy frequent flyer account balance rather than my job. If you find me in business class it will usually be because I paid for it.

In fact, when a magazine asked me to contribute to a piece about how to get upgraded I replied I could probably write more authentically about what it's like to be downgraded! My best downgrade experience was on a flight from Frankfurt to London when I found myself in the British Airways check-in queue with Mark Ellingham, one of the founders of Rough Guides. I had a business-class ticket, Mark had an economy one and we wanted to sit together. If you were British Airways checking in the publishers of the two travel guide series which dominate the British travel market and had to choose between upgrading Rough Guides or downgrading Lonely Planet, which would you choose?

Correct. British Airways chose downgrade.

My son has had better luck at being upgraded than I have. In 1995, when he was twelve years old, I sent Kieran back from London to Melbourne by himself. 'How was the flight?' Maureen asked him when he arrived back in Australia.

'Oh, I ended up sitting next to an English kid flying to Australia by himself,' Kieran announced. 'His parents worked for the airline and he recognized one of the flight attendants. She got us upgraded so we both came back business class.'

Damn it, that would never happen to me.

Sometimes we think the users of our books should be led astray more often. It's not our fault that some people use our books like an instruction manual.

'It's supposed to be a guide, not a blueprint,' we regularly point out, but to no avail.

I was really pleased when we heard from one traveler who reported that he used our book as a list of places not to stay in. By avoiding the places we mentioned he reckoned he'd find less crowded accommodation.

Our best piece of unintended leading astray goes back to 1975 and the first edition of *South-East Asia on a Shoestring*. Starting at Sibu near the north coast of Borneo, Maureen and I had been up the

Rejang River to the town of Kapit. Then we backtracked to Sibu and took a ship further east along the coast to Bintulu. Today there's a road connecting Sibu and Bintulu, but back then it was impenetrable jungle. Boats ran inland into the jungle along the Kemena River from Bintulu as well. A woman from the local tourist office pointed out that if we had continued another day upriver to Belaga we would have reached a spot where the two rivers came close together. It would then have been possible to walk for a day or so through the jungle to the Kemena River and catch a boat down to the coast, arriving 120 miles east of our starting point.

This seemed quite feasible. We knew boats continued further up the Rejang River, we knew boats came down the Kemena River and on the map we could see the rivers approached close to each other. So we suggested in the book that this was a possibly interesting, but untried, trip.

A year later a traveler dropped into our office in Melbourne and told us about his travels around the region. He commented that he'd made the jungle trip in Borneo.

'Oh, the day-and-a-half walk from the Rejang River to the Kemena River?' I queried.

'Yes, that one,' he said and then, after a pregnant pause, 'six weeks.'

After the first week of hacking his way through dense jungle, sleeping with headhunters and portaging dugout canoes up and down rapids he would have quite happily strangled me he said. But after the first couple of weeks he decided he was having the adventure of his life and just went with it.

'Thank you very much,' he announced.

Today, logging roads and tourist development have made it a straightforward trip.

We ask a lot from our editors. In addition to the usual editorial tasks, they also have to ensure the author can tell north from south, right from left, gets all the phone numbers correct, uses the same street names in the text as on the maps and spells that obscure king's name exactly the same way in the history section as when describing his statue in the main square.

It's a lot to ask and since authors do make mistakes it's hardly surprising that we occasionally have problems like the Irish 'Disneyland lady'. There are hundreds, even thousands of telephone numbers in a typical guidebook and every once in a while a digit does get transposed, which is what happened to Mrs O'Something in somewhere or other in county something in Ireland. In fact, it was the popular village hostel whose number we got wrong, with the result that Mrs O'Something got phone calls intended for the hostel. She was rightly annoyed and we did everything we could to fix the situation. We corrected the mistake with the next reprint of the book, we offered to pay to have her phone number changed, we offered to put a message on the system redirecting her calls, we offered to pay to have any stationery reprinted or to cover the cost of notifying her friends and acquaintances. None of this was good enough for Mrs O'Something—she wanted a trip to EuroDisney for her entire family! We were not a travel agent or tour operator, we had to politely point out.

Over the years, though, we've had remarkably little trouble with phone number screws-ups or wrong addresses. Sometimes, however, much more serious errors creep through. In one case it was a deliberate one.

In 1989 we published *Trekking in Turkey* at a time when Turkey was really booming as a destination and we thought that walking might also become popular. It didn't, but that's another story. The author wrote that getting cooking gas for camping stoves or finding the Camping Gaz compressed gas cylinders that are popular with walkers in Europe was very difficult in Turkey. So he suggested hiding them in your baggage to sneak them on board flights. This was seriously bad advice. Quite apart from the fact that it's illegal, I certainly wouldn't want to be on a flight where passengers are hiding inflammable, even explosive, material in their baggage. The author shouldn't have written it, but the editor certainly should have picked it up, deleted it and ticked off the author for even thinking about it. He didn't and we, quite rightly, got told off by IATA, the International Air Transport Association.

In this politically correct era editors all too often are inclined to turn 'a classic John Wayne cowboys and Indians flick' into something involving 'cowpersons and native-Americans'. I usually side with the author when they complain that when they wrote 'statue of a fisherman' they definitely meant 'man' not 'person' because they can guarantee there is not a single non-male fisherperson in the whole country.

When Chris Baker wrote in our Bahamas book that in island casinos 'bare feet and swimwear are not permitted, and skimpy clothing is frowned upon. Tastefully elegant minimalism, however, such as a miniskirt, décolletage, and high heels, is welcomed', an editor fretted that this was potentially sexist and inappropriate. Fortunately, it got through—if we let the good taste police win every case our books would be as bland as a workshop manual.

My favorite over-editing tale involving my own text came with the first edition of our San Francisco guide. After a year and a half in the Bay Area in the mid-1980s and many subsequent visits I felt I knew the city fairly well. Even better, I'd seen it from both sides, as a resident and as a visitor, so when the decision came to publish a California and Nevada guide and a San Francisco city guide I volunteered to lend a hand. I ended up writing up the whole Bay Area from Silicon Valley in the south to Marin County to the north and also covered the coasts further north and south, so Point Reyes, Bolinas, Santa Cruz, Monterey and Carmel all came into my territory and, to overfill my glass, the Napa and Sonoma wine country valleys as well.

Like any over-eager writer I turned up lots of interesting little stories which, for space reasons, ended up on the cutting-room floor. Like the Berlin airport terminal on Treasure Island, the US Navy base in the middle of the Bay, halfway between San Francisco and Oakland. The island was created with the rock cut out of adjoining Yerba Buena Island when the tunnel was cut through the island in the early 1930s to link the two halves of the Bay Bridge. The island was the home for the International Golden Gate Exposition of 1939–40 and it was intended that it would become an airport able to handle both land aircraft and seaplanes. World War II intervened and the airport was never built, apart from the terminal itself which is still there, housing a small museum. It even looks like an airport terminal, a fact which you can confirm by watching *Indiana Jones and the Last Crusade*, where it appears as the Nazi-era Berlin Airport.

Marilyn Monroe was nearly edited out as well. In 1954 baseball hero Joe DiMaggio married Marilyn Monroe and, after the wedding, the happy couple was photographed outside the church of Sts Peter and Paul, a noted landmark in San Francisco's North Beach district. It's a famous photograph outside a famous church, but I was careful not to say it was taken after their wedding in the church. Because it wasn't. Joe was a staunch Catholic and it was his second marriage (Marilyn's too), so there was no way he could get married in a church. The wedding took place at San Francisco City Hall, only the photographs were taken outside the church. A careful editor checked the facts and found out, just as I had, that Joe and Marilyn weren't married in the church, but then dug further. Fifteen years earlier Joe DiMaggio had indeed been married in the Sts Peter and Paul Church, to his first wife. So Marilyn Monroe got axed and replaced with Dorothy Arnold.

Fortunately, I read the edited copy and caught this very accurate, but rather less interesting, correction and reinstated Marilyn. Incidentally, the church also made a notable movie appearance. In Cecil B. De Mille's 1923 version of *The Ten Commandments* the church foundations (it was being built at the time) appeared as the construction scene for the Temple in Jerusalem.

10
Other Activities

Our London operation had only been going for a year when we began to think about another European office. This time we turned our attention to France.

The first foreign translation of a Lonely Planet guide dates back to the late 1970s and by the early 1990s we had books translated into French, Italian, German, Japanese, Spanish, Hebrew and a number of other languages. All of it was hit and miss and none of it was very profitable. Translating guidebooks is not easy, we quickly discovered. For a start, English is the most important language when it comes to books. You're simply not going to sell as many copies in Spanish, Italian or German as you're going to sell in English. Second, guidebooks are not very good candidates for translation. Translate a novel once and you've translated it for ever; translate a guidebook and in two years time there will be a new edition and you'll have to translate most of it all over again.

That's not the end of the problems. There are parts of the book you can't translate at all. German readers don't want to know about flights from Los Angeles, Sydney or London to Bangkok; they want to know how to get there from Frankfurt, Vienna or Zurich. French readers don't want to know where to find the Canadian or Irish embassy in Rio de Janeiro; they want to know where the French or Belgian embassy is located. Well, perhaps they do want to know where the Canadian embassy is if they're from Quebec.

There are also lots of cultural differences between guidebooks. The French want to know more about cinema and they'll definitely demand a bigger section on food and cuisine. The Germans are likely to be sticklers about railway-timetable accuracy. Plus there's the little problem that a guidebook which is already overlength and overweight in English is going to be even bigger and bulkier in other languages.

For these and various other reasons we had not developed a real policy about translations. Some of the foreign-language books looked like Lonely Planet English-language guides; others looked entirely different. If translators asked us about making their books look like the English edition we were often less than helpful. We worried that a poor translation would be bad for our reputation.

In France a number of our books were translated by Arthaud, but not as French editions of our books and in many cases not the books which had the most potential. They translated Turkey, but bypassed Thailand because they already had a French-originated edition. Then Arthaud cut back on their publishing program and we decided to do the translations ourselves. Working out how to do it effectively would turn out be a very difficult process.

In early 1991 Charlotte, our UK manager, and I flew over from London—Eurostar was not yet in operation—and spent a few days making a circuit of bookshops in Paris. Our sales in France were handled by the utterly charming and very French Gerard Boulanger who took us from shop to shop (always driving at high speed), introducing us to the bookshop people and explaining the French market for travel books. We were pleasantly surprised to find how well known Lonely Planet was already, even though we only had books with our name on them in English.

A year later we sent Michelle de Kretser from the Australian office to set up a small office in Paris, recruit French staff and get our French publishing operation under way. Michelle was the perfect person: born in Sri Lanka, she emigrated to Australia with her parents as a child, studied French at the Sorbonne, joined Lonely Planet as an editor and worked her way up to be our senior editor. Michelle's one of those people who has 'very intelligent' written all over her.

Our French operation didn't go smoothly at first—it was a steep learning curve—but our first French guidebook, to Cambodia, came out in 1992 and we soon had a nice little list of French-language titles. Producing our own books in French had a pleasantly surprising side effect. The sales of our English-language books also increased. On a per capita basis our English-language sales in France may not have been as healthy as in, say, Sweden or the Netherlands where people accept that on many topics the only option will be a book in English (or sometimes some other foreign language) rather than their native tongue, but they were still pretty good. If a French traveler is going to the Solomon Islands they have to accept that there is never going to be a French-language guidebook—English is the only option. Or more correctly, the Lonely Planet guide in English is the only option.

In 1994 Zahia Hafs joined us to run our French operation. She'd worked for the UN in New York and had discovered Lonely Planet when she traveled around India with our guidebook in hand. We soon outgrew our small office and moved to a new office at 71 bis rue du Cardinal Lemoine, an address with an interesting literary background—James Joyce had lived there. We weren't likely to find any forgotten Joyce manuscripts under the floorboards since the building had been totally demolished and our office was in a very modern new complex on the same site. In fact, there wasn't even a sign to identify the connection, although round the corner an upstairs apartment where Hemingway lived did sport a small plaque under the relevant window.

A few years later our British operation also moved to a new home with a bookish history, though a publishing rather than a literary one. Paul Hamlyn had his first office at the same Spring Street, Kentish Town, address. Hamlyn was a publishing maverick who outraged the old school tie British publishing brigade by selling books colorfully, aggressively and, much worse, making money at it.

In 1995 we published *Australie*, the French-language edition of our best-selling Australia guide, and the Australian embassy in Paris offered to host a launch for us in the embassy building. Australia has a wonderful embassy and ambassador's residence, overlooking the Seine from beside the Eiffel Tower. We invited French media, bookshop and publishing people, and Zahia convinced me that I should make a speech in French. The ambassador showed how it was done, speaking in fluent French, and I followed, speaking in much less fluent French. I apologized for how bad my French was, promised that it would improve and said how pleased I was that Lonely Planet now had a guidebook to our own home country in the French language. I spoke about the numerous connections between France and Australia, particularly the many French explorers who have left their names on Australian maps. In fact, I explained, if La Perouse had turned up one week earlier, the history of Australia might have had much more French influence and I might not have had to apologies for my poor French. (La Perouse had sailed into Sydney's Botany Bay only days after the First Fleet had arrived with the convicts who would establish the first British colony in Australia.) People laughed, so I knew my French had worked well enough to tell that little joke.

'The English speaker always starts off by apologizing for how bad their French is,' an attractive French journalist told me afterwards, as if you could hardly expect anything different from an Anglo-Saxon. 'And then they make their speech in English,' she continued. 'That is no problem. Today, if you are a journalist you have to speak good English. We all,' she indicated the journalists dotted around the room with a sweep of the hand, 'speak excellent English.'

'But tonight was different,' she concluded. 'First you apologized for how bad your French was. Then you went on to prove it.'

That reception at the Australian embassy was not the only time my execrable French provided some amusement. In 1996 we put on a small reception at Brentano's, the wonderful American bookshop on the Avenue de l'Opéra. During the course of the evening I put my half-full glass down on a bookshelf while I used both hands to emphasize some point in the discussion I was having. When I reached out to retrieve my wine a few minutes later I was surprised to find it had been cleared away and announced, 'Oh c'est gone,' which quickly became the standard expression in our Paris office for reporting anything that was missing.

Ten years into our French operation we had seventy Lonely Planet titles in French, we'd become an important player in the French travel book market and we were selling as many books in French as we were in the whole English-language market at the beginning of the 1990s. The only problem was we didn't make any money from it.

Although we could charge a higher retail price for our guides in French, the smaller sales of the French editions, plus the huge costs of everything in France—salaries, taxes, office rent, you name it—made life very difficult. In the early years we'd made the mistake of producing books not totally aligned with French demands, but increasingly we concentrated on books that precisely fitted the local market, such as a Quebec guide instead of a Canada guide or even guides produced in French from scratch, but it was never enough. In late 2004 we sold our French operation to PSB, part of the Editis Group, the second-largest publisher in France.

The closure of our Paris office brought our French operation into line with what we have been doing in other parts of the world. In Italy, EDT in Turin have been producing Lonely Planet guidebooks for many years and doing a wonderful job. EDT often split an English-language book into two smaller and more profitable guides. With 150 books in total, EDT/Lonely Planet is the number one travel publisher in Italian and I'm regularly surprised by how well known the Lonely Planet name is in Italy.

We have a similar arrangement in Spain with GeoPlaneta, in Japan with Media Factory and in South Korea with Ahn Graphics. Smaller numbers of Lonely Planet titles are translated into Russian, Swedish, Polish, Dutch and other languages. One of our most successful overseas deals, despite the small size of the market, is in Israel where the energetic Ohad Sharav of SKP produces around a hundred Lonely Planet guides in Hebrew. The first Lonely Planet guides (other than bootleg copies) in Chinese were published in mid-2006 with the Chinese publisher SDX.

At the same time we finally launched Lonely Planet in Germany with MairDumont. It's surprising this took so long because Germans are probably the world's most energetic travelers; some of the first translations of our books appeared in Germany and we sell a lot of books there in English. Through the 1990s many of our books were translated into German by Stefan and Renate Loose under their eponymous imprint in Berlin and by Udo Schwark of Verlag Gisela E. Walther in Bremen. These books did not appear as German Lonely Planet guides, however; they were simply books in the publishers' own range. As we moved towards getting more control over our imprint in important markets we decided this had to change.

We intended to set up Lonely Planet Germany in conjunction with Stefan and Renate Loose, but in the late 1990s the deal became complicated, the Looses started to get cold feet and with the figures from our French operation continuing to look discouraging everything ground towards a halt before September 11 killed it completely. In mid-2006 our new partners published the first dozen Lonely Planet German language guidebooks.

A 1959 Cadillac propelled Lonely Planet into the digital world.

As a teenager I'd spent six years in the United States, first in Detroit and then between Baltimore and Washington DC when my father was working there for British Airways, or BOAC as it was then. Much more recently, Maureen and I, with our young children, had lived in the San Francisco Bay Area in 1984–85 when we set up the US office. So I'd lived on the East Coast, the West Coast and the Midwest, a pretty good selection of the 'lower 48'. Maureen and I had also traveled around the US, but we'd never done that all-American road trip, that sea to shining sea odyssey. In 1994 we did.

Crossing the USA in a modern, antiseptic rent-a-car didn't seem right. Route 66 and Toyotas simply did not go together. No, we wanted a real car, something from the days when Detroit iron ruled the interstates. Something with a thundering V8 engine, enough chrome to empty a mine and fins that soared towards the sky. Something like a 1959 Cadillac.

Our US office faxed me the 'old car' ad columns from the *San Francisco Chronicle* and soon our dream mobile turned up. It was a baby-blue Coupe de Ville, with a 390 cubic inch engine (about 6.5 liters), the biggest tail fins Detroit ever hoisted skywards and no brakes to speak of. Slowing down this behemoth, we soon discovered, was like redirecting the *Queen Mary*. Freeway exits required miles of advance planning, starting with a gentle whisper that a turn was coming up and building to a delicate foot on the powerfully assisted brakes, all of which resulted in a barely discernible change in our velocity. Never mind, it did have a trunk so big you had to climb in to redistribute bags towards the front. And a cigarette lighter for every seat. They don't build them like that any more.

The Caddy may have been venerable, but we had some high-tech gadgets on board. We weren't only planning to get off the freeways and onto the old Blue Lane Highways; we were going to get off the real roads and onto the virtual ones. Our Caddy was wired up to travel the information superhighway. The Internet has wormed its way so effectively into our lives it's almost unbelievable to insist that you could be an Internet pioneer in 1994, but we were. Well, to be honest, GNN or Global Network Navigator was the pioneer. We only came along for the ride.

Sure we knew the Internet existed, but back in 1994 it was still something for the military, academics and computer nerds. Very few people had access to it although there were already some people who saw the revolution around the corner. One of them was O'Reilly, the Bay Area computer book publisher who specialized in, amongst other things, books on the arcane delights of Unix, the original key to the Internet. Serendipitously there were also some travel enthusiasts at O'Reilly, led by Allen Noren, who suggested we take a laptop computer with us and post a daily diary of our travels on the groundbreaking Internet magazine they were about to launch. Today it would be called a blog. At the same time, Jeff Greenwald was about

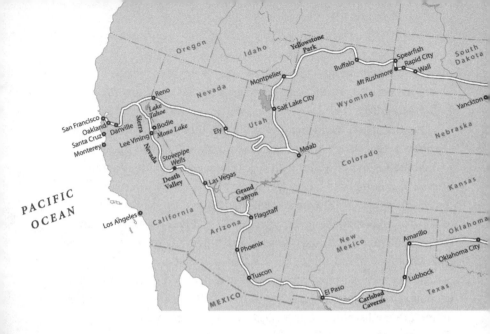

to set off around the world, sticking strictly to sea level and also making regular reports back to GNN. His travels later ended up as the book *Size of the World*.

Hewlett Packard came to the party with a very compact little OmniBook laptop computer. A car phone (which plugged into one of our multitude of cigarette lighters) and a host of modems and phone couplings, most of which never worked, were also slung aboard. I ended up wasting lots of time in payphone booths trying to link through to O'Reilly with an acoustic phone coupling. We even messed around with an early-model digital camera, but trying to send images over the web was clearly a project way ahead of its time.

In late March we pointed our lead sled eastwards. It was school holidays down under and our intention was to get all the way to Boston, park our dreamboat in author Tom Brosnahan's driveway and return to Australia for the next school term. Next school holiday, in June, we'd come back and do the trip in the reverse direction. (Tom was the author of our Turkey guidebook, another project which had emerged with perfect timing just as Turkey, after years of being right off the tourist map due to political troubles, suddenly became a hot destination.)

For more information, check out the original travel blog at:
http://www.lonelyplanet.com/tonywheeler/travel_blogs/

We drove east nearly to Lake Tahoe then wandered south through the time-warped ghost town of Bodie, paused at Mono Lake and arrived at Stovepipe Wells in Death Valley to find there was no room at the inn. We ended up sleeping in camp beds on the stage in the auditorium. From there we pointed the Caddy's acre of chromed nose towards Las Vegas, where we saw a fire-breathing dragon at the Excalibur, an exploding volcano at the Mirage and rode 'the best ride ever' (according to Tashi and Kieran) at the Luxor. The Mirage's volcano (every fifteen minutes after dark) was visible from the kids' room and each eruption probably used enough fuel to propel the Caddy for, oh, twenty miles.

From Las Vegas a stretch of the old Route 66 hustled us onto the Grand Canyon, where we walked down into the abyss and the Caddy posed for photographs with Japanese visitors and was pronounced 'a cracker' by a Scotsman staying at our motel. Then it was Flagstaff, another Route 66 town, by which time, my diary records, the OmniBook and I were on good terms and getting the emails home was no problem.

In Tucson, we stayed with Lonely Planet author Rob Rachowiecki, then exited the town past the Davis-Monthan air-force base where surplus military aircraft are mothballed, in case there's another war big enough to need them.

En route, Maureen and I pondered American coffee. Tea and the British go together yet they can't make it for beans, ditto for coffee and Americans. OK, there are coffee centers like Seattle, Portland and San Francisco, but out in the heartland the coffee is almost always terrible. What makes it worse is the difficulty of getting anything natural to put in it. Maureen and I both like milk in our coffee, but almost always the choice in American restaurants is cream (yuk) or various powdered or plastic-containered substances which are probably petro-chemical in origin.

In Lubbock, Texas, we paused to inspect the Buddy Holly memorial, where his name was spelt 'Holley'. Roy Orbison was also from Lubbock. Amarillo demanded a pilgrimage to the Cadillac Ranch where a line of Caddys from the 1950s and '60s are 'planted' in a field, their tail fins pointing skywards at, it is said, the same inclination as the Pyramid of Cheops. We never saw Amarillo itself, just a succession of shopping malls, and we never tested if Oklahoma City is 'oh so pretty' as the Rolling Stones had claimed, slipping by to the north of the freeway. In Little Rock it took six stops before we found a place to stay, but after parking the kids in their room Maureen and I went down to the bar for a drink, where a band was playing 'Pink Cadillac'.

Initially, Memphis was kind of disappointing. In daylight it looked quite fun, but after dark, downtown at least, it was plain dull. Beale Street was the only spark of life in the place and, tacky though it was, Graceland was simply too small to be over-the-top, inspired tacky. Elvis didn't come over as a really big spender—the swimming pool wouldn't be out of place in a small suburban house and his 1975 Ferrari was bought used in 1976. This was not pop-star excess. The Graceland hype was so overpowering it was kind of surprising to find two other attractions (one low key and one big budget) which we ranked way ahead of the Presley extravaganza. The low-key one was Sun Studios, where Elvis, Carl Perkins, Roy Orbison, Jerry Lee Lewis, Johnny Cash and many others (more recently U2) had recorded. The big-budget one was the Lorraine Motel where Martin Luther King was murdered. Today it's the Civil Rights Museum and walking through it is a powerfully moving experience. Visitors wind their way through a series of exhibits in the gutted and rebuilt old motel to finally emerge in room 306, from which King stepped to his death.

My diary recorded various mishaps as we wended our way north to Pennsylvania. In West Virginia one night there was no phone in our room and my cellular phone didn't want to connect, so I ended up sending the files through to GNN via a payphone. I had to hold the computer in one hand, angling it to catch the light from a streetlamp and typing in one-finger instructions with the other hand while a cold West Virginian mist, with a distinct smell of burning coal, wafted around me. Then we got comprehensively lost trying to find Frank Lloyd Wright's house Fallingwater although, once located, this sixty-year-old, but still modern as tomorrow, masterpiece was definitely worth the effort. Even the kids seemed mildly impressed.

Naturally, we made a stop in Amish country. By shunning the modern world the Amish have managed to create a major tourist industry with all the worst tourist excesses, all of it dedicated to watching them. One wonders if they won't get fed up with it and move away, leaving the Amish-watching industry without Amish to watch. We went to a bank where, to my amazement, a horse-drawn carriage pulled up and its Amish driver stopped to negotiate with the ATM, just like the postcard I'd chuckled at earlier in the day.

A couple of months later we were back in the US for the return odyssey. In the interim I'd walked across England from coast to coast and had a bicycle accident in Australia good enough for a case of road rash and some stitches in my eyebrow. We arrived back in Boston minus Tashi who had opted to go on a school trip to Malaysia. The trip from the airport to Tom's place in Concord was enlivened by our Ethiopian taxi driver explaining why O. J. Simpson was, at that instant, driving slowly along a Los Angeles freeway pursued by half the LA police force.

The westbound half of the return trip started by heading east, visiting Glenda Bendure and Ned Friary, two more of our authors, on

Cape Cod and then heading out into the Atlantic for a spot of whale-watching. Turning west we made a pilgrimage for Kieran to the Basketball Hall of Fame in Springfield, then overnighted at Stockbridge, a strong contender for the title of Middle Americaville because it is also Norman Rockwellville. Another rock and roll stop followed at Woodstock although it seems somewhat unfair that Woodstock (the town) should be doing so well out of Woodstock (the event) when back in 1969 the good citizens of Woodstock actually banned those three days of peace and love, which ended up taking place over fifty miles away in Bethel.

The next stop was Niagara Falls which I'd visited once before in the early 1960s. Two things about it fascinated both Kieran and me. One was the sheer idiocy of going over the falls in a barrel (and the wooden barrels, steel drums, foam-skinned capsules, giant spheres and devices made out of huge inner tubes all provided the same morbid interest!). The other was the story of an involuntary, but successful, trip over the falls by a seven-year-old boy in 1960. The boy and his seventeen-year-old sister were out on the river with a neighbor in his boat. The outboard motor failed, the boat overturned and they were carried towards the falls. The boy and the man were swept over the falls, but the girl managed to hang onto the boat and, miraculously, was grabbed at the very brink of the falls by two onlookers. The man died, but the young boy survived and was, until very recently, the only person ever to go over the falls without a barrel and live to tell the tale.

The only thing that enlivened the next day's grey and miserable drive was the borrowed place names. Could nobody in this part of Ontario think up a new name? In short order we passed Paris, London, Delhi, Dresden and Melbourne, paused for the first fast-food meal of the trip in another Woodstock and finally left Canada at Windsor.

Detroit turned out to be a surprisingly accessible place; it was quiet, but not the disaster zone it's assumed to be. Back in the late 1950s and early 1960s, when I lived there as a kid, and when our Caddy rolled off the assembly line, it was absolutely fine. Greenfield Village and the Henry Ford Museum are still worth the trip. Finally, before continuing on to Chicago, we made another rock and roll visit, this time to the Tamla Motown studios.

At dinner that night in Chicago we headed out for the obligatory deep-dish pizza and bumped into exuberant Spanish soccer fans olé-ing around town. The World Cup was on and they'd just beaten Bolivia. At the pizzeria one group announced, very politely, that they had better have an outside table as they intended to be rather rowdy. In fact downtown Chicago as a whole was pleasantly bright, energetic and rowdy—poor Detroit made a sorry contrast.

'I come from Des Moines,' lamented Bill Bryson in *The Lost Continent*. 'Somebody had to.' The Midwest metropolis gave us the first indication of the communication power of the web. At a restaurant one night, Maureen and I went to sample the salad bar, leaving Kieran at the table. We ate our salads, the main courses arrived and Kieran suddenly announced he was not feeling very well and departed for the bathroom. A few minutes later he returned and announced he was feeling not merely unwell, but awful. Then it was panic stations; he was pale and clammy, sweating and writhing around complaining that his stomach was going to explode. He looked terrible.

In Iowa this clearly was not a sudden onset of cerebral malaria, but we were very concerned and abandoned the meal to get some medical attention. We asked for the bill, called for a taxi and I hustled Kieran off to the bathroom to see if he could throw up. But when I got there I started to put two and two together. When Maureen and I had returned from the salad bar she'd asked me if I'd poured her a glass of wine before we stood up. I certainly thought I had, but her glass was empty. Where had that full glass of wine gone? Straight down an eleven-year-old's throat, perhaps? I quickly added a gallon or so of water to whatever he'd already had and, surprise, surprise, he started to feel much better. Yes, I had a drunk-as-a-skunk kid on my hands. I posted this little tale of pre-teen misadventure on our diary account that night and for the rest of the trip we bumped into people who asked if we were the parents with the underage drinker.

By the time we got to San Francisco, right where we started from, we'd covered twenty-four states and logged over 10 000 miles. It was a great trip, but next time I'll do it in something much younger and more reliable. We ended up outside the Rand McNally travel bookshop on Market Street where we had a little lunchtime reception and got fined twenty dollars for parking on the sidewalk. Somehow the permission we thought we'd obtained to park there hadn't percolated down to the cops on the beat. When I tried to argue about it they demanded to look at my driving license and then suggested that if I wished to continue I might find there were expensive rules about whether or not an Australian license allowed you to drive ancient American cars. We quickly decided twenty bucks to park on the sidewalk in the center of San Francisco for a whole lunchtime was pretty cheap, but our Caddy (soon sold and gone) continued to generate publicity. Our slide show and across-the-USA-by-Caddy talk became a bookshop favorite in Britain.

Ten years later our Caddy expedition helped to inspire another Great American Road Trip. Our Oakland office rented an ocean-liner-size RV, decked it out with Lonely Planet signage and on May 8 2004 set off from New York on the 'Everywhere You Are' bookshop tour. With Gary Todoroff, our US trade sales director, on board for the whole trip and other LP-ites including our marketing manager, Robin Goldberg, and our US head, Todd Sotkiewicz, for shorter sections they covered 6000 miles, across twenty-six states in twenty-seven days, to visit 100 independent bookshops in the east, south and Midwest of the country. The trip was intended to strengthen the strong tie between independent Lonely Planet and independent bookshops, but the odyssey inspired far more warm and fuzzy feelings than we'd hoped for. It also focused attention on America's independent bookshops and by the time Myles, as the hard-working vehicle had been dubbed, rolled into Chicago in time for the annual US publishing shindig, our road trip had gone down as one of our best-ever publicity blitzes.

In October 1994 Lonely Planet had been in existence for twenty-one years. We decided to celebrate: Lonely Planet would have a birthday party.

We invited all our friends—fellow publishers, distributors, authors and staff. Anybody who had been working for us for twelve months on our birthday, we decided, would be flown back to Australia for the occasion. Jim and I were in Oakland mid-year and took our staff out to lunch at a local Thai restaurant. At the end of the meal we stood up to thank everybody for their hard work and tell them how pleased we were that Lonely Planet was about to reach twenty-one years of age.

'So we're going to have a party in Australia to celebrate,' Jim announced.

'And you're all invited,' I continued.

'Yes,' said Jim, 'we're flying you all to Australia.'

There was more than a shocked silence—there was a delicious moment of utter incomprehension! A few months later, in Australia, Dave Skibinski, one of the guys from the Oakland warehouse, leaned over to me as the Lonely Planet bus took us out to a winery outside Melbourne.

'Tony,' he said, 'any time you ask me to jump I'm only going to say one thing: how high?'

We gathered together staff from all the offices, many of our authors, and some of our long-term competitors/friends, including Bill Dalton from Moon Publications in California, Hilary Bradt of Bradt Publications in Britain, and even our new arch rival Philippe Gloaguen of the Guides du Routard in Paris.

Why not make it a public event as well, we thought? So we booked the Malthouse, a small complex of theater spaces also used for the Melbourne Writers Festival, and planned two days of public events. We invited Eric Newby, author of the classic travel tale *A Short Walk in the Hindu Kush*, and Pico Iyer, best known for *Video Night in Kathmandu*, as two stars of the show.

There were many highlights, but one that stood out was at the close of the public events at the Malthouse. We'd had talks, slideshows, how-to events and we'd packed the place out. When it all wound down, Maureen and I walked out to our car, exhausted but elated, and started to drive away. A couple walking by in the street flagged us down: 'Fantastic,' they said, 'that was the best weekend ever. You guys are great.' They didn't need to tell us, we felt great.

This week-long celebration also launched Lonely Planet onto the Internet. 'Let's create a multimedia product for the event,' we had decided. Rob Flynn and Paul Clifton were locked away in a dark room with computers, digitizers, photographs and text, and before we knew it we had an internal interactive website which told the story of Lonely Planet and showed various historic (i.e. better forgotten) pictures of Maureen and me and even included our first 'destination profile' on Bali.

From there it was only a blink of the eye to launching a real website, still a pretty pioneering thing to do in 1994. Soon after our 'E-Team', which included Rob Flynn, David Collins, Peter Morris, Janet Austin, Brigitte Barta and Chris Klep, launched our website in April 1995. How early was this in the history of the web? Well Yahoo! went commercial just one month earlier. The Internet, websites and email have all become such a familiar part of our lives (even my eighty-year-old mother keeps in touch with her friends by email), it's hard to remember they were virtually unknown, except to real technology geeks, in the early 1990s.

The Internet Advertising Report (1997, Harper Business, New York) was produced by Morgan Stanley's technology team and included 'A Time Line of Internet Advertising', starting with the launch of GNN in November 1993, the first recorded instance of advertising on the Internet. Those early advertisers included Mountain Travel, Sobek and, of course, Lonely Planet.

We had made an abortive foray into the realms of digital publishing earlier, an expedition which even included a meeting with Bill Gates. In 1994 things were changing so fast in the digital information world that it's hard to believe only a year before the launch of our website nobody had really foreseen the impact the Internet would have. It was assumed at the time that digital content would come to computers by way of CD-ROMs.

In early 1993 we were approached by Microsoft about producing a digital version of our guidebooks. Microsoft staff visited our Oakland office, and our staff made the trek north to the Microsoft campus in Seattle. In September Jim Hart and I also flew to Seattle and spent a couple of days kicking around how an interactive guidebook might work on CD. But it wasn't going to work. CD-ROMs are static things which work very well for encyclopedias and dictionaries, but the web, still lurking in the wings in 1993, would soon march on stage and comprehensively trash any ideas about putting guidebooks on CD-ROM.

Nevertheless, a year later Bill Gates made a brief visit to Australia and, so the story goes, had only two names on his 'must see' list: Paul Keating, at the time Australia's prime minister, and Lonely Planet. Jim and I flew up to Sydney and spent forty-five minutes with the world's richest man. It may have been more than our fifteen minutes, but it was the end of any deal with Microsoft. During our Seattle visit there had been murmurs about selling the company, if we weren't interested in simply licensing the information. Fortunately, we weren't interested.

Our website quickly became very popular, but making money from it was never easy. That was partly our fault, since taking on advertising or selling things from our site didn't qualify for approval as 'the Lonely Planet way' of doing things.

Our success in the annual Webby awards was one measure of the popularity of our site. Often described as the 'Oscars of the Internet', Webby awards recognize outstanding achievements on the web in various categories including travel. They're awarded by members of the International Academy of Digital Arts and Sciences, a group which ranges all the way from David Bowie to Larry Ellison. There's also the People's Voice awards, determined by the general public. In 2005 we picked up that award in the travel category for the sixth consecutive year. Like Amazon and Google we've also been double winners—in 2002 we picked up the Best Travel Website award as well.

Webbys are nice to have, but it is the Thorn Tree travel forum which we regard as our website's success. All we really provided was the stage—the Thorn Tree enthusiasts turned it into the most popular travel information center on the web. The formula is simple: anyone can post a travel question and, inevitably, there will be somebody who has an answer. Of course, the Thorn Tree, like any website chat room, has had its problems. At one point we were so plagued by the dark side of the web, the idiots who only want to abuse people and post garbage, that we decided, reluctantly, to require people to register before they could post messages. Remarkably, it had no effect on the Thorn Tree's popularity. Today we have over 200 000 registered users who post over a million individual messages a year.

Of course, even registration won't totally suppress website troublemakers so keeping the Thorn Tree neat and clean requires around-the-clock supervision. Apart from our own personnel we also have experts who live in different time zones around the world and who contribute to the upkeep of the forum. When I was in Iran in 2004 I spent a day with a Thorn Tree regional expert who lives in Tehran.

The popularity of our website and our digital expertise has also given us foot-in-the-door status for all sorts of projects, from a travel information site on Nokia phones in Europe to travel information covering nearly 300 destinations on Airshow, an inflight entertainment system carried by many of the world's major international airlines.

What about a digital version of our guidebooks? We have played with a digital guidebook called CitySync to load onto Palm Pilots. It came complete with maps and later with a regularly updated entertainment and activities module. I tried it out on a number of city trips and at the end we covered twenty-two different cities, but it was clunky and never worked as well as a paper guidebook. It was launched in 2000 and we eventually sold nearly 50 000 of them, plus there were about half a million free 'demo downloads' from our website. We never made a penny of profit from CitySync and we eventually closed it down in 2004.

CitySync was a step towards that digital guidebook of the future. As handhelds, laptop computers and cell phones converge there probably will be a digital guidebook which you can load onto something you carry round just like a real guidebook. Perhaps you'll load the latest version just before you start your trip. Perhaps you'll update it by connecting to something like an ATM at the airport—and swiping your credit card, of course! Or maybe you'll get the latest version off the Internet while you're on your flight.

When an idea's time has come it pops up from all directions. So, when the idea of a Lonely Planet TV series began to percolate in the early 1990s, we suddenly had several people running with the idea. Eventually Simon Naisht and Ian Cross, two Europe-based Australian TV veterans who had been associated with the *Beyond 2000* TV series, convinced us they were the people to make it work. They did, but it took a long time.

It was Ian who became the moving force behind Pilot Productions and in 1992 a program based on a trip through Indonesia was shot. The Australian broadcaster SBS put up most of the funding to shoot the pilot, but moving the project on from there was akin to building a house of cards. Each card was another network willing to put money into it, but when it seemed the whole edifice was standing high enough to launch the project somebody would pull their card out from the bottom and the whole construction would tumble to the ground. Eventually the British Channel 4 network joined the game, giving the whole project enough momentum to launch it. The first programs—Morocco, Vietnam, Brazil, Central America, Alaska, the Pacific—were shot and I spent an evening in Pilot's London editing suite looking at that first batch as they neared completion.

The Lonely Planet TV series soon took off, although Ian Cross' initial plan that travel should be the most important element, not the presenter, went straight out the window when Ian Wright, a pint-sized, one-man energy source with a peculiar accent, became immensely popular. The series showed all over the world and also became a regular on airlines. A few years down the track, when Channel Four began to lose interest, the series was picked up by the Discovery Channel.

This was all fine and we certainly appreciated the exposure—I would regularly bump into people in strange corners of the world who knew the name Lonely Planet, but through the TV series, not the books. Nor were we too unhappy about the programs themselves. At first we'd insisted on veto rights over what got made, but after watching the early shows fairly carefully we became confident that Ian wasn't going to damage our reputation and we let him run with it.

There were other areas of the relationship we weren't so happy about. We got a flat fee for each installment made, but the series never seemed to make enough money to pay anything beyond that starting fee. Nor was Pilot always completely scrupulous about what it produced, so we began to see programs we were less happy about, such as the series of beach out-takes that were strung together to produce a Best Beaches show. Plus, we could see the time would come when faster access and digital media production would make video an important part of our website, in which case we wanted to control it. We'd even dipped a toe in the video water ourselves by producing a series of airline arrival videos.

So when the Pilot/Lonely Planet contract ran its course we let it lapse, set up our own LPTV division and launched our own television series titled *Six Degrees*. It's already in its third series with Discovery Asia and we've also produced a number of other programs including Going Bush with Aboriginal Olympic hero Cathy Freeman.

I: Maureen and I are regularly asked, 'What is your favorite place?' It's an impossible question to answer, since we like one place for its beaches, another for its food, another for its culture. If we're pushed, we say how much we love Nepal or how the Australian outback gets beneath your skin, or I comment on my short attention span and how I always like wherever I was last week.

The other inevitable question is, 'What's the most dangerous thing that's ever happened to you?' Well, there was a bus once, heading down from Banos in the Ecuadorean highlands to Guayaquil on the coast. All South American bus drivers are a little crazy, but this guy was crazy big time. Remarkably, the speedometer worked (usually South American speedos are permanently pegged at zero) and, unfortunately, I could see it from my seat. Quite often the needle was spinning right off the end of the dial and looking like it was going to have a go at making a second circuit. As we sped through towns I'd look out the back window to see every chicken in the village dead in the street.

Finally, we agreed that this was impossible; our daughter was four, our son only two, and the chances of them reaching five and three seemed remote if we continued much further with this madman. Grabbing our bags and lurching down the aisle, Maureen commanded him to stop there and then. He slammed on the brakes and screeched to a halt and I summoned up my limited supply of Spanish to tell him that his balls were much bigger than his brain. He seemed pleased with the news.

But that's about as far as I can go in a search for dangerous moments. The simple fact is that all it takes is to be in the wrong place at the wrong time. This came home forcefully to me in November 1996 when a hijacked Ethiopian Airlines 767 crashed into the sea off the Comoros Islands. One of those who died was the respected Kenyan photographer and travel publisher Mohamed Amin. Amongst other achievements, it was Mohamed whose video work alerted the world to the terrible famine in Ethiopia in 1984, bringing back photographs from a country that was virtually shut off from the outside at that time. I didn't know Mohamed well, but we certainly greeted each other if our paths crossed in the aisles at the Frankfurt Bookfair.

Fortunately, our airline stories are usually funny rather than harrowing. In 1985 our US office manager Camille Coyne, Maureen and I were flying from San Francisco to New York with the much-loved, but short-lived, pioneer of cut-price American aviation, People Express, and our tickets were a knockout bargain at $99! Who could fail to love an airline that would fly you coast-to-coast for a mere $99? We were thrilled when the captain announced that last week they'd cut their coast-to-coast fare by a full fifty bucks, so you could now fly to New York for a mere $49. The flight attendants came down the aisle, and gave anybody with a $99 ticket a $50 refund! We duly collected three crisp $50 notes. And soon thereafter pondered why on earth this fine airline had gone bankrupt.

Things were similarly casual nearly seven years later on an Air Cambodge flight from Angkor Wat back to Phnom Penh in Cambodia. We'd been kicking around the ruins with a young German who worked for Lufthansa as a flight attendant and there were no seats left when he boarded. The Air Cambodge flight attendant ushered him up to the flight deck. I was pleased to find both halves of a seat belt at my seat, until I discovered they were both the same end, but things weren't quite so well equipped up front. As we waited for our bags in Phnom Penh, our German friend explained that not only was there a pilot and co-pilot up front but also two training crew and the flight attendant. Our friend was given a bamboo chair to sit on while the others stood for the duration of the flight. The crew were very interested in working conditions with Lufthansa—the aircraft's Russian pilot was paid US$1000 a month while the Cambodian co-pilot took home part of his pay in bags of rice.

Alaskan Airlines, always an airline keen to keep a smile on the passengers' faces, gave us one of the best safety quips. Before concluding the flight with a request that we consider flying Alaskan again, 'anytime our travel plans called for flights anywhere from Puerto Vallerta to Dead Horse', our flight attendant pondered why we had been free to wander around the aircraft while it hurtled through the stratosphere at 500 mph but were being firmly admonished to stay belted down in our seats as we taxied in to the gate at 5 mph.

Then there was the British Airways flight attendant who ticked us off, in her best school-marmish voice, for not listening to her safety announcement. 'In fact,' she continued, 'I'm going to do the whole thing again. Now listen this time.'

At the tail end of 2001, as we taxied into the terminal at Denver International Airport on a United Airlines flight, the announcer warned us to open the overhead lockers with care, 'because,' after which there was a pregnant pause, '. . . because shit happens.'

Despite the success of our website we were never caught up in the 1990s 'new economy' boom. We didn't boom, but nor, of course, did we bust. Not that we couldn't have joined the craze—lots of people suggested we spin off Lonely Planet Digital and make lots of money, but why? Where was it going to go? What was it going to do? I remained a digital skeptic the whole time. I spent a lot of time surfing the web, booking airline tickets and making rent-a-car reservations online. Rarely do I send a check these days if I can pay a bill on the web, but buy clothes? Forget it. Trade in my local supermarket for online shopping? No way.

I still only half-believe Amazon as a business model. Have the profits it now makes ever covered its set-up costs? However, I consult it almost every day and regularly buy books from it—and, of course, Lonely Planet sells a hell of a lot of books there. For that last reason alone, I hope Amazon finds a way to make lots of money and survives to a healthy old age, but it's simply another way of selling a rather old-fashioned (though very nice!) product. I still buy far more books in bookshops than over the web. I like bookshops, they're a social as well as a shopping experience. I like browsing, finding things I wasn't even looking for, going in to buy a book and coming out with an armful of magazines instead. I'm not going to give up that pleasure to sit in front of a computer screen.

If having a successful website was one new-economy litmus test for the 1990s, having a recognizable brand was the other. In fact, the two often seemed to be inextricably linked. You raised a huge amount of money through an IPO and spent the money on advertising to create interest in your brand which then fed people through to your website. What nobody seemed to ask was what that website was all about and why people would go there even if they did recognize your name.

We began to realize in the late 1990s how valuable a brand Lonely Planet had become. We had created that brand not by hype or advertising, but by simple word of mouth. We'd created something that people valued and respected and, as a consequence, they knew our name and trusted it. We were absolute believers that what we did, we did better than anybody else. Because we were often the biggest—the mythical 300-pound gorilla—we could spend more money, more time and more effort making sure what we did was the best, whether it was the most comprehensive and exhaustively researched guidebook or the most up-to-date website. We were also independent; we weren't part of some conglomerate book empire where travel was only one field of interest and where our name could be tacked on to almost any other activity so long as it looked like making money. For us, travel was the start, the finish and everything else in between.

The standing of our brand came home to us more and more often. Sometimes it was through Lonely Planet fans, people who believed in what we were doing and praised us when we did it well or damned us if we didn't. Sometimes it was through people who had no idea what Lonely Planet was all about, but recognized the name: it might be a young Japanese guy who'd seen the television program, a sari-clad Indian woman who had noticed the young travelers clutching our book or a Vietnamese cyclist puzzling over the Lonely Planet Café, the Lonely Planet T-shirts for sale and the signs announcing 'recommended by Lonely Planet' on establishments in Hanoi.

There was even recognition of our name's value in the business world. In Interbrand's 2004 Readers' Choice Brand of the Year survey, Lonely Planet came in as the sixth best brand in the Asia-Pacific region. We were beaten by Sony, Samsung, Toyota, LG and Singapore Airlines, but the rest of the top ten were Virgin Blue, Honda, HSBC and Mazda so we were in good company.

The digital world is sexy and we're putting lots of effort into it, but books are still where we make most of our money. We're hoping that in the years to come books will be as important as ever dollar-wise, but as a proportion of our total turnover they will go down and down. Which is not stopping us from putting lots of effort into expanding our range of books.

Guidebooks and Lonely Planet are like bread and butter or fish and chips, although in fact our fourth book was a walking guide, Stan Armington's guide to trekking in Nepal. Now in its eighth edition, it's still our most popular walking book. Over the years many other walking titles have joined the list, ranging from very popular walking regions like New Zealand (where you 'tramp' rather than walk) and Ireland to more unusual destinations like Patagonia and Japan.

I've had the opportunity to try out many of our walking titles over the years. We included a substantial walking section in our first Britain guide and then expanded it into the separate and very popular *Walking in Britain*. As well as some shorter strolls, I walked Britain coast to coast by following Hadrian's Wall, covered the beautiful Cotswold Way from just south of Stratford-upon-Avon to Bath and concluded by walking the Pennine Way, a 260-mile jaunt which starts in the Peak District in the northern Midlands and travels up the mountainous and often surprisingly remote central spine of northern England, eventually crossing the border to finish in Scotland.

The Cotswold Way was a beautiful walk and logistically easy. There was no need to carry food since each night there was a pleasant English pub serving dinner. There was no need to carry a sleeping bag or camping gear either, as comfortable bed and breakfasts dotted the route. The Cotswold Way could almost be luxury walking—how many walks include Michelin-starred restaurants?

Later that year, at the Frankfurt Bookfair, I spoke with Hilary Bradt, publisher of the Bradt Guides. I enthused about what fun the Cotswold Way had been and what a change such 'civilized' walking could be, but Hilary, who divided her time between work and leading treks through the jungles of Madagascar or across high Andean passes in Bolivia, looked at me as if I was slightly crazy. Clearly, what I was going on about was more like a Sunday-afternoon stroll to the village shops than a real walk. Three years later, however, Hilary collared me at Frankfurt to give me an enthusiastic account of the walk she'd just led through the Cotswolds.

'Nobody died,' she said, as if deaths were a daily occurrence on a normal stroll with Hilary, 'and if they had I would have pulled my mobile phone out, dialed 999 and the problem would have been over.'

In recent years walking has become a regular part of our annual itinerary. So often guidebooks are done at high speed, racing from place to place to get the book finished and out on the shelves before the information gets out of date and inaccurate. Walking is different; the world passes by at a speed more in tune with thought and contemplation. We've always enjoyed walking and almost every book we do includes some walking, but for the past ten years I've contrived to make at least one long walk each year. As a result, there have been many trips to Nepal plus walking trips in Australia, New Zealand, France, Italy and Switzerland.

For many years our phrasebooks were a back-burner project. We specialized in odd and obscure languages (nobody else had a phrasebook for Quechua, for example, the language of the Incas of the Andes). The big languages we left to Berlitz and the other language specialists until, in the mid-1990s, our phrasebook publisher Sally Steward launched into European languages with more comprehensive phrasebooks which broke new ground with useful sections such as Frisky French. This offered the sort of phrases which could be useful if you were going 'to get laid' (*s'envoyer en l'air*), in which case you might need expressions like 'touch me here', 'you're fantastic' and 'let's do it again!' Or 'tie me up', although our French office pointed out, with serious concern, that we didn't follow up with 'and now untie me'.

To our delight, we found we could produce phrasebooks which were just as comprehensive and usable as the established competition. Furthermore, they sold incredibly well and, unlike guidebooks, they didn't need updating all the time. We also enjoyed some high-level help: it's always nice to get photographs of well-known people using our books and one of the best showed Bill Clinton stepping out of Air Force One and hurriedly checking something in his copy of Lonely Planet's *Latin American Spanish*.

We also had fun with three English-language phrasebooks for those who wanted to communicate in American English, Australian English or British English. The *British Phrasebook* got a huge amount of publicity in Britain, particularly for its theory that the British were 'moving towards a sort of Zen English in which *fuck* will be the only word—shaped, nuanced and spat out to convey every thought and sentiment'.

Of course, there were some more horrible screw-ups along the way. It was the guys in the warehouse, once again, who picked up that we'd left the 'h' out of 'phrasebook' on the spine of our first Quechua phrasebook. Far worse was the mess we made with language cassettes. Packaging a language cassette along with the phrasebook seemed like a good idea. The parallel idea that we'd put them out in neat little culturally appropriate folders—a Thai silk one for the Thailand phrasebook and cassette, a batik one for the Indonesian version—turned out to be horribly expensive, complicated and a complete marketing failure. Furthermore, when the first batch of cassettes (Bahasa Indonesian) arrived at the office, I grabbed one to try out in my car as I drove somewhere that afternoon. I am no linguist and my Indonesian is strictly of the market variety, but a few miles down the road I pulled off to the side, breathing heavily. We had got the numbers wrong. I couldn't believe that with all the Indonesian expertise we had around the office I had to be the one to find this horrible mistake, but the first batch of cassettes ended up crushed, crunched or whatever the cassette equivalent of pulped may be.

Journeys, as we named our foray into travel literature, kicked off with four titles in 1996. It was an idea which had been germinating for a long time, but it was Michelle de Kretser's return from establishing the Paris office which got the list out of the garage and onto the road. It's been an interesting and satisfying range to publish and pleasantly profitable without, yet, producing a bestseller.

We weren't interested in doing a book for only one market until we began to find travel literature titles which we really liked but could only purchase the rights for in one region of the world. Eric Newby and his wife Wanda had come to Australia for Lonely Planet's 21st-birthday celebrations. Eric was born in 1919 so he was hardly a youngster, but he and his wife were such irrepressible enthusiasts for living (Wanda could drink you under the table) they even won over our children. In 1942, Eric was only twenty-three when he was taken prisoner by the Germans after a bungled commando raid in Sicily. When the Italians pulled out of the war, Eric escaped and spent the next year on the run, aided, it sometimes seemed, by half the population of Italy. Remarkably, he even found time to fall in love with Wanda, the teenage daughter of one of his helpers.

Eventually Eric was recaptured by the Germans and spent the rest of the war in a prison camp in Czechoslovakia. When the war was over, he headed straight back to Italy, tracked Wanda down and married her. They lived happily and vividly ever after and the book he wrote about his Italian adventures, *Love and War in the Apennines*, was made into a tele-movie in 2001. Eric went on to write a string of books, one of which, *A Short Walk in the Hindu Kush*, is one of the classics of travel writing.

In 1997 Sandye Wexler, co-owner of the Savvy Traveller bookshop in Chicago, asked if I had any suggestions for good titles for her travel literature reading group.

'What about A *Short Walk in the Hindu Kush*,' I suggested.

'A great book,' she replied, 'but it's out of print in the US.'

I couldn't believe it—it was regularly listed in top tens of the best travel titles ever—but when I checked it out, sure enough it was out of print. As were all the other Newby titles. They were readily available in Britain and Australia, but in America none of them was listed. A year later we had acquired the American rights to seven Newby books, including *Short Walk*. I would never have imagined, when I first read Eric's wonderful book, that one day I would be able to say, 'I'm his publisher.'

Another range joined the list when we bought the American

Pisces series in 1997. The list of diving and snorkeling guides fitted with my personal interest and we set to work to upgrade and expand the list. By the end of 2001 we had nearly forty guides in the series, less than a dozen of which dated from the old Pisces list. In fact, we had been talking about starting a scuba-diving series for years and I knew we would continue to talk without doing anything. Taking over an already established list, even if it was not as high quality as we would wish, would propel us into action.

By 2001, I'd managed to try the diving in twenty-two different countries and had helped to write one of the new Pisces titles, a guide to the diving in Tahiti and French Polyncsia, but unhappily we hadn't managed to make the series work properly. From the start I was concerned that we would find ways of improving the quality, but if we weren't careful we would also push the costs upwards. That was exactly what happened and in the round of belt-tightening we were forced into after September 11 our scuba-diving series ended up on the back burner although in 2006 we relaunched the diving series in a new format.

If we could produce books and other publications for individuals to buy, why not produce them for companies to give away? That simple idea was the start of our special publishing department, which has produced everything from a travel safety booklet for the New Zealand tourist office to a London shopping guide. Sporting events have been particularly popular for this field—we've done an international Grand Prix guide for Foster's Beer, a host of projects for the 2000 Sydney Olympics and guides for both the 2002 and 2006 soccer World Cups.

Once upon a time another publisher said, 'The images in Lonely Planet books look as if they were taken by the author using an Instamatic borrowed from his mother.' Although I took all the photographs in some early books it was never with my mother's Instamatic and by the 1990s our standards were much higher. As the standards rose we spent increasing amounts on buying images from photo libraries. It was time to establish our own photo library. This was a case of necessity being the mother of invention—we were using so many photos that simply managing all the color transparencies floating around the office meant we needed some sort of photo-management system. Getting Lonely Planet Images (LPI) off the ground took longer than we'd expected but the decision to make LPI a digital library put us at the forefront of photo library technology and we now have one of the best travel collections in the world.

Around the same time I was involved in some photographic projects, although not behind the camera. I'd always been fascinated by rickshaws, those bicycle-powered taxis of Asia, and in 1997 Richard I'Anson, who would later manage LPI, and I set off on a circuit of twelve Asian cities that had interesting rickshaw fleets. It was the start of a firm friendship and the resulting book, *Chasing Rickshaws*, looked terrific and sold pretty well but cost so much to get on the shelves it never made a cent. That was not a problem for me—the book was really a personal extravagance, a labor of love.

Unfortunately, we followed up with several other photographic books—coffee-table books as they're known—which also failed to become more than mildly profitable. With Peter Bennetts, another talented photographer who has become a good friend, I made trips to the Pacific island nation of Tuvalu in 2000 and 2001 to tell the story of a country threatened by global warming and rising sea levels. Despite support from the country's government, *Time and Tide* was too specialized to be commercial. Our Tuvalu book faced a few other problems. The prime minister of Tuvalu gave the project his personal backing, signed the contracts with me and died of a heart attack twenty-four hours later! Then Peter and I had a spell as castaways when we were dropped off by a fishing boat on the island of Nukufetau and what should have been a 48-hour visit turned into a week when the boat failed to come back for us. Richard I'Anson and I also did another Asian circuit, this time to tell the story of rice, the world's most important food, in the book *Rice Trails*, another project which I have to admit was more a labor of love than commercially realistic.

Roz Hopkins took over our special publishing projects in 2002. Her titles included coffee-table books and she turned the list around, beginning with *One Planet*, published in late 2003, which proved we could produce a profitable photo book. She followed that with the hugely successful *Travel Book* in 2004 and *The Cities Book* in 2006. Plus Richard I'Anson has written two editions of his very successful guide to *Travel Photography* which has prompted a series of specialist spin offs. Nobody makes any snide suggestions about Instamatics any more.

In the mid-1990s the desire to live overseas began to affect us again. Perhaps it was a period of stability at the office; perhaps it was rediscovering Europe as our first Europe guides moved through the system; perhaps it was an urge to shake the kids up; or perhaps it was our two European offices offering an excuse to try a different environment. Whatever the reasons, it came to a head in 1995. I'd been in San Francisco and on the way home I'd stopped in at both our London and Paris offices. Naturally, I'd had a great time in all three cities and back in Australia I brought up the idea of another one-year upheaval.

'If we're going to do it we should do it right now,' suggested Maureen. 'Tashi only has three more years at high school, so a year overseas next year would be OK. I don't think it would be fair to ask her to cope with that in her last couple of years.'

Within half an hour we'd not only convinced ourselves to do it, we'd narrowed the choice down to Paris (we'd already tried life in London and San Francisco) and only had to sell the idea to the kids.

'No way,' was their immediate response.

'It's bad enough dragging us somewhere every vacation,' they complained in chorus. 'But a whole year away would be unsurvivable.'

'Our friends would all forget us,' they continued.

'Our social lives would come to a complete halt for evermore,' they moaned.

'A whole year would be the end of civilization as we know it,' they concluded.

'Big deal, we're going right after Christmas,' we heartlessly responded.

We arrived in Paris on an icily cold and grey morning. Arno Lebonnois and Laurence Billiet from our French office had driven out to the airport in two cars to meet us and convey our large collection of bags into Paris, a redundant operation since British Airways had left all our bags behind in London when we'd transferred flights. I'd tentatively looked for an apartment during my October visit, but for interest only, since any place we found would have been rented by Christmas and given the sky-high Parisian rents there was no way we were going to rent a place months in advance.

Easily the nicest apartment we found was in the 16th arrondissement, close to where the kids would go to school, but this was quickly blacklisted.

'You cannot live in the 16th,' our French office unanimously reported. 'It is bourgeois; it's full of diplomats and the employees of multinationals. If anybody finds out you live there, Lonely Planet's reputation will be ruined.'

It was imperative that we live somewhere more interesting. In fact, that was excellent advice; the 16th would have been irredeemably boring, something you could never say about the colorful eighteenth-century apartment we ended up with in the Marais district of the 4th arrondissement. From the bedroom window of 39 rue St Paul you could look straight down rue Neuve St Pierre to the window of the apartment at 17 rue Beautreillis where Jim Morrison of the Doors had died back in 1970.

Would we need a car—and thus a parking space—in Paris? That was one of our pre-departure questions, but we decided we'd do without and worry about it after we'd been there for a while. Perhaps we'd get away with renting a car when we needed one. In fact, in our entire year in Paris, we only once rented a car in France, during a weekend trip to Brittany. We certainly rented cars during the year—in Portugal, along the Turkish coast, on the Greek Islands, on a visit to Maureen's brother in Ireland, even on a trip to the US. But in France? Not necessary. Not owning a car was one of the real delights of Paris. On the other hand, Paris did provide the constant intrigue of that most Parisian of skills: car parking. How on earth do they get their cars into those tiny spaces? We'd notice, as we went into a restaurant, that the car outside was utterly wedged in with much larger and bulkier vehicles parked hard up against it at both ends. When we'd emerge, the trapped vehicle would have disappeared, as if a flying saucer had come down and spirited it away.

Mid-year I made a quick trip back to the Melbourne office and when the aircraft flew out of Singapore and crossed the equator it occurred to me that I'd be going from the longest day of the year in the northern hemisphere to the shortest day of the year in the southern—simultaneous solstices. I'd just finished reading *A Year with Swollen Appendices*, multimedia enthusiast and musician Brian Eno's intriguing diary for the year 1995. I'd kept diaries on our overland trip in 1972 and for our year-long journey in 1974, but they were perfunctory accounts. That night I started a real diary and kept it assiduously for precisely one year. When I reread bits of it I still find it interesting. It totaled over 200 000 words, the equivalent of a 400-page book, so I clearly put a lot of time into it.

My return down under was partly business, but also to see my father, who was very ill and very unhappy about it. Two years earlier, when his health had taken a real tumble, my parents had moved to Australia permanently. My sister and her family had been living there for ten years and after my mother, a school teacher, had retired, my parents began to spend half of each year in Australia. Despite his hospitalization my father rallied, went home and lingered on for another unhappy year.

From Australia I traveled to California and returned to Paris on the night of a Neil Young concert at the Bercy. Maureen, never a Neil Young fan, didn't go, but Kieran, Tashi and I did—separately. The kids met their respective friends before the concert, while I wandered in by myself and gravitated, like an overgrown teenager, to the oldies' mosh pit down the front. What a concert—absolutely fantastic from the opening chords of 'Powderfinger' to the last ringing note. In fact, my ears rang for days. I never saw the kids until we all reappeared at the apartment, but on the metro on my way home I bumped into

Kieran's schoolteacher, who had also been at the concert.

A couple of months later, we went to London for the weekend by the high-speed Eurostar train service. When we discovered that Steely Dan, one of our favorite bands, would be playing on the Sunday night, we sent Tashi and Kieran, fifteen and thirteen, back to Paris ahead of us. We put them on the train at Waterloo, told them to get themselves to school the next morning and we'd be back in Paris that afternoon.

Our year in Paris included a terrific six-week Mediterranean circuit, island-hopping from Athens through the Greek islands to the Turkish coast and then traveling along the coast to Gallipoli and on to Istanbul. In November we were in Berlin for Stefan Loose's fiftieth birthday, and only a few weeks later it was my own fiftieth at a surprise party with the French office. We spent Christmas with Maureen's brother and his family in Northern Ireland and then went back to Australia. We arrived on New Year's Eve, little realizing that we were about to embark on several very strange years. Looking back on the second half of the 1990s we would wonder how the business could go so well and we could have so many wonderful moments, and yet at the same time be so miserably depressed.

11

Not Always the Good Guys

We had no idea the trouble Burma would cause us in later years when we made our first visit in 1974. Burma had only recently opened its doors to visitors and by only the narrowest amount. North Korea has been a reclusive hermit kingdom for much longer than Burma, but back in the 1950s and '60s getting into the 'Golden Land' was difficult. For a long time visitors were not allowed at all and when visas were first issued they were for a mere twenty-four hours. Finally, the seven-day visa arrived, allowing travelers a single week to race around as much of the country as they could, but the areas open to visitors were severely circumscribed.

There were various reasons why the government kept such a tight rein on visitors. One was that they had only the most tenuous control over much of the country. Even today, one of our writers commented that traveling around Burma you realize that 'the country is still run like a loose-knit collection of warlord states'. In recent years, the government, using heavy-handed tactics, has brought some of its independently minded border regions to heel. In some regions that has caused great hardship and floods of refugees into neighboring countries, although in other areas, government control, even by a bad government, has brought improved conditions.

The fact that Burma, away from the central plains, wasn't really under Burmese control didn't have much impact on us during that first visit. We scurried around the country as quickly as we could and then retreated to Bangkok, blown away by what we'd seen. Burma was quite unlike anywhere else in the region. In 1974, McDonald's was making its first inroads into the big cities in Southeast Asia. Coca-Cola had been a familiar drink for some time, and the roads were beginning to fill up with Toyota cars and Honda motorcycles. Singapore was getting ready to transform itself from a kitten to a tiger, and tourists were starting to appear in larger numbers. Not in Burma.

Visiting Burma was like passing through a time warp. The shops were empty, Western brands were few and far between, everybody wore a sarong-like *longyi*, the roads were quiet, the handful of buses ancient and hopelessly overcrowded and the even smaller number of cars all dated from the British era, which ended soon after World War II.

At the same time the ancient deserted city of Pagan was easily the most astonishing sight we had seen anywhere in Southeast Asia and the people were amazingly friendly and outgoing. It was love at first sight—we wanted to come back and see more.

How had Burma backed itself into this corner, shut off from the outside world and economically far behind the rest of the region? Some of the problem went back to the British era. Between 1826 and 1886 the British had taken over the country in three giant bites and tacked it onto their great Indian empire. It's debatable why the British needed even more territory, but the country's wealth of timber and the fine port of Rangoon must have proved irresistible. Sorting out the chaos on the borders of their lucrative Indian holdings was equally important. Burma at the time was a shambolic mess; a series of weak and ineffective kings had resulted in the country being squabbled over by greedy officials on one side and ruthless gangs on the other. It was hardly surprising many people found efficient British rule a pleasant change, and the British discovered that doing business in Burma was equally satisfying. The Burmese were efficient rice producers and their forests were full of valuable teak.

Britain ruled the country with an iron hand, but in the years leading up to World War II the push for independence grew stronger, mirroring the movement led by Gandhi in neighboring India. In Burma a young university student named Aung San was one of the leaders of the independence movement in the late 1930s until a British arrest warrant prompted him to hightail it to China and then Japan. Aung San wanted independence for his country, the Japanese offered to help him get it, and his siding with the Japanese is probably as simple as that. In February 1941 he was back in Burma to recruit his 'Thirty Comrades' and return with them to Japan for training. Later that year Aung San, still only twenty-six years old, was at the head of the Japanese-financed Burmese Independence Army in Bangkok. Soon after Pearl Harbor, Rangoon fell to the Japanese and Aung San was now firmly in the Japanese camp as the British were driven north.

By the end of 1943 it looked like Aung San had achieved everything he wanted, but it was all about to fall apart.

Now a Major-General, as the title Bogyoke indicated, he was decorated with the 'Order of the Rising Sun' by the Japanese emperor. In August of that year the Japanese announced that Burma was independent, but Aung San discovered that although the Burmese had been 'struggling like bullocks under the British' they were being 'treated like dogs' by the Japanese. It would be a step forward, he avowed, 'to get back to the bullock stage'.

In November 1943 he smuggled a message out to the British forces offering to switch sides. In May 1945 he renounced the country's 'independence' under the Japanese and when the Allied forces marched back into Rangoon, only weeks before the Hiroshima and Nagasaki atom bombs brought the war to an abrupt halt, Aung San was at their side. Quite how popular their new ally was with the British is hard to gauge. British and Australian prisoners of war had been starving to death on the Thailand-to-Burma 'death railway' while Aung San was being feted by the Japanese. After the war it was hardly surprising that the central Burmese government found they had enemies within their own borders.

Nevertheless, Burma gained real independence on January 4

1948, less than six months after India achieved the same thing. It did not come soon enough for Aung San: he had been assassinated along with his older brother and five other government leaders in July 1947. Aung San's vision of a democratic, socialist, unified Burma fell apart piece by piece in the subsequent years, but the young leader was to have a surprisingly long-lasting influence on his country. In 1942 Aung San had married Daw Khin Kyi and in 1945 they had a daughter: Aung San Suu Kyi.

I have no sympathy with governments that maintain absurd exchange rates and profiteer from visitors by making them change money at unrealistic 'official rates'. Inevitably, black markets spring up and the government wastes huge amounts of money trying to enforce the unenforceable. On our first visits to Burma the exchange rates were absurd and there were draconian punishments for anyone who changed money on the black market.

Fortunately, there was a wonderfully simple solution to the exchange rate dilemma. You just had to buy a carton of cigarettes and a bottle of whisky (total price about US$10) at the duty-free shop at Bangkok airport and sell them on arrival in Rangoon for about US$100. Not any cigarettes, they had to be 555; and not any whisky, it had to be Johnny Walker Red Label. A budget-minded couple could not only get around Burma for the seven-day duration of their visa on their combined US$200, they might find themselves with enough money left over for a slap-up final meal or some souvenir shopping.

I'd returned to Burma in late 1978 and early 1979 to write our first guidebook to the country and in 1983 I was back again. The list of places foreigners could visit had been slowly growing, but nevertheless I was going to try to see 'accessible' Burma in one flat-out week. At that time Union of Burma Airways were dropping their aircraft out of the sky at an even more frightening rate than in the 1970s, so I was not at all enthusiastic about flying. Years later one of their engineers told me that in a fifteen-year period they'd crashed ten aircraft—eight F27s and two Twin Otters. For a tiny airline this was a horrific accident rate.

On my earlier visits, Burma's automobile fleet had been chiefly notable for its small numbers and decrepit condition. Most cars at that time were English and American vehicles dating back to the early 1950s. Now things were changing. Burmese merchant seamen were allowed to import used vehicles when they came back from overseas and small Japanese pickup trucks were starting to appear on the road in larger numbers. I'd heard it was possible to rent one of these for trips out of Rangoon, even though it was officially illegal. I wandered over to the tourist office to see what time it opened and before you could say, 'Psst, wanna rent my Toyota Hilux?', I'd been approached by a Burmese gentleman and we were negotiating a one-week rental.

Before dawn the next morning we set off from Rangoon, bound north for Prome, Pagan and Mandalay. By the time we'd explored the north and turned round to head back south to Inle Lake I was running on empty. My driver and guide were putting in the same miles, of course, but when we reached our destinations they were able to put their feet up while I had to run around.

The final stint was going to be an all-night drive from Inle Lake to Pegu before returning to Rangoon in the afternoon. When I announced I didn't have the energy to spend another night bouncing around in the back of the truck they came up with an alternative. I could take the overnight train from Thazi to Pegu, sleep on the train and they'd meet me in Pegu later in the morning. There was only one catch. The train went straight through Pegu without stopping.

'No problem,' my resourceful crew announced, 'the train goes through the station very slowly, so you can jump off.'

They were right. The next morning we crawled slowly through the station, I jumped down to the platform and my sleeper compartment companions tossed my bag down to me. Later, I met up with my pickup truck and we drove back into Rangoon.

What a trip! But it was my last Burma visit for over ten years, as Joe Cummings took over writing the Burma book. Meanwhile the Burmese 'road to socialism' had proved to be a steadily downhill route and by the late 1980s the long-suffering Burmese had simply had enough. Despite the assassination of Aung San and his key followers, Burma had remained a democratic country through the 1950s, but it was a country in chaos. The economy had been badly mismanaged, the fractious border groups resented central Burmese control and the country's income fell as steeply as its military expenditure rose. In 1962 it all fell apart: the government of U Nu was overthrown and Ne Win's military dictatorship took over and turned a genteel decline into a headlong downward tumble.

In 1966 nationalization was extended right down to retail shops. Many everyday items were only available from 'People's Shops' and, as a result, they were not available at all, except on the black market. Huge numbers of people who had been working in shops lost their jobs. Indians, hated as exploitative money lenders, but also important to the economy since they ran so many of the shops and restaurants, were expelled. People of Chinese descent got similar treatment and anti-Chinese riots in 1967 led to hundreds of deaths. As many as a quarter of a million Indians and Chinese left Burma during the 1960s.

Isolation and economic mismanagement were compounded by the government's hopeless attempts to combat money hoarders by demonetization. In 1966 the government announced that effective immediately the larger-denomination 50- and 100-kyat notes were now worthless. They were replaced with 25-, 35- and 75-kyat notes! This did nothing for the economy except to make people bitterly mistrustful of the kyat and ensure that wherever possible they converted Burmese money into something else, whether it was dollars, gold or precious stones. Nevertheless, in 1987, the government tried the same trick again, this time dumping the 25-, 35- and 75-kyat notes and foisting 45- and 90-kyat notes on the poor Burmese. This led to bitter protests and the violent reaction from the government in 1988.

In the middle of this confusion Aung San Suu Kyi, the daughter of the country's founding father Aung San, returned to her homeland. She had grown up first in India and then in Britain where she went to Oxford University. She was married to an English academic, but back in Burma, where she had returned to care for her elderly mother, she was quickly swept to the forefront of the opposition National

League for Democracy (NLD). In 1990 the military government, for unfathomable reasons, decided to permit an election, the first one since 1960. To nobody's surprise, except perhaps army generals with their heads in the sand, the NLD swept to victory, taking 392 of the 485 contested seats. The elected parliament has never been allowed to sit and Aung San Suu Kyi, 'the Lady' as she is universally known in the country, has spent long spells of the subsequent decades under house arrest and Burma has become an international pariah-state.

Meanwhile, Maureen and I maintained our close interest in the country. In late 1997, photographer Richard I'Anson and I went to Rangoon to work on *Chasing Rickshaws*. Both of us had been to Burma before, but it was my first visit since 1983 and Richard had not been there since 1986. Although politically there was no change, and the government was the same bunch of medal-dripping military goons, economically there had been major changes. If traffic was an indicator of economic progress then Rangoon was doing very well indeed—the streets were full of cars, trucks, buses and motorcycles. Sure, most of the taxis had already had one productive lifetime on the streets of Tokyo or Singapore, but compared to the backfiring wrecks of the 1970s these were super cars. The previously empty streets now featured traffic jams which wouldn't have been out of place in Bangkok or Manila.

It was the same story in shops, where the shelves groaned under stacks of Japanese electronic gear and all the fake name-brand clothing found in markets throughout the rest of the region. On my last visit, Rangoon had looked as if there hadn't been a single new building since World War II and most of the old ones hadn't had a splash of paint in that time. Now it was a construction zone with new buildings ranging from air-conditioned shopping centers to modern office blocks and lots of new hotels—most of them empty. The expected tourist rush had not materialized. Restaurants, few and far between on our earlier visits, were also much more widespread. Officially, the country had also been renamed Myanmar.

The 1990 election of Aung San Suu Kyi focused attention on the country and its nasty military dictatorship. And us. In early 2000 the

London-based Burma Action Group announced that by publishing a guidebook to the country we were encouraging people to visit Burma and, therefore, we were arm-in-arm with the dictatorship. Their 'boycott Lonely Planet' movement kicked off. In fact, our Burma book has always shown how to avoid putting money in the government's pocket and even includes a 'should you visit Burma' section detailing the pros and cons of visiting the country. Since the campaign started I have ensured that every single person who writes to me gets an individual reply and during that period I have accumulated over 1000 pages of correspondence on the Burma question.

By the end of 2000 I'd become fed up with repeatedly correcting the same misconceptions. No, you did not pay a US$300 fee to the government to enter the country. Yes, you had to change that amount (later reduced to US$200) on arrival, but you got 200 bucks worth of kyats (and at a real rate) in exchange, just as you would if you changed money on arrival in London or New York. No, you were not forced to stay in government-run hotels, eat in government-run restaurants and travel on government-owned transport. The near total government control at the time of my first visit had mostly disappeared, and there were only a half-dozen or so government-owned hotels amongst a much larger list of possibilities. You could go pretty much where you pleased and when you pleased and, contrary to what so many of the London-based Burma activists insisted, people were not only keen to talk to you about the politics of Burma, they were also alarmingly nonchalant about it. 'Government spies are everywhere,' the London activists insisted, 'nobody will risk talking to you.' In fact, I found that people might be cautious about talking, but once they were certain they were not likely to be overheard, talking was what they most wanted to do.

So in early 2001 Maureen and I returned to Burma on our own little fact-finding mission. We talked with diplomats, business-people (both Burmese—and Shan and Karen for that matter—and expat), journalists (from outside and inside the country), ex-political prisoners, the families of current political prisoners, NLD members, aid workers, people in the street, people who were dirt poor and people who were well off. For part of the trip we were accompanied by Ron Gluckman, a journalist from the Hong Kong–based news magazine *Asiaweek*.

If there was one place where everyday Burmese wanted tourists it was on 39th Street in Mandalay, the home of the Moustache Brothers. Two of the brothers, U Lu Maw and U Par Par Lay, are indeed brothers. The third, U Lu Zaw, is a cousin, but the threesome are Burma's most famous comedians in the time-honored *a-nyeint pwe*, a traditional vaudeville combining singing, dancing and skits. In 1996 two of the brothers were sentenced to seven years imprisonment for telling jokes about the military government. When I visited U Lu Maw, the only brother at liberty, the nightly performances he and his wife put on for tourists were the sole support for the entire extended family.

At Inle Lake we met with U Ohn Maung. I'd met this one-man power station in 1979 when he had opened the first non-government guesthouse at the lake. In 1990 he ran for election as an NLD candidate, won, of course, and was sent to jail by the military dictatorship. U Ohn Maung spent one and a half years in jail, the first year in a ten foot by ten foot cell with seven other men. When he was released he went back to his hotel, then opened another one and had recently opened a third hotel, this one a very classy lakeside resort.

More importantly, he'd become involved in all sorts of projects around the lake, including one to build a bridge for a village called Maing Thauk. Most of the village facilities were on dry land—the schools, health center, monastery and so on—while the villagers mainly lived in stilt houses out on the lake. The villagers had to ferry their kids to school by canoe, so the children often had to leave for school very early, because their parents were going fishing or heading off to work in their fields. At the other end of the day, the kids had to hang around waiting for their parents to finish work before they could get home. Building a bridge from the village homes to the 'land village' would solve the problem and also let people walk to the health center. The trouble was the bridge would be 1100 feet long and U Ohn Maung needed about US$15 000 for materials—the villagers would provide the labor. Maureen and I agreed that Lonely Planet would finance it.

Maureen and I returned to Burma in early 2002, this time with our daughter Tashi and friend Stan Armington. At Inle Lake we walked across the completed bridge and met with the villagers who told us what a huge improvement it had made to their lives. We've subsequently helped finance the building of a new health center and will continue to work on projects in the area in the future.

In Mandalay, the Moustache Brothers were reunited after U Par Par Lay and U Lu Zaw were released from jail. They were as enthusiastic as ever.

Boycott proponents usually point at South Africa and the demise of apartheid to prove that their ideas work, but in general I believe the evidence is against them. For decades Burma had its own self-imposed boycott and it didn't loosen the generals' grip on power. The savage boycott of Iraq after the 1991 Gulf War, complete with air attacks and no-fly zones, made life hard for Iraqi civilians, but it didn't get rid of Saddam Hussein. The idiotic US boycott of Cuba only reinforces Castro's position; there may be plenty of Cubans who don't like the 'Maximum Leader' but they like US Cuban policy even less.

Quite apart from the money tourists put directly into the local population's pockets, there are a host of reasons why a visitor to a country with an unpleasant government can be a good thing. One is that visitors are witnesses. Would we have known about Tiananmen Square if it had taken place during the Mao era when nobody got into China to see anything? Repeatedly, Burmese have told us how important it is for them to have contact with visitors. 'They're an umbrella between us and the government,' one Burmese explained. Every time the Burma boycotters in London crow that they've persuaded another clothing manufacturer to withdraw from Burma I wait with bated breath for them to explain how this is going to improve life for the workers who are now out of a job.

Australia has been one of the few Western nations to have maintained some sort of dialogue with the country, even if this has earned it much criticism. The ASEAN nations' policy of engagement may have no backbone, but it ensures they have some influence, even if they are irresolute in using it. Of course, there is one country which is happy to deal with Burma and even happier to see its Western rivals deal themselves out of the game: China. The big power to the north sees Burma as a useful client state, a direct route to the Indian Ocean and, of course, China is no friend of democracy.

The 'boycott Lonely Planet' push reached its height in 2000 and has bubbled along on a lower heat ever since. It could easily boil up again, but while it might make good sense financially to cave in, we're not going to withdraw our Burma guidebook.

M: 'This will be the second year in a row we've made a real profit,' Jim announced at one of our regular Sunday-night meetings.

Our sales for the 1986–87 financial year were approaching $3 million and we looked like making $300 000 in profit after tax.

'A large slice of that money comes from books on Third-World countries,' Tony pointed out. 'Perhaps we should try and put some of it back into the places we're doing books about.'

'Like Ethiopia,' I suggested. Images of the famine which had devastated the country in the mid-1980s were still on everybody's mind. 'We still have the only guidebook to Africa.'

That evening we mapped out a plan which we would follow fairly resolutely for over a decade. It was admirably straightforward: so long as our profits permitted, we would donate one per cent of our gross revenue to organizations and projects in the countries our books covered.

'So who's going to administer it?' Jim queried.

Tony and Jim both looked, pointedly, at me. 'I will, I guess,' I said.

We had been so cost-conscious for so long that the $30 000 we gave away that year seemed like an enormous sum. I was worried about the responsibility of deciding where it should go, and determined that it would be spent well.

I started by phoning the main organizations such as AusAID

and Community Aid Abroad, asking for details of their finances and projects they were involved with in specific countries. Having traveled extensively in developing countries, I had seen how aid can be wasted, but also how much impact well-managed programs can have. We asked that our donated funds be earmarked for projects we felt corresponded most closely with our goals. I also asked our authors to seek out and nominate worthy projects they came across while traveling.

We were very impressed with the Fred Hollows Foundation and annually supported their 'eye camps' in Nepal. I remember being really thrilled when one of the medical staff sent us a photograph showing a long line of people waiting their turn to be assessed beneath a banner bearing the Lonely Planet logo. A follow-up photo showed the patients seated like a classroom of pirates, each with a patch over one eye following a successful trachoma operation.

Although a lot of the money we've donated over the years has gone to big aid organizations we have supported smaller projects, often way outside the mainstream. In the late 1980s a young man in Sulawesi, concerned that male prostitutes in the port town of Makassar were unaware of the AIDS epidemic sweeping the West, sent in a submission. He wanted to open an office, translate, print and distribute leaflets and provide counseling. I wasn't sure how much could be achieved by just one person, but I was moved by the sincerity of his account. We sent him a small sum, less then $5000, but later that year one of our authors visited the office in Makassar and wrote to me fully endorsing the operation. A few years later we received a submission for seed money to start a 'bank' to lend small sums of money to enable Sulawesi transvestites to have other options than prostitution. Within a few years the fund was self-financing and going very well, but now there is a need to provide anti-retroviral drugs, an expensive and heartbreaking process since the drugs cannot be provided to everybody who needs them.

We also helped Surf Aid get started, an organization founded by two surfers, one of them a doctor, to provide healthcare
to people on the Sumatran islands of Mentawai. People had
been resettled on the islands and then virtually abandoned by
their government. The two Surf Aid organizers came to visit me
at our office and I was impressed not only by their vision, but
also by their practical approach. Sleeping under mosquito nets
impregnated with insecticide can cut down on the incidence of
malaria very effectively and are cheap and easy to distribute.
We put in $28 000 to fund a health worker for a year.

When Tony and I visited Cambodia we were horrified at the
number of land mines which still lie buried across the country.
We spoke to people working on mine removal and became
involved in this vital cause.

We've also been long-term supporters of Greenpeace. Their
efforts to stop French nuclear testing in the Pacific were particularly important for us and Tony even ran in the Greenpeace
team in the Sydney City to Surf Fun Run in 2004 and 2005 (he
was the first Greenpeace finisher in 2004). Amnesty is another
organization whose efforts we strongly believe in and we offer
any support possible.

Lonely Planet helped build a boarding school in Nepal for
children in the Manang region on the popular Annapurna
trekking circuit. In 2001 we walked the circuit with Australian
business identity John Singleton. 'My other business partners
take me out to lunch or for a few beers,' John announced. 'Not
on a bloody three-week walk!' When we stopped by the school,
John immediately took over a classroom of bemused Nepali
children and within minutes had them all singing 'You Are My
Sunshine'. In newly independent East Timor we helped fund a
reading room developed by Kirsty Sword Gusmao, the
Australian wife of the country's first president. And, of course,
there have been our projects in Burma.

In 2001 we donated nearly three-quarters of a million dollars, a big jump from the $30 000 of fourteen years earlier.

Many of the projects gave us a real sense of achievement so one of the hardest decisions to make when we were hit by the post-September 11 downturn was to discontinue the donations policy. With the travel industry making a comeback we introduced a new donations policy in 2005, kicking off the Lonely Planet Foundation with one million dollars, half of which went to tsunami-relief projects.

Burma has not been the only place where we've been accused of being the bad guys. Some people reckon that Lonely Planet is right in there with Nike, McDonald's, Toyota and Sony, working on the globalization of everything. We've been accused of the Lonely-planetisation of the world.

'The way things are going,' the critics insist, 'we'll all be driving the same cars, wearing the same shoes, eating the same burgers and using the same guidebooks and the world will become dull and bland and uniform.'

Well, we don't want this either, but is it really happening? The First World may have exported McDonald's, KFC and Pizza Hut, but we've brought back Thai, Mexican, Indian and Japanese food to balance those exports. Live in almost any big city these days and restaurants from places as far afield as Ethiopia, Tibet, Korea, Afghanistan, Burma or Argentina are no longer unusual.

Sure, Balinese kids may listen to Western rock music on their Walkmans as they zoom around on their Yamaha motorcycles, but come nightfall they'll still be practicing their gamelan music and rehearsing for the next *kecak* dance. France, with arguably the world's biggest tourist flow, may feel like it's being overwhelmed around the Eiffel Tower on a hot August weekend, but are the French any less French for all that international attention?

On the other hand, there is no question that we can get a little too ubiquitous. Our China guidebook is very popular—it's the book most visitors tote in a country where a guidebook is nearly essential if you're going to find your way around by yourself.

'I'd arrived in China after a long flight from Vancouver,' a traveler reported. 'Then I jumped straight on a train. I was jet-lagged and several times during the trip I'd put my book down. I was reading *Lord of the Rings*. Every time somebody would remind me I'd left it or bring it over to me, but they never said, "Here's your book." It was always, "Here's your Lonely Planet." '

Traveling around Iran in 2004 I was surprised how many interesting conversations and encounters I had in a country where the general level of friendliness and the command of English (and other European languages) regularly surprises visitors. But those English speakers are usually members of an educated and wealthy elite. Taxi drivers are not so likely to speak English, nor, you would think, policemen.

Emerging from the chaotic South Tehran bus station one afternoon I stumbled out into the Islamic Republic of Iran's capital's frenetic traffic, thumbing through my Iran guide to find which way to head for my hotel.

'Hey, Lonely Planet,' yelled the cop directing the traffic. 'Which way you going, man?'

In early 2006 I spent a week traveling across Iraq—I'm not crazy, my travels were all in the safe, Kurdistan region of northern Iraq. In Erbil, a town which disputes Damascus' claim to be the oldest continuously inhabited city on earth, I discovered the recently opened Kurdistan Textile Museum and within five minutes of signing my name in the visitor's book I was cornered by the museum's director.

'Are you from Lonely Planet?' he asked. 'Does this mean we can expect a Lonely Planet guide to Iraq?'

We're regularly asked if we feel guilty for what we've done to—choose your destination—anywhere from Bali to Thailand, Nepal, Cambodia or Vietnam. Soon I'm sure we'll be asked if we feel guilty about what we've done to Afghanistan. The implication is that Lonely Planet has all by itself created Kuta Beach and other similar tourist enclaves. Somehow our little guidebook-publishing company has expanded the airport, bought the aircraft, increased the flight frequencies, sold the package tours, built the hotels and restaurants, equipped the rent-a-car fleets and convinced all the visitors to go there.

Of course, we haven't done that. My reply to these accusations is that if Lonely Planet was as all-powerful as many people seem to think we are, airlines all over the world would be falling over themselves as we approach. It would be, 'Oh Maureen and Tony Wheeler, let us upgrade you.' Unfortunately, that simply does not happen!

It's worth remembering that in the 1930s the Mexican artist Miguel Covarrubias, whose book on the art and culture of Bali still remains a classic, worried that too many tourists would ruin the place. At that time there were no flights to Bali and ships arrived every month or so. When I first went to Bali in 1972, Kuta Beach still had sandy little tracks running down to the beach and accommodation consisted of the Kuta Beach Hotel and perhaps a dozen or two little *losmen*. The first surfers were rediscovering Bali after the Soekarno era.

So has tourism wrecked Bali and all those other destinations which have seen so many changes since we made our first trip through the region? In general, the answer is no. Some of the changes are not for the best—we would all like the roads anywhere in the world to go back to the less crowded state of a generation ago—but overall most people would agree that in most places, and particularly in the developing world, we have seen progress in our lifetime. Of course, tourism is far from the only agent of change. Plus it's very patronizing for those of us in the developed world to think people should maintain a simpler life to please us: 'It was so nice when you didn't have electricity and cars and motorcycles and life was simple.' I've yet to see a Third-World village that didn't rejoice when electricity arrived or cheer when they could enjoy motorcycle traffic jams instead of walking to work.

There is, however, one serious downside of travel which worries me: it burns up energy. At the moment the contribution to global carbon emissions by airlines is comparatively small, but it is growing faster than any other category and is expected to grow by a factor of five over the next fifty years. It's not that airliners use more fuel than other forms of transport. To shift a human being from A to B takes fairly similar amounts of energy whether you do it in a car, train, boat or plane. It's that we go so much further when we fly places. Typically, people in the West drive about the distance from London to Sydney in a year. So one round trip between Europe and Australia is equivalent to two years of regular car usage.

The scary amount of travel we're inclined to do once we get on a plane is exacerbated by the fact that airlines are generally exempt from fuel tax for international usage. No other form of transport gets that sort of tax break. When I was speaking at the Pacific Asia Travel Association's annual conference in 2005, I brought up some worrying figures. Like the fact that all the fuel-guzzling race cars in a Grand Prix use about the same amount of fuel the 747 flying them to the next race uses in half an hour. Or that in a typical year of travel I'll personally use more fuel on airliners than all the cars for a whole Grand Prix.

One of the big trends in travel over the past twenty years has been long-haul flights. With airlines now operating non-stop flights of nearly twenty hours duration, we are almost able to fly from any point on earth to any other point. But do we need to? Aircraft use far more fuel on long flights than they would on two shorter sectors. Plus, long flights are bad for destinations like the Pacific islands which are now routinely overflown and, as a result, are increasingly hard to get to.

Despite all its drawbacks and problems, travel is enormously important. It is the biggest business in the world—more people depend upon travel and tourism for their employment than any other business—but travel is much more than money. It is through travel that we meet and understand other people and at this time, when there is so much anger and misunderstanding in the world, travel is more important than it has ever been.

There are often occasions where the book itself is more important than any contribution it might make to our bottom line. There are places we feel we have to cover simply to reinforce the message that we will go anywhere and everywhere. There are also books we publish for very definite reasons, such as our coffee-table book on Tuvalu which we hoped would increase consciousness about the damage climate change could do to one small nation. In 2001, soon after the emergence of independent East Timor, we published a phrasebook for Tetun, the main language of the new country. Xanana Gusmao, the principal leader of the independence struggle and the new nation's first president, wrote an introduction to the book. We didn't expect for a moment that we would make money from this phrasebook for a very specialist language, but we felt it would be our own small contribution to East Timor's independence and it did become standard issue for many UN personnel and aid workers going to the island.

In late 2003, laboring up the long hill to the Tengboche Monastery in Nepal behind a group of British trekkers, Richard I'Anson and I overheard a conversation which made us feel very uncomfortable.

'I really enjoyed my time in Australia, but they're horribly racist, aren't they?' the young English woman commented.

'Yeah, I felt the same way after I'd been there a month,' agreed her companion.

Richard and I dropped back to discuss where they'd got this idea. Like most Australians we didn't consider Australia was a racist country and yet, we concluded, it probably wasn't so surprising that these young backpackers had come away with that impression. They'd probably spent a lot of their time in the central Australian outback or in the north of Queensland, both places where they were more likely to encounter attitudes that would be quickly squashed in Australia's big cities. If a visitor to the US spent all their time in certain parts of the Deep South or a visitor to England restricted themselves to specific areas of cities in the Midlands they could easily come back with similar views about racist attitudes in the US or UK.

Visitors to Alice Springs are quite likely to hear complaints about Aborigines as welfare layabouts, collecting their checks and spending it on booze. And yes, you do see groups of Aborigines camped out in the dry riverbed of the Todd River in the center of town, sur-rounded by a litter of bottles and cans. Yet if you spend any time in Alice Springs you'll meet people who work with Aborigines and are keenly aware of the problems and challenges they face. Lining up at a supermarket checkout I overheard one those interactions which underlined how big that challenge can be.

'How much money do you have?' the checkout operator asked the Aboriginal woman in front of me. When she was told she glanced again at the overloaded shopping trolley before saying, politely, 'I don't think you've got enough money for everything you've got here. Why don't we start by ringing up the things you really want, then we can see how the money is going?'

A few years later I overheard precisely the same exchange in Alice Springs all over again. It's the sort of collision between an age-old people and the twenty-first century which takes place in parts of Australia every day and while those supermarket workers handled it perfectly there's no doubt that some people don't.

Being branded as a racist, indifferent or uncaring country isn't nice and unfortunately the Australian government blindly reinforced those negative images with its 'Pacific Solution' to arriving refugees in 2001. This ill-considered policy kicked off when the Norwegian container ship *Tampa* picked up more than 400 survivors from a sinking refugee ship close to Christmas Island, an Australian territory in the Indian Ocean to the south-west of Java. At first the Australian government tried to force the *Tampa* to take them elsewhere and then quickly negotiated to dump them on the bankrupt Pacific client state of Nauru. Nauru was isolated and firmly under Australia's thumb so it was easy to exclude journalists, lawyers and anybody else who might get in the way of what was clearly a shameful activity.

In 2003 we published *From Nothing to Zero*, a collection of let-ters from refugees imprisoned as part of Australia's detention policy. It was our small attempt to shed light on our government's inhumane treatment of refugees, to make a publishing statement and to help right something which we felt was very wrong.

'I remember when we first arrived in Australia people back home asked us how we could live in a place where racism was so entrenched,' Maureen said to me over breakfast one day. 'We saw progress taking place in attitudes towards Aborigines and how well Australia's immigration policies had worked. So for years I've been correcting that misunderstanding. Now I'm beginning to wonder if it was me who was led astray.'

'Look at how we were treated when we first arrived,' I agreed. 'We met nothing but kindness from when we first stepped ashore from that yacht. Now we've got a government that treats people appallingly and seems to be proud of it. Yet I can't believe that everybody agrees with them.'

In mid-2004 the *Sydney Morning Herald* contacted me for a comment on figures showing that visitor numbers to Australia were declining when in other countries, in particular New Zealand, the numbers were going up. There were many reasons for the drop, ranging from problems in our neighborhood (Indonesia's dramatic downturn in visitors has to rub off to some extent) to the rise in the Australian dollar making things more expensive, from the increased risk of terrorism due to our joining George W's badly planned Iraqi adventures to simply no longer being the flavor of the month.

To my mind, there was also the fact that our treatment of refugees had, to put it bluntly, made Australia a place that was 'on the nose'. The story appeared in the newspaper and that afternoon the Minister of Tourism slammed me for commenting that his government's policies had any effect on the drop in tourist numbers. 'Lonely Planet is simply trying to drum up business and gain some cheap publicity,' he stormed. Furthermore, my statements were the result of 'anecdotal observations and highly subjective analysis'. He ignored a parliamentary study that 'overseas reports suggest that adverse international publicity over Australia's policies on asylum seekers and Aborigines may have also contributed' (to the decline in tourist numbers).

12
The Highs, the Lows

The second half of the 1990s was a time of great highs and miserable lows. There were no disasters. Nobody died or suffered terrible tragedies, we didn't go bankrupt or have to lay staff off, but the whole period seemed to gyrate between elation and depression. Some mornings I would drive to work thinking: next week I'll be heading off somewhere incredibly interesting, I'm running an amazingly successful company, I'm sitting in my very nice Ferrari, so why am I so miserable?

M: In many ways Lonely Planet's 21st-birthday celebrations in 1994 marked a high point. We had weathered the various periods of a company's evolution, from surviving by the skin of our teeth, to growing and expanding, to becoming a leader in our field. Our relationship had mirrored that evolution. We had grown up together and we'd also allowed each other to grow, even when that meant taking separate paths. The children were coming into their teens, healthy, smart and old enough to be real travel companions.

For years we had juggled travel with children, travel for business and Tony's travel for guidebooks. I had always tried to be there to pick up the children after school and had been sparing in my use of after-school care. When we both traveled

I tried to limit my trips to no more than two weeks, even less when the kids were very young. Tony and I usually split the business travel, the bookfairs and overseas office visits, despite which there is no doubt that Tashi and Kieran's lives, in fact all our lives, were subsumed to the demands of Lonely Planet. I know Tashi found those parental departures hard when she was young. 'You wouldn't believe how much I worried about you,' she would tell us years later.

Tashi also told me that she had enjoyed traveling each holiday, but hated telling her friends when she got back where she had been, because it sounded like 'showing off'. Since every school vacation was spent overseas, both kids began to feel they were missing out on the long, lazy summers, hanging out with friends. Both of them wanted to experience 'normal holidays'. When they returned after the long trips, they always felt they had missed out, new cliques had formed, friendships had to be renegotiated. We didn't understand this at the time—everyone envied their incredible travel experiences—but things feel a whole lot different to a teenager.

In 1997, when we returned from Paris, we found ourselves in that parent hell known as the 'adolescent years'. Both Tashi and Kieran embraced teenage rebellion with a fierce enthusiasm worthy of James Dean in *Rebel Without a Cause*. Neither Tony nor I coped at all well!

At first we presented a united front in trying to reason with them, set boundaries, be understanding, be flexible, be there. But to no avail. Over the next few years life became unbearable; home was a battlefield and there were nights when I would drive around the block several times summoning up the courage to walk through the door. Tony was in no better shape; in some ways I think he found it even harder than me since he simply couldn't understand how his children could behave so irrationally. We certainly weren't alone. Other friends with much more settled lives experienced even worse cases of teenage hell than we did. And teenage hell does have one valuable side effect—it sorts out real friends from the fair-weather ones who desert you as if you have leprosy.

Of course, it didn't take long before this affected our relationship. I resented the fact that Tony could escape on another trip. It was quite legitimate for him to travel, but it was also too easy. He could 'volunteer' himself for any interesting project while I felt I had spent a lot of time alone and this crisis-filled time of our lives was no exception. On top of this I was concerned about the business. People were too complacent, too much money was being spent and, I thought, wasted. It seemed our children and our business were both going through adolescence together—it was a real test of our managerial and parental skills.

Work was often not a great deal of fun. With Jim nothing happened quickly and there was likely to be a lot of thinking and talking before any action. Some time in the mid-1990s Jim began to talk about departing Lonely Planet, cashing in and going off to do something else. The relationship between Jim and Maureen and I had been fine for about fifteen years although it certainly hadn't worked out the way we'd expected. When Jim joined us we thought it was going to be for his publishing and editing expertise, but, as it turned out, that really wasn't where he shone.

Jim more than earned his keep helping us with computers, a field we hadn't even thought about when he joined us. Jim's university degree was in mathematics and he'd specialized in computers. Jim and I both shopped for Lonely Planet's first accounting computer, but it was Jim's expertise which really drove it, Jim who did all the hard slog getting our accounting program up and running, Jim who steered us into word processing and Jim who oversaw the proliferation of computers around the place. There was a phase when it became a familiar sight to see Jim elbowing through the front door with yet another Kaypro 4 under his arm.

When we set up our London office it was Jim who mapped out what we had to do and made sure it happened, and for many years he was the main communication between Melbourne and all our overseas offices. The emails which ricocheted back and forth between Jim and Michelle de Kretser, setting up our Paris office and launching our French publishing operations, kept the whole office entertained. Furthermore, while I worried about the publishing side, it was Jim who managed our sales and marketing.

Today we have a whole department full of techies and a sales and marketing division, but back then it was Jim or nobody. Then things began to change and Jim lost interest and began to look for another life outside Lonely Planet. But not too fast.

At first we weren't in too much of a hurry either. After all, it made no difference to us; we couldn't afford to buy back Jim's share of Lonely Planet, so the money had to come from outside. But we didn't want the question hanging around for ever and we began to worry about who our new business partner would be.

There was plenty of interest in taking over Jim's share of Lonely Planet. It was a successful company with a good track record in three very sexy areas of the business world. A company involved in travel, media and technology had to be a good bet. Often, however, that interest tended to evaporate when some of the pre-existing conditions became known. First, it was only Jim who was selling out; Maureen and I were quite happy where we were. So anybody coming in was going to be in a minority position without much leverage to make us change our plans. Second, and this was a big turn-off for many potential investors, we would make no promises about selling out or going public. There were unlimited supplies of investors who would love to have sunk their money into Lonely Planet with the idea of gearing it up for an IPO (Initial Public Offering) or some other sell-out within a few years. There were far fewer who wanted to join a long-distance ride to an uncertain destination. Equally, there were lots of publishing houses keen to take Lonely Planet on board, but the idea of being swallowed up by a competitor or dissolving into some larger company didn't appeal either.

What Jim could expect to get for his share of Lonely Planet did start to emerge from the mists and in 1998 he appointed advisors to find somebody to buy his shares. It was a totally sensible thing to do, but somehow it was also the signal that things were changing from a friendly separation to a divorce. Later it would start edging towards a messy divorce.

Mid-1998 was an example of an up amid the downs. I was asked to give the keynote speech at the graduation ceremony for new MBAs at the London Business School and I picked up the Alumni Achievement Award for my troubles. It was a nice footnote to my LBS career. My first university degree was nothing to write home about. I'd emerged with a 'gentleman's degree', a 2.2 or, as writer Simon Winchester dubbed it, a 'Desmond', after the crusading South African Bishop Desmond Tutu. I reckon LBS got some mileage out of my spell there, since my name regularly seems to pop up in hit parades of people who've emerged with their degrees.

In late August 1998, Maureen was at the office in San Francisco and an email I sent her at that time described a meeting I'd just had with Jim, his advisors and some potential investors. 'Jim said this was a first meeting with just him and one other person,' I explained and went on to describe how I'd felt seriously outnumbered.

By this time Maureen and I had retained Barrie Dobson as an advisor. 'In future,' I wrote, 'we will have Barrie present for any such meeting. There was nothing wrong with these guys, but nothing right either and I wouldn't have any enthusiasm at all for working with them. All they would bring to the party is money, but we're going to have to get some ground rules in place for these situations. Do we simply say, "No, we don't like them?" Or what?'

It was not only at the office where things were going off the rails. Most of the rest of that email message was devoted to problems with the kids and schools.

Maureen and I played tag team at the airport at the end of the month; she flew in from the US and I flew out to Nepal. We had planned for over a year to make a trip to Tibet to walk the circuit of Mt Kailash, but at the last moment Maureen decided that the combination of our business problems and our teenagers' problems were too worrying to leave behind. She would stay in Australia.

I flew in to Kathmandu, met up with the rest of our trekking party and ten days later, having walked for a week across western Nepal up to the Tibet border, I tried to call Maureen from the phone office in the Tibetan border town of Purang. Unsuccessfully. It didn't matter if I tried our home, Maureen's cell phone or the office, the phone simply would not ring. By this time it was early afternoon in Tibet, late afternoon in Australia and, I calculated, our office in London was just opening in the morning. I got through to them instantly.

'Thank goodness you've called,' answered Charlotte, our UK manager. 'Maureen's desperate to talk to you.'

Charlotte got through to Maureen within seconds and we then carried on a conversation by me (in Tibet) talking to Charlotte (in London) who relayed the message to Maureen (in Melbourne) and vice versa. Maureen was concerned that more company information was being divulged than we were happy about and after discussing the issue with Jim he'd decided it was better if he sold his stake in the business as if he was an outside investor, not an executive of the company. We'd been partners with Jim for eighteen years—this was a major split.

In November 1998 I got a most unexpected phone call.

'This is John Singleton,' said the voice at the other end of the line. 'I hear you're selling some shares in your company. I'm in Melbourne this afternoon, could I come in and talk about it?'

'Singo' may not be a household name in other countries, but in Australia he *certainly* is. His name first started to pop up in the early 1970s when Maureen and I were living in Sydney and working on our first guidebook. He'd started a fledgling advertising agency which specialized in loud and very in-your-face television commercials. Raucous or not, his ads proved to be amazingly successful and over the years his advertising business became more respectable until eventually he was the agency for such household Australian names as Qantas and Telstra. He then merged with Ogilvy & Mather to create Singleton Ogilvy & Mather and along the way bought Channel Ten, one of Australia's three commercial free-to-air television networks, when it was in deep trouble and later sold it when it was doing very well indeed. Singo was not short of the odd dollar.

Out of the office his life was even more newsworthy. There were six Singleton children and six Singleton wives or partners, one of whom had been Miss Australia. Then there was his well-known interest in horse racing. The following year a Singleton horse, co-owned with former prime minister Bob Hawke, came in the winner at a Sydney race on fifty to one odds (and Singo had put a $20 000 bet on it). On that successful afternoon he announced, 'The piss (yet another Australian expression for beer) is on me,' and picked up the tab from all the race course's bars (except the members' reserve!) for the rest of the day. Singo's million-dollar winnings suffered some shrinkage by the time he went home. In short, he seemed like the very last person to buy in to Lonely Planet.

'Got to admit I'd never heard of your books,' he confessed immediately. 'But Mark Carnegie told me about them and said you were looking for somebody to buy out your former partner. I was going to Hawaii so I bought the Hawaii book and it was terrific.'

Within half an hour I was convinced that of all the people we'd talked to so far, this was the one I could most imagine working with. Despite his colorful reputation he was easy to talk to and seemed utterly genuine in his admiration for what we had done with Lonely Planet. Furthermore, I knew that beyond his reputation for being a big spender he was also known as generous, and he assisted many community and charitable projects.

'Guess who's interested in buying Jim's shares?' I told Maureen (who was in the US) on the phone that night. 'Singo.'

'No way,' said Maureen. 'He's so crass, not a chance.'

'Look, he isn't at all like you'd imagine,' I said. 'He's talking about coming down to Melbourne again. At least meet him.'

M: John came in, sat in my office and within twenty minutes I was completely charmed. He was so easy to like, but he was obviously no fool. A few weeks later Mark Carnegie came down to talk through some of the business issues. We were a bit nervous—we had heard that Mark, his advisor, was smart and tough. One of the first questions he asked us was why we had a Burma book. I was impressed. This was obviously someone who was thinking about our company in a very different way from the other people I had interviewed. We talked for quite a while, but afterwards we were even more convinced that John and Mark were people we wanted to work with.

By this time Jim had a definite offer to buy his shares although we were still less than enthusiastic about the proposed investor. Singo had come in from left field, not via Jim's advisors, and although we felt we would be happy with him as a new partner we didn't want to jump into bed on the first night. We devised a plan to match the offer Jim had been given. John would buy about half of Jim's interest in Lonely Planet and Maureen and I would guarantee to buy back the rest over the following three years at an agreed price. Of course, we expected we would have to go back to John, or some other investor, for help with those future tranches. Lonely Planet was still likely to be growing rapidly and using up all the money we could spare.

With Singo's arrival on the scene the question of Jim's shareholding was settled, but by the end of 1998 we still felt we were going crazy. Kids, schools, the ongoing business hassles had all combined to drive a wedge between us although, even at its worst, we were generally able to stand back and think about what we were going through and why it was happening.

'When you feel like most of the time you're simply battering your head against a brick wall,' I surmised, 'at least battering against each other produces some sort of reaction.'

M: Towards the end of the year I remember looking at Tony and saying, 'I can't live with you and the kids, we can't keep fighting each other and them. I think you should move out for a while.'

It was a hard decision to make, but we were both exhausted and depressed. We needed some space.

'I'll move to England,' he replied.

'I didn't mean that much space,' I shot back.

'Tony's moving out,' I told Steve Hibbard the next day, but the news was already out.

'You know, Maureen, the word is that you are sending him away,' Steve responded.

'Well, maybe,' I said, 'but I didn't expect him to go that far!'

Tashi was about to finish school and had suggested going to London. I was concerned about her being so far from home at such a young age, but I was even more worried about the people she was spending time with in Melbourne. Perhaps going away might be good for her and having Tony there would be even better.

Plus, I had always felt that I could get along with Kieran more easily when he and Tony weren't constantly rubbing each other up the wrong way as were Tashi and I. So separating the family down the middle began to make some sort of sense. But it wasn't going to be easy. Although Tony and I had spent a lot of time apart, it had always been because one of us was traveling. Living apart was another matter.

A year afterwards we agreed that putting a continent between us had been a good idea—certainly telling the kids that their parents were about to split up was the first time we'd got their full attention for several years. Later, we would also realize that we had already hit rock bottom and were on the way back up when we made the announcement.

In fact, the twenty flying hours that divided us didn't result in as much separation as we'd expected. In 1984, when we'd lived in San Francisco, neither of us had returned to Australia for the whole year. In 1996, when we lived in Paris, I had made only one trip back. In 1999, however, I returned to Australia a couple of times, Maureen came to London a couple of times, and we met up at other places around the world on various occasions. At the end of the year we'd spent far more time together than we'd expected.

Other events contrived to make 1999 a ridiculously busy year. I'd managed to get involved in three book projects. For years we'd been talking about producing a South Pacific guidebook, but various factors had stalled it. We'd covered all the major Pacific island nations and colonies in individual books, but pulling them all together and covering the tiny places in between simply hadn't worked out. Furthermore, David Stanley's *South Pacific Handbook* for Moon Publications was long established and had no real competition. David was a friend, he'd written two books (Eastern Europe and Cuba) for us and we felt a little leery of confronting him with competition.

Nevertheless, we decided to tackle the South Pacific. I'd do French Polynesia, essentially taking the French Polynesia book I'd written with Jean-Bernard Carillet and condensing it down. My visit to Pitcairn Island the previous year would provide that chapter. (Sure it would be a bit out of date, but we doubted any other guidebook writer had been there.) I would also cover the tiny island of Niue on my way to Europe in March and in July I would visit the French colony of Wallis and Futuna. I was looking forward to the opportunity of visiting some very out-of-the-way places and contributing some manageable little chapters to the book.

Since I was going to be passing through Tahiti in both directions Jean-Bernard and I, both keen scuba divers, contrived a plan to produce a diving guide for the Pisces series as well. The book came out with the evocative subtitle 'Shark Diving Capital of the South Pacific', a reminder that sharks are regular companions for divers in the region. I'd already been diving in Rangiroa, the French

Polynesian atoll regularly rated as the world's best dive site for meetings with sharks, and thirteen consecutive dives had involved shark encounters.

There was a third book. Richard I'Anson and I had enjoyed our rickshaw project in 1997 so much that we'd agreed to pursue a second round-Asia project. This time we'd follow the story of rice, the world's most important food staple, the most visually delightful crop and the grain which probably features in more cultural and ceremonial activity than any other food. So visits to Bali, Burma, Cambodia, Vietnam, Thailand, the Philippines, China, Japan, India and Nepal were also penciled into my diary. Would I have any time at all in that apartment I was about to rent in London's Camden Town?

Also, Maureen and I were finally going to visit Syria, a place that had been on our 'must do' list for years. And we were taking a laze-on-the-beach break at the start of the year in Fiji. Plus I'd promised to make a couple of promotional trips to the US and one to the Middle East, where we sell a surprising number of books both about the area and for expats working there who make trips to Africa, the subcontinent and other places in the region.

Then, when 1999 was booked out, Channel Nine in Sydney asked if we would be guest presenters on the popular travel show *Getaway*. Yes, if we can choose the destinations, we said. Trips to Lebanon, Bali and London (at least that one wouldn't involve much travel for me) were factored into the equation, along with a spell in Northern Ireland for Maureen. She wanted to show off the real Northern Ireland that she knew and loved, not the one that appeared so often on the nightly news. Both of us had done plenty of television before, from thirty-second book-tour guest appearances where the interviewer has never heard of you until he's told who's on next during the commercial break, right up to programs that took a week to shoot. But we'd never done so much TV in a relatively short period of time.

We weren't very good at it (they didn't ask us back for the next season) and we both found it incredibly tedious. Would I rather be a travel guidebook writer or a travel show presenter? I'd take guidebook writing ten times over. The people involved with the show were terrific. It was a small team on each shoot—a producer, cameraman and sound recorder—and we were always impressed with their professionalism and the sheer hard work they put in to get things absolutely right. On the other hand, standing around, shooting things over and over, waiting for just the right moment and the ridiculous number of hours it took to produce five minutes of television drove us up the wall. We both look at television with new respect, but if anybody asks us to do it again the answer is no.

I managed to spend only fifty-eight nights in my Camden Town apartment and another week or two in various hotels (and one overnight train) around the UK. Tashi, by now eighteen years old, made more use of it than I did, turning up in London a couple of months after me and spending the rest of the year working for Lonely Planet and Pilot Productions, making forays to Amsterdam and Paris and in July joining 1.5 million other ravers and techno-heads for Berlin's Love Parade. She also joined Maureen for the 'back to Ireland' TV shoot and in between times she hung out with a rowdy bunch of New Zealanders, South Africans and Australians with whom she developed an unexpected enthusiasm for cricket when those three countries, along with Pakistan, were the four semi-finalists in the 1999 World Cup.

Our son didn't get left out. He came to England with Maureen on one of her visits and later in the year Kieran, his girlfriend Abby and Maureen went to Nepal to trek up to the almost mythical Tibetan border region of Lo Manthang, also known as Mustang. Bob Pierce, who was seventy-four when he'd trekked around Mt Kailash in Tibet with me the year before, came along too.

Although we were definitely on the rebound in 1999, the year still ended in gloom. All the hassles at home and work over the past couple of years seemed to weigh down on us and on New Year's Eve we went to bed before midnight, not even staying up to see the new millennium fireworks.

13

September 11 and All That

Kieran phoned me. 'Turn on the TV, Dad,' he urged. 'A plane's flown into a building in America.'

It was just after 11 p.m. on Australia's east coast, and the second plane had just slammed into the South Tower of the World Trade Center.

Before dawn I'd had phone calls from all over the world. Steve Hibbard, our CEO, called me from the streets of Paris where, grappling with the news in French, he was still unclear about what was happening. Jennifer Cox rang from London.

At the office on the morning of September 12, still early evening on S11 in New York, we convened an emergency meeting. We were already tracking down any authors who might have been working on East Coast USA projects and checking if any of our staff were in the region, on business or privately. It was clear this was going to hit travel hard and we immediately looked for ways of cutting costs. We dumped our free quarterly newsletter, delayed books to areas which we felt were going to face tourist downturns or where we could reasonably put off a new edition, suspended new staff recruitment and began to look for other ways we could cut costs. Within days we'd rolled out an extended leave-without-pay program, hoping that it would save us from actually having to cut staff numbers. Although many staff took up the opportunity to do what Lonely Planet is all about—travel—it wasn't enough.

Remarkably, the International Map Trade Association, a group of map dealers, cartographers and other people involved in the map business, was about to start their annual international convention in Melbourne's World Trade Centre and I was scheduled to deliver the opening address the following morning. It would still be September 12 in New York, but I'd already drawn a number of conclusions about the terrorist attack and they're on the record in my speech.

'Two nights ago,' I said, 'I saw a map being changed in front of my eyes. The World Trade Center towers in New York disappeared. At the moment, it's mere speculation who perpetuated the outrage in the US, but did the suicidal anger and rage which must have been there to drive people to such horrific action spring from other changes on other maps? From borders forcibly redrawn, countries created and destroyed, populations mercilessly shifted?

'Perhaps sometimes we need to stand back from our maps and realize there is a human story behind them and that changes thoughtlessly made to one map can result in totally unexpected and often horrific changes to another. There is no excuse for the recent carnage and horror wrought upon innocent people in the US, but perhaps we need to look at what mere lines and dots really mean. We need to look beyond maps of no-go zones in Iraq. Maps showing the proliferation of refugee camps on the borders of Afghanistan. Or maps detailing the settlements which seem designed to underline who holds the absolute power on the West Bank.'

There was no genius in my perception of what was going on in the world. It was clear to a great many people, not only me, that the embargoes on Iraq were probably shoring up Saddam Hussein's control rather than weakening it. Like many other people who had visited Afghanistan and been heartbroken by the way the country had become just another pawn in international power struggles, I'd been outraged by the way the country had been flooded with arms and then cast aside as soon as its role was finished. I'd noted that cynical CIA quip about 'fighting the Soviets to the last Afghan'. And like many people who'd maintained an interest in the Middle East, I was keenly aware that an awful lot of the problems in the region circled around Palestine and, immensely difficult though the issue was, simply putting it in the 'too hard' box wasn't going to get us anywhere.

M: September 11 hit travel worldwide and over the next twelve months would make life at Lonely Planet very difficult, but we were determined it was not going to halt our own travel plans. If we stopped traveling, how could we expect our readers to keep going? Less than a week after the New York attack I flew to Italy to meet with a group of twelve women friends from California (the 'wild writing women'), and the only one who didn't turn up was detained for other reasons, not S11 related.

Then in November, with Tony, Kieran and his girlfriend Abby, photographer Richard I'Anson and John Singleton, we headed off to Nepal to walk the Annapurna Circuit. Halfway round the three-week walk Tony and I celebrated our thirtieth wedding anniversary and a few nights later we listened to a confused and scratchy account of the first bombing raids on Afghanistan on a shepherd's transistor radio in a Himalayan hut.

Guidebook sales did indeed plummet and often in unexpected ways. If sales dropped we obviously had less income, but if a book fell off the edge when a new edition was soon to arrive we could also find ourselves saddled with big stock write-offs on the old edition. Ideally, the last copy of the old edition sells out just as the new one arrives. If we have to choose between having too few books in stock (and losing sales) against having too many (and having to write off the last copies) we generally prefer the latter option, but only within limits. Our India book, with all the trouble in adjacent Pakistan and Afghanistan, was only one of a number of titles which suffered unexpected elevated end-of-edition write-offs.

At the same time as we were writing off tens of thousands of books to destinations suddenly perceived to be 'unsafe', we had to increase print runs to the 'safe' places. Toss in the costs of rescheduling books, mix in disgruntled authors whose projects had been shelved, factor in a half-dozen other hidden costs and guidebook publishing was not a happy business.

S11 wasn't the only problem to hit Lonely Planet. Over the next couple of years SARS, the Bali bombing, the Iraq invasion, the Madrid bombing and other downers would create a 'Perfect Storm' for anybody involved in the travel business. Plus we'd created a few problems of our own making.

Through most of the 1990s it seemed like we could do no wrong when it came to publishing. Most of the books were healthily profitable and we had excuses for the ones that weren't. Books like Yemen, Mongolia, Iran or Ethiopia simply underlined that we were the sort of travel publisher who would bravely sally forth where nobody else dared.

Unfortunately, by the late 1990s we were running out of big destinations. Those hefty doorstop books with big price tags and big sales stats were an endangered species. With the US and our all-Europe books out of the way in 1999 we really couldn't see any more megadestinations to cover. There were always new editions and, spurred by competing travel publishers and by the continuous updating of travel websites, we were bringing them out more frequently than in the past. New editions every two years had become the norm for the vast majority of our titles. Plus we were constantly dicing and slicing established titles. Our Australia guide had been followed by books on each state, on the outback, the Great Barrier Reef and on Sydney and Melbourne, along with a walking guide and a scuba-diving guide.

In the late 1990s we launched a whole catalog of new travel series. Some of them, like our pocket-sized 'Best of' series, did very well while our Journeys travel literature series was nicely profitable without producing the mega-selling Bryson or Theroux we would really have liked. Our World Food series was a great little range of books, but expensive to produce, and it never really found a niche, seeming to disappear in the bookshops halfway between the food and the travel sections.

Some of the new series were much less successful. The cycling series looked like a nice companion to our walking guides, but it also proved to be a fine example of not having our eye on the bottom line. For years we'd been confident that no matter how big and complex the book, the sales would justify the expenditure. Those days had passed, but having a budget didn't mean we always kept to it. All the way up the line people managed to ignore cost over-runs with the cycling series. It was always 'unexpectedly high development costs on the first titles; they'll drop with subsequent titles'. They did, but never enough.

The cycling series books were great, although produced at a cost which we'd never recover, but our restaurant series, Out to Eat, was a half-baked idea badly carried through. The inspiration was that we were already gathering lots of restaurant information for our guide-books, so why not recycle that expertise into restaurant guides? Of course, we'd pump the info up to a higher level for these new books and then we could spin it back into the regular guides, a real virtuous circle. When the first examples of these books emerged they looked terrific. Too terrific.

'How did we produce something that looks so good at so low a cost?' I wondered, studying the arty halftone photographs of restaurant interiors.

The answer was we couldn't. The crew producing these books had tossed the budget forecasts out the window and set out to produce the most beautiful books imaginable, completely ignoring the cost constraints we thought we'd placed on them. They'd ignored the rules and we hadn't checked up on them.

At the end of the day, the buck should have stopped with us, but it didn't. In fact, Maureen had begun to have her doubts, but somehow I'd remained convinced that these over-the-top titles would still work. Too many times they didn't.

There were a host of other problems in the late 1990s. We'd never become fully entangled with the dot-com madness, but we'd still spent a heap on developing our website. We'd wasted huge amounts of time, although, fortunately, not huge amounts of our own cash, on an international phonecard project which never justified its developer's sky-high claims. We still offer the card, but at arm's length—we're no longer directly involved in it. The Pilot Productions TV series had never provided much return and we were becoming increasingly worried about the program going off in directions over which we had no control. The final straw was when Discovery Channel decided to tour Ian Wright, the series' star presenter, round Australia. We put lots of effort into promoting it for Discovery only to discover the effort was strictly one way. Ian didn't even have time in his schedule to say hello while he was in Australia.

All this activity inevitably demanded cash and we found ourselves going cap in hand to the bank for more financing. Ever since a chance hitch-hike into Sydney back in 1972 had led to Westpac becoming the Lonely Planet banker we'd stuck with them and our line of credit had gradually climbed to ten million dollars. There had never been any problems on either side, and we'd always met our commitments to the bank, but suddenly that relationship started to go sour as well.

This was the worst time to get hit by accounting problems. In the early days we'd followed a very simple, and by accounting standards very conservative, policy on our book costs. We'd written off all the development costs—the author fees, the editorial and cartographic work and so on—on the first print run of each book. So in our accounts our first print runs were expensive, but the subsequent ones were much cheaper. I believe that if you deal with any bank or accounting firm for long enough, eventually they'll do something to seriously annoy you. Our accountants had convinced us that we should write off costs over the whole estimated print life of the book. It made things more profitable at the start of a book's life, but when, post S11, we unexpectedly found ourselves writing off far more books at the end of the cycle, it simply increased our already painful losses. Today we've switched back to our earlier accounting policy (and changed our accountants), but it was another problem at a time when we had quite enough to wrestle with.

To top off this mess there was our US office. For twenty years the US had been our single biggest market, although in per capita terms it had never come anywhere near the Australian or UK markets. Despite the five to one population difference, our US sales were only marginally higher than the UK and as an office the UK, with all of Europe, Africa and the Middle East to look after, was actually bigger than the US, which also handled Canada and Latin America.

Our US production program had started badly with the first regional titles which went so haywire back in 1994–95, but by the late 1990s books were streaming smoothly out of the Oakland office. But at a cost.

Dot coms and Silicon Valley had pushed the San Francisco Bay Area's always high salaries to absurd levels. At the same time, the US dollar had been soaring ever higher while the Australian dollar, lumped in with the neighboring Asian currencies which had tumbled with the 1997 Asian economic meltdown, had dropped ever lower. By 2000 it sank below sixty cents to the US dollar and stayed there. The downward path continued in 2001, hitting rock bottom right after S11 when a US dollar would buy two of the Australian variety. So we were paying higher salaries with more valuable dollars. Often an editor or cartographer cost us as many 'dollars' in Oakland as in Melbourne and each of those Oakland dollars was twice the size of a Melbourne one.

Add in much higher office rental costs in the US and the story was even worse, but this unhappy equation was mitigated by US efficiency, right? Wrong.

By every measure we applied our US office was less efficient than our London or Melbourne operations. We'd always tracked how many hours went into every book and noted how many hours it took per page of text or map. Of course, each book has its own text and mapping problems. We expect our China book, with so many Chinese characters integrated into the maps and text, to cost more per page than a book without script problems. Even simply having a different language to cope with can push the costs up. Whatever the comparisons, it seemed to take more hours to edit a page of text or draw a page of map in the US than in Australia or the UK. When those editing and cartographic hours cost twice as much, the impact on our profitability was severe.

We never got to the bottom of why things didn't work smoothly in the US. Undoubtedly, our US cartographic costs had been pushed higher by a badly conceived decision to concentrate on databasing our mapping. The theory was we'd have the whole of the US data-based on one map. From this super map we could then pull out New York state and from New York state pull out New York City and from New York City pull out Manhattan and from Manhattan pull out Central Park. Of course, we weren't planning to map the whole of the US in the same detail that we mapped Central Park, but all the mapping would be tied together and interrelated. If the city authorities ever decided to rename Central Park as the Big Manhattan Park, that change, made on one map, would flow right up the line. However, this central databasing cost a heap and employed a 'cartographic corral' of map makers without ever providing any real advantage.

Why US editing should cost more we never worked out, although we joked that the US enthusiasm for nit-picking political correctness may have played some part!

Although salary costs in London were not as high as in Oakland, and although the production efficiencies were comparable to Melbourne levels, our office rentals were even higher so production in the UK was also more expensive than in Australia.

In early 2002 it was clear that our post-S11 cost-cutting measures weren't doing the job. We were still hemorrhaging money. More drastic measures were called for. Simon Westcott, our forceful new Global Publisher, bit the bullet on a move which for everybody, but for Maureen and me in particular, was extremely painful. We would centralize book production in our Melbourne office.

We could still have the advantages of a US and UK publishing presence even if we were doing most of the editing and cartography in Australia. We would still commission books from those offices, still draw up the book specifications there and supervise the authors and researchers and check the general structure of the book before handing it over to Melbourne. We'd still get local expertise and flavor into the books and be closer to the markets, but without the higher production costs we were facing.

Unfortunately, these changes would mean losing about half of our 150 US staff as well as a smaller number in the UK. In Lonely Planet's nearly thirty-year history we'd never had to lay off staff and we didn't want to start, but the more we looked at the figures, the clearer it became that there was no choice. We had to restore profitability, and this was the only way to do it.

Maureen and I had sleepless nights arguing out the inevitability of downsizing our overseas operations, but we quickly came to one firm conclusion. If we had to do it, then it was going to be done personally. We decided to make the announcements at all our offices simultaneously. Maureen would stay for the Australian announcement, but if half of our US staff were going to lose their jobs then I would tell them myself. So in mid-March 2002 I followed Steve Hibbard and Ian Posthumous, our human-relations chief, to the US and the next day dropped a bombshell which, sadly, our staff had already seen coming.

I didn't realize when I flew to the US that it was going to be an opportunity to see Americans at their resilient best. The overwhelming response was the same: they were understanding about why we had to make the changes, they were pleased we'd turned up to explain the reorganization personally, they reiterated that Lonely Planet had been a great place to work (and that they weren't going to hold this against us!) and in many cases they thanked us for treating them with dignity, respect and (when it came to the question of dollars) generosity. When we knew how tough this news was for so many of our Oakland staff, it was embarrassing that many of them came over to say, 'I know this must be really hard for you,' and 'We'll still love Lonely Planet.'

After our announcement the mood at the office was like a funeral and many of our staff headed across the Bay Bridge to a San Francisco bar to drown their sorrows. At their invitation I joined them.

There was, however, a final coda to our San Francisco changes.

'If a job comes up in Melbourne,' asked several of our departing American staff, 'could I apply for it?'

'Sure,' we replied. 'There are no guarantees, and if you got the job it would be at Australian salary levels plus you'd have to get to Australia yourself and, although we'd do anything we could to help, it would be up to you to sort out visa problems and work permits. But you know what Lonely Planet's about, so if you applied you'd certainly be a front runner for any position going.'

A half-dozen of our American staff ended up moving to Melbourne.

Simon Westcott also had a comprehensive program to increase the efficiency of every stage of our book production. His plan was not going to get an easy ride because we'd no sooner made the US changes than the US dollar's long rise and the Australian dollar's long decline both switched directions. From flirting with the fifty-cent level in late 2001 it sat in the mid-fifties for 2002 then climbed to sixty cents in early 2003. It rose to seventy cents by late 2003 and has been in the seventies ever since.

This dramatic change didn't only make cost savings at our Australian office much more difficult, it also whacked our sales. In 2004 the US was accounting for about thirty per cent of our worldwide sales, but US$10 million of sales when the Australian dollar was worth just fifty cents US translated as A$20 million. When the Australian dollar soared to the eighty-cent level that same US$10 million only meant A$12.5 million.

In mid-2002 our spirits had never been lower and on paper the problems Lonely Planet would face over the next couple of years looked horrific. Apart from exchange rates pushing our costs up and our income down, we also had the Bali bombing in October 2002. Once again, travel numbers dropped and a host of our popular Asian titles fell on their collective faces. Then in early 2003 we were hit with SARS. With horrible timing, 50 000 copies of the big new edition of our China guidebook arrived in our warehouses just as every-body stopped going to China. We were about to print a new edition of our Beijing guidebook, but instead we popped it in the freezer for twelve months.

Topping all this bad news was the crazy decision to invade Iraq, giving travel in general, and the Middle East in particular, another hard thump. Our Israel book had already ground to a near halt so at least there was one title in the region which couldn't go downhill any further. I had trouble finding anybody who thought the decision to march into Iraq made sense, although I wouldn't have been at all sur-prised if they had managed to 'find' those imaginary Weapons of Mass Destruction. I was quite ready to believe they were in storage in a warehouse in Kuwait ready to be trucked into Iraq as soon as the first American troops arrived in Baghdad. Heather Harrison, our feisty US sales manager, got herself arrested in a San Francisco anti-war protest.

This series of blows forced us into another round of redundan-cies, which this time hit our Australian operations. On June 13 2003 I talked with each of the nineteen people we were forced to let go and, as at our US office a year earlier, was touched to find that nobody blamed us for the predicament—even Valerie Tellini, who had been with us for sixteen years, could see that this was the last thing we wanted to do. Valerie had been with us through three differ-ent offices and was the fourteenth person Lonely Planet employed.

With cruelly precise timing a batch of sixty-five postcards arrived on my desk that morning. Each one showed a bloody hand back-dropped by a beach and on the reverse sixty-five Australians prom-ised that they would never buy another Lonely Planet guidebook. On this occasion it was the ACTU, the Australian Council of Trade Unions, who were supporting the British Burma activists and hoping we'd go out of business. I wrote to Sharan Burrows, the president of the ACTU, and pointed out that it was remarkable for an Australian trade union organization to campaign for Australians to lose their jobs, but I never received an answer.

There were changes right across the board. We increased the

height of our regular guidebooks from 184 to 197 millimeters, a simple little seven per cent change which meant, other things being equal, we could get the same number of words onto seven per cent fewer pages and reduce our printing costs. We looked at every title and reassessed exactly how big that book needed to be. Most travelers going to Jamaica are only going to spend a week or two, so did they really need a 640-page guide? No, we decided and reduced the next edition to 352 pages. (Unfortunately, all the potential saving on that particular title got wiped out when the author made a somewhat intemperate accusation about a former prime minister. The editor failed to pick it up and we had to pulp the entire print run.)

Despite the financial pressures, we also pushed through an across-the-board redesign of all our destination guides, from the shoestring guides (we aimed them more tightly at their key young, long-trip users, a group we nicknamed 'global nomads') to the city guides (we made them more stylish and more useful for short-term visitors as enthusiastic about the travel experience as saving money). We'd never been big on market research, but for the relaunch of our guides we did everything from focus groups to surveys. One of the important changes was to move the boring (even if it's necessary) stuff to the back of the book and bring the excitement (Why am I going there? What are the sights I'll never forget?) up to the front. There was also a great deal of clever redesign which used space, always a commodity in short supply with guidebooks, more effectively and new mapping which made finding locations easier and faster.

The 'new look' guides were on bookshop shelves at the beginning of 2004 and we immediately had our best sales month ever. Despite the huge changes, we also managed to bring these books in at a much lower cost than their predecessors. There were some key titles where we actually halved the production costs.

I've regretted that our tighter focus post-S11 has meant the encyclopedic quality of some of our books has had to be reined in. Today when we tell a writer their section will be 60 000 words and have fifteen maps we really mean it. Despite these hard-edged realities it's important that we do keep our hand in with those 'unusual destinations', which is why I'm pleased to be involved with projects like East Timor and the Falkland Islands, cutting-edge destinations which I wrote and we published in 2004.

The dwindling US dollar hammered what should have been a nicely upward sales chart, but if we couldn't count on soaring sales to make life look better, our own hard work did the trick. Our cash flow steadily improved, our bank borrowings began to slide steadily downwards and by mid-2004 we were more profitable.

One day we realized we no longer knew everybody at Lonely Planet and once we'd reached that plateau the numbers we didn't know seemed to accelerate. 'Anybody whose name I can't remember I just call mate,' suggested Singo when I brought up this problem. Suddenly, the familiar names at the top all seemed to be changing as well.

Charlotte Hindle, who'd joined us in Melbourne in 1988 and returned to London in 1991 to set up our first UK office, decided to leave in 2002 to look after her young family. She's continued to work with us, but other departures were more final. Rob van Driesum and Richard Everist, both stalwarts of our Melbourne publishing operations, and Carolyn Miller, who headed up our US marketing effort and had been with us longer than anybody else at our Oakland office, were other sad departures.

Sometimes people who are perfect at one stage of a company's life cycle are wrong at another. Sometimes you can engineer a new role for a person, but more often there's a parting of the ways. Even before S11 we had begun to make changes. We sat down with Steve Hibbard in 2000 and planned a department-by-department change strategy which even moved Steve out of his job, bringing in a new CEO who would take us to the next level. One of Steve's prime skills had been finding the right people and once again he did a fantastic job of identifying the gaps and finding the people who would fill them.

For a couple of years our management team seemed to be spinning through a revolving door. Eric Kettunen, who'd been with us in the US for thirteen years, departed soon after the dramatic changes in 2002. Eric had come with me to French Polynesia and to Mt Kailash in Tibet so he was far more than just our US head and his departure was especially sad. Todd Sotkiewicz, who replaced Eric, had survived the ups (he'd done very well out of working for *Wired*) of the dot-com era and also the downs (he'd been on board a disastrous startup called Bigwords, intended to be a sort of Amazon of college books).

There was a wholesale switch around on the publishing side at all the offices as we reassessed the successes and failures of the new series we'd launched in the late 1990s. Simon Westcott had a mandate to change anything he needed and instructions to approach the list with financial rigor and production savvy. Tony McKimmie, our new sales and marketing manager, came in with similar instructions for that side of the business.

For years Lonely Planet had been driven by two teams: a big editing and cartographic production unit and a smaller sales and marketing department. All that other stuff—accounting, financial, legal, personnel—took a back seat. That changed when Carolyn Sutton joined us as a Chief Financial Officer who would actually say 'no' (even to us) to anybody who even hinted at running a project over budget. We even got a company lawyer, Chaman Sidhu, and before long discovered we needed a second one.

The events of S11 accelerated the rate of change; we no longer had the luxury of evolving at our own pace. The final, and biggest, piece in the puzzle was a new CEO. Steve Hibbard had joined us almost by accident, coming on board after doing a business-school case study on Lonely Planet and then convincing us we should let him run the place. After an exhaustive search we appointed Judy Slatyer. Judy had been a high-flyer at the Australian phone company Telstra and left them to head up the Australian end of a wireless Internet startup before joining us. Judy had zero publishing experience, but we reckoned she had what we wanted. The fact that she had cycled from Greece to Norway one summer didn't hurt. One of Judy's beliefs was that once you'd set a target, hitting an unexpected problem didn't give you an excuse for failing to reach your goals. You simply had to work harder or find some totally new way to get there. The invasion of Iraq and the unexpected outbreak of SARS soon gave her that challenge.

Like anybody involved in a small company that becomes a much bigger one, the roles Maureen and I play at Lonely Planet have been steadily changing. In some respects they have simply been whittled away. It's a long time since I drew maps, designed books or went round the bookshops to sell them. I'd pulled back more slowly from wearing the publishing hat, but I'd made the mistake of stepping back from hands-on-management without ensuring that everybody else who'd stepped up could really handle the job.

In retrospect we could probably have saved ourselves a lot of headaches and heartache if we'd been more aggressive about budgeting and keeping our attention really focused on the bottom line years earlier, but if you don't make mistakes and take risks you're never going to do anything interesting. If Lonely Planet had been run by accountants rather than two crazy travelers, would we ever have done most of the books which have made the company what it is? Warren Buffett, of all people, summed it up pretty well at Berkshire Hathaway's 2004 annual meeting: 'If every shot you hit in golf turned out to be a hole in one, it would get pretty boring. You need to lose a few in the woods now and again!'

The interesting transition, and one which seemed to take place without either of us even noticing it at first, was that we each began to gravitate towards different sides of the business. For some time we'd been equally involved in being the company spokespersons, the motormouths in a business which required a lot of talking. I'd tended to be the creative publishing person, the dreamer who conjured up new projects or saw the directions they should go. We'd both been involved in the business side, but my interest in that dwindled and it was now often Maureen who saw what was going on and made the hard decisions about it. It was Maureen who pushed things forward even when it was painful.

Many other changes flowed through Lonely Planet in the first couple of years of the new century. We'd finally ended our 25-year banking relationship with Westpac and moved to ANZ. We also shifted into a new office beside the Maribyrnong River in Melbourne's inner-west. Converting a derelict, century-old cotton warehouse into a state-of-the-art office and warehouse complex was an amazing task managed by Maureen with considerable help from Anna Hardwick, a new employee who did a fair impression of the Hindu god Shiva, arms whirling in every direction, as she juggled a hundred tasks simultaneously. Our techies pulled all-nighters and Tashi joined in as Anna's assistant in the final shift across town. For the first time, Maureen and I had our own parking spaces. It was a symbol of the new, businesslike Lonely Planet which was inevitable, but it was also an 'improvement' I wasn't really happy about.

14
Where to Now?

So, where to now—for guidebooks, for Lonely Planet, for us?

I'm frequently asked if the guidebook can survive when so much information is available instantly updated and for free from the Internet.

'People will still read guidebooks,' is one of my answers. 'I just don't know if they'll be printed on paper.'

Or, 'I've got the guidebook of the future right here,' I might say, holding up my cell phone, my GPS (Global Positioning System) and my handheld computer or PDA (Pocket Digital Assistant). 'We just have to weld the three together. Then I'll look up Italian restaurants in the guidebook loaded onto the PDA, the GPS will point out how far the one I choose is from my current location, I'll press a button and the phone will call up so I can book a table. Then I just have to follow the GPS to the front door.'

So, we'll still be producing 'guidebooks'. We'll still be sending out our researchers to check out restaurants, bounce on hotel beds and decide what's really worth seeing and what can be missed, but the end result might be digital rather than printed. On the other hand, the printed guidebook still has a long future—the batteries never go flat, the connection never drops out and the information is reliable. Let's face it, there's plenty of misinformation on the web.

Printed or digital, we expect guides will remain Lonely Planet's core activity, although we also expect to become less dependent on them. Over the years all those other projects, from the website to the photo library, special publishing to television, mapping to cell phones, have gradually become more important and we expect that trend to accelerate.

It's important to keep an eye on changes because serious competition is unlikely to sneak up in your rear-view mirror. Real competition is far more likely to ram into you from the side. It's probably going to be that much over-used phrase the 'paradigm shift'. Look at what's happened to free-to-air-television, losing 'eyeballs' to cable and satellite TV, to rental videos and DVDs, to Internet surfing. Or big general-interest magazines, losing newsstand space to a host of specialist magazines catering for ever-narrower market segments. Or *Encyclopedia Britannica*, its long-lasting business model shunted off the track by digital versions and then by the Internet.

If the business is changing then so are we. With specialists for everything from computers to finances, what is there left for us to do? It's a question Maureen and I often get asked and expectations seem to be at one extreme or the other—either we spend all our time behind our desks, acting just like any other businesspeople (except I never wear a tie), or we spend our days lounging around swimming pools, sampling the latest restaurants or exploring exotic locales with just the occasional phone call home to make sure everybody is working hard. The reality is we're still vitally interested in everything Lonely Planet does and although we're no longer in the driver's seat, we're involved in all the major decisions.

T: Sitting on the beach in Noosa in 1992 I drew up a list of fifteen 'must dos'. Two of them are still to be done: the Karakoram Highway across the eastern outlier of the Himalayas from Pakistan to Kashgar in China and the Trans-Siberian Express to Moscow. Everything else I've done, from walking the Mont Blanc Circuit (with Kieran in 1995) to diving the World War II wrecks in Truk Lagoon in Micronesia in 2000. One item was to buy something, rather than do something:

a Ferrari.

I can't defend cars, but if you're an addicted gear head with the cash to spare it's almost inevitable you'll end up with a Ferrari in your garage. So in 1993 I bought one, seven years old, but the real thing, a Mondial, Quattrovalvole, 3.28 liter, V8, quadcam, in that shade of red only Ferrari has perfected, totally impractical and enormous fun.

To make space, the 32-year-old Austin-Healey Sprite which Maureen bought (and restored) for my fortieth birthday went to another gear head. The 24-year-old Marcos had a more exotic departure, shipped off to join a small museum of unusual British sports cars in Tokyo.

My Ferrari was perfect. It was amazingly economical, saved huge amounts of time and kept me fit. In seven years I only had one Ferrari speeding ticket and that was on the first weekend. On the other hand, I did get it past 200 kph on several occasions, quite legally, when the Ferrari owners' club rented a racetrack for the day (speed does thrill). But its ability to go fast wasn't how my car saved me money and time and kept me fit. That was due to all the times I didn't use it. You cannot use a Ferrari to go five miles; it has to be properly warmed up. So I took my bicycle to work much more often.

Counting the time spent looking for a parking space, you can get most places faster by bicycle, but the real time saver had nothing to do with getting from A to B. It was the time I'd wasted reading car magazines. I used to guiltily think that if I could kick the car magazine habit I'd free up enough time to learn German, understand Tibetan Buddhism or do something else really useful. Owning a Ferrari cured me of car magazines. They seemed pointless. Unfortunately, I didn't devote the free time to German or Buddhism, but it must have gone somewhere.

The Ferrari finally went as well. It was replaced by another interesting car. A 32-year-old Volkswagen Beetle, which was followed by a Lotus Elise. The nicest thing about my Lotus, apart from its utter impracticality (there's something about a car which has power nothing, no carpets and barely enough trunk space for a laptop), is that the handbook actually suggests if you're not going very far it's better for the environment if you walk. Get some exercise, it recommends.

The other 'must dos' on my 1992 list, and the years they got crossed off, were Angkor Wat (Cambodia, 1992), Birdsville Track (classic outback road, 1993), USA coast to coast (Caddy trip, 1994), Milford Track ('best walk in the world', New Zealand, 1997), Mt Kailash Circuit (Tibet, 1998), Lhasa (same trip), Damascus (oldest city in the world, Syria, 1999), Gunbarrel Highway (another outback classic, 2000), Thorsborne Trail (on the coast of Hinchinbrook Island, 2001) and the Annapurna Circuit (Nepal, 2001).

'Lonely Planet? They do books for backpackers.'

I've felt obliged to correct that misconception almost as many times as I've had to answer, 'What's your favorite place?' We're not strictly a backpacker publisher. We publish books for almost every market segment, from young family groups to city weekend escapees, Tokyo business travelers to Africa safari explorers. Although I still sample backpacker places every year (in some places there's no alternative), I also have a taste for hotels where rooms come with their own swimming pools.

Nevertheless, backpackers are still an important category and one we work very hard to keep happy. They're a vitally significant part of the travel market for all sorts of reasons. Those global nomads are often the travel pioneers, the people who open up new destinations and new markets. They often go to places no other tourists bother about, going beyond the big cities and big resorts to spend tourist dollars in the backblocks, the small towns, the forgotten corners. They don't ask for big tourist infrastructure; they'll get by without swimming pools or air-conditioning and put up with difficult and uncomfortable transport to get to the end of the road. Furthermore, the money they spend often goes in at ground level, straight into the local population's pocket, not leaking back out to some faceless tourist operator.

Plus backpackers are often young people starting out on a lifetime of travel experiences. They may not stay backpackers for ever, but they're likely to remain invcterate travelers. So backpackers may not be our only market, but they're certainly a very important one.

Backpackers are travel trendsetters when it comes to technology as well. Recently Maureen and I spent a decadent week at some very luxurious island resorts. Each resort had a computer set up for their high-paying guests to access the Internet or check emails. It was a good job that these resorts were not only luxurious but also small, because each of them had just one computer. Plenty of backpacker places offer far better Internet access to their guests. The same week, one of our researchers commented about a backpacker guesthouse which offered free broadband access in every room for backpackers toting their own laptops. Rock-bottom backpacker places have to offer better technology than the five-star places because young people expect it.

A far higher proportion of backpacker bed nights compared to regular hotel bed nights are booked over the Internet. So what's going to happen in ten years' time? Those backpackers are going to grow up and move on to booking regular hotels rather than hostels. So once again the backpackers are technology leaders.

The major international hotel group Accor has recently started a backpacker chain known as Base. Why on earth would a company with brands like Sofitel and Novotel, as well as Ibis and Formule One at the cheaper end of the scale, want to move into competition with youth hostels? Because they want to grab those first-time travelers at Base level and then move them up their hotel chains over the years? Or, equally probably, because they can see China about to take off and calculate that a lot of the potential China market is going to be in the no-frills bracket?

M: In a way Lonely Planet was our first child and I think it demanded a great deal of our family as a whole.

Giving children the experience of travel is seen as a great gift, but there were costs for all of us. At one point I realized that I was being introduced to people as 'Maureen Lonely Planet' and I remember wondering who I would be if we hadn't created the company.

When your children are very young it is impossible to imagine a life where they will not live with you, where you will not see them every day or know what they are doing. As they grow up, you gradually untangle your 'self' from their 'selves' until the day arrives when you look at your child and see a separate adult, and realize the role you play in their life is no longer a central one. It's hard to recognize that your child is independent, but it's also incredibly liberating.

In much the same way a company grows up. When the point is reached where you realize that you are no longer central to the success or even existence of the company, it can be either threatening or liberating. Along with the realization that there is life after children, has come the realization that there are many other things I can be involved in outside Lonely Planet. That was exciting, but it was also unnerving. I felt panicky at the thought of not having to go to the office. I was afraid that without a role at Lonely Planet, I might have no role at all.

When I was asked to join the board of Tourism Tasmania I accepted and did two terms as a director. I enjoyed the experience very much, not just because the other people on the board were great to work with, but also because I fell in love with Tasmania, the island state to the south of mainland Australia. I was also asked to become patron of the Ronald McDonald House at Monash in Melbourne, where seriously ill children and their families stay while the child is undergoing treatment at the nearby medical center. The people there are a huge inspiration and it's gratifying to be able to make even a small contribution. In various other ways I have enjoyed stepping out of the world I have been so enmeshed in for the past thirty years to learn something about how other businesses work.

I have been riding a roller coaster for so long that I have consciously not planned anything for the future. I need to leave a space to see what comes next; I want to be open to whatever fate hurls at me. I don't think I will ever be completely detached from Lonely Planet, but I would like to think that there are new horizons, new worlds and new Maureens to discover.

I am still a travel junkie. Put a ticket in my hand and I'm heading for the departure lounge. Lonely Planet started by covering destinations which other publishers hadn't even looked at and that's still my greatest interest.

Although I'm unlikely to be involved with our big books, in 2004 I worked on two small new guides. I'd visited East Timor in its Portuguese, Indonesian and now in its independent incarnation so I was keen to publish the first book on the new nation. Plus I traveled down to the remote Falkland Islands and on to the amazing sub-Antarctic island of South Georgia where I joined a group of intrepid walkers to follow explorer Ernest Shackleton's famous walk across the frozen island. That trip led to our Falkland Islands and South Georgia book.

The number of countries we manage to cover each year in our Africa guide is always a fine gauge for how hard we're working to cover difficult destinations. In 2006 I was delighted to be called in to rewrite the Central African Republic chapter, Maureen and I had managed to visit that little visited corner of the continent in late 2005.

George W. Bush's evil axis also inspired some personal travel plans. I'd already been kicking around the idea of writing about pariah countries before Bush drew up a list for me. Recently, I've traveled in Iran, North Korea, Libya, Saudi Arabia and Syria and in 2006 I spent a week, by myself, in Iraq and later returned to Afghanistan for couple of weeks.

Our travels almost always have a purpose attached to them, even if it's only to try out a new book. Most of the time we confirm that the book is as good as we hoped it was, but Maureen and I are Lonely Planet's fiercest critics and even when we come back absolutely delighted we're likely to have pages of notes for things that must be fixed, improved or added. We joke that our writers quake when they hear we are going to the place they write about and sometimes they're wise to do a little quaking.

We started Lonely Planet because we loved to travel and firmly believed in the importance of travel. That love and that belief have not altered over the years. Today, we each have our particular interests in the business (Maureen is vitally interested in the Lonely Planet Foundation; I'm determined that we should keep at the cutting edge when it comes to covering new and challenging destinations) but it was travel that inspired us, travel that drove us and travel is still what Lonely Planet is all about.